How Humans
COOPERATE

How Humans
COOPERATE

CONFRONTING THE CHALLENGES
OF COLLECTIVE ACTION

Richard E. Blanton with Lane F. Fargher

UNIVERSITY PRESS OF COLORADO

Boulder

Published by University Press of Colorado
5589 Arapahoe Avenue, Suite 206C
Boulder, Colorado 80303

AAUP The University Press of Colorado is a proud member of
The Association of American University Presses.

The University Press of Colorado is a cooperative publishing enterprise supported, in part, by Adams State University, Colorado State University, Fort Lewis College, Metropolitan State University of Denver, Regis University, University of Colorado, University of Northern Colorado, Utah State University, and Western State Colorado University.

ISBN: 978-1-60732-513-0 (cloth)
ISBN: 978-1-60732-616-8 (pbk)
ISBN: 978-1-60732-514-7 (ebook)

Library of Congress Cataloging-in-Publication Data

Names: Blanton, Richard E., author. | Fargher, Lane, author.
Title: How humans cooperate : confronting the challenge of collective action / Richard E. Blanton ; with Lane F. Fargher.
Description: Boulder : University Press of Colorado, [2016] | Includes bibliographical references.
Identifiers: LCCN 2016019924| ISBN 9781607325130 (cloth) | ISBN 9781607326168 (pbk) | ISBN 9781607325147 (ebook)
Subjects: LCSH: Cooperativeness. | Cooperation. | Social action.
Classification: LCC HM716 .B53 2016 | DDC 302/.14—dc23
LC record available at https://lccn.loc.gov/2016019924

The University Press of Colorado gratefully acknowledges the generous support of Purdue University toward the publication of this book.

Contents

Acknowledgments

We gratefully acknowledge the support for this book and critical commentary on an early draft provided by our colleague Stephen Kowalewski. Rich's wife, Cindy Bedell, has devoted untold hours to reading multiple drafts, arranging permission for image reproduction, and bibliography checking. We also benefitted from comments by Michael Smith and Audrey Ricke, from three external reviewers for the University Press of Colorado, and from audiences who responded to presentations at Arizona State University, at the Human Relations Area Files, and at meetings of the Society for Cross-Cultural Research and the Society for American Archaeology. The ideas presented here reflect the discussions we have enjoyed over many years with colleagues, especially Gary Feinman, Linda Nicholas, Carol Ember, Melvin Ember, and Verenice Y. Heredia Espinoza. However, all errors or omissions are our sole responsibility. The National Science Foundation of the United States has been our principal source of funding (0204536-BCS and 0809643-BCS), and we also acknowledge the support of the Center for Behavioral and Social Sciences, Purdue University. We gratefully acknowledge the help and support provided by Jessica d'Arbonne, Darrin Pratt, Laura Furney, Daniel Pratt, and Sonya Manes of the University Press of Colorado.

How Humans
COOPERATE

I

Introduction

How will humans decide to address today's "Grand Challenges" of resource deple-
tion, climate change, ethnic and religious conflict, and natural and man-made
disasters? Grand Challenge problem-solving will demand an unprecedented
degree of cooperative effort and effective policies based on well-grounded theories
of human nature and of cooperation. Yet, as I searched through the relevant literatures I was disappointed to find inconsistent ideas and research methods, even
disagreements about the kinds of questions we need to be asking about humans
and about cooperation.

The key barrier to cooperation research is the lack of coordinated efforts between
a camp of collective action theorists and a camp of evolutionary psychologists.
Differences are evident between the two camps even in something as basic as the
questions: What is the nature of cooperation, and what is the goal of cooperation
research? Collective action theorists understand cooperation to be a particularly
difficult challenge for humans owing, in large part, to the tension that may arise
between individual and group interests. Much of their research and theory-building
has aimed at learning how humans confront cooperator problems through the construction of institutions (rules and associated forms of social organization and culture) that can foster cooperative behavior.

Unlike the collective action theorists, to evolutionary psychologists cooperation is not a serious problem because, when required, it arises spontaneously as
an expression of a prosocial psychology. Thus evolutionary psychologists ignore

DOI: 10.5876/9781607325147.c001

institution-building, and, while some may consider the importance of culture, ultimately they understand cooperation to result from instincts that have a deep evolutionary history in our species. As a result, they pay little attention to the "proximate" time frame of collective action theory, which addresses how humans solve cooperator problems in particular social and cultural settings. To evolutionary psychologists, the key research question pertains to the "ultimate" sources of cooperation, namely, how did humans evolve into a "groupish" species over hundreds of thousands of years of bioevolutionary history?

In this and later chapters of this book I tilt strongly toward collective action theory, but always from a critical perspective toward both collective action and evolutionary psychology. I find collective action theory superior to evolutionary psychology for a number of reasons, chiefly because its theoretical proposals can be evaluated in the light of data gathered from real human experience, a way of thinking and working that is in line with the expectations of scientific epistemology. I find this empirical dimension admirable. At the same time, I fault the collective action literature for its tendency to emphasize Western historical experience. I also fault its lack of ability to link cooperation to the psychological foundations of human thought and social action—the human nature question. Evolutionary psychologists do bring psychological factors into the conversation about cooperation. Yet, I find their highly formal methodologies, which depend heavily on experimental game research and computer simulations, unable to match the complexity of real human psychology or of social experience that we find outside the sterile confines of the lab or the computer screen.

THE LIMITATIONS OF PREVAILING COOPERATION
THEORIES AND A CALL FOR REVISION

Some researchers have attempted to overcome the divide between empirical and formal (by which I mean experimental game and computer modeling) approaches to cooperation research by presenting both side by side. However, this strategy has not been successful, in my view, even in the writing of some of the bright lights of cooperation studies such as Russell Hardin, Dennis Chong, and Elinor Ostrom (who won the Nobel prize in economics for her work on the collective management of resources). The difficulty I see is an uneasy tension between an empirical dimension, consisting of narrative accounts drawn from particular ethnographic or historical examples, and a formal dimension, the latter based on mathematical modeling and experimental games. The problem is that narrative and formal modes of presentation are highly dissimilar forms of knowledge that are not well integrated.

Oddly, it is often the case that while the narrative accounts document successful instances of cooperation, formal analyses often point to how cooperation is unlikely. For example, computer simulations show that cooperation is not likely to evolve biologically, a perhaps counterintuitive finding that has engaged the imagination of the evolutionary psychology community and prompted much new research that I describe in chapter 2. Similarly, experimental games show that based on the rational decisions of individuals (a characteristic feature of most experimental game research), highly cooperative outcomes are uncommon. For example, in "public goods games" players selfishly strategize to "free-ride" to gain individual benefit from pooled resources. And, in these games, if cooperation does appear, it usually is not sustained and may even decline within games and across multiple repeated games, again, owing to the free-rider problem. And yet, humans have sometimes built cooperative social formations in the real world, away from the game-playing laboratory, some of which have been sustained over long periods. This says to me that the emphasis placed on experimental games as a path to understanding cooperation may be misplaced.

As I mentioned, in the cooperation literature we often encounter formal analyses interspersed with narrative accounts based on ethnographic or historical sources. Typically I find the latter compelling and useful, while, at the same time, I realize that the description of selected isolated examples fails to realize the important goal of placing cooperation study on a firm foundation of scientific understanding. In spite of this shortcoming, what I find worth noting in these narratives is the way that institutions form a bridge between the individual, who is tempted to behave as an egotistical free rider, and the collectivity, which thrives on each person's group-oriented choices; cooperation is more likely to thrive when well-crafted institutions are able to shape individual choice toward cooperative action.

Interestingly, the same process of institution-building may be observed even in some specially designed experimental game scenarios. For example, in one experiment conducted by Elinor Ostrom, James Walker, and Roy Gardner, free-riding declined and cooperation increased when players were able to identify free-riding players and were able to decide on rules for imposing punishments and rewards, illustrating a rudimentary form of institution-building in an experimental context (Ostrom et al. 1992; see also Ostrom and Walker 2000). But such examples are far from edifying when we consider that the cooperating groups in games like this typically consist of a small number of middle-class US college students, often even sharing the same academic major. In the real world, persons attempting to forge cooperation often do so in contexts of vastly larger social scale and in situations of social and cultural heterogeneity in which communication is challenging and contention and opposition present obstacles to institution building and to cooperation.

THE REVISIONIST GOALS OF THIS BOOK

It is in these contexts—large scale and social and cultural heterogeneity—that I situate the theory-building project of this book. In doing so I not only separate my work from the experimental games and computer simulations, but I also depart from the common practice of those cooperation theorists who focus their research efforts on small-group contexts in which, typically, cooperators share social standing and cultural background and in which monitoring, sanctioning, and rewarding, enacted in face-to-face contexts, are the principal strategies to minimize cooperator problems. Cooperation and institution-building in small groups have an important place in cooperation research viewed broadly, yet, I suggest, what is most needed is for cooperation study to shine its light on groups whose large scale renders direct monitoring of behavior problematic and in which not everyone will agree what form cooperation should take or whether it is a good idea at all.

Another goal of mine is to avoid the divide that separates formal analysis and descriptive narrative accounts, to instead unite these two highly separate forms of knowledge. I do this first by suggesting that we unmoor cooperation research from its ties to evolutionary psychology, experimental games, and bioevolutionary simulations. I propose this reorientation not to distance cooperation study from psychology or other biological factors, or quantification. Instead, I will propose ways to build cooperation research on a rich empirical foundation while also aligning it with a branch of psychological research very different from evolutionary psychology, one that studies human cognitive capacity, especially what is called "Theory of Mind." The study of cognition is important because, as I argue throughout this book, properties of human psychology intersect in important ways with cooperative social action and with institution-building for cooperation.

My revisionist perspective is also a turn away from particularistic descriptive accounts of successful cooperative groups to deploy, instead, the method of systematic cross-cultural comparative research. This method, developed by anthropologists and psychologists, draws from a vast body of ethnographic, archaeological, and historical sources from multiple world areas, cultures, and time periods. By taking a comparative direction, I am able to illustrate the diverse social and cultural patterns within which cooperative social outcomes have been realized. At the same time, the cross-cultural approach provides me, and my coauthor, Lane Fargher, with a method suited to the evaluation of causal theories that identify those factors that inhibit or enhance the possibilities for cooperation.

THE PLAN OF THIS BOOK

In chapter 2 I bring together ethnographic and other anthropological data to show how ideas proposed by evolutionary psychologists concerning cooperation can be critiqued. I argue that their understanding of humans is a poor fit with what is known, from descriptive accounts, about how humans behave and about the kinds of social groups they build. I follow up on the critique by asking, and, I hope, answering, the question: Why has evolutionary psychology gained so much credibility as a source of cooperation theory?

In chapter 3, I present two building blocks for a cooperation theory: the notion of collective action and associated ideas about the rational human. I also point to how collective action theory is applied by way of institutional analysis. The goal of chapter 4 is to address the seemingly puzzling fact that the discipline of anthropology, my home discipline, has had little role to play in developing or evaluating theories of human cooperation. However, I also point to some recent developments, what I call a "new anthropological imagination," that will provide a path forward to better incorporate the discipline's vast store of knowledge and insights into the conversation about cooperation.

The goal of chapter 5 is to provide an additional building block for cooperation theory. Here I suggest that we turn away from evolutionary psychology to instead benefit from recent discoveries by psychologists and primatologists, especially ideas surrounding Theory of Mind cognitive capacity. This will be an essential path to cooperation study that allows for an integration of biological evolutionary questions and the institution-building that is central to collective action.

In the following chapters, to realize my goal to situate cooperation study beyond small-scale and socially homogeneous contexts, I address institution-building that enables broad participation in commercial transactions (chapter 6), how collective action can become a central goal of state-building (chapters 7 and 8) (with Lane Fargher), how collective action is staged across the territorial expanse of a polity and in populous urban centers when established social ecologies and physical infrastructures inhibit the implementation of collective strategies (chapters 9 and 10) (also with Lane Fargher).

In chapter 11 I address the issue of how collective action entails the construction of cultural designs that reimagine the mind and the self in society, inspires aesthetic transitions in forms of representation, and involves innovation in forms of performance and ritual to enhance consensus in the face of social cleavage. In the chapter's last section I point out that in instances where high levels of cooperation have been established, we see a pattern of reconsideration of the role of religion in civil life.

In chapter 12 I bring together themes developed in previous chapters to place cooperation in a material framework of environment, production, exchange, consumption, and demography. My analysis shows how these factors mutually interact to establish what I identify as a "coactive causal process" that, once set into play, is a spur to demographic, technological, social, and cultural change. In this chapter

I also address the question of causality—what are the initial conditions in which cooperation, and the coactive process, are likely or not likely to be established? The final chapter summarizes the central themes of the book's project and identifies possible policy implications of an expanded collective action theory.

2

What Does Evolutionary Psychology Tell Us about Human Cooperation?

Theories of cooperation promoted by evolutionary psychologists, regarded by many as exemplifying the best recent thinking on this subject, pay no attention to collective action or to institutions. Instead they see the foundations of cooperation in biologically evolved prosocial instincts ("moral intuition"). In this chapter I critique evolutionary psychologists using an empirical approach that demonstrates how ethnographic and other data challenge their assumptions and raise doubts about their claims. I do that by evaluating five foundational ideas of the evolutionary psychological theory: (1) that cooperation reflects an evolved propensity toward altruistic social action in which, to benefit others, individuals will incur costs to themselves; (2) that, as a result of altruism, human populations tend naturally toward high levels of cooperation; (3) that human populations in the past tended to be biologically bounded so that group members are likely to mate with others carrying the same DNA sequences ("phenotypic assortment" or "positive assortment"); (4) that individuals will display consistent behavioral patterns in relation to cooperation or defection from cooperation; and (5) that biological evolution is "multiscaler" in the sense that it operates at individual and group levels. Group-level selection is regarded as an important context for the evolution of cooperation because, it is argued, groups displaying high levels of cooperation will out-compete less cooperative groups, thus setting the stage for a broad evolutionary trend toward prosocial instincts.

The group of evolutionary psychologists I focus attention on, that I term the "biomathematicians" (based on their propensity to depend on formal mathematical

DOI: 10.5876/9781607325147.c002

methods), apply Darwinian theory as a way to explain the foundations of human cooperation. The claim is that, ultimately, cooperation results from a prosocial psychology driven by what some call "mental modules" of the brain, neurological features that evolved biologically over the deep history of our species. The analytical heart of their Charles Darwin–inspired scheme—the natural selection idea— understands that both human biology and culture are replicated across generations. In the competition for resources such as food and reproductive opportunities, some individuals and cultural practices will replicate at higher levels (i.e., they are "adaptive") to the degree that their characteristics bring relatively greater reproductive benefits to their carriers. These variants eventually will accumulate in a population. Further, they argue, populations with higher frequencies of successful genetic material and cultural practices will, over time, replace less well-endowed populations.

A key claim of the evolutionary psychologists is that a prosocial psychology evolved in the context of small-scale hunter-gatherer societies of human Pleistocene prehistory. In the kinds of small groups they imagine—and assuming, as they do, rigorous conditions of the "Ice Age" (although no climatological or other specifics are provided)—social actions consistent with cooperation must have been advantageous for individuals in small groups. This behavior includes a willingness to cooperate as well as to punish noncooperators. Further, both aspects of cooperative behavior, cooperation and punishment of noncooperators, are understood to represent an evolved propensity toward *altruism* in which cooperators and punishers sacrifice personal benefit for the good of other group members.

The idea that altruism, the Holy Grail of the biomathematicians, must be the cornerstone of the human capacity for cooperation is based on the following logic: All we have to do is look around us to realize that humans are a highly social, "groupish" species. As Robert Boyd and Peter Richerson express it, "Human Societies are extraordinarily cooperative compared with those of most other animals" (Boyd and Richerson 2006: 453); similarly, Martin Nowak and Roger Highfield describe humans as "SuperCooperators" (Nowak and Highfield 2011). An altruistic human nature, it follows, must be the basis for cooperation because the alternative—a selfish human nature—would bring social chaos. According to the economists Samuel Bowles and Herbert Gintis, without "prosocial emotions, we would all be sociopaths, and human society would not exist, however strong the institutions of contract, governmental law enforcement and reputation" (Bowles and Gintis 2003: 433).

Below I comment on the main arguments supporting the notions of altruistic psychology and the human SuperCooperator. But I begin my discussion here by pointing out that to pursue this research direction would take us into very stiff headwinds when we consider what is known about human psychology, social behavior, and culture—which I detail here and in later chapters. For example, the idea of SuperCooperation seems quaint when we recall the numerous examples in which the social fabric of a society is constructed principally out of the coercive and exploitative power of a particular person, faction, or social class. It is true that where coercion is the principal organizing force of a society, those persons making up the dominant faction will face the challenge of cooperating among themselves to maintain effective control over others, itself not an easy cooperation problem to solve. Yet, considering the society as a whole, we would be unwise to conclude that such a society exemplifies anything like "SuperCooperation." To build a more productive and realistic understanding of cooperation we need a way to understand the conditions that might favor the growth of societies in which coercion has been overcome and the benefits of broadly based cooperation gained. This topic will be addressed in later chapters of this book.

WHY ALTRUISM?

It may seem confusing to the reader, as it does to me (and biologists I cite), that evolutionary psychologists concerned with the roots of cooperation base their theory largely around altruism. One source of my confusion is that I cannot detect any sure way their method allows them to distinguish cultural altruism (i.e., ideas that valorize it) from altruistic acts that might result from a biologically evolved psychology. Thus, I think it would be important to consult the data of culture history before attributing a behavior to altruistic psychology. Donald Pfaff (2015: 126) notes that acts of charitable giving have been noted to activate a reward center in the brain (as detected from brain scans). Is this admissible as evidence that our altruistic brains make us "naturally good"? I doubt it. I would suggest in this case that a favorable response to charitable giving could also be understood as an example of an emotional response to an internalized and culturally specific value.

To have the capacity to make a distinction between cultural values and instincts would seem to be a basic starting point for a method that emphasizes an evolved altruistic psychology. Since the term "altruism" was first coined by the sociologist Auguste Comte (1798–1857), philosophers have mostly regarded it as a cultural artifact. Different forms of cultural altruism have been identified, starting with a distinction made between "beneficence" and "justice" obligations. Beneficence obligations are those that in a particular culture are considered to be virtuous but optional (e.g., saving a drowning swimmer when no lifeguard is present), while justice obligations are socially obligated duties, for example, when a lifeguard is obligated to rescue a drowning swimmer. Given that in different cultures beneficence and justice obligations are differently defined and have different purposes, it is virtually impossible to assess the degree to which expressions of altruism are likely to reflect shared social conventions versus expressing what Herbert Gintis (2012: 417) identifies as a "deep structural psychological principle."

An additional shortcoming with the biomathematicians' theory of altruism is that it ignores the possibility that a social act benefiting others may also benefit the actor, meaning that what are perceived as altruistic acts might entail mutual benefit and thus actually constitute a form of collective action. Evolutionary psychologists ignore this possibility—but why? Stuart West and his coauthors help us understand the altruism preference by pointing out that for researchers committed to Darwinist theory, altruism presents a challenging evolutionary problem to solve; in fact, it is the "core dilemma of cooperation" (Henrich and Henrich 2007: 43). According to West (et al. 2011: 242), many biologists "prefer their research problem to be altruism. This reflects the common feeling that mutually beneficial behaviors are somehow less interesting . . . A contributing factor here may be the often quoted statement from the sociobiology book of Wilson (1975: 31) that: the central problem of sociobiology [is]: how can altruism, which by definition reduces personal fitness, possibly evolve by natural selection?'" It does seem to be the case that the evolutionary puzzle of altruism challenges the mettle and arouses the best efforts of some cooperation theorists and thus has had, in my opinion, a longer-than-expected life span as a subject of cooperation research. Although this puzzle is compelling only to those researchers, editors, and readers who equate cooperation with altruism, to them the puzzle appears real and deserving of attention.

One also wonders how evolutionary psychologists are able to address their "core dilemma" methodologically, given their focus on such a complex subject as altruism, and given the evidentiary problems of understanding the nature of biological evolution in the deep human past. Their solution has been to develop a strongly formalist rather than empirical research design in which mathematical models of biological and cultural evolutionary processes are considered to be valid substitutes for observation and empirical data analysis. This lack of real-world grounding extends to the psychologists' dependence on findings from experimental games. This branch of cooperation research purports to discover elements of human psychology from observing the strategic interactions of subjects playing games in carefully controlled laboratory conditions. However, broad claims made about human psychology from experimental games are widely recognized to be suspect because subjects are drawn almost exclusively from "WEIRD" societies ("Western, educated, industrialized, rich, and democratic," e.g., Henrich, Heine, and Norenzayan [2010]), and thus are not highly representative of our species as a whole. The cultural and social baggage carried into the games by WEIRD game players is no doubt influential in the determining of the players' game strategies, but is rarely ever described or analyzed. the cultural and social baggage carried into the games by WEIRD game players. This baggage is no doubt influential in determining the players' game strategies, but is rarely ever described or analyzed. And, although the goal of experiments is to learn about cooperation, in most games subjects make their choices privately and without communicating. Further, in the most commonly used game, the "Prisoners Dilemma," the goal is for each game participant to strive for maximum individual payoff—not a good starting point to learn about cooperation! As interesting as these games may be to some people, I find them not at all useful as guides, especially when we consider the challenges of cooperation in very large and socially and complex populations studied in this book. I am not alone in this assessment. As the cooperation researcher Michael Hechter (1990a: 244–45) puts it, "Game theorists have not yet been able to provide a robust basis for the solution of collective action problems."

A CRITIQUE OF EVOLUTIONARY PSYCHOLOGY

The biomathematicians' main research tactic is similar to experimental games in the sense that they develop strategic games and "play" them, using recursive computer simulations, to mimic multigenerational (bioevolutionary) time. Given the limited availability of data, and to keep the simulations within a manageable level of complexity, imaginary groups are populated by imaginary individuals whose behavior is driven by a limited repertoire of imaginary motivations, for example, when game players are unrealistically programmed to behave as "inherent cooperators," altruistic punishers," "timid punishers," "defectors," "norm violators," and so on. Then various levels of payoffs and costs are attributed to types of mentality in strategic interactions, and other variables are introduced such as group size or group boundedness. Under varying conditions, individuals whose behavior allows replication at higher levels over repeated simulated interactions "win" the evolutionary game, and eventually those genetically caused mentalities will predominate in subsequent generations.

Normally, in these scenarios, cooperators and punishers will fare poorly in comparison with defectors and nonpunishers (because defectors avoid the costs of cooperating and punishing), except in the hypothesized circumstances that I critically discuss next.

KIN SELECTION

An oft-repeated argument of the biomathematical community is that altruism can become biologically fixed in groups if altruistic acts provide benefits to biologically similar others. This is called "kin selection" or "inclusive fitness." As a consequence of kin selection, the propensity to behave altruistically can accumulate in a phenotypically assorted population (i.e., when members are all close biological kin). This assumes that the population in question is bounded so there is little migration or other sources of gene flow from other populations. According to biomathematical theory, kin and inclusive selection have resulted in the biological evolution of a human predisposition to behave altruistically toward closely biologically related others, what they refer to as "kin psychology" or "familial sociality." One context for this evolutionary pattern is that owing to the extreme energy costs of human child development, cooperative breeding involving individuals other than the mother and father (e.g., the "grandparenting effect") has provided evolutionary advantages in the context of human evolution.

Some Stumbling Blocks for Kin Selection

I follow the lead of earlier critics by relating five concerns about the usefulness of a kin selection scenario to understand the evolution of cooperation in humans:

1. Inclusive selection obviously does operate in what are called "eusocial" species such as social ants, where worker castes sacrifice their own reproductive capacity to benefit other hive members who are biologically closely related. Yet, surprisingly, research on the eusocial species, with their evolutionary foundations in inclusive fitness, has exerted a powerful influence on biomathematical theory concerning human cooperation. By contrast, it is not uniformly accepted in the social science literatures that biologically caused kin preference for cooperation exists. One reason for this may be that empirical demonstration is challenging. Any possible expression of kin psychology will be difficult to disentangle from the personal bonds that grow from day-to-day interaction, as well as culturally based pro-family values and sanctioned obligations among close kin that are found in most cultures. And, as the economist Gary Becker (1981: 172–201) argues, while family members may choose not to cooperate on rational grounds, in some instances intrafamily cooperation could result from rational economic choice rather than a compulsive social instinct. In this case cooperation may be a strategy to gain access to family-provided resources, and thus is a reflection of collective action. I should mention that primatologists have noted a similar behavioral pattern. For example, David Watts (2002: 366) concludes that the "formation of low-risk coalitions in which all participants stand to make immediate net gains is widespread in primates and may even incorporate much presumed 'altruism' among kin."

2. It is well established that positive maternal behavior toward offspring is facilitated by a suite of hormones, including opioid peptides, which reduce

anxiety, and oxytocin, which increases sociability. Some neuroscientists argue that hormones such as these are instrumental in enhancing sociability beyond the confines of parenthood, but research suggests otherwise. Most notably, though oxytocin production is increased in the context of social encounters with well-known others, it is not enhanced in social encounters in other social settings.

3. Kin selection seems an unlikely bioevolutionary basis for human cooperation also when we recall that kin sentimentalism, no matter the cause, will be a potential source of cooperation problems. For example, Edward Banfield's (1958) ethnographic research in a southern Italian village demonstrated that a cultural preference for kin-based cooperation ("amoral familism," as he called it) brings in its wake antagonism between kin groups and thus limits the possibilities for community-scale cooperation and economic development. Kin preference would be an especially acute problem in the kinds of human groups discussed later in this book that form around either common-property management or other forms of collective action. In these cases, cooperation is sustained when there is trust that a sufficient degree of accountability of group leadership will be maintained. Here, kin favoritism would threaten participants' confidence in the collectivity when persons in positions of authority, and who control group resources, treat kin and nonkin unequally. In fact, in such cases kin favoritism often is recognized as a potential threat to cooperation, and, as a consequence, nepotism among governing officials is carefully monitored and is considered a punishable offense. Obviously, the social lives of humans would be very different today if people had not developed ways to not only manage kin favoritism but also to engage in predictable social relationships that transcend those based on kinship.

4. It is also important to note that sociability in the context of family formation must take into consideration factors beyond the promotion of favorable maternal behavior. In other respects the family context is problematic for an inclusive selection theory. Biologists have emphasized that mammals invest heavily in parenting, most notably humans with their extended period of neonate and childhood dependency. Evolutionary biologists have pointed out how such offspring dependency could lead to sibling competition for parent-provided resources. As a result, rather than positive selection for cooperation, individual ability to compete effectively might be evolutionarily advantageous. It is true that competition and conflict can be found in human family life, as Becker (1981: 32) reminds us when he writes that "malfeasance within a family is not simply a theoretical possibility but one that has been recognized for thousands of years." Further, he suggests, the high cost of monitoring for and punishing selfish behavior is among the factors limiting families to relatively

small size worldwide (usually no more than five to seven persons). Certainly, conflicts with close kin are well documented ethnographically in Western as well as other cultures. For example, as Donald Donham (1981: 537) finds in his study of the Ethiopian Malle culture, families "are composed of a number of persons, not one" (I provide additional ethnographic and other sources in the bibliographic essay).

5. Another factor to consider in relation to kin selection is that humans often understand kin in sociocultural frameworks that extend beyond biology. We see this in the fictive kinlike ties that have considerable emotional and economic force such as the practice of co-parenting found in many cultures; examples include old English *godsib*, Russian *kum-kuma*, and Spanish *compadre, comadre*.

RECIPROCAL ALTRUISM

Another argument made by biomathematical researchers is that cooperation may be fostered, even beyond close kin, when altruist sharing is based on a propensity to participate in reciprocal exchange between cooperating partners ("reciprocal altruism" in Trivers 1971). Such reciprocity is hypothesized to have provided advantages in the context of rigorous Pleistocene Period climates. Some evolutionary psychologists have argued that this kind of behavioral propensity results from an evolved bioprogram (or "mental module," analogous to a computer program) that is a "social contract algorithm" (Ermer et al. 2007).

STUMBLING BLOCKS FOR RECIPROCAL ALTRUISM

The claim that human behavior is due to a biological social contract algorithm cannot be confirmed when we consider ethnographic accounts of pressure for generosity without the expectation of reciprocity, including demand sharing (e.g., when food is demanded from a successful hunter), when we consider tolerated theft of food, or when we consider secretive hoarding to avoid obligations. In addition, in the case of food-sharing, especially valuable meat, anthropologists have noted that its main purpose may be male prestige rather than as an adaptation to food insecurity. Economic anthropologists have documented numerous different social and cultural factors shaping patterns of reciprocal social exchange across cultures and time periods, including such factors as the degree to which reciprocal exchange is more optional or strongly culturally valued and how social distance between persons or groups determines the kinds and importance of reciprocal exchange transactions. In addition, sharing also may involve a complex process of rational accounting of multiple social factors, as we see in the account written by Polly Wiessner

(1982: 79): "In deciding whether to work on a certain day, a !Kung may assess debts and debtors, decide how much wild-food harvest will go to family, close relatives and others to whom he or she really wants to reciprocate, versus how much will be claimed by freeloaders. A person may consider whether the extra effort is worth-while, or if time would be better spent gathering more information about the status of partners and trying to collect from one of them." It seems unlikely we can reduce a complex decision-making process like this to a simple social contract algorithm lodged in the brain that provides the human with a "cerebral disposition" to share (from Marlowe 2004).

ALTRUISTIC PUNISHMENT

A third argument of the biomathematicians is that while punishment of defectors is argued to promote cooperation, it is costly to the punisher because of the time and energy required and the potential for retaliation. As such it would reduce the punisher's fitness compared with nonpunishers. Punishment could become biolog-ically established, however, according to their argument, so long as punishment is coordinated by multiple group members, which minimizes the costs per individual. Punishment could also evolve in a situation in which members of a population share cultural notions, for example, religious beliefs that reduce the need for punishment and also enhance fear of supernatural reprisal for malfeasance. The latter argument about shared values introduces the element of culture into a bioevolutionary sce-nario. This is the argument that refers to "gene-culture co-evolution" that I address below under the rubric of "group selection."

Stumbling Blocks for Altruistic Punishment

Punishment is central to how humans uphold moral codes, including those per-taining to cooperation. However, the idea that the human brain is equipped with an evolved propensity directing humans to the punishment of antisocial behavior can-not be verified. Instead, cross-culturally, the degree and severity of forms of punish-ment are variables reflecting cultural and social factors. For example, from a cross-cultural comparative study using an experimental game called the "Ultimatum Game," researchers found less propensity to punish for asocial actions in very small-scale and weakly commercialized societies by comparison with societies with highly developed commercial economies. This result suggests that punishment is not an evolved altruistic social instinct. I also point to the cross-cultural comparative work of Nicolas Baumard (2010). In his wide-ranging review of ethnographic literature, he found little evidence for acts of punishment. Instead, in small-scale foraging societies people tended to simply switch away from partners when cooperation fails. In more complex societies, while acts of antisocial punishment are present, for the most part punishment is institutionalized so that specific persons are rewarded for punishing and are legally obligated to punish. I should also mention the interesting results from a study by Benedikt Herrmann and colleagues (Herrmann et al. 2008). They found that in societies scoring low on rule of law, there was some evidence that it was cooperators who were punished in acts they call "do-gooder derogation."

GROUP SELECTION

From computer simulations, biomathematicians also claim that cooperator genes can become established in a population if cooperators interact mostly with others carrying the same DNA sequences, a process called "positive assortment." This is identical to the inclusive fitness mentioned earlier. Further, based on the results of bioevolutionary game simulations, it is argued that altruists can flourish when members of a population are likely to internalize prosocial values and "groupish" cultural practices such as ethnic signaling devices and initiation rites. In these cases, a process of gene-culture coevolution is initiated because where there are cultural preferences for cooperation, violators of community values will be shunned so cooperators will interact most of the time with other cooperators (thus the "cost" of cooperation will be lower). In addition, in such groups punishment will be coordinated, also reducing the costs of punishment for an individual.

A cultural group selection approach begins with the assumption that in the deep human past social organization was based on multiple discrete and highly biologically bounded local populations. Then some population isolates are argued to have somehow developed cooperative behavior from prosocial psychology and cultural norms. These cooperative populations are argued to have biological evolutionary advantages (higher average fitness) when in competition with groups featuring less cooperatively oriented psychologies and cultures. Group selection then ensued, and prosociality proliferated when cooperative groups drove into extinction groups with lower frequencies of cooperation-driving social instincts and cultural values. In this scenario, less-cooperative groups are predicted to emulate the cultural values of the more cooperative groups to avoid extinction.

Stumbling Blocks for Group Selection

Group selectionists display their Darwin adoration by inevitably quoting the following passage from Darwin's *Descent of Man: And Selection in Relation to Sex* (Darwin 1874: 150): "There can be no doubt that a tribe including many members who . . . were always ready to give aid to each other and to sacrifice themselves for the common good, would be victorious over most other tribes; and this would be natural selection." However, the advocates of group selection have been too willing to accept the truth of Darwin's "no doubt" modifier here, as his claim had little empirical support at the time he wrote it and still does not. As an example, I point to Charles Wagley's (1969) study of two Tupí-speaking tribes of Brazil: the Tapirapé and the Tenetehara. The Tapirapé featured a social arrangement involving cooperative hunting and ritualized food-sharing between families, whereas the Tenetehara—a riverine-oriented group—featured relatively little interhousehold cooperation or feasting, as fishing was better pursued by individual families. Wagley documented how, under the pressure of European influence, including the introduction of epidemic diseases, the more cooperatively oriented of the two tribes, the Tapirapé, experienced severe population decline as it became increasingly difficult to assemble the personnel needed for group hunting and food-sharing. Conversely, the Tenetehara not only survived in the new environment, but their population appeared to be growing at the time of Wagley's study. In this case there was no tendency for the more cooperatively organized group to spread at the expense of the less cooperative. In fact, cooperation proved to be disadvantageous in light of changing circumstances. Of course one example is no disproof of a theory, but it points to how we should keep in mind that high levels of cooperation may entail both costs and benefits.

I find the group selection ideas less than convincing for additional reasons. For one, the gene-culture coevolution argument would be more plausible if it were possible to better specify the conditions favoring the emergence of a cultural pattern of cooperation. Instead, in cultural group selection theory cultural variation between groups is simply conjured out of nowhere with no hypothesized causation. The lack of a causal theory is troubling, but an even more damaging argument against the bioevolutionary scenario is the positive assortment assumption. As Nowak and Highfield point out, group selection doesn't work when there is migration or an exchange of genes between stable local population isolates (Nowak and Highfield 2011: 265). The value of this assumption, however, is brought into question when we consider a rapidly expanding body of data from archaeological, ethnographic, and genetic research demonstrating high levels of intergroup interaction and flux. As the archaeologist Jennifer Birch (2012: 649) expresses it, "human communities are not in any way static."

While there are a few documented cases of relatively stable and relatively bounded population isolates, they are exceptions. From his investigation of historical records, Robert Netting (1990) finds that the population in Törbel, Switzerland, had endured over dozens of generations. Rather than illustrating a "natural" state of humans, however, there is a compelling reason for demographic continuity in this case. For hundreds of years, the community maintained tight controls over grazing resources and wooded uplands. Rights of access to these valuable resources were passed down between generations and were restricted to community members. As a result, community members preferred not to emigrate or marry out, and outsiders rarely immigrated. It is interesting to note, however, that even in this comparatively bounded community, Netting found that ancestral families were responsible for only 62 percent of the community's genetic constitution.

Evolutionary psychologists appear to be relying on early anthropologists who often painted a picture of a premodern world peopled by highly bounded cultural isolates, each distinguished by its local culture and adaptation to local environmental circumstances. But this picture is now understood by many scholars to be an antique notion that cannot be empirically confirmed. Not even at the scale of families is the image of bounded and static isolates realistic, let alone at the population scale. Families may at times have an ephemeral quality, as in the concept of "tacit households" or "family communities" in which households form when—as described by Martine Segalen (1986: 14–18)—in "troubled times, during wars, epidemics and calamities of all kinds, people formed groups for mutual help and support and to work together."

From historical sources we are well aware of the massive scale of human diasporas and other forms of migration, processes that were accelerated with the growth of the modern world-system over the past five centuries. But, we also know these processes have a deeper history. From a growing body of work in regional-scale archaeology, and stable-isotope analysis of human remains, and from ethnographic and historical sources, we have been able to document a dynamic human past. This past included migration, slavery, creolization and coalescence, processes that describe how disparate cultural schemes and languages are recombined or reimagined to form novel cultural patterns. These processes also minimized the likelihood that phenotypic assortment was a constant factor of the human past.

I point to some elements of a dynamic human past long predating the rise of modernity. Regional archaeological surveys have often found abandonment of even once densely populated regions as well as evidence for local and large-scale migrations and variation over time in degree of settlement aggregation hundreds or thousands of years before the modern era. We also recognize that captive taking was often a goal of prehistoric warfare, with women most often the victims. Slavery and slave trading are well documented long before the rise of early capitalism, even in societies of comparatively small scale such as the Southwest and Northwest Coast Native American regions. Small-scale communities are often noted to be subject to disruptive and sometimes settlement-transforming processes such as factional disputes and wars leading to fissioning of groups and dispersal followed by coalescence into new communities. For example, from his detailed genealogical research among the village-living Yanomamö of the South American tropical lowlands, Napoleon Chagnon (1988: 990) concludes that "village membership changes chronically and fissioning redistributes individuals in such a way that . . . [persons] . . . will have close kin living in distant villages."

Migrations, factional disputes, fissioning, and wars are causes for some cases of population dispersal or other kinds of disruptions of population boundaries, and the ethnographic record points to additional causal factors of this type. Tim Ingold (1999) reminds us that earlier anthropologists mistakenly imagined hunter-gatherer lifeways in which highly stable local groups were composed of closely knit kin who cohered around endurable reciprocal exchange relations. As Ingold points out, however, in reality it is more typical for forager bands to consist of flexible associations of unrelated families who come together for specific shared activities, often for short periods. Ingold's point is supported by a thirty-two-society study of contemporary hunter-gatherers, demonstrating that generally speaking, residential groups are made up of biologically unrelated individuals. As a result, "inclusive fitness cannot explain cooperation in hunter-gatherer bands" (Hill et al. 2011: 1286).

Group selectionist ideas also fail to reflect a century-long argument among anthropologists regarding the nature of hunter-gatherer lifeways. The isolationist perspective favored by the biomathematicians sees foragers in archetypical terms as isolated and highly bounded populations that are food-sharing and endogamous collectivities. But "revisionists" question just how culturally, biologically, and historically isolated foragers have been, based on accumulating evidence that individuals, households, and local groups participate in larger social fields involving trade, migration, and gene flow. For example, Alan Fix (2002: 195) notes that gene flow is common among forager groups, who have quite large average mating distances, even, on average greater than agriculturalists. And he points out that the degree of gene flow between populations is highly variable depending on whether marriage rules favor exogamy (marrying out) or endogamy (marrying locally).

Various cultural practices have been noted that blur group boundaries and promote intergroup social interaction, such as the obligate exogamic marriages and related cultural practices that facilitate interaction between linguistically distinct groups. The native North American Kiowa, in particular, are recognized for their frequency of intercultural interactions including marriages ("many Kiowas recall Arapaho, Cheyenne, or Crow ancestors" (Hickerson 1996: 75). Ethnographers have noted a widespread phenomenon in which forager women often will "marry up" into a more settled group ("hypergyny") in spite of cultural and linguistic difference. In one of the most important social processes found in western New Guinea, groups with highly fluid memberships, and based in part on "nonagnatic" (non-kin) recruitment, form around successful "Big Men" (faction leaders). According to Andrew Strathern (1982: 37), Big Men "use descent talk . . . to give an impression of [group] stability where empirical events suggest flux." Katherine Ann Spielmann (1986) summarizes the extensive ethnographic literature pertaining to small-scale egalitarian societies that are linked across ethnic or other social boundaries through various forms of social and personnel exchange.

According to one expression of group selection theory, prosocial behavior is selected for when there is a pattern of competition between local populations. But the ethnographic reality makes this claim appear misleading when viewed from the perspective of small-scale "tribal" societies. Ethnographies have noted situations in which villages are autonomous political units and where no state exists to tamp down intervillage warfare. These conditions are associated with a persistent causal nexus linking in-group favoritism with homicide, blood revenge, and warfare between groups. If biological selection were to take place at all in these situations it would probably favor violent and aggressive behavior, not prosociality. Marc Howard Ross (1992) confirms this from his cross-cultural study in which groups scoring high on frequency of wars also scored high on harsh socialization practices that potentially could result in a pattern of aggressive behaviors in adult males. Could this be in any way consistent with biological selection for prosociality? I doubt it. As Randolph Nesse (2001: 9) reminds us, group selection could as easily select for "tendencies to dehumanize, exploit, and kill members of out-groups, hardly typical examples of moral behavior."

The shortcomings of group selection theory are on full display when we consider the well-known aboriginal societies of highland New Guinea. From his cross-cultural comparative work, D. K. Feil (1987) identifies two community patterns, one featuring high levels of in-group solidarity and relatively closed boundaries, the other featuring more fluid group boundaries. The latter cases, predominately in western New Guinea, occur where competitive Big Men and their factions engage in pig exchanges across expansive networks of interacting households, a pattern associated with a relative decline in both community life and shared religious ritual. Interestingly, in the other, predominantly eastern New Guinea social pattern, Big Man competitions are less common. Instead, high levels of intragroup balanced reciprocity and shared religious beliefs are coupled with elaborate ritual cycles that enforce comparatively high levels of social solidarity in tightly bounded nucleated communities.

According to Darwin's notion, and modern group selection theory, the eastern groups should be more successful, and tend to spread, at the expense of the Big Man formations, but the reality is quite the opposite. It is in the east where there are more pronounced adaptive problems stemming from intergroup competition expressed as a destructive pattern of "total" warfare with few rules of engagement. This pattern results in generally higher per capita male and female mortality rates from wars, by comparison with the western region, up to as high as 32 percent males per generation killed in battle. In addition, in the eastern region average group size is smaller than in the west, and overall population density is lower. In the western region, wars are viewed as disruptive to the long-distance exchanges between groups and the exchange cycles that serve as showcases for prestige competition. Correspondingly, Big Men promote institutions including war compensation payments, similar to the ancient Anglo-Saxon practice of wergild, that "deflate" the intensity of war.

Lastly, there is the matter of religion's role in service of group cohesiveness and group selection. Generally, biomathematicians see positive evolutionary outcomes from shared religious belief in the evolution of cooperation because religious belief systems typically will foreground the importance of moral conduct and thus exemplify a key argument of gene-culture coevolutionary theory. However, this argument also fails the test of explanatory adequacy because even when group members share religious precepts, they often face cooperation problems. As Mary Douglas and Aaron Wildavsky put it, "In religious sociology it is agreed that frequent schism and dissolution are the normal lot of sects and communes" (Douglas and Wildavsky 1982: 111). Given their finding of a high frequency of dissolution and schism encountered in such groups, some researchers have turned to a new perspective to understand the role of religion and ritual in the development of group sociality, one that is consistent with collective action theory. This perspective, referred to as "costly signaling theory," points out that in spite of shared religious views and ritual, group survival depends on each member having confidence that others will act with group benefit in mind. From his comparative study of religious groups, the economist Laurence Iannaccone (1992) identifies one way the confidence problem may be at least partially solved. He notes that the lifespan of religious groups was longer when the demands made by the group's conventions—for example, frequency of ritual cycles—were more onerous in terms of the time and energy they required. He interprets such obligations as a form of "costly signaling" (or "reputational symboling" in the phraseology of T. K. Ahn and coauthors [Ahn et al. 2004: 131–35]), a notion first proposed by Amotz Zahari (1975). Zahari points out that signals that are costly to the signaler namely, that are a handicap, will be perceived as having more reliability and thus are more likely to enhance confidence in the signaler's intentions than would be possible from lower-cost signals.

WHY DOES THE DARWINIAN-INSPIRED BIOMATHEMATICAL APPROACH TO COOPERATION ENJOY SUCH CREDIBILITY?

"A cottage industry has grown in recent years around theories
purporting to explain how our brains produce empathy,
morality, and good will." (Oren Harman 2015: B7)

In spite of its untestable findings, its inadequate theory of human psychology that reduces motivations to a few rigid categories, and its biological reductionism, the biomathematical theory of cooperation has gained considerable credibility in academic circles and in the broader culture. For example, the prestigious journals *Nature* and *Science* (the latter the principal journal of the American Association for the Advancement of Science) frequently publish reports on the evolution of human cooperation based on nothing more than an experimental game or a computer simulation (I can only conclude that the phrase "computer simulation" glistens in the eyes of editors). My task in this section is to try to make sense out of what I see as an unwarranted acceptance of a misguided theory. I revisit the question of evolutionary psychology's favorable treatment in the final chapter, where I consider the implications of evolutionary psychology for policy-making around issues of cooperation.

A BRIEF VIEW OF DARWINISM IN CULTURE AND SCIENCE

The theoretical foundation of the biomathematical approach is Darwin's natural selection theory, and he is typically cited in this literature with great reverence. Is this attention to Darwin deserved? Of course Darwinian theory is foundational to much of biological thinking, but historically Darwin's ideas have not always been viewed as favorably as they are currently. Today's adoration of Darwin is a phase in the history of a theory that has experienced ups and downs in popularity and prestige in Western science and popular culture since the time of the founder. Darwinism peaked in late nineteenth century and early twentieth century during which time social differences across the spectrum of human experience typically were viewed through the lens of biology, especially race. This strongly biological perspective was discredited during the early decades of the twentieth century as ideas about race and racism changed, and in concert with a growing condemnation of eugenics, a movement inspired originally by followers of Darwin.

Today, Darwinism is resurgent, striking a positive chord in the cognitive pathways of researchers and among the public, not so much, I hope, owing to a return of race thinking, though anthropologists fear this could happen. Rather, it seems, resurgence has many causes, including rapid advances in genetic research and the recent surge in prestige of the STEM (scientific) disciplines in schools and universities. Darwinian thinking was also given a boost by those biologists who theorized that aspects of animal social behavior, including human behavior, could be understood from a natural selection perspective. One approach to this "sociobiology" claimed to elucidate the evolutionary basis of human competition and violence, thus envisioning what Robert Sussman and Audrey Chapman describe as a "radically selfish and individualist account of human nature" (Sussman and Chapman 2004: 3) This view came to prominence especially in the post–World War II period, when people generally were skeptical about the possibilities for a peaceful human. Books like those of Konrad Lorenz (1963, *On Aggression*) and Desmond Morris (1967, *The Naked Ape*), both best sellers, conveyed what was then known about primate behavior to build a model of the biological evolutionary foundations of an innately aggressive human. In recent decades, however, as the memory of World War II receded, and as new views of primate sociality emerged from more sophisticated field studies (that observed reconciliation as often as agonistic encounters), some Darwinists realized it might be better to turn away from thinking about competition and aggression and turn to the study of cooperation.

The interesting work of biologists Vero C. Wynne-Edwards (1962) and E. O. Wilson (1975) also turned the heads of evolutionary psychologists. Wynne-Edwards and Wilson write about biologically adaptive forms of cooperative social behavior, a theme raised originally by Darwin himself. Wilson's work on social insects was pathbreaking, but personally I was most impressed with Wynne-Edwards's book. I have a copy of it, which I've had since my graduate student days, and still find it an interesting and compelling argument connecting cooperation and group selection, made at a time when this was not the prevailing opinion. The pages are filled with fascinating descriptions of territorial conventions and the uses of signaling to denote population density and dispersion in varied animal species among the birds, amphibians, and mammals. However, the question "How much of this is relevant to understanding human cooperation?" remains a very big one indeed.

ADDITIONAL EXPLANATIONS FOR THE POPULARITY OF BIOMATHEMATICAL THINKING

"Mathematics . . . A splendid subject, an education in thinking, without the encumbrance of knowledge." (Zia Haider Rahman 2014: 234–35)

"People sometimes seem to treat the output of formal models as data in and of itself." (Michael Price 2012: 48)

Stimulated by the work of Wilson and Wynne-Edwards, the biomathematical approach to cooperation has attracted many researchers and is now regarded in many quarters as exemplary science in spite of what I see as its host of misguided ideas and its lack of secure empirical grounding. To explain this phenomenon I suggest we look at a confluence of social factors and culturally entrenched habits of mind that together endow both mathematical reasoning and biologically reductionist explanations of human behavior with considerable prestige. Among the causal factors at play, I point to the 1950s discovery of DNA as the main source of genetic programming. This discovery has established biological research as one of the most active areas of scientific research, and its influence adds a patina of legitimacy to all forms of biological investigation. I would also allude to the impressive conceptual and methodological advances in the mathematical analysis of data from experimental games. This has become a highly respected research strategy since its inception in the early decades of the twentieth century, based on the idea that experimental games expose basic mechanisms of human cooperative psychology, in spite of the fact that, as I mentioned previously, research subjects typically are Western European or North American college students.

Experimental game research was growing in prestige coincident with the work of mathematically inclined biologists who, beginning during the 1920s and 1930s, first devised the basic elements of mathematical population genetics. This approach has been greatly enhanced by the use of computers to simulate long-term biological evolutionary scenarios.

I suggest that the biomathematical approach, which has turned to mathematical reasoning as a substitute for empirical observation and data analysis, has gained traction also because many people in the industrialized nations tend to share in the largely unexamined conventional wisdom, really a habit of mind, that mathematical reasoning is the epitome of scientific rigor and clarity. As a result, irrespective of the quality of the resulting work, in a variety of disciplines formalist mathematically informed research generates an inordinate amount of scientific prestige for its practitioners and continues to do so in spite of what has become a steady drumbeat of opposition. The economist Thomas Piketty, for example, commented on how his mathematically inclined economics colleagues expressed little interest in empirical or historical work: "What I found quite surprising when I was at MIT was that sometimes there was a level of arrogance with respect to other disciplines in the social sciences, which is really quite incredible" (qtd. in Eakin 2014: B9). His insight about the elevated prestige of mathematical work reminds me of the Nobel–prize winning economist Paul Krugman (2009: 37), who warns us not to mistake "impressive-looking mathematics for truth." And, interestingly, similar critiques originate from the voices of biologists. One of the most prominent cooperation researchers, E. O. Wilson (2013), disagrees with the claim of mathematical rigor. As he puts it, "Discoveries emerge from ideas, not number-crunching," a sentiment similar to that of another prominent biologist, Stephen J. Gould (1980), who describes evolutionary game research as nothing more than "evolutionary storytelling."

A key problem with formalism as a research strategy is that human behavior is not easily analyzed using computerized evolutionary game scenarios in which human motivations are, by necessity, distilled into a few simple categories. Instead, behavior is better understood in probabilistic terms. For example, as I discuss at more length in the next chapter, compliance with social obligations is predicted to be more likely, and defection from obligations or exit from a group less likely, when the conditions favoring cooperation have been met. The "likely" adjective refers to the reality that human social life is complicated; people's behavior is not predictably rational, nor are people always able to accurately gauge the costs and benefits of cooperation or defection or the probable behaviors of others.

Given the complexities and difficulties associated with cooperation, in my view a research design that will best answer questions about cooperation is an empirical one grounded in the reality of social action in real social and cultural formations. In this way the work will realize a form of understanding that is attentive to the need for "richness, texture, and detail, rather than parsimony, refinement, and (in the sense used by mathematicians), elegance" (Ortner 1995: 174). There is a tension, however, when one must make a choice between elegance and richness. While it is important to make the reader aware of the confusing welter of information and the great diversity and variability of human social action, at the same time there is danger in a "radical empiricism" that devolves into pure description. To take a middle ground between pure formalism and empiricism requires that we describe data, but also search for broad patterns that allow us to evaluate existing theory and develop new theory. That is the goal of this book.

I should also make clear that the critical stance I take toward a biomathematical approach, and my preference for empirical work is not a condemnation of quantification. In fact, much of what is reported on in this book is quantitatively grounded, involving the testing of hypotheses based on statistical analysis of empirical data. I have also at times have used simulation (not for purposes of this book's contents), but always with the goal that the simulation would serve to identify expected empirical outcomes from theoretical predictions. The important thing about this use of simulationist epistemology is that simulation is followed by an empirical, hypothesis-testing phase of the sort the biomathematicians typically pay little attention to or cannot possibly carry out. Thus their method fails to attend properly to that critical aspect of scientific investigation described by John Cartwright (2008: 81) as the "rigorous interplay between theory and experience." And, while conclusions drawn from simulations can never be considered as a form of evidence, I see a disturbing kind of nonreality creeping into the biomathematical community when others cite the results of one person's simulation as established fact. This tendency illustrates a form of knowledge production referred to as "narrative knowledge," which, unlike scientific knowledge, "is not subject to procedures of verification, but, rather, is self-verifying through its very recitation" (Peregrine 2013: 645).

My critique does not condemn quantification, and neither is my critique a condemnation of biology, or even of Darwin, whose work, unlike today's biomathematicians, was strongly grounded in natural history empiricism rather than in anything like the formalism of computer simulations or the artificiality of experimental game research. Rather than a polemic against biological thinking, my argument has been a reasoned critique based on what I perceive to be a very poor fit between what the biomathematicians propose about human nature and what is actually known from empirical observation. And, in chapter 5 I point to important developments in some branches of biological research such as primatology and social neuroscience that I think provide useful insights from biology—based on empirical observation—that can productively inform cooperation research.

3

The Path to Cooperation through Collective Action and Institutions

Imagine a group of Jane Austen devotees who form a club with the goal to learn from the sharing of knowledge and ideas. We might imagine that the members' appreciation of Austen's novels will provide the impetus for the club's success. Yet, even a devoted "Janeite" will think about the value of continued participation in the club, considering costs (setting aside valuable time preparing for meetings, foregoing other opportunities, travel, etc.) in relation to the perceived benefits of lively discussion. Because club benefits are, to use the terminology of cooperation theory, "jointly produced," members will hold each other accountable for the club's success, and so will be aware of each other's actions: For example, are members benefiting from the conversation but coming unprepared? Are all members genuinely interested in Jane Austen, or do they appear to have other motives for participating? In short, are other club members acting in a manner consistent with group goals?

Successful cooperation in a Jane Austen club and in many contexts like it is possible only when group members perceive that their claims of mutual accountability are being realized. If not, cooperative failure is a possibility. However, resources such as time or the foregoing of other opportunities are not strongly implied in all forms of cooperation, and thus group formation and success are not so threatened by self-interest. Cooperator success is more likely when resources figure less importantly and when group members coordinate their actions voluntarily, such as when we agree to drive on one side of the road, when municipalities and nations conform to the standard red and green colors for traffic signals, and when automobile manufacturers

DOI: 10.5876/9781607325147.c003

place the turn signal switch to the left of the steering column. This form of cooperation, referred to as *coordination*, is relatively simple to realize because it brings benefits to everyone and individuals perceive few or no incentives to disobey.

Cooperation in the form of *collective action*, however, like the Jane Austen club, is considerably more problematic because resources are involved and, with them, incentives to behave selfishly. While a multiplicity of factors may problematize the enactment of collective action (discussed in later pages of this book), the key cooperation problem is the incentive to disobey, namely, the temptation to act selfishly in relation to the production or use of communal resources. Selfishness may take the form of free-riding, which is to derive benefit from group-provided or managed resources while disobeying rules or minimizing contribution to group effort. Selfishness also manifests itself as what collective action theorists refer to as "agency" in which persons charged with the management of communal resources misuse them for personal benefit.

Owing to the potential for selfishness, two conditions must be met for cooperative success: group members must agree to accept limits on their own potentially egotistical behavior, and they must have confidence that others will act with accountability in relation to collective benefit. A potential cooperator who sees others taking the egotistical path may decide to do likewise (why should I absorb the cost of cooperating when others are not?) or may decide, depending on the availability of alternatives, to exit from an unsatisfactory group. But under what conditions are individuals likely to accept limits on their behavior, and how is it possible to know whether or not others' actions will be cooperative in tandem with self? In recent decades, collective action researchers have studied cooperative groups and have identified conditions in which potential cooperators are able to assess the balance of costs and benefits of egotistical or cooperative social action and to gain confidence that others will act accountably in relation to communal interests. This work provides a firm foundation on which to expand the scope of collective action theory.

FORMS OF COLLECTIVE ACTION

While coordination is an important dimension of human cooperation, collective action, owing to its potential for cooperator problems, has been the central focus of research, and within the domain of collective action viewed broadly we find two somewhat dissimilar kinds of cooperative arrangements and associated theoretical ideas. In "common-pool" resource management, the goal is the sustainable exploitation of a particular and degradable resource, for example, a fishery or a grazing commons. Common-pool management succeeds to the extent that group members abide by rules limiting exploitation of the resource in line with the goal to maintain sustainable levels of production. In common-pool management, because any exploitation of the resource by nonmembers will diminish the value of agreed-upon rules, cooperation will be limited to a highly bounded social space where the resource is found and a particular subgroup of a society.

By contrast, in a "public goods" system the cooperative goal is to gain mutual benefit from collectively (jointly) produced resources. The public goods form of cooperation could occur within the confines of a demarcated group, analogous to a common-pool system, in the case of what are called "club goods" and "toll goods." Here resources are jointly provided and consumed, but only by the membership of a delimited group such as a country club or a book club. However, most of what has been written about public goods systems places collective action in a wider social field where joint supply and mutual benefit refer to the population of an entire society and where the management of jointly produced resources is a responsibility of the society's governing institution. Where there are public goods, ideally, at least, no person, family, or other entity contributing to the production of communal resources can be denied access to their benefits, nor are any excluded from the responsibility to contribute to joint production.

THE RATIONAL SOCIAL ACTOR IN COLLECTIVE ACTION THEORY

A basic premise of collective action theory is that in the context of a book club or other forms of collective action, each person's social actions in relation to the group are a result of rational decision-making. Thus, for the collective action theorist, the starting point to build a theory of cooperation is to abandon the problematic notion of an evolved altruistic human nature and to emphasize instead the rational instrumentality of the *contingent cooperator*. Rather than a mentality driven by prosocial instincts, the contingent cooperator is a cognitively active information processor and decision-maker possessing the ability to collect, store, retrieve, and process information, and to then rationally identify the most satisfactory course of social action among perceived alternatives. Of course, as the economist Herbert Simon (1969) noted decades ago, it is mistaken to assume that such a "rational" decision-maker will necessarily identify an optimal solution that would best exemplify an approximation of true rationality. This is the case because it is likely that information available to an individual or to a group is incomplete.

COLLECTIVE ACTION AND RATIONAL CHOICE THEORIES

The notion of the rational human found in collective action theory is very much unlike the instinctive altruist of evolutionary psychology. Instead, the contingent cooperator's mind is one that exhibits features more in line with the rational choice theory found in disciplines such as economics, political science, and sociology. However, to abandon altruism in favor of rational choice does not imply that we must turn our backs on the findings of the psychological sciences. As I will argue in chapter 5, what psychologists call Theory of Mind ability is key to understanding the social rationality of the contingent cooperator. This ability allows a person to mentally simulate possible negative or positive outcomes of a social action based on memory of others' and self's past actions along with other factors that I discuss in that and in other chapters.

Collective Action Theory and Economic Theory

Collective action theory assumes a rational social actor, but I find it difficult to know how to apply, or even define, rational choice theory. Part of the problem is that the theory implies different things in different disciplines. For example the theory as applied here has little in common with the highly individualized wealth-maximizer central to much of traditional economic theory (*Homo economicus*). Nonetheless, given the rationality implied in the notion of the contingent cooperator, some social scientists imagine that collective action theory must align with economic theory. This is an unfortunate misunderstanding that has led many anthropologists and sociologists to avoid any rational choice approach at all and to instead focus attention on how human behavior reflects primarily the structured properties of social and cultural systems. Unfortunately, their approach leaves little room to consider the thinking subject.

Technically, it is true that the perceived human social actor of collective action theory is in some ways like the rational wealth-maximizer of economic theory. Both share the idea that social actions are not motivated principally by emotional-cultural values and beliefs. Instead, while culturally acquired beliefs and values figure into the conditional cooperator's thinking and actions, ultimately collective action theory starts from the assumption that the human has the ability to act socially in a manner that is instrumental, ends-oriented, and problem solving. How does the view of human nature envisioned by the concept of the contingent cooperator differ from traditional economic rational choice theory? I see four main differences:

1. **Self or others or self and others:** According to economic rational choice theory, the subject's choice-making is a path to the maximization of self-interest through individual behavior that ignores the costs and benefits to others. This holds true whether in the context of the "formal" calculative economic rationality of the marketplace, for example, when the goal is to maximize

wealth, or in the case of "substantive" rationality in which behavior aims for noneconomic goals such as the maximizing of prestige or power. By contrast, collective action theory sees a subject whose goal may be self-interest, but whose social actions may also aim to benefit both self and others. Some economists would regard this kind of group-oriented logic as one in which choice is influenced by "expressive" or "affective" factors such as commitment, and thus is not really rational choice. Yet, even when expressive or affective factors play a role in a person's choices, group-benefitting social action is individually rational to the degree that the subject depends on the vitality of the group in question.

Certainly, the idea that other-oriented actions may be individually rational is not new or radical. For example, 150 years ago Alexis de Tocqueville described the American tendency toward what he called "enlightened self-interest." But some have trouble imagining how that could be true; many anthropologists, for example, equate rationality with amoral selfishness. Evolutionary psychologists find the source of cooperation to be in the social instinct of altruism rather than rationality, which they equate with selfishness and social chaos. Samuel Bowles and Herbert Gintis, for example, argue that selfishness and cooperation are two separate outcomes of biological evolution that sit side-by-side in human psychology ("evolution can not only foster self-interest, but also promote . . . generous and ethical behaviors") (Bowles and Gintis 2011: 7). That the two might be compatible is not considered.

2. **Complexity of the decision-making task:** Other-oriented rational social action has implications that transcend the usual subject matter of economic decision-making. While economic theory would appropriately address the logical operations involved in a simple economic behavior—such as choosing between the purchase of a pair of shoes or a shirt—this kind of decision is not an essentially social act, because it is not likely to entail social or moral considerations concerning costs and benefits to others. By contrast, as Becker (1976: 253–82) notes, economic choices made in relation to both self and group are complicated because they consider how self's actions impact others in a cooperative group and impact the success of the group as a whole. I would add to his notion the fact that such choices are made within the context of social institutions that are sources of rules and culturally defined beliefs, moral values, and norms. Culture enters into the decision-maker's calculus when the choice-maker considers the question: Will my actions violate my own and others' notion of what is right? This does not imply that internalized cultural values will determine social action, but it does point to the fact that prevailing beliefs, values, and norms will count among the mix of factors considered by the

conditional cooperator prior to social action. Lastly, the conditional cooperator will take into consideration aspects of the institutional environment to estimate whether an amoral social act is likely to be detected and, if so, punished, or whether a moral act will be noted and rewarded.

In short, the conditional cooperator's decision-making is complex because it considers the possible benefits that might be individually gained by free-riding on group resources in relation to the potential for loss (the possibility of punishment, loss of reputation perhaps jeopardizing future cooperative interactions, the experience of regret and embarrassment, and possible negative outcomes for the group). Cooperating entails both a potential loss (removing the possible gains from free riding) and a potential benefit (contributing to the vitality of a group I depend on, maintaining my reputation, and avoiding punishment, regret, and embarrassment).

3. **Signal sources:** While the rational economic actor's wealth-maximizing choices are influenced by price and demand signals in the marketplace, the contingent cooperator's choices are influenced by signals emanating from other sources in the social environment indicating whether intentions and actions of others will be consistent with collective benefit. Especially in small groups, face-to-face interaction provides visual signals indicating that other group members are behaving in a manner conducive with cooperation. And, even in larger-scale contexts ritual events or other obligated public behaviors, for example, that promote the intermingling of members of a population may also provide such signals.

4. **Human cognitive capacity:** In chapter 11 I point to additional forms of visual signaling, including artistic representation, that will figure in how persons might make sense of others' degree of commitment to group benefit in the context of collective action. The ability to analyze such signals is due to the exceptional capacity of the human brain for visual signal analysis of actual persons as well as artistic representations of persons. The abilities in question include analysis of visual cues such as shared gaze, facial expression, and body co-presence to estimate others' states of mind that might be relevant to estimating their likelihood of cooperating (discussed in chapter 5). From these considerations, the conditional cooperator is able to mentally simulate likely social outcomes of possible courses of action. Simulation ability also allows the social and cultural architects of cooperative groups to conjecture about possible institutional means that will increase the probability of compliance with group needs in a community of conditional cooperators.

COLLECTIVE ACTION THEORY AND "AGENCY THEORY"

Although not universally accepted, rational choice theory (usually described as "agency theory") is sometimes found in the writings of political scientists and sociologists. The key problem addressed in this literature relates to the actions of principals (the chief decision-making officials of an organization such as a state or firm) in relation to their agents, the latter charged to enact the policies and directives of the principal. The problem arises because the goals of principals and agents may not coincide, so, to maintain a viable organization, principals must strategize to control the behavior of agents.

As will become apparent, there are some similarities between agency theory and collective action theory in the context of the principal-agent dynamic. However, my sense is that agency theory is more often concerned with power and control—how principals strategize to control agents—and less with cooperation. Collective action theory thus has more in common with what is sometimes referred to as "group solidarity theory" than with agency theory. In the group solidarity approach, the key cooperation problem pertains to how groups solve cooperator problems, especially free-riding on collective resources. A key to cooperative success is to build confidence among group members that others' behavior, including that of both principals and agents, is consistent with collective benefit. From this perspective, the principal-agent dynamic does have a power dimension, because agents must be monitored and controlled. But the underlying logic is that social solidarity will be threatened if group members lack confidence that there are sufficient institutional controls to inhibit malfeasance by both principals and agents.

THE CHALLENGES OF COLLECTIVE ACTION

The central notion of collective action theory is that, while humans have the capacity to realize the benefits of cooperating, to do so is challenging. In a successful cooperative group, members will have confidence that others will act in accord with collective benefits. But confidence, and, probably, the group itself, may be shattered, and future cooperation curtailed, when others take the self-interest path. As a result, cooperative groups are not likely to form at all, or, if they do, to succeed for the long run, in the absence of highly specialized and effective institutions that can foster prosocial action in spite of the contingent cooperator.

How often have humans realized collective action? Judging from the historical cases I am familiar with, its challenges were not often overcome, although, on the other hand, I would not view collective action as anomalous. For example, in the case of state-building, historically it has been more common that the armature of political structure has been the ability of one faction to exercise coercive domination over society in a manner that by no means can be described as cooperation. At the risk of jumping too far ahead, I illustrate this by referring to some results reported on in chapter 8, in which Lane Fargher and I compare a sample of thirty premodern states with a sample of thirty contemporary states. Of these samples, fully 40 percent of the premodern and 43 percent of the contemporary polities show a strong tendency toward authoritarian governance coupled with ineffective and corrupt administrative apparatuses. This reality raises the questions: Where and how have humans managed to achieve "real" cooperation in which benefits extend beyond those gained by a dominating faction, and what are the conditions favoring cooperation over dominance? Obviously, the advent of "modernity" alone will not suffice as an explanatory theory of cooperation.

Ostrom (1990: 90; cf. Ostrom and Walker 2000: 238–39) identify several conditions conducive to building cooperative groups, emphasizing common-pool situations. I list those conditions most relevant to introducing this book's subject matter: (1) small group size that allows for low-cost direct monitoring of behavior, (2) a socially homogeneous group where there is a shared sense that all members are able to participate in the crafting of operational rules, (3) dissatisfied members can easily exist, and (4) an existing pattern of trustworthy leadership that will act to enhance joint benefit. However, in the present volume, Lane Fargher and I address how cooperation is realized in large and socially heterogeneous contexts—in marketplaces, states, and cities—where Ostrom's conditions are not met. In fact, as will become clear from the discussion later in the book, we are more interested in cooperation-building that was by necessity forged out of quite challenging conditions.

By challenging conditions I refer to large group size, sometimes very large, which problematizes the possibilities for direct mutual behavioral monitoring. The management of communal resources in large group contexts implies the need for a hierarchical organization consisting of principal and agents, which brings in its wake a host of potential cooperator problems I alluded to above ("agency"). I also refer to situations in which the social composition of a society is ethnically and religiously heterogeneous and highly socially stratified into subgroups who may display a mutual lack of trust or even overt antagonism. Typically, where there is social divisiveness it is accompanied by a dualistic folk theory of the human mind. These notions distinguish between an elite, alone thought to possess the innate capacity to govern, and commoners, who are thought to be mired in irrationality and thus are unable to productively participate in society on an equal basis.

A dualistic folk theory of mind will limit the degree to which some persons will have the ability to exercise choice or to have a voice in societal decision-making, resulting in a "moot" social rationality. Dualism must be overcome by those striving to install high levels of cooperation across social sectors. Another challenging situation for cooperation is one in which potential cooperators have been ensnared in what is called a "social trap." Here, free-riding and other deceitful behaviors are common, and no person wants to be the "sucker" who breaks out of the trap by behaving cooperatively. In many cases a social trap has presented itself as one more obstacle for those persons—I'll call them "change agents"—whose goal is to enhance possibilities for cooperation. But how is it possible to instill confidence in others and compliance with obligations in such a noncooperative social environment?

It would seem almost impossible for cooperation to emerge under the challenging conditions I refer to, yet, it has happened, although, it appears, only rarely, and Lane Fargher and I wanted to know how and why. The prevailing Western social science literature provides a rather simple, but easy-to-falsify accounting of this phenomenon (discussed further, especially in relation to previous theories of polity-building in chapter 7). Basically, the argument is this: Over the long history of human societies, cooperation eventually did develop, but was a phenomenon unique to Mediterranean and European history that eventuated in modern democratic polity-building. The idea of democratic modernity then traveled from the West to the rest of the planet, making it possible for non-Europeans to escape the yoke of despotism. But I wondered: Had it been possible to enact collective action outside Western history? And, is the theory of collective action a suitable guide to understanding the conditions favoring or inhibiting cooperation?

COLLECTIVE ACTION AS A PROBLEM-GENERATING STRUCTURE

To resolve cooperator problems in collective action entails a process of problem solving, and thus I see collective action as one example of what Gudmund Hernes (1976) termed a "problem-generating structure." I use this metaphor to refer to the fact that given the rational and conditional human cooperator, when collective action is a goal there are key issues to resolve irrespective of sociocultural setting. In all cases, means must be found to allow group members to assess the balance of costs and benefits of cooperating and to generate confidence that others will be accountable in relation to joint interests. Additional cooperator problems are found when the goal is to extend cooperation across a socially, economically, and culturally heterogeneous group in which people have diverse preferences regarding how to realize cooperation, and in which there may be little consensus about what benefits and costs might accrue from collective-friendly policies. A particularly difficult-to-solve problem is that the traditional privileges of an elite often are inconsistent with the realization of joint interests considering society as a whole. A turn to collective action, particularly public goods systems, will have an overall egalitarianizing outcome that reduces elite privilege and enhances commoner welfare, and this will be true whether the impetus for change is a reform movement intended to weaken elite privilege or a political ploy by one faction to gain supporters. Whatever the motivation, collective action brings previously excluded subaltern categories of persons more firmly into a civic unit and its economy, not always something that is congenial to all parties. Opposition to cooperative reform may also result when the elite are obligated to contribute to joint production but benefit little from public goods ("demand asymmetry" in the language of collective action theory), for example, when a system to enhance food security provides more benefit to less affluent than to more affluent families.

Collective action is also difficult to build and sustain because, as will become clear in later chapters of this book, it implies the construction of a highly interconnected social system featuring substantial flows of people, material, energy, and information—all of which strain the capacities of communication and transportation infrastructures and technologies. These practical entailments, especially at large social scales, bring high transaction costs, which must be funded by an increase in wealth production. And wealth is important in another respect: collective action will be inhibited if many potential cooperators are unable to contribute to the jointly produce wealth of the collectivity.

Given the conditional cooperator and the practical difficulties inherent in establishing and sustaining collective action, it is predicted to occur only rarely and only under ideal conditions such as those discussed in chapter 12. What I find surprising is that in spite of the numerous challenges humans have faced in realizing collective action, in some cases they have succeeded through the innovative development of highly functional institutional structures, some of which represent important turning points in the history of human cooperation.

CONFIDENCE, TRUST, AND COLLECTIVE ACTION
"The twin of trust is betrayal." (John Dunn 1988: 81)

Collective action is impossible in the absence of a shared sense that the actions of group members will be in accord with mutual benefit. In what follows I use the term "confidence" to describe the form of that sense most suited to understanding the foundations of collective action. With its etymological affinities to words such as "confide" and "confirm," confidence is suited to characterizing the kind of thoughtful analysis of social signals that will occur prior to cooperative social action. The concept of trust, by contrast, is less useful in a discussion of cooperation because it is more commonly thought of as a cultural valorization of trusting, that is, that others who share my moral sentiments should be trusted.

Trust as a moral sentiment (sometimes referred to as "moralistic trust") is thought by some social scientists to be an ideal state of mind, as it allows sociability and cooperation to emerge spontaneously. One example is Francis Fukuyama (1995: 34) in his argument that economic development is most likely in a society where people express trusting as a culturally "inherited ethical habit." Yet, to valorize trust as a cultural habit as Fukuyama does is to render it a private matter and a belief system similar to faith, a kind of trusting that can be counterproductive for cooperation when trust is excessive and not based on sufficient information and analysis. Indeed, I found little evidence for a valorization of a trusting mentality in the highly cooperative societies discussed in later chapters of this book. I point to the example of Classical Athens, where people tended not to express much confidence in the inherent moral capacity of their fellow Athenians. Their institutional response to a lack of trust was to build an elaborate institutional system to accommodate what they saw as the inevitability of personal moral failure. The system they developed provided the many advantages of a democratic society, including freedom of speech, careful control over the actions of governing officials, public goods, and citizen participation in governance (and, I might add, a flourishing market economy), but there was no notion that a cultural valuation of trusting would somehow bring a spontaneous form of sociability and cooperation.

SCALE AND COLLECTIVE ACTION

Cooperative outcomes are facilitated in small groups where it is possible to directly evaluate others' commitment to collective benefit through personal knowledge of others and through face-to-face monitoring of behavior (although, even in such contexts we often see the use of institutionalized rules that shape cooperative behavior). The personalized aspects of knowledge of others and monitoring alludes to one aspect of what will be termed human "social intelligence" (in chapter 5) in which the possibilities for cooperation are relatively enhanced in groups, up to a scale threshold of about 150 to 300, in which each person is able to accumulate a dossier of memories of others' past actions and use that as a guide to their probable future cooperation.

Much of the collective action research has been focused on socially homogeneous small groups. This is locally developed or "bottom-up" collective action that we might see in an irrigation cooperative or a grazing commons. Many collective scholars claim that cooperation is best achieved in bottom-up fashion because in social formations of larger scale and complexity, cooperation is more challenging and thus is likely to be imposed through "top-down" coercive and hierarchical forms of control. An important source for this idea is Mancur Olson, one of the originators of collective action theory, who points to how societal scale would impact the potential for cooperation, arguing that "the larger the group the less it will further its common interests" (Olson 1965: 36).

However, I find the traditional assumptions about "bottom-up" versus "top-down" thinking not all that useful. For one, many theorists have pointed out how coercion is likely to fail as a strategy to enhance cooperation because it only provokes opposition and disorder. An additional problem with claims about the disadvantages of large group size is that there has been little empirical work on this issue. As will become evident in subsequent chapters, Lane Fargher and I found ample evidence for cooperation at large scales in the absence of coercion. This finding calls for new thinking about the relationship between scale and collective action that, I suggest, will focus on the issue of institution-building. While social intelligence, direct monitoring, and social memory are essential aspects of small-group cooperation, at large social scales the central fact of collective action will be found in the construction of institutions that foster—or it is hoped, will foster—prosocial action among contingent cooperators.

BUILDING INSTITUTIONS FOR COOPERATION

The study of institutions has gained traction in the social sciences in recent decades. Elinor Ostrom and her colleagues have written extensively about how even in small-group contexts, effective institutions enable the management of common-pool resources. Economists have also recently turned attention to institutional study in spite of their discipline's long history of centering its theory-building around the self-regarding and socially isolated individual economic maximizer. Douglass North (e.g., North 1981) and other "new institutional economists" have pointed to the importance of considering institutions (to them, rules) in the analysis of economic systems, for example, rules such as those protecting private property and for regulating contracts. From this economic perspective, rules serve to maximize wealth generation through their capacity to reduce the uncertainties in the marketplace stemming from selfishness ("human factors"). While I have benefited from the ideas of North, Ostrom, and other new institutionalists, this book extends their interests beyond market efficiencies gained through rule-making (North), or the social organizations of small-scale common-pool cooperatives (Ostrom), to address cooperation problems encountered in large and socially complex societies.

INSTITUTIONAL CAPITAL FOR COOPERATION

It is useful to consider an institution able to foster cooperation as a kind of social resource—a form of capital. Thus I refer to the degree to which a group's institutions are able to enhance cooperation as its "institutional capital for cooperation."

The study of institutional capital is well suited as a research design for cooperation because it approaches institutional study in relation to how cooperator problems are solved in particular social domains such as a local community, an irrigation cooperative, a state, a city, or a marketplace where problem-solving takes place in light of the problems generated by the collective management of particular resources. Thus, the term "group" here refers to the network of individuals who participate in a system of activities specified by the charter of a particular domain-purposed institution. Unlike common-pool or club goods cooperation, in a complex society there will be multiple different institutional contexts for cooperation that sit side by side. For this reason, while there might be overlap of cooperator problems and institutional features across domains, an institutional approach often will be at odds with social science theories claiming that the goal of social analysis is to identify those social and cultural structures that impart a deep unity and systematicity to society. As examples of this sort of unifying approach, I point to various notions claiming that a society will have a dominant mental pattern or "mythogram" (e.g., Claude Lévi-Strauss), a dominant cultural pattern such as an "episteme" (Michel Foucault), a dominant "mode of production" (Karl Marx), or shared culture (anthropologists generally).

BUILDING INSTITUTIONS IN COMPLEX SOCIETY

What would constitute appropriate institutions to foster cooperation in large and complex social formations? In later chapters I address this question from the vantage point of a comparative, empirical study of a wide range of premodern social formations. To do this, with my colleague Lane Fargher, I developed methods for institutional study that build on some suggestions of Ostrom (1986) and others cited in the bibliographic essay. In the following I modify Ostrom's scheme, which grew out of the study of small-scale common-pool management, to make it more suited to application to larger and socially and culturally heterogeneous societies. Although there will be many variations across space and time owing to local history, culture, and functional goals, I suggest that an institutional system devised to foster cooperation will include the following elements:

1. **Role structure:** In socially complex and large-scale groups, persons occupying specialized roles coordinate their actions in a way consistent with the functional integrity of the cooperative group. Because collective action depends on the ability to assess signals of compliance with, or defection from, obligations, each role is carefully defined so as to specify the limits of its holder's privileges and obligations vis-à-vis shared interests. Thus, it becomes possible to gauge the degree of compliance or malfeasance that will be subject to reward or punishment.

2. **Recruitment:** There will be established procedures for recruiting persons into roles, as well as appropriate methods for socializing or training persons for position service. Equitable recruitment from across social sectors is important in light of the goals of transcending social cleavage and of enhancing the potential to unite a socially heterogeneous populace into a cooperative network.

3. **Reliable communication channels:** The conditional cooperator depends on reliable information to assess whether others are contributing to group efforts and whether an institutional system is performing as expected. The need for information places pressure on change agents to devise strategies for the production of signals that will be judged as valid, including new forms of artistic representation as I discuss in chapter 11.

4. **Physical infrastructure:** Collective action in large and complex groups brings in its wake problems with coordinating the actions of persons linked into a cooperative network. This implies a growth in the physical movement of people, information, and materials, for example, to provide public goods. To enhance coordination and movement, institution-builders must provide a suitable built environment including features such as transportation infrastructure, city plans that are legible, and other built features to manage high transportation and communication loads. For example, in chapter 10 Lane Fargher and I point to standardized rules that apply to urban space use and infrastructure development such as specifications about road construction and use.

5. **Fiscal system:** The dense communication networks, physical infrastructure, monitoring, and other entailments of collective action discussed in later chapters bring collective benefits but also high "transaction costs" in the language of institutional economists. This places pressure on institution builders to devise equitable systems of fiscal support to sustain a group's activities, while avoiding overtaxation that would be counter to the goal of maintaining high levels of voluntary compliance.

6. **Institutionalized patterns of interpersonal interaction:** Humans possess elaborate cognitive abilities purposed for the analysis of others' intentions. These abilities are mobilized in interactions such as market bargaining and some forms of rituals. These interaction patterns are designed so that even strangers are able to gauge each other's intentions by evaluating visual cues such as the correct performance of conventionalized interactive behavioral sequences. Interaction is also organized by scheduling that brings people together for specific activities at set times and places.

7. **Cultural designs for cooperation:** Any attempt to devise effective institutions for cooperation will stimulate discourses surrounding rationality. Are all categories of persons endowed with sufficient rational capacity to participate in a group based on cooperation? Is rational capacity (or its absence) inherent or acquired, and if acquirable, how? Should positions of governing authority be restricted to an elite, or open to all? In addition, in culturally and socially heterogeneous contexts, to build a cultural design suited to cooperation often will require the questioning of orthodoxy with the goal of realizing new forms of consensus that transcend existing patterns of social cleavage. In later chapters I address how this kind of cultural production is seen in modes of ritual practice and artistic production that serve to communicate novel cultural notions consistent with cooperation.

COLLECTIVE ACTION AS EVOLUTION, SOCIAL TYPOLOGY, OR PROCESSUAL STUDY?

This book's primary goal is not to establish a typology of societies based on degree of collective action, nor is it an attempt to identify a standard evolutionary sequence of developmental stages leading up to fully developed collectivity as a final progressive stage of social development. Typologies and evolutionary schemes are made problematic, first, by the fact that cooperation entails the solving of a particular set of local problems, so there is not likely to be any ideal or archetypical form of collective social formation suited to every situation. Also, institution-builders will emphasize specific collective strategies reflecting local cultural preferences, the influence of prior social formations, and other local peculiarities including local environmental factors. In connection with the problem of typology, I should also point to the fact that collective action occurs ephemerally and as such does not constitute a final developmental stage in some kind of progressive evolutionary sequence. In fact, as I point out in chapter 7, some very early polities were highly collective, while many contemporary polities lack much in the way of institutional capital for cooperation. This suggests a lack of overall progressive evolutionary development.

Rather than societal types and evolution, the perspective I find more useful is to consider cooperation to be a social, cultural, and technological *process*. A process approach better addresses the reality that pathways to cooperation will be diverse and historically complex. While it is possible to identify broad cross-cultural similarities in patterns of institution-building, achieving cooperation in any particular case typically entails a lengthy and protracted process of confronting problems, some of which are more general (the free-rider problem), some more local (e.g., an entrenched aristocratic elite opposed to social and cultural change). The efforts of change agents may also be complicated by the fact that strategies contrived to resolve problems at one moment in time may prove inadequate for the long run and may not be carried forward into subsequent institution-building episodes. And change agents may devise what they imagine will be an effective system for cooperative capital, only to see unanticipated behavioral outcomes. Given these complexities, I conclude that my most productive investigative strategies will be, first, to identify elements of both similarity and difference in how humans have solved cooperator problems in different times, places, and contexts, and then to search for possible underlying causal conditions that might have played a role in either enhancing or inhibiting the likelihood of cooperation.

4

Anthropology

The Missing Voice in the Conversation about Cooperation

The anthropologist's mission is the study of humans across all of their diverse expressions of biology, technology, society, and culture, and some have taken on the additional task of applying that knowledge to solve practical problems. However, as curious as anthropologists are concerning the human condition, and as interested as they are in problem solving, only a few have thought about cooperation or have considered it a topic worthy of investigation. This is in spite of what I see as a great deal of disciplinary potential to do so, as I detail in the latter sections of this chapter. The lack of interest is indicated by the fact that I could find only one reference to cooperation and related concepts such as rational choice, institutions, and collective action in any of the dozen or so general anthropology textbooks sitting in my office (the one exception, not coincidentally, is in a textbook coauthored by one of my ex-students). And in a recent collection of articles intended to capture the main themes of recent anthropological theorizing (Moore and Sanders 2006), while there are fifty-seven index entries under the subject "culture," there are none for collective action, cooperation, or rational choice. Before I argue that anthropology does, in fact, have the potential to contribute to cooperation research, it is important to understand why most of its practitioners might not agree with me.

I should point out that researchers in other disciplines similarly see little role for anthropology in cooperation research. Many biologically based investigators find it difficult to imagine that anthropology, or any other social science, will have a meaningful role to play in cooperation study, and have instead pointed to the

DOI: 10.5876/9781607325147.c004

advantages that would accrue from uniting the physical, biological, and social sciences under a Darwinian banner to achieve a "consilience" of disciplines. An important source for this notion is the Darwinian manifesto of John Tooby and Leda Cosmides, who justify consilience when they argue that "after more than a century, the social sciences are still adrift, with an enormous mass of half-digested observations, a not inconsiderable body of empirical generalizations, and a contradictory slew of ungrounded, middle-level theories, expressed in a babel of incommensurate technical lexicons" (Tooby and Cosmides 1992: 23). This harsh language has to be understood as more rhetorical than factual, and is meant mostly to prepare the reader for what the authors are pitching, namely, that we will most positively advance our understanding of humans by abandoning social science as we know it to embrace a Darwinian approach. However, there is more than a grain of truth in their rhetoric, and here I explore that reality as a way to understand why anthropology has not figured importantly in cooperation research.

ANTHROPOLOGY AND SOCIALLY CONSTRUCTED
VIEWS OF THE INDIVIDUAL IN SOCIETY

One of the key issues that any human cooperation theory must address is how we understand individual social action in relation to the operation of societies. This is a key question addressed at length in other chapters of this book. An objective understanding of the self in society is important for cooperation study, but typically the Western social sciences, including anthropology, have tilted toward "socially constructed" views. By this I mean ways of thinking that are more likely to be ideologically inspired than scientifically valid. As an aside, I should mention that several anthropologists have noted a degree of social construction as well in the case of Darwinian bioevolutionary theory, which, they argue, shares features with the prevalent economic thinking of late nineteenth-century England (e.g., Sahlins 1976: 101–7; McKinnon 2005).

As an example of socially constructed knowledge, I point to the *Homo economicus* idea of economic theory. In this theory, social benefits accrue when rational individuals act largely independently to realize individual want-satisfaction (utility); in this view, social obligations inhibit economic efficiency. The individualizing preference has a lengthy history in Western thought, perhaps first expressed in Bernard Mandeville's *Fable of the Bees: Private Vices, Publick Benefits* and his comments on it (Mandeville 1924, orig. 1732). In this work he challenged the commonly expressed idea of the period that human society grows in part out of innate senses of compassion and understanding of right and wrong ("apriorism"). This theme is evident, for example, in the writings of David Hume and Adam Smith, especially in the latter's first book, *The Theory of Moral Sentiments* (Hume 1978). It was only with the publication of Adam Smith's second book in 1776 (*An Inquiry into the Nature and Causes of the Wealth of Nations*) (Smith 1993) that he departed from strict moral apriorism by allowing that in the domain of commerce, there can be favorable social outcomes from self-regarding behavior. By making this argument he foregrounded a utilitarianist economic theory.

I mention the idealization of individualism and the associated utilitarian behavioral model of economic theory because this idea, to a considerable degree, created a theoretical environment that influenced the growth of anthropology and its notion of human nature. This has been true because, historically, a central goal of the anthropologists has been to give the discipline not only a distinct subject matter (the non-Western "other"), but also a distinct theoretical identity. Specifically, anthropology's notion of the human was designed to separate the discipline's main ideas from the prevailing rational utilitarianism and individualism that they perceived as having little applicability beyond the unique experience of recent Western European civilization.

To build their particular theory of the human, anthropologists aligned themselves in many ways with a Romanticist tradition of philosophy. Romantics had mounted a critical reaction to the French and British Enlightenment literature and its notion that social harmony arises from rational social action. Counter to rationalism, Romantics (or Romantic nationalists), such as the eighteenth-century German author Johann Gottfried von Herder (1978, orig. 1774), argued that a society is better understood as a particular group of people who are united through their shared commitment to custom, language, religion, law, and their communal history and destiny (*kulture*).

During the early twentieth century, anthropologists looked back to German Romanticism at a time when promoters of social reform movements, such as Franz Boas, saw that during the nineteenth century the ideas of the French and British Enlightenment had devolved into socially damaging pseudoscientific theorizing. The social and cultural evolutionary theories of Lewis Henry Morgan, for example, served to legitimate claims of European social, cultural, and racial superiority. Evolutionary theories such as his legitimated colonial expansionism, slavery, separation of races, and, eventually, even eugenics (the latter promoted by followers of Charles Darwin). During the early decades of the twentieth century, anthropologists distanced themselves from Morgan and other social and biological evolutionists by turning to German Romanticism and its humanistic understanding of societies and cultures. This approach prioritized the spiritual and emotional aspects of human experience over the utilitarian, biological, and rational. The turn to *kulture* implied that anthropology would replace the study of society viewed broadly with the particularist methods of local study of the shared language, custom, and culture history of particular groups ("historical particularism"). Thereby, it would avoid broad explanatory theories, the study of human universals, social evolution, and comparison.

I should point out that the anthropological turn to Romanticism and particularism also denied any role for a general science of psychology. To historical particularists, the human brain was a blank slate, with the consequence that the only feasible form of psychological study is one firmly situated in each local culture. As Clifford Geertz puts it: "A cultureless human being would turn out to be not an intrinsically talented though unfulfilled ape, but a wholly mindless and consequently unworkable monstrosity" (Geertz 1973: 68). As a result, he made a plea to separate the study of "mental knowledge" (psychology) from anthropology's concern with the public communication of symbols (cultural study).

To understand the discipline's resolute focus on culture, I should also point to the challenge anthropologists faced, or thought they should face, to secure meaningful boundary lines around their discipline's purpose and subject matter. From this perspective the idea was promoted that any attempt to subsume anthropology into biology or psychology would be a false conceptual unification of unrelated phenomena ("reductionism"). The gulf between the biological and the cultural was further widened because many anthropologists were, and still are, concerned that a return to a strongly biologically based human study will rejuvenate nineteenth-century and early twentieth-century racialist and eugenic thinking that was anchored in Darwinism and social evolutionism.

FUNCTIONALISM AND NEOEVOLUTIONISM

While under the sway of German Romanticism, anthropologists had rejected theory-building, but theory came back into play as particularism waned just before mid-twentieth century, particularly under the rubrics of functionalism and neoevolutionism. The economic sociologists Émile Durkheim and Marcel Mauss were (and continue to be) widely cited as sources of inspiration for anthropology's antieconomic, nonutilitarianist approach that is called functional analysis—the study of how social factors themselves maintain social integration and cohesion—leaving no role for the strategic actions of persons. In the Durkheimian perspective, in premodern small-scale societies the self is not a self-aware agent. Instead, the potentially amoral self becomes thoroughly embedded in society through the mechanism of shared participation in emotionally charged communal ritual (in what appears to be a secularized version of the Christian theory of original sin and rebirth through baptism). They argued that the powerful emotions generated in ritual elevate the autonomous individual, who is selfish and amoral, to a new level of consciousness as a social person.

The way that Durkheim deeply embedded the social person in society was especially appealing to anthropologists. They liked it because it depicted a sharp divide between the compassionate social human of the past and the self-awareness and self-interestedness that appeared only with the advent of Western modernity and the decline of community. In this view, the individualistic person emerged as the dominant form of consciousness, but this brought with it a pervasive sense of social isolation and loss of purpose. Durkheim's nephew Mauss provided another twist on the functionalist theme, arguing for a new social economics consistent with the idea of the compassionate person. His insight was that outside of capitalist economies, the exchange of goods and services is more than an "economic" act aiming for individual want satisfaction. It is, instead, a "total" institution serving to create enduring social bonds between persons and groups based on the mutual obligation of reciprocal exchanges among members of a moral community.

The neoevolutionist path to a more comparative and scientific anthropology was unlike the Durkheimian in some respects but also was centered around a concept of a selfless premodern human. To build their theory, the neoevolutionists brought back to life the critique of utilitarianism and capitalism originally proposed by Karl Marx, as envisioned by the economic historian Karl Polanyi. According to Marxist/Polanyist theory, a growing pattern of private ownership of the means of production ultimately brought the demise of communal living, replacing it with individualism, competition, class divisions, class conflict, and exploitation. These processes are exemplified, it is argued, in the rise of a European commercial bourgeoisie. This bourgeoisie morphed, over hundreds of years of social evolutionary change, into a dominant and exploitative class of capitalist owners of industry and managers of commerce who eventually were able to assert their influence over government policies in capitalist societies.

Functionalist and neoevolutionist thinking represented a sharp turn away from Enlightenment philosophers such as John Locke, and its argument that social harmony arises from thinking persons who strive to build institutions that will bring a peaceful and functional commonwealth. To those who drew from Marxist theory, rationality and individualism, associated only with a commercial bourgeoisie, brings social atomization and anarchy. For example, Marx and his colleague Frederick Engels singled out the anarchic state of capitalism by arguing that in earlier social evolutionary periods people were lacking in the narrow individualistic economic rationality that propels the growth of commerce in the modern world. They also proposed that the core egalitarian and moral qualities of these early developmental stages, and their communal sensibilities, could be restored through a revolutionary overthrow of private property and capitalism and its predatory bourgeoisie class.

Marxist theory also contributed to anthropological theory-building the argument that the evolution of social complexity has taken two distinct paths, Asiatic and Occidental. Anthropological researchers have largely ignored the latter because its market systems (price-making markets) and democratic political institutions are thought to have developed uniquely in Western experience. For example, Polanyi described the rise of the West as a "discontinuity" in history created by the emergence of the uniquely European rational "marketing mind." Anthropologists cared little for European history or commerce and turned instead to Marx's sense of the Asiatic form of society (his "Asiatic Mode of Production"). In this framework, the monarch was the central fact of the political system. They were able to maintain total dominance over society and avoid revolutionary overthrow because members of the "presocial" (to use Marx's phrase) subaltern (rural) sector of society were mired in an irrational "herd mentality" ("the despotic regime hovering over the little communes" [Marx 1973: 474]). According to the Marxist scenario, it was only in the recent history of Europe that the herd mentality was transcended, bringing in its wake a form of revolutionary consciousness that "would in time subordinate the whole world" (quoted from Vitkin 1981: 445).

While anthropologists typically did not adopt the revolutionary implications of Marx's critical economic theory, his ideas resonated with anthropologists who saw in them resources for a more materialist and evolutionary—and therefore, in their view, scientific—discipline to replace historical particularism. One aspect of Marx/Polanyi thought that anthropologists accepted without question is the idea that in the premodern world, most humans, excepting the governing elite, lived in "primitive collectivities" whose economy was deeply moral in that it was based on shared religious ritual, reciprocal exchange of goods and services, and shared ownership of the means of production. So, when market exchange is found in a non-Western setting, it follows that it must reflect a process of "penetration" of the community by outside capitalist interests. This antimarket mentality drove anthropologists away from market study; at the same time they assumed that the local moral community (their main area of interest) could be understood in terms of Durkheimian and Marxist ideas.

INDIVIDUALIST OR COMMUNITARIAN?

As will become apparent in the pages of this book, neither of the posited perspectives of human nature, highly individualist or socially embedded, is ideally suited to understanding how humans solve cooperation problems. In fact, both concepts, the individualist or "undersocialized" self of economic theory, and the socially embedded "oversocialized" self (borrowing terminology from Dennis Wrong 1961) of anthropology, are both socially constructed forms of knowledge. Each is imagined with the goal of promoting particular social, cultural, or political ideals. The individualist view is intended to promote notions consistent with libertarian market fundamentalism. The oversocialized notion is designed to mount a critique of modernism, capitalism, and capitalism's utilitarianist economic theories.

An unfortunate outcome of the anthropological view of the socially embedded human is that it rendered the study of cooperation largely unnecessary. In this scenario, community life molds the self into a moral and social person, while, at the same time, communal ownership of resources restricts the potential for the development of anything like bourgeois individualist mentality. This way of thinking renders cooperation a given, not a question that requires research attention. Unfortunately this imagined "authentic" human is a limiting construct incompatible with cooperation study because it fails to embrace the possibility that a self-aware subject may exhibit rational choice and self-interest that may threaten cooperation. And, as I outline in chapter 6, the focus on a communitarian human has pushed anthropological research away from market study, which is argued to be of little importance outside capitalist economies. Yet, recent research demonstrates just how important markets have been in noncapitalist and precapitalist conditions. And, I suggest, market study should be a key venue for cooperation research because markets have presented among the earliest and most important kinds of cooperation problems humans have faced during the post-Neolithic Period. As I discuss in chapter 12, the problem solving developed in the marketplaces might have had important implications for the evolution of cooperative social institutions in other social domains.

THE NEW ANTHROPOLOGICAL IMAGINATION

"I urge the reader to study the tradition, begin where you
are, get off your home turf, play with ideas, practice dis-
belief, observe emphatically, theorize wildly, think ahead, and
conduct exploratory analyses." (John Gerring 2012: 37)

From my studies I have arrived at the conclusions that human cooperation is devilishly complex to understand. Thus it compels the researcher to creatively integrate many lines of evidence ranging from bioevolution, primatology, archaeology, history, psychology, and contemporary societies to realize the kind of diverse and exploratory research design Gerring (2012) describes. The path to discovery that I find most capable of facing up to this difficult challenge in a meaningful and useful way is a processual and transhistorical one. This path has as its goals the discovery of causal regularities across time and space as they can be inferred from the observation of concrete biological and social realities. In spite of my discipline's historical avoidance of cooperation topics, anthropology's "new imagination," as I call it, has the potential to serve as an important source of this kind of deeply empirical and comparative inquiry that can serve as a useful complement to work done by collective action theorists.

One aspect of the anthropological imagination I foreground here and that is not new to the discipline is its strong history of empirical work. While the Darwinist Alex Mesoudi promotes the value of mathematical formalism because "researchers can conduct experiments under controlled conditions in the lab without distractions or confounding factors . . . can accurately record data . . . manipulate variables to test specific hypotheses, and . . . can re-run history to replicate evolutionary trends" (Mesoudi 2011: 138), this is not a commonly expressed idea among anthropologists. Although anthropology's history is checkered with antirationalist and antireductionist ideologies, its practitioners have, for the most part, persisted in seeing their discipline as having a primarily empirical rather than formal-mathematical basis.

The idea of sitting in an office writing equations and running computer simulations ("computer squeezing" as some critics describe it), or recording the actions of student subjects in an experimental game, are not at the soul of the anthropological imagination. Anthropologists will pack their suitcase with Imodium, slather on the insect repellent, get their boots wet, excavate, observe, listen, record, measure, and interview—in the field. This empirical orientation has allowed them to produce a large body of data that, in my opinion, is highly relevant to evaluating current theories of cooperation and of stimulating new ideas about it. In addition, in recent decades many of its practitioners have rejected anthropology's tendency toward socially constructed notions of the human, and I see these new ways of thinking as productive pathways to cooperation study. I include especially the following developments:

1. Recent discoveries made by cognitive researchers and primatologists, especially that related to "Theory of Mind" described in the following chapter, throw light on the psychological foundations of the conditional cooperator.

2. Psychological anthropologists now regard any simplistic dichotomy of Western and non-Western kinds of persons to be misleading, a major rethinking of the relationship of self to society and culture that had originated long ago with Durkheim, Mauss, and Marx. Indeed, Geertz's famous claim that "the Western concept of the person as a bounded, unique . . . dynamic center of awareness, emotion, judgment, and action . . . and set contrastively both against other such

wholes and against its social and natural background is . . . a rather peculiar idea within the context of the world's cultures" (Geertz 1983b: 59) can now be amended to read, "a typology of the self (or of personality) that consists of only two types—a Western and a non-Western—is much too restrictive to accurately describe either, and only serves to distort both" (Spiro 1993: 144). As I argue in later chapters, this rethinking makes it possible to build a more objective and empirical anthropological understanding of the self in society and by doing that it is possible to imagine the broadly human approach to the study of cooperation found in the chapters of this book.

3. Marketplaces have not been a favored as a research site for anthropological investigation. Yet, marketplaces have been important sites where new forms of cooperative social action first emerged during the post-Neolithic Periods. The potential for amoral, noncooperative behavior is exaggerated in market contexts, especially where transactions occur among strangers, yet, from archaeological and historical sources it is evident that humans have found ways to overcome such difficulties. The evidence is found in a lengthy history of institutional change, at least 5,000 years in some world areas, that set the stage for the evolution of modern commerce. But how was it possible to overcome inherent cooperator problems in marketplace venues? Although anthropologists have shown little interest in market behavior and commercial institutions until very recently, still, there is some suitable ethnographic descriptive material that I am able to draw from to begin to theorize about how people have solved cooperator problems. I follow up on markets in the concluding chapter where I suggest that it was in marketplaces where problem solving for cooperation set the stage for the rise of modern economies and also influenced social change in other social domains, including polity-building.

4. Much of the theory applying collective action ideas to the evolution of polities has been done by political scientists interested in collective action, mostly by reference to Western history. While their very interesting work will be cited extensively in chapters 7 and 8 (with my colleague Lane Fargher), we extend collective action theory outward so as to incorporate an extensive literature on non-Western polities coming from anthropological archaeology, history, and ethnography. These sources allow us to evaluate the usefulness of a collective action approach as a general theory of human cooperation.

5. Cross-cultural comparative research has a long history in anthropology, more than fifty years, and it has seen considerable methodological development since it was first envisioned and then institutionally strengthened by the creation of

a massive file of ethnographic materials known as the as the Human Relations Area Files, or HRAF (now eHRAF http://ehrafworldcultures.yale.edu). Much of the work presented in this book has a strong comparative orientation and in some cases makes use of statistical methods to evaluate hypotheses.

6. Anthropologists have a long enough history of engagement with the cultural aspect of human experience to address how symbols and performances motivate thought and social action. I benefit from my discipline's store of knowledge and concepts in these subjects, because, as I discuss, particularly in chapter 11, while cooperation is largely a problem-solving process of social construction, it will entail, as well, the formulation of shared conceptual structures and systems of symbolic meaning that are expressed through visual and other media. Those who follow the logic that scientific inquiry is inconsistent with the humanistic concern with symbolism and meaning ("natural sciences versus humanism") may see cultural study as counter to the goal of discovering process through a comparative method. However, as I point out, it is possible to discover processual regularities in some aspects of how people situate meaningful experience into the construction of social formations, including those based on cooperation.

FINAL COMMENT

To promote a distinct disciplinary identity, anthropology's practitioners built their discipline around a human subject they constructed as counterpoint to the hyperindividualism implied by *Homo economicus*. Correspondingly, anthropologists judged their subject to be an "authentic" human, or "noble savage," a naturally prosocial cooperator deeply embedded in community life and thus exhibiting a way of life, as Eric Wolf (1974: xiii) writes, "once led by all men and still by some, a life richer and more intricately human than our own." While, historically, this approach strongly shaped aspects of anthropological thinking, now, at least in some circles, it is losing force. Not only would many find it unacceptable to judge some human ways of life as more authentic than others, it turns out there are theoretical downsides to this kind of idealistic thinking. A key drawback is that it fails to provide a sufficient basis for understanding what humans must do to overcome the challenges of cooperation in all kinds of social settings, including the non-Western. Further when we understand the self to be deeply embedded in the culture of local group, community or otherwise, we are not as likely to ask how it is that humans have been able to transcend the myriad forms of group identity—including community, class, faction, caste, ethnicity, religion, and gender—to build large-scale and inclusive cooperative groups in the face of heterogeneity.

Burdened with their historical particularism, their often idealistic sense of the self, and their unwillingness to address the issue of human nature, anthropologists created an "explanatory vacuum" (to quote Walter Goldschmidt 2011: 271) in regards to the subject of cooperation, and to a considerable extent, as Goldschmidt points out, this vacuum has been filled by evolutionary psychologists. I would point out that the vacuum has been filled also by collective action theorists in sociology and political science, both venerable and well-developed disciplines, but whose practitioners display little interest in or experience in human behavior outside Western history. The goal of this book is to take steps to overcome anthropology's "explanatory vacuum" problem.

5

The Contingent Cooperator as Seen from the Perspectives of Neurobiology and Bioevolution

In his monumental *The Growth of Biological Thought: Diversity, Evolution, and Inheritance*, Ernst Mayr expresses a concern that his discipline is split between "two biologies" (Mayr 1982: 68–69). One, he notes, addresses proximate questions such as the functional study of organisms in present time, while the other attends to ultimate questions pertaining to biological evolution over long time spans. His concern is that biology as a discipline could be more productive if proximate and ultimate camps were not so "remarkably self-contained." I, too, worry that progress in cooperation research is impeded by a similarly divided research community. While the biomathematical theory limits itself to ultimate questions, collective action theory addresses the proximate, and neither camp has attempted to integrate the two perspectives. In this chapter, I propose a strategy aimed to unify ultimate and proximate by moving away from a faulted biomathematical approach and, in its stead, bring to the table the results of research on the "social brain" and its unique cognitive capacities that are foundational for the contingent cooperator.

This is an appropriate time to build a bridge between cognitive sciences—the study of the brain—and sociocultural sciences to better understand the foundations of cooperation. In recent decades, considerable progress has been made in a "new psychology" that studies cognitive abilities, coming from fields as diverse as primatology, cognitive neuroscience, psychology, primate and human paleontology, art psychology, and cultural anthropology. Even the collective action researcher Ostrom alludes to the need for psychological study, for example in her claim that the "model of the individual is the animating force that allows the analyst to generate predictions about likely outcomes given the structure of the situation" (Ostrom 1986: 18), but she and other collective action theorists have not seriously attended to this issue.

To fold cognitive science into a conversation about cooperation will, I suggest, enhance our ability to understand the interplay of biology and human social behavior. And it will do so in a way that challenges the evolutionary psychologists' claim that human sociality reflects instinctive other-regarding preferences. As one example of how the new psychology has the potential to contribute to cooperation study, I point to the discovery that genetic composition has a less determinative role in brain functioning than was understood previously. Thus, while Theory of Mind ability stems from the biological nature of the ape/human brain, its set of cognitive abilities is known to be enhanced through experience, in what Peter Smith (1996: 354) calls the "ontogeny of mind-reading skills." In this case, the dedicated neurocognitive mechanisms that provide the bases for social intelligence may be enhanced owing to what cognitive scientists refer to as neural plasticity and epigenetic processes (gene-environment interactions). These enhancements may result from experience during brain development, or even in adulthood, that shape what is called the "epigenome." Possible examples include chimpanzees who, enculturated by human contact and training, show enhanced skills in deception, pretend play, gaze following, and shared attention, all important dimensions of Theory of Mind ability. Cecilia Heyes and Chris Frith suggest that, for humans, mind-reading skills have an important learning component that is passed from generation to generation by verbal instruction (Heyes and Frith 2014).

In addition to brain plasticity and behavioral flexibility, new research points to the neurophysiological basis for conscious decision-making that is made possible, in particular, by the functionality of the brain's prefrontal cortex region and related neurophysiological structures. Psychologists have known for some time that in humans a properly functioning neocortex plays a critical role in sustaining productive social interactions. This is the case in part owing to the fact that the neocortex serves as an executive area able to assert control over some of the more primitive functions of the "subcortical" brain regions, for example, limiting the possibility for outbursts of impulsive behavior and (under normal conditions) avoiding the expression of emotionality over rationality. I mention under "normal" conditions because, in a state of mental exhaustion, the neocortex may relax controls, opening the door to a more emotional state of mind; in chapter 11 I follow up on this finding when I address how this interplay of neocortex and lower brain is expressed in different forms of ritual practice.

The neocortex expanded greatly in later mammalian evolution, most notably in the primates, and especially our genus (*Homo*), adding new dimensions to cognitive capacity that transcended the specialized functions of the subneocortical limbic regions. It makes perfect sense that the biomathematicians pay little heed to brain functionality, especially the executive functions of the neocortex, in their goal to demonstrate the existence of prosocial instincts. To do so would undermine their theory. As J. Panksepp (2007: 179) puts it, "We are fundamentally mammals, with a long and glorious heritage that was capped, only recently in brain evolution, with a massive neocortex that permits sophisticated forms of learning and thinking. However, one must wonder about the extent to which our capacity to have all kinds of creative higher-order thoughts now coaxes us to see evolutionarily specialized 'modules' in the higher reaches of our brains."

PRIMATE SOCIAL INTELLIGENCE

From paleontological evidence, studies of living primates, and psychological investigations of humans, it is possible to develop a basic model of the underlying cognitive processes that make the rational contingent cooperator a possibility. This aspect of what is termed "social intelligence" is found in humans and to some degree, most notably, in certain apes (including orangutans, gorillas, chimpanzees, and bonobos). But it is also present, to a limited degree in monkeys and even in some nonprimate species. The centerpiece of social intelligence is a mix of abilities, including the elaborate neurophysiological structures that allow for face and emotion analysis, summed up by the concept of "Theory of Mind." Theory of Mind allows for a kind of "mind reading" in which it is possible to consciously analyze the states of mind, beliefs, and intentions of others ("state attribution") and from that to predict their possible social actions. Theory of Mind ability also allows for the retrodiction of motivations for past actions. As I point out in chapter 11, the ability to make sense of a person's past actions is a key feature of the judicial apparatuses we see in the more collective polities.

Elements of Theory of Mind capacity evidently have a deep bioevolutionary history in primates, long antedating forms of symbolic communication, which first appeared in our species some 150,000 years ago. Primates generally, especially the anthropoids (monkeys, apes, and humans) are noted to have relatively highly developed social skills by comparison with other mammals. This is exemplified in the development of social bonds—even with unrelated individuals—through reciprocal grooming, among other behaviors. However, monkeys, among the anthropoid group, display the least developed Theory of Mind capacity. This probably accounts for the fact that as a whole, they tend to exhibit fewer and more invariant behavioral patterns in their relatively rigid and hierarchically structured social formations. Apes, in contrast, are described by primatologists as having many more categories of behavior and a greater tendency toward individualistic behavior in their comparatively fluid, less-structured social groupings. Enhanced individualism, however, does not imply an absence of capacity for cooperation. In fact, among chimpanzees we see novel forms of cooperation not seen in monkeys. These include, possibly, the active teaching of skills, an expression of what is called shared attention, one dimension of Theory of Mind ability.

The phylogenetic trend away from the more genetically structured behavioral patterns found in monkeys to the more fluid and variable interaction found in apes, in which interaction between group members is more individualized, has interesting ramifications. First, to base cooperation on individualized social memory of others, as Dwight Read (2010: 199) has noted, "places exponentially greater cognitive demands on individuals having to cope with a social unit composed of behaviorally individualized members." This would have placed evolutionary pressure on enhanced memory capacity to a greater degree in the hominoids compared with other primates. One possible outcome of this kind of pressure is "encephalization" (increase in relative brain volume)—apes have relatively larger brains than monkeys—and encephalization was carried considerably further in the case of our genus, *Homo*. However, in spite of encephalization, memory limitations imply scale limits for personalized human social networks, depending on the degree of familiarity required for a group to function effectively. Where high levels of close attention and detailed social knowledge are required for group functioning, for example, in families, as few as five to seven individuals is a limit often found. Larger groups are possible, of course, but where some degree of direct personal knowledge of others is required, maximum group size is estimated to be in the neighborhood of approximately 150 to 200 individuals. Humans have devised more impersonal cooperative groups vastly exceeding that number, a fact addressed in later chapters. However, even in humans, comparative researchers have noted a significant organizational threshold, a limit that requires enhanced organizational capacity to overcome, at approximately this same 150- to 200-person scale.

ELEMENTS OF SOCIAL INTELLIGENCE

The primatologist Robin Dunbar has defined social intelligence (sometimes referred to as "behavioral modernity") as the cognitive capacity that allows an individual (ego) to estimate the intentions of others and to gauge the possible responses by others to ego's actions (including possible responses to deceptive actions). Social intelligence is a complex variable exhibiting a spectrum of possible expressions. The range of possibilities extends from a comparatively simple set of cognitive abilities found widely among the higher vertebrates to the fully developed Theory of

Mind capacity of humans. The simpler form, referred to as "behaviorist" analysis (or "smart behavior-reading" in Whiten 1996), is a "lean" form of state attribution that allows an individual to understand the probable intentions of others based on a knowledge of routinized sequences of behaviors (similar to what psychological anthropologists call a "schema," "a simplified interpretive framework used to understand events" [D'Andrade 1992: 48]). Many animals have this ability. My cat Poco, from his experience, is quite good at gauging whether or not I'll respond positively to his begging to be taken out for a walk, to be fed, or to be played with, depending on what I'm doing and what time of day it is (although he sometimes violates his own social algorithm when he wakes me at 5:00 A.M. instead of the allowable 6:00). Poco also uses specific ritualized movements and sounds to communicate his intentions—to be fed, brushed, played with, and so on—and to which he knows I will normally respond, a simple and direct form of social intelligence.

A schema is not very complete, but may allow the viewer to hypothesize about a person's mental state and intentions based on past actions (a kind of pseudo mind-reading). Theory of Mind is a more complex, or "rich," form of state attribution. Although Theory of Mind has been a focus of primatological, psychological, and neurophysiological research only within recent decades, it is known to have several component elements. One of these is exemplified in behaviors of savannah baboons in Africa and recorded by the primatologists John Watanabe and Barbara Smuts. Although, generally, monkeys, by comparison with apes, have only limited capacities of this sort, this example is useful to relate because it points to some elemental aspects of Theory of Mind capacity that distinguish it from simple behaviorist analysis.

Watanabe and Smuts (1999, 2004) discovered a complex form of social communication in baboons that results in a more generalized, less time-specific, and less task-specific potential for cooperative action by comparison with Poco's schemas. This enables "partners to transcend the here and now of short-term failings in their relationship" (Watanabe and Smuts 2004: 289) in spite of the fact that their baboon male subjects ordinarily are involved in quite antagonistic and competitive interactions. It is only through a process of formalized ritual greetings that they are able to overcome aggression to realize a greater potential for mutual coordination of social action. The greeting sequence is initiated by one male, who uses a specific kind of gait as he approaches his target animal, followed by the instigating of a shared gaze, lip smacking, and making what the investigators referred to as a "come-hither" facial expression. If successful to this point, hind-end presenting or even the mutual touching of sexual organs and embracing follow. At any point the other animal may fail to respond, break off the sequence, or even attack the initiator. If successful, however, the ritual cycle serves to confirm the existence of a bond of cooperative potential between the greeters. It can be enacted in various possible contingencies, including the avoidance of antagonistic encounters between the two and the possibility of allying against threats from dangerous younger baboon males. Interestingly, the ritualized communication evidently is not inherent and instead is mastered only with experience. As a result, it is mostly older males who are able to successfully bring the behavioral sequence to a successful conclusion, giving them an advantage in competition with the physically stronger young males.

Savannah baboon ritual communication is worth noting because of the way the greeting ritual serves to establish the potential to achieve generalized, nonspecific cooperative goals. It accomplishes this by employing elements of Theory of Mind mentality that I outline below. These include some degree of what is called temporal displacement, in this case the ability to imagine that the benefit of the ritual will be realized in some future but unspecified contingency. The ritual cycle contains other elements found in higher primate cooperative ability, including shared gaze and other aspects of mutual attention-sharing ("entrainment"). Analogous behaviors are seen in the scripted interactive ritual chains that can be a prelude to cooperative social intercourse in more advanced primates and humans.

ORIGINS AND EVOLUTION OF THE PRIMATE SOCIAL BRAIN

Primate paleontologists point out, judging from cranial morphology, that key evolutionary changes leading to Theory of Mind abilities most likely first appeared during the Miocene geological epoch (sometime in the range of 24 to 5 million years ago). These changes are most apparent in, although not restricted to, one branch of the superfamily Hominoidea (apes and humans). This branch, the Hominidae, was directly antecedent to gorillas, orangutans, bonobos, and chimpanzees (who are genetically closer to humans than any other primate species), and also is antecedent to the bipedal hominids, which includes our genus, *Homo*. *Homo* first split from the other hominids roughly 3 million years ago and is distinguishable owing to the rapid burst of encephalization (brain growth), a process that continued at varying rates for another 2 million years. Interestingly, areas of the neocortex, where the most notable brain expansion occurred, are those that house the decision-making capacities central to advanced forms of cooperative social behavior and Theory of Mind ability. Some researchers have postulated that it was the changing nature of social groups and social action that provided the selective pressures favoring neocortex evolution (the "Social Brain Hypothesis"), though I should point out that the causes of brain evolution are not well understood at this point.

While it is important for my research goals to summarize the nature of cognitive capacities associated with our branch of the Hominoidea, the bioevolutionary basis of them is not the central topic of this book. Instead, the purpose of this review is to identify those cognitive properties found among the pertinent living alloprimates and humans that provide a neurobiological basis for human social action including cooperation. Anyway, the evolutionary history of Theory of Mind ability is not clear and probably will remain so for the time being because of the severe evidentiary limitations of any investigation of neurobiological change that occurred millions of years ago. What is clear and very interesting is that advanced cognitive abilities would have exacted high energy costs related to the growing and supporting of the neural tissue itself ("expensive tissue" in the terminology of Leslie Aiello and Peter Wheeler), with significant bioevolutionary and social consequences (Aiello and Wheeler 1995). Melvin Ember and Carol Ember, based on their cross-species comparison, demonstrate that due to the exceptional costliness of reproduction and child rearing, human mothers would need help, prompting change in social behavior including pair bonding and biparenting (with both parents caring for offspring) (Ember and Ember 1979). Energetic stress also explains the unique life course of our genus that extended the period of brain development and social learning across stages from a baby phase to a lengthy juvenile phase. Another pathway to funding the high costs of neural tissue was to reduce the proportion of the body's energy budget devoted to mastication and digestion coupled with a relative loss of muscle tissue by comparison with other primates. Reducing mastication and digestive costs entailed, across the long phylogenetic history of genus *Homo*, improved technologies. These included chipped stone tools that improved the efficiency of scavenging, served for premasticatory food preparation, and eventually made possible big-game hunting, a source of increased food quality. The cooking of food, for which there is evidence as early as 800,000 years ago, can be added to the list of factors reducing mastication and digestive costs.

Human chipped-stone tool-making is one factor that may have figured into the evolution of behavioral modernity, even beyond its role in scavenging and food preparation. This technology, nearly 3 million years old, is unique among all animal tool-making, even among other primates. The advent of chipped-stone tools not only reflects changing "foodways," but it is also considered a possible source of selective pressure amplifying neuroevolutionary change, assuming that more adept toolmakers would have gained reproductive advantages over less capable knappers. This makes sense, as chipped stone tool-making is a uniquely cognitively demanding technology. For example, because not all classes of stone have equal value for knapping, to obtain desired materials depends on a rudimentary geological knowledge. The planning of acquisition trips required temporal displacement ability or "mental time travel," and superior knappers would also have the ability to effectively participate in social networks that served as raw material supply chains. Tool-making also places demands on working memory. To imagine a finished product that will emerge from raw material requires considerable capacity for visualizing desired outcomes, and each tool type requires the knapper to remember a set sequence of production steps. The earliest tool types of nearly 3 million years ago required only a few sequential steps, but tool production got very complicated by the Upper Paleolithic Period (after about 50,000 years ago), by which time some tool types required hundreds of sequential production steps.

THEORY OF MIND

Theory of Mind is defined as "the ability . . . to explain and predict the actions, both of oneself, and of other intelligent agents" (Carruthers and Smith 1996a: 1). It does so by endowing the individual with the ability to understand that others have thoughts, to understand that others can have false beliefs, to understand pretending, to understand desire and intention, and to understand the difference between appearance and reality (Baron-Cohen and Swettenham 1996: 161). Theory of Mind is found in its fullest expression in apes and adult humans (normal human children are lacking in some Theory of Mind abilities until about age four), but humans understand intentionality at a higher level of abstraction than apes. For example, as Robin Dunbar (2007: 23) points out, the sentence "I intend that you suppose that I want you to understand that I believe," is comprehensible to most adult humans, but not to apes, who are thought to understand only one level of abstraction.

The neurobiological basis for Theory of Mind cognitive ability is not well understood. One proposal emphasizes the importance of mirror neurons found in humans and other species, although at present the process is not well understood. In this scenario, mirror neurons are one aspect of a premotor neural mechanism that has two structures. One, connected to the corticospinal pathway, activates muscles to create movement, while the other will discharge, for example, when observing another's actions, but it only simulates movement rather than causing it. The latter mechanism may account for how we perceive what a person is doing and perhaps also how we estimate what the person's state of mind is while doing it, for example, to conjecture about why the person is doing it. And the mirror mechanism may allow for the simulation of state of mind and the corresponding action response of self, or another, through pretense (simulation). For example, a person might pretend to face a moral dilemma, which is then evaluated through the decision algorithm they would employ for that context. The predicted response is then used to imagine how another person would react to the same dilemma and to predict their possible behavioral response to one's own action.

THE ELEMENTS OF THEORY OF MIND CAPACITY

Representational Understanding

Theory of Mind is predicated on what Richard Byrne (1997: 298) refers to as a "representational understanding of the world" (or mental time travel), the ability to envision the probable consequences of courses of social action as a "mental rehearsal of action" (as phrased in Carruthers 2006: 230). Representational capacity is foundational to both envisioning the outcomes of one's social action but also to "mind-read" others to gauge their emotional states and even intentions. This includes the ability to predict the behavior of others through the process of simulation, projecting "ourselves into another person's perspective, simulating their mental activity with our own" (Carruthers and Smith 1996a: 3). Representational understanding also makes possible imaginary play as well as tactical deception. The latter is a strategic social behavior found in monkeys and apes, most elaborately in chimpanzees and humans. Mental representation also provides the ability to imitate the motor actions of others, by replicating in action something that has been visualized. This, again, has been noted primarily in chimpanzees (with human training) and humans. It is not unreasonable to suppose that representational understanding is related to those aspects of technical intelligence, including tool use—found in humans and also some great apes such as chimpanzees—who have been observed to prepare tools for future use ("displacement"). Monkeys, by comparison with some apes, are comparatively deficient in their degree of displacement ability and tool use and also lack full Theory of Mind capacity, although savannah baboon ritual communication implies some degree of anticipation of future benefits from cooperation.

Inner Speech

Language ability is not a requirement for Theory of Mind (apes possess some Theory of Mind abilities but do not use language communication in natural settings). However, language enhances Theory of Mind ability in the sense that grammatical constructions provide an accurate way to represent the mental states of others ("I believe that Sally thinks that the chocolate might be in the drawer"). Further, language in the form of "inner speech" (or "inner monologue," or "inner dialogue") is argued to be a strategy for developing an understanding of one's internal sense of self (one's subjective Theory of Mind), while also providing an effective form of representational understanding that makes possible mental rehearsal for social action. In this sense, Theory of Mind notions challenge the distinction made by Geertz (1973: chap. 1) in his plea to separate the more individually centered study of "mental knowledge" (psychology) from anthropology's concern with the public communication of symbols (cultural study), because simulation and inner speech are both preludes to social action.

FACE ANALYSIS AND BODILY ENTRAINMENT

The cognitive scientist Eric Kandel (2012: 287) notes that "the human brain is highly specialized to deal with faces." This aspect of Theory of Mind includes the ability to perceive facial expressions and eye movements, especially shared gaze, as sources of information that allow the viewer to gauge the emotional states of others and their probable intentions. For example, facial analysis allows one to determine whether or not another is devoting full attention to a potentially cooperative interaction. Behavioral analysis is made possible in part by the fact that compared with other primates, the human eye has the largest proportion of exposed white sclera (the white of the eye) surrounding the darker iris, and the eye outline is markedly horizontally elongated. Hiromi Kobayashi and Shiro Kohshima suggest this morphological difference enhances the capacity to analyze gaze, even from a distance (Kobayashi and Kohshima 2001). In addition, elaborate neural pathways of the "oculomotor plant" enable a high degree of control over eye movements, for example, to maintain shared gaze while the head is moving (visual analysis requires a physiologically costly apparatus: the optic nerve through which much of this information is communicated contains approximately one million axons). However, of these abilities, the analysis of shared gaze attention provides a key source of nonverbal information pertaining to the analysis of intention. When directly facing another, a dedicated neural circuitry allows humans to detect even very slight angular deviations from direct gaze that would signify a less than fully shared attention.

Gaze analysis is coupled with other perceptive abilities. Patterned interactional sequences such as greeting rituals, turn taking in conversation, and other joint activities that involve bodily entrainment are also elements of Theory of Mind capacity. In later chapters I point to the role of shared attention and forms of patterned interactional sequences in fostering cooperation, following the suggestions of the sociologist Randall Collins. He argues that "sustained cooperation on practical matters" is only possible when utilitarian exchanges are embedded in social ritual (Collins 2004: 40). The latter, which he terms "interactive ritual chains," consist of the following elements of most interest to the study of cooperation: stereotyped formalities, bodily co-presence, mutual focus of attention, shared mood, and rhythmic entrainment. It is also interesting that shared attention abilities provide humans with an important means of cultural transmission that transcends learning by imitation that is found in many animal species. With the possible exception of chimpanzees, humans alone possess teaching ability, in which the teacher becomes entrained with the learner, maintaining mutual inter-action during the learning process so as to provide feedback that can improve the quality of the learning experience.

Entrainment constitutes a spectrum of behavioral forms ranging from those that are less formally specified and everyday to those that are more formalistic and found in the extraordinary circumstances of public ritual. Among less formal expressions of entrainment, I include behaviors such as waiting in line, bargaining (as I discuss in chapter 6), and engaging in mutual conversational exchange. More formalistic entrainment behaviors are found in the context of group activities, such as collective performances or rituals that require considerable training and practice to carry out and that are structured by the force of liturgical practice or scripted instruction sets such as music scores and choreography. In later chapters I consider the roles of both informal and formal aspects of bodily entrainment in relation to how humans construct and sustain cooperation.

Folk Theory of Mind

In all human societies a "folk theory of mind" (sometimes called a folk psy-chology) is a commonsense cultural construction of mind that provides a means to gauge others' likely states of mind and intentions and to predict their actions, even of persons beyond one's immediate social network. Especially in large-group contexts, folk theory of mind will play an important role in shaping the potential for cooperation, making it one of the points of intersection between cooperation research and cultural study, and one that I address at length in later chapters.

The most important point of departure for folk theory of mind study is that typi-cally collective action must be carved out of a cultural pattern in which folk theory of mind specifies that some categories of persons lack the mental and moral capac-ity to actively participate in society. This kind of thinking is not consistent with collective action, in part because it implies that the simulation of other person's state of mind is not possible. Lacking the ability to simulate, a person might avoid or limit social interactions with those others, not a behavioral pattern consistent with the kind of social entanglement implied by collective action. And, with no ability to simulate, it will not be possible to devise governing policies consistent with broad participation in a collective social unit. In later chapters I suggest that any attempt to realize the advantages of collective action will fail in the absence of a suitable folk theory of mind, and I also suggest that aspects of a folk theory most consistent with collective action are as follows: to recognize that all social catego-ries of persons have minds similar to self, to acknowledge that others are able to comprehend the relationship between privilege and obligation (moral capacity), to acknowledge that the needs and preferences of others may be different from self's, and to understand that behavior is a reflection of intention.

CONCLUSION: AN EMERGENT PERSPECTIVE FOR COOPERATION STUDY

By turning attention to cognitive capacity, I have laid out a pathway to an expanded collective action theory of human cooperation that makes no reference to an inherent altruistic psychology or other aspects of moral intuition. Rather than altruism, the notion of human nature that is foundational to cooperation research is one that recognizes a potential cooperator whose social actions are best understood to have an emergent and contingent quality shaped by the person's social and cultural context. An emergentist perspective for cooperation study gives us grounds for a divorce from the endless and fruitless arguments between social science and biological science. Instead, it allows us to draw insights from multiple stores of relevant knowledge and methods. Emergentism also dissolves the difference between ultimate and proximate causes in the study of human cooperation. The difference between ultimate and proximate are not relevant considerations when cooperation is understood as an emergent phenomenon that has its foundations in the biological structure of the human brain, but not in a highly content-specific manner.

6

Cooperation or Competition in the Marketplace?

Anthropologists have often centered their research in the community, where, they imagine, the moral capacity of the social person is shaped. By contrast, marketplaces have not been favored as research sites because, in the anthropological view, commerce implies individualism, amoral competition, and evidence for capitalist "penetration" that destroys traditional ways of life. This antimarket mentality is most unfortunate. For one, any concept that equates capitalism with commerce paints a sharp contrast between the condition of a commercially oriented capitalist modernity and a past in which the principal institutional environment for human life was the community. I take issue with this dichotomizing scheme because it ignores the reality that humans have a long history of marketplaces and of commercial transactions. This is a history we need to understand because marketplaces not only have provided economic and other resources for households, but they also have been important sites of cultural and social foment and change.

A further reason to study marketplaces is that they have been important venues in which humans devised institutional means to address cooperation problems. This aspect alone is bound to attract the interest of a cooperation researcher, but I would also point out that from the perspective of the cooperation theory developed in this book, marketplaces are a fascinating research venue because they are sensorially rich environments in which human cognitive abilities are pressed into full service. In the marketplaces, participants search for price and demand signs that influence economic decision-making, while, at the same time, they search for

DOI: 10.5876/9781607325147.c006

signals pertaining to the truthfulness of persons. The search for truthfulness strains the cognitive abilities of the human brain, most notably those neurophysiological apparatuses related to Theory of Mind ability that allow us to analyze verbal cues, gaze, entrainment, and facial expression.

Marketplaces are also unique problem-generating structures for cooperation in the way they encompass cooperative action at multiple social scales. The essential cooperative activity of a marketplace consists of transactions between dyads of marketers engaged in buying and selling (below labeled the "microsociology of market behavior"), which presents challenging cooperator problems when the transactions take place among members of a socially and culturally heterogeneous population of strangers (Figures 6.1, 6.2). In addition to the fleeting encounters of potentially socially diverse buyers and sellers, however, there is also a collective element of cooperation at the scale of the marketplace itself. Marketplace "organizational entrepreneurs," as I will call them, whose goal is to build thriving marketplaces, must develop workable and cost-effective institutions for marketplace management. Because this institutional structure is funded by market participants (as market taxes), market participants will have an interest in seeing that services are provided in a way consistent with joint interest—the joint interest in this case being to provide a well-organized, efficient, safe marketplace and a trustworthy and egalitarian system for dispute resolution. A regional scale enters the picture in the sense that, at least in the cases of what I will term "open" markets, market participants may choose between multiple marketing destinations. This choice dimension places pressure on organizational entrepreneurs to provide market services at reasonable cost in a competitive environment.

MARKETPLACE EXCHANGE IN HISTORY AND PREHISTORY

Marketplace commerce is an ancient form of human social intercourse that had its origins thousands of years ago, developing independently in multiple cultures and regions. Ethnohistorians identify commercial transactions in early literate societies, such as Mesopotamia, from texts recorded as much as 4,000 years ago. Commercial exchange is difficult to detect archaeologically, but it very possibly had a deep history in nonliterate societies. I infer this from the fact that commerce has been noted by ethnographers in small-scale societies, such as the *gimwali* trade of the Trobriand Islands, and in marketplaces linking upland and coastal populations of horticulturalists in New Guinea, among many other examples similar to these. In most historical agrarian civilizations, markets were an important resource for household economy. For example, Brent Shaw (1981) points to the importance of periodic markets in the Roman Empire, and markets were clearly a part of the fabric

FIGURE 6.1. Elite and commoner intermingle and buy and sell in a marketplace in Antwerp. *The Meir on a Market Day*, Anonymous, ca. 1600. © Royal Museums of Fine Arts of Belgium, Brussels / photo: J. Geleyns / Ro scan.

FIGURE 6.2. *Trading at Pecos Pueblo*, by Tom Lovell. Reproduced with permission of the Abell-Hanger Foundation, photo courtesy of the Permian Basin Petroleum Museum. This painting depicts commercial exchange as it took place between Plains and Pueblo Indians in the American Southwest, which, according to archaeologists, had its origins as early as the Late Prehistoric Period (1250 CE). Goods included bison products from the plains exchanged for maize, cotton, and turquoise from the Pueblos (e.g., Wilcox 1991: 131, 143).

of urban life in China as early as the eighth century BCE, but probably had much earlier origins there, as elsewhere.

We are just beginning to learn about market prehistory as archaeologists have developed methods designed to identify marketplaces. From these limited data and from ethnographic and historical sources, I think it is reasonable to suggest that during the span from the Neolithic to the present (i.e., in the last 10,000 years) markets have been one of the most important venues in which humans solved challenging cooperation problems. Challenges arise most notably because a party to a commercial transaction will suffer losses when encountering opportunistic self-interest- seeking behavior, especially, again, when marketplace transactions consist of fleeting encounters with strangers. The latter is problematic both because of the potential for cheating, but also because transactors from different cultural or social backgrounds may not agree on the relative values of goods and services. By the same token, market transactors may not share the same moral concepts of market conduct or forms of marketplace etiquette. As a result, they may underestimate or overestimate the likelihood of market cooperation by others. Another problem arises when marketplace participants fear they will suffer from unfair treatment in the adjudication of marketplace disputes, for example, when commoners lack rights vis-à-vis an elite or when ethnic, gender, or other forms of bias or sectorial interest preclude fair judgments.

GIFT, BARTER, AND THE RISE OF THE PERIODIC MARKET

Economic anthropologists identify two major categories of social exchange: gift and commodity (an unfortunate overly simple scheme that ignores common-pool, public goods, and club goods economies). Although some features of gift and commodity are overlapping in practice, still it is the case that the main goal of a commodity transaction is to satisfy each transactor's need for a utility, that is, a desired good or service. Reciprocity in gift exchange aims less to satisfy a utility through a single transaction than to create and maintain an endurable social tie between two persons or groups (with a commodity transaction, once complete, there is no leftover business, implying that the good or service is alienable). By contrast, to alienate a gift—by destroying, selling or regifting—signifies the weakness of the social tie, while the reciprocal aspect of continued exchange between the two parties confirms the durability of the social tie.

The relatively impersonal and potentially fleeting nature of commodity transactions present cooperation problems, but also raise the issue: How is the value of a commodity determined? In gift exchange the potential for disagreement about value is minimized because what is important is the gifting and reciprocity, and, typically, value is counted in largely customary terms. But in commodity exchange the transactors may not always agree on value, so the transactors will either engage in bargaining to arrive at a mutually agreeable solution (referred to as "barter" exchange), or will depend on a market mechanism to provide information on prevailing prices. However, even where a market mechanism exists it may not always function well for every category of good or service. This is true, for example, for craft, art, or other goods that may be one-of-a-kind. The market for used cars is an example in which each car has its own history of use, mileage, and condition. In these cases bargaining is found side by side with a market-based pricing mechanism or is a supplement to it.

Barter is an inefficient mode of commodity exchange, mostly because the bartering takes time and because parties to the transaction may attempt to misrepresent the value of the commodity. Most of us have experienced exactly this trying to buy a used car, and there are many ethnographically known examples of barterers in diverse other cultural contexts making up elaborate stories about the danger or difficulties they encountered in obtaining or producing a good as a way to drive up the price. The most common institutional solution to inefficiency, deception, and cheating inherent in barter is found when selling and buying decisions can be made with a knowledge of supply and demand conditions that influence price. The earliest such price-making mechanisms are what we call "periodic markets" (or "traditional markets"), in which buyers and sellers congregate during specified days and times in designated marketplace locations.

In the periodic markets, market days are information-rich social events that make it possible for vendors and their potential customers to gauge market conditions by observing market attendance and the quantity and quality of goods offered and thus to assess whether the prices asked are reasonable in light of market conditions (ideally, in the marketplaces, vendors of similar goods are grouped together to facilitate comparative data gathering on price, quantity, and quality). In this kind of commodity economy, most transactions will take place on-site, in the marketplaces. Off-market transactions are problematic in part because they occur outside the marketplace's umbrella of institutional control and thus will be more subject to deceptive practices. In addition, off-market transactions will be secret and thus diminish the important communicative role of the marketplace, where participants can readily see goods offered and buying and selling of goods, in full view. Information is critical for market participants, and public transactions are a key to finding out about market conditions.

The social and cultural evolution of the periodic or traditional marketplaces will be the focus of this chapter. Periodic markets have existed in multiple world areas for thousands of years and can be found contemporarily even in advanced economies, for example, as farmer's markets. Today periodic markets are economically important in developing countries where they are an important resource for millions of households. Periodic markets differ in some important respects from modern economies with their national or world-scale capital markets, firms, and factory production, and their multiple electronic and other media that provide information about market conditions. Typically, a system of periodic markets connects rural households and rural to urban households at regional scales rather than the national- and world-system scales of modern markets. Also, although even in a modern economy there is some periodization of activities (e.g., the New York Stock Exchange is closed on weekends), in traditional markets periodicity is much more marked so that buying and selling take place in specific marketplace locations that convene on specific days according to a set schedule, one that typically determines the length of a week in a local public schedule. And, unlike modern markets, which are dominated by firms, in traditional markets most transactors are households who are simultaneously producers, sellers, and buyers. Correspondingly, there will be more household-produced rather than industrially produced goods (and, correspondingly, more bartering for price). And, because households, not industrial corporations, are the major producer-vendors, capital markets are weakly developed.

BARRIERS TO THE STUDY OF MARKETPLACE COOPERATION

Only rarely have economists or other social scientists proposed market evolutionary theories (below I mention Henry Maine's theory). This chapter takes a step toward a market evolution theory by considering, in comparative and processual senses, how market cooperation problems have been solved. To do this I benefit from culturally and temporally diverse data collected by anthropologists and geographers, although I will point out that because anthropologists have paid little attention to markets, the data are more limited than I would like. Economic theory and data are also of limited value. Economists have developed mathematical models of modern markets, but rarely provide insights about the nature of long-term institutional evolution of market cooperation. This deficiency is due, in part, to the fact that in the eighteenth century, most economists turned to a timeless and placeless notion of a product market understood to consist of those factors influencing the demand, supply, and price of a particular commodity ("the market for . . . "). This perspective starts from the assumption that a social and culture foundation for cooperative market exchange is in place, such as contract and consumer protection laws and their associated judicial apparatuses. But market analysis in this sense leaves unanswered the question: How did people originally build institutions to solve cooperation problems? To get at this question, in this chapter I follow the lead of "New

Institutional" economists by turning away from the timeless and placeless notion of the product market to investigate how people have solved cooperation problems in the physical and social context of the marketplaces and other venues.

Another barrier to the study of markets arises from the fact that the subject has been mired in culture wars. For example, historically, markets have been depicted in elite ideological discourses and religious canons as amoral or dangerous, as in the *Iliad* and the *Odyssey*, where commerce is associated with "disreputable" Phoenicians. Hermes, the Greek god associated with merchants and marketplaces, became the patron god of thieves. In Medieval European Christianity and the African Christian Church of the post-Roman Period, dogma condemned merchants, markets, and priests or others who engaged in market activities (Figures 6.3 and 6.4). A fourteenth-century preacher's handbook indicates: "A marketplace or fair is now filled with people, stocked with all sorts of goods, joyful and magnificent, and in a little while everyone goes back to his home, one with profit, another with loss, and the place becomes deserted, ugly, dirty, and contemptible" (qtd. in Davis 2012: 2). As late as the seventeenth century, in Early Modern England (following "Aristotle and the Bible" [in Hawkes 2001: 6]), it was thought that the behavior of capitalists—who make money with money—was idolatrous because such transactions encouraged persons to develop a material rather than spiritual view of the world. And antimarket sentiment is found beyond the bounds of Western history, for example in pre-modern Chinese and Japanese philosophies based on Confucianist principles that idealized an agrarian-based economy of highly self-sufficient producer households.

Even well into twentieth century, in the discipline of history and in the social sciences, Aristotle has been an influential antimarket source based on the contrast he made between the moral sensibilities underpinning the "natural" and proper economy of the autarkic household (*oikonomia*) and the "unnatural" market economy (*kapelike*). The latter, he argued, is problematic because it "equalizes things and thus challenges the natural order of things" (qtd. in Booth 1993: 153). In European history, the opposition to market and an expressed preference for domestic and community autarky echoed from its sources in Classical Greek philosophy. These ideas gradually gave way to a new perspective in the writing of John Locke and other Enlightenment authors who saw the market as an emancipating force freeing people from the coercive bonds of the prevailing social order. Similarly, liberal economic theorists such as Adam Smith pointed to the social benefits of commerce and self-interested behavior. The new liberal theories of the seventeenth and eighteenth centuries came to view the market as a force for opposition to aristocratic privilege and as a way to dampen emotion-driven social strife and wars by stimulating a turn to rational thought and social action. The marketplace was seen as a source of social

FIGURE 6.3. Peddler depicted as a simian. From the English Book of Hours, early 14th century. © British Library, London, MS Harleian 6563, fol. 100r.

progress owing to its *douceur* effect, a civilizing influence that "softened" social relations in situations where people will strive to maintain a favorable reputation.

During the nineteenth and twentieth centuries, however, liberal ideas were rejected by critical theorists, such as Karl Marx, in reaction to the social inequality and horrible working conditions that came in the wake of nascent industrialization. As I described previously, socialist economic historians such as Polanyi, M. I. Finley, and John Murra carried critical theory forward into twentieth century anthropological thinking and practice. Interestingly, the growing critique of capitalism in some respects revived the antimarket ideas that had informed classical Greek and Medieval Christian thought. Anthropologists as market critics came to view commerce as an alien force that penetrates society, transforming the social bonds of the traditional household and community, destroying what anthropologists understand to be a "natural" or "authentic" way of living.

Anthropologists embraced an antimarket and community-focused moral economy approach for decades. But recent empirical work finds fault with this largely ideologically motivated way of thinking. Anthropologists (and geographers)

FIGURE 6.4. Baker and alewife being taken to hell, from the Holkham Bible, ca. 1325. © British Library, London, MS additional 47682, fol. 42v.

began to pay close attention to markets as early as the 1960s, following the lead of G. William Skinner, who demonstrated that retail location theory ("Central Place Theory") could be productively applied to understanding the spatial distribution and retail functions of marketplaces of the Chinese Late Imperial Period (after the fourteenth century CE). But retail economics is only part of what he discovered. Local marketplaces, what Skinner calls "standard marketing communities," were also important elements of rural social organization in a way not previously recognized. In his view, "Anthropological work on Chinese society, by focusing attention almost exclusively on the village, has with few exceptions distorted the reality of rural social structure. Insofar as the Chinese peasant can be said to live in a self-contained world, that world is not the village but the standard marketing community" (Skinner 1964: 32).

Since Skinner's seminal publications, both anthropologists and rural geographers have done much work centering on marketplaces. Even now, however, it is rare to find an ethnographic account done with as much care and detail as Geertz's study of rural Morocco that I draw from below. While there are scattered useful sources from many world areas, historical and ethnographic work in Medieval and Early Modern Europe and in North and sub-Saharan Africa are particularly rich sources for this chapter. Mesoamerica has also been an area where economic anthropologists as well as archaeologists and ethnohistorians have devoted considerable attention to marketplaces and commodities.

THE NORTH AFRICAN MAGHRIB REGION AS A CASE STUDY

"In order to understand what a market originally was, you must try to picture to yourselves a territory occupied by village-communities, self-acting and as yet autonomous, each cultivating its arable land in the middle of its waste, and each, I fear I must add, at perpetual war with its neighbor. But at several points, points probably where the domains of two or three villages converged, there appear to have species of what we would now call neutral ground. They were the Markets. They were probably the only places at which members of the different primitive groups met for any purpose except warfare . . . The Market was then the space of neutral ground in which, under the ancient constitution of society, the members of the different autonomous proprietary groups met in safety and bought and sold unshackled by customary rule. Here, it seems to me, the notion of a man's right to get the best price for his wares took its rise and here it spread over the world." (Henry Maine 1872: 192–93)

In this chapter I follow up on Maine's useful insights, carrying them forward into twenty-first-century cooperation theory. To begin the discussion of marketplaces and their institutional changes, I briefly summarize the example of the rural market-places of the North African Maghrib (or Maghreb) region, encompassing what is now Morocco, Algeria, Tunisia, Libya, and Mauritania, elegantly described in the work of the Roman economic historian Brent Shaw (1981) and in other sources cited in the bibliographic essay. I chose this well-described situation because it illustrates several key points about marketplaces that I develop in relation to my goal of understanding the beginnings of market cooperation in broadly processual and comparative senses.

The Maghrib is a topographically and environmentally complex region featur-ing a lowland zone along the Mediterranean coastal plain that is bordered on the south by a rugged upland zone. In the recent colonial and postcolonial terminol-ogy, a distinction is made between the societies and their marketplaces occupying the low-lying coastal areas, the Bled el Makhzen ("Land of Government"), and the upland zones occupied by loosely connected segments of Berber tribes, the Bled es Siba ("Land of Insolence"). These contrastive zones also feature contrastive forms of periodic markets, although all share the same general term, *suq* (pl. *aswâq*) (Table 6.1). The upland suq are more rural institutions by comparison with their lowland counterparts, serving mostly in trade between village communities. But they some-times served to connect the populations of uplands and lowlands, especially those marketplaces situated along borders separating regional zones with complementary forms of upland and lowland production.

The lowland zone features market systems of a type that will be familiar to anthropologists and geographers who study contemporary periodic or traditional markets in places such as Mexico and China. In the Bled el Makhzen, a suq is part of a hierarchically structured, regional-scale network of marketplaces that provides multiple potential marketing destinations for both vendors and consumers and that links the small local marketplaces of the countryside to those in the cities. The net-worked quality of the market systems in the lowlands is evident in the coordinated periodicity of market days that allows merchants or other market participants to attend various different market locations in a predictable sequential circuit.

The upland-lowland distinction in market types has a deep history. During the Roman Empire, two kinds of Maghribian markets were recognized that correspond to the modern terminology. *Nundinae* were the rural markets of the uplands, while the *mercatus* (or *macellum*) were elements of hierarchically structured, regional-scale networks of marketplaces linking rural to urban in the lowland zone. The urban markets convened in the *fora*, a feature always present in the standardized configuration of Roman cities. As a structured element of the city's social and physical environment, the mercatus constituted an extension of the official concept

TABLE 6.1. Terminology for Maghribian marketplaces.

	Upland Zones Bled es Siba (Land of Insolence)	Coastal Lowlands Bled el Makhzen (Land of Government)
Roman Empire	Nundinae	Mercatus (a hierarchically organized regional market system linking city and countryside)
Contemporary	Rural suq (pl. aswâq)	Lowland suq (pl. aswâq) (a hierarchically organized regional market system linking city and countryside)

of city function; was governed within the established authority structures of city, province, and empire; and was an important source of revenue for the polity.

NUNDINAE AND RURAL ASWÂQ

The nundinae and rural aswâq served principally rural trade, and they did so in a less economically systematic manner than the periodic market systems of the lowlands. For example, nundinae and rural aswâq cannot be fit within the retail locational logic of Central Place Theory, and, although they convene at preset intervals, their market-day schedules are not coordinated to facilitate intermarket travel. In fact, rather than integrated systems of markets with coordinated weekly market-day schedules, each nundinae and rural aswâq operated as an independent entity. Today they sometimes even have market-day schedules that conflict with other marketplaces. This is true, I would argue, because in this kind of developing market situation, there is often competition between marketplaces for regional preeminence.

The upland markets were and still are also unlike those of the lowlands in terms of their relationship to political structures. Lowland states (including the Roman Empire in North Africa) might attempt to assert control over the upland markets and tax them. However, this kind of control is difficult to assert owing to logistical and military limits placed on state authority in upland mountainous and marginal environments dominated by powerful tribal groups. In addition, local populations have been known to resist a central state's meddling in their marketplaces. As a result, the nundinae and upland aswâq feature a degree of self-organization. This is true in the sense that these were marketplaces that developed institutionally largely outside the official structures of states that, since pre-Roman times, controlled the coastal and lowland areas. Nundinae and upland aswâq were also in large part separate from control even by members of the local Berber governing elite, because, as Shaw (1981: 53) puts it: "An attempt by one chieftain or segment to exert control over the market immediately excites the suspicion and resentment of the other tribesmen." As a result, marketplaces developed as a social domain separate from village community and polity. For example, in the recent history of upland markets, the coming together of potentially opposed clan segments or ethnic groups to trade (as well as to engage in other forms of social intercourse) required the managerial authority of the *aggarum*, Berber holy men "whose magical powers . . . not only ensure the peace of the market but also its prosperity" (Shaw 1981: 53). The fact that holy men are not members of the Berber governing elite affords them a degree of social neutrality suited to maintaining peaceful marketplace commerce and to maintaining an acceptable level of neutrality in resolving marketplace disputes.

The nundinae, and the aswâq of the Bled es Siba can also be distinguished from the lowland marketplaces in terms of their relative roles in society. While the lowland markets served mostly commercial purposes, the upland markets are identified by Shaw as "total" institutions that served more than economic functions. They are (and were) arenas in which disputes can be mediated between warring tribal segments and also where a Berber leader "begins his ascendency . . . spreads his patronage...and can conclude alliances" (Shaw 1981: 56). Marketplaces serve also as meeting grounds where subversive political action took place that could threaten even imperial interests. For example, Benet (1957: 193) repeats E. Doutte's claim that in such markets "political information is passed on, the announcements of the authorities are made and the reaction to these are formed . . . political conspiracies started, public outcries raised, broadminded proposals mooted and crimes hatched." It was this combining of commercial and political functions, as Shaw attests for both the Roman Empire and more recent colonial and later periods, that made the rural marketplaces central to the social fabric of Berber society at a scale larger than village, clan, or tribe.

BOUNDARY MARKETS

I follow up on Maine's proposal about market origins by suggesting that in situations such as the Roman nundinae, and the more recent upland aswâq, we are provided with a window into an important kind of setting in which humans first solved cooperation problems. While in some cases geographers and anthropologists have turned their attention to markets, they mostly emphasized the hierarchically structured periodic marketplace systems analogous to the Roman mercatus. For my purposes, however, I would argue that periodic market systems of this type are of less interest for cooperation theory because they represent the results of thousands of years of social change, including, in some cases, a process of incorporation of the marginally located boundary marketplaces into the official structures of states and their established judicial and other institutional orders. By contrast, the more rural marketplaces such as the upland aswâq and nundinae were "boundary markets" located in marginal social environments. These contexts were rich with the potential for novelty and social change as people were motivated to solve market cooperation problems in ways that required them to challenge the moral assumptions of the traditional political domains and to devise new forms of highly incorporative social intercourse.

It is important to bring the rural and marginal into the conversation about social and cultural change. During earlier developmental phases of state formation in all early civilizations, social landscapes analogous to the Bled es Siba presented problems and opportunities for market-builders. The fields of power of all early agrarian states were limited territorially owing to the logistical problems of governing at a distance with technologically limited forms of transportation and communication. As a result, the spatial patterning of early polities consisted of discrete patches of closely administered territories surrounded by weakly governed zones. Thus, rather than the (usually) clearly defined borders such as exist between modern states, interpolity spaces were boundary zones with weak authority resulting from the underlapping of the sovereignty of competing states, or where control was overlapping and contested. Either way, these boundary "shatter zones" between polity cores typically were only weakly governed, were often populated by bandits, and featured travel risks compounded with the potential for warfare that may arise between contesting polities. With North Africa as a useful example, next I develop a framework for understanding how key aspects of market cooperation might have been first forged in such marginal, interstitial contexts, starting with a comparison of forms of cooperation in what I call "restricted" and "open" markets.

THE TRANSITION FROM RESTRICTED TO OPEN MARKETS

Nundinae, and the more recent upland aswâq of North Africa display some of the characteristic aspects of market cooperation I develop in this chapter pertaining to what I will call open markets, but to place such marketplaces in context I first point to the nature of what I call restricted markets. By restricted I refer to market systems in which broad participation by common persons is inhibited, either owing to a lack of suitable marketplace institutions or to the power on the part of elite commercial actors to stifle free marketplace competition, or both. In this and the following section, I discuss institutional strategies that enhance free competition and broad participation in some very early marketplace systems. The opening up of markets had important implications for social and cultural change, as I discuss here and in chapter 12, but I should point out that social forces favoring market restriction are always present, as we see even in modern economies, for example, as a result of insider trading and when monopoly and oligopoly often render market competition imperfect.

The Social Embeddedness of Restricted Markets

Geertz (1980: 198–99) describes the marketplaces of the traditional Balinese commerce of the common person as follows: "The market system in classical Bali was confined to very small-scale retail trade in everyday consumables such as foodstuffs, simple implements, and fuels, and staffed almost entirely by women . . . who brought their produce from home to sell. Such markets . . . were held in the mornings and rotated on a three-day "market week" cycle . . . [rotating between markets in an area] . . . comprising seven or eight *desa adats* [clusters of closely related villages]."

While the potential for cheating is present in any form of market trading, in situations such as the local Balinese markets, cheating and other cooperation problems, such as agreement on the value of goods, are minimized owing to some combination of the small size of the population of potential exchange partners and the ethnic and social uniformity of market participants. These features serve to "embed" market transactions in established social relationships and local values, placing pressure on the behavior of parties who wish to reap the gains from future transactions. Following the economic sociologist Mark Granovetter, to embed a commodity transaction is to impart to it some of the personal characteristics of a gift exchange because transactors are related through family ties, are involved in other kinds of ongoing social exchanges, or are known to each other by reputation (e.g., Granovetter 1985). "Market clientelization" is an example of the embedding process, in which a buyer tends to return to the same vendor rather than search across multiple vendors to compare prices and quality of goods. This strategy relieves the buyer of some search costs while at the same time placing pressure on the vendor to behave honorably.

Clientelization or other expressions of embeddedness minimize the possibilities for cooperator problems with little need for an institutional system of rules to minimize marketplace uncertainties. Yet, embeddedness entails economic costs given that most persons will be unable to expand their scale of commercial activity beyond the narrow geography of their local marketplace. I illustrate this by situating the local Balinese marketplaces within a larger social field in which local small-scale and long-distance trade are seen to be strongly differentiated in terms of the personnel involved and the material and social gains to be realized. In Bali, long-distance trading linked the island's separate polities but, more important, also linked the Balinese polities into the Southeast Asian seaborne commerce that was carried through internationally oriented trade entrepôt on Bali's north coast. Periodic markets played no role in these centers, and instead trade was controlled entirely by some combination of local Balinese rulers and, as described by Geertz (1980: 38–39), "large-scale Chinese entrepreneurs, who were granted commercial

patents by one or the other Balinese lords in return for tribute in money and
goods . . . [and who could] . . . themselves become quite splendid local figures, living
in grand palace-like houses . . . [and who might even] . . . gain significant informal
influence as backdoor advisors to their patrons."

POWER AND THE RESTRICTED MARKETS

Power is not often addressed in relation to the "perfect markets" of economic
theory. In the perfect market concept, the highly individualized buying and selling behavior of each market participant is considered to have an equal impact on
market dynamics such as price formation, and exchanges are assumed to occur independently of the identities of the transactors ("faceless buyers and sellers"). Both
assumptions are unrealistic in the real world of marketplace exchange where we
find that factors such as gender and status bring power and privilege into the marketplace. Economic sociologists, however, have been more sensitive to the role of
power as it is expressed in the differential ability of market participants to shape
markets in ways beneficial to themselves. Power differential is, in fact, commonly
associated by economic sociologists with what I am calling restricted forms of market cooperation; as Laurel Smith-Doerr and Walter W. Powell put it, where economic transactions are strongly socially embedded there will always be "winners
and losers" because some economic actors will be excluded from valuable social
networks (Smith-Doerr and Powell 2005: 391). In the cases considered here, an economic elite will dominate the most valuable and potentially profitable trade circuits
involving the movement of goods across long distances and across environmental
divides and polity boundaries, where travel for commoners is dangerous and logisti-
cally challenging and where there will be the potential for cheating in transactions
between total strangers. The difficulties for commoners are compounded when, as
would often be the case, the transacting parties face each other as potential enemies
or social unequals. In this case, a person probably could not expect that a market
judge in a nonlocal setting would provide the outsider, especially a commoner, with
fair adjudication of a marketplace dispute.

The linking of economic zones with different resource endowments can be a
source of profits, but commoners mostly restricted to their local-scale marketplaces
will find it difficult to operate in such territorially expansive economies. A governing elite, however, are more likely to possess "network capital" that facilitates trade
at larger spatial scales and across zones of different resource endowments. Their
large scale of trade also brings the potential for profit asymmetry because economic
actors operating at large spatial scales will have access to information on supply and
demand factors that more localized market players will lack. From a cooperation

perspective, however, the key difference between elite and commoner trading is found in the difference between two forms of social embeddedness. While the trust basis for local restricted market exchange is found in community life at the local scale, in the more territorially expansive network capital of an elite, trade is a natural expression of their interpolity activities such as diplomacy and other social ties across local social boundaries forged through shared genealogy, intermarriage, and reciprocal gifting, all of which can be sources of reputational symbols that enhance trust and create the possibility for commercial transactions.

TRADE DIASPORAS AND ALIEN TRADERS

The example of Bali noted above points to another form of embeddedness that shares some features with the governing elite as commercial actors. In this case trading is in the hands of entrepreneurs who are able to maintain social ties at a distance, and who often combine their network capital with expertise in arranging credit and contracting at a distance, social technologies not required in local-scale marketplace cultures. Philip Curtin (1984) terms this form of restricted markets "trade diasporas." In these cases the trust basis for market transactions often is a consequence of shared religion or ethnic affiliation ("ethnically homogeneous middleman groups" in Landa [1981]) and personal ties among group members. As an example, I point to Avner Greif's (2006: 58–90) study of the eleventh-century Maghribi merchant coalition of North Africa. Grief illustrates how a relatively small group of specialized Jewish merchants was able to constrain the actions of their distant agents by coordinating among themselves the punishment of those agents who behaved dishonestly. Coordination among coalition members was feasible because the population, no more than about 300, was close to a scale threshold for human group size in which each person will have personal knowledge of others.

Max Weber used the phrase "alien traders" to describe the coethnic and coreligionist embedded economic phenomenon, the study of which is now a branch of economic sociology referred to as "middleman minority theory." Well-known middleman minorities include Jews and Italians in Medieval Europe and the Mediterranean; Parsees in India; Sikhs, Orma, Hausa, and Julas in Africa; the overseas Chinese in Southeast Asia and elsewhere such as those who operated in Bali, as well as the Putun and Itzá merchant groups of late pre-Hispanic Mesoamerica.

Alice Dewey (1962: 49), from her research on markets in Java, illustrates some of the advantages Chinese traders have by comparison with local Javanese merchants: "Chinese will buy goods on description or from a sample when dealing with other Chinese and feel relatively sure that the quality and amount ordered will be forthcoming on time. Javanese feel they must themselves inspect all goods being considered (from Javanese suppliers), and, when delivery is made, check the quality and quantity. No payment is made until then. Such a rationale makes it difficult to calculate future expenditures and delays resale negotiations as well as adding to costs in time and money spent in personal supervision of even simple transactions."

What is the basis for the network capital enjoyed by the Chinese merchants? For the Chinese, potentially trustworthy trading partners can be identified through difficult-to-fake signs including linguistic competence and ethnic signaling (clothing, gestures, etc.) that indicate with some degree of surety that the person, even if a stranger, is likely to share a code of market ethics and a knowledge of financial instruments for conducting commercial transactions at a distance. In addition, as Granovetter (1992) points out, Chinese diaspora groups are economically successful in Southeast Asia because they form small, close-knit communities based on shared clan membership or places of geographical origin. Within the close-knit networks, "credit is extended, capital pooled, and authority delegated without fear of default or deceit" (32). No doubt this "close-knit" aspect of the Chinese social networks helps us understand how the assurance problem is solved, in part. In addition, China has a long and complicated history of institution-building to facilitate commercial transactions, including long-distance trading. Comparatively, Indonesians had less experience with the development of institutions for long-distance trading.

As described in the ethnographic record, not only the Chinese but other ethnically homogeneous middleman groups typically operate as foreigners who have migrated from regions where elaborate institutions for market cooperation are in play. Jean Ensminger's (1997) research on trading during the eleventh to nineteenth centuries in sub-Saharan Africa gives us another perspective on sources of network capital of middleman minority groups by pointing to the importance of religious conversion as a form of reputational symbol. Ensminger documents how Islam followed the major trade routes, sometimes displacing pre- or non-Islamic ethnic trading groups, by providing several advantages not available in the context of commercial systems of smaller scale. Islam brought a shared language of trade and "a monetary system, an accounting system, and a legal code to adjudicate financial contracts and disputes . . . making outsiders, insiders" (Ensminger 1997: 7). The considerable personal costs of religious conversion—which included giving up alcohol, devotion to fasting, costly pilgrimages, and the building of mosques—mitigate the assurance problem because they constituted costly signals demonstrating a deep commitment to religious values shared with other traders. At the same time, the high cost of religious conversion served to restrict access to the profits of the long-distance trade to a successful and privileged few who could become important merchants and maintain profitable monopolistic control of long-distance trading, and who would benefit from maintaining a favorable reputation among the relatively small number of major traders.

Do Alien Traders "Serve" Society?

To the degree that a governing elite or a merchant diaspora group is able to maintain domination of interlocal trade, and if commoners are able to satisfy their consumer needs principally through a local market, the two-tiered commercial system that sharply separates elite and commoner in their respective forms of restricted markets could result in the persistence of, in Geertz's (1979: 141) terminology a "culturally encysted trading class, half intruder and half pariah, so common in . . . parts of the world (Southeast Asian Chinese, East African Indians, Medieval European Jews)." Greif (2006: 398) advances a more positive view, arguing that trading groups "served" society in European history through their linking of European producers and markets to larger world-system commercial networks, and in the way their behavior foregrounded the importance of virtues such as individualism, thereby hastening the development of democracy. My sense, however, is that Greif and other European economic historians making similar claims overemphasize the importance of trade diasporas in the rise of democratic modernity. Trading coalitions not only monopolized profitable trade connections, thus depriving others of opportunities for commercial activity, but they also allied themselves primarily with elite sectors of society, even propping up the failing economies of the feudal aristocracy and authoritarian political regimes of the late Medieval Period.

Geertz's notion of an encysted pariah group may be closer to how people felt (and feel now) about the trade diasporas. The history of market change from restricted to more open markets is not well known for most world areas, but from what evidence is available for England it appears that local merchants were jealous of the way that alien traders were given royal favors. To change the trading system was not easy, and appears to have been contentious. This is illustrated by the expulsion of Jewish traders from England in 1290 CE and riots against Italian and other foreign merchants that erupted in various locations during the late Medieval Period, as I discuss in chapter 12. Expulsion of the long-distance trading specialists was one factor that contributed to the growth of a more egalitarian, broadly based economic system of more open markets that had important implications for social change in England and elsewhere in Western Europe.

CONTINUITY AND CHANGE IN RESTRICTED MARKETS

The cooperation theorist Robert Axelrod (1984: 59–60) argues that "the great enforcer of morality in commerce is the continuing relationship, the belief that one will have to do business again with this customer." But this is a theory only applicable in restricted market contexts. Things get a lot more complicated when transactions are between persons lacking social ties or the likelihood of continued future interactions, and where some may aim for windfall profits while anticipating few social costs. I propose that market change that allows for cooperation in these more impersonalized, socially disembedded contexts is the result of radical institutional and cultural changes that negate the inequality inherent in the embedded economy and restricted market. To disembed makes possible the kinds of market transactions that are more in line with economic theory in the sense that buyers and sellers in the market are "faceless" so that the identities or social connectedness of the parties have little bearing on the nature of the exchange transactions. The unrestricted ("open") markets thus provide even commoners with enhanced market choice. However, this enhanced market freedom is not the same thing as the notion of freedom as it is proclaimed by today's market fundamentalists, that is, that market participants ideally should become more socially independent. To function, the open marketplace still requires rules and other attributes of institutional capital for cooperation because market participants are dependent on the moral actions of others and on market-based forms of institutional capital for cooperation.

To overcome embeddedness, with its potential to restrict access to markets and profits, institutions must be crafted that facilitate broad market participation. Yet, those who benefit most from restricted markets—the governing elite and wealthy trading groups—command more of the symbolic and material resources they can then use to resist change. In the following sections I propose several institution-building strategies that have made market change a reality in spite of barriers to change. I look first at those microsociological practices that allow strangers to interact productively as buyers and sellers. Next, I identify a process of "piggybacking" of marketplace activities on existing institutions and cultural codes. I also point to evidence indicating that marketplace organizers made use of the identity-transforming process of "liminality" to enhance an egalitarian sensibility in the marketplaces. I then look at how market-building organizational entrepreneurs (to use the terminology of Robert Salisbury 1969) constructed systems of paragovernmental market organization to enhance the autonomous institutional capital of the marketplaces.

THE MICROSOCIOLOGY OF MARKET BEHAVIOR

Bargaining is an apt beginning point for the study of marketplace cooperation, because it involves a classic cooperation dilemma. Although arriving at a mutually agreeable price will bring benefits to seller and buyer, to do so is challenged by differing preferences regarding the ideal terms of the transaction, and because cheating is always a possibility. I suggest that detailed studies of bargaining behavior will afford an opportunity to understand how it is that bargainers may realize mutually agreeable outcomes. Even though bargaining is commonly observed in the traditional markets studied by anthropologists, there has been little attention devoted to this aspect of market behavior. Anthropologists' antimarket attitude has also led them to mischaracterize bargaining. For example, in the widely repeated scheme of types of gift reciprocity developed by Marshall Sahlins (1972), in small-scale societies the closest approximation of marketlike behavior he identifies is "negative reciprocity." This is an antagonistic form of exchange taking place beyond the domain of kin and community in which the goal is to "get something for nothing with impunity" (Sahlins 1972: 195). Only a few researchers have faulted or expanded on Sahlins's view. The economist Ralph Cassady (1968), from his analysis of marketplace interactions in Oaxaca, Mexico, understood bargaining to be a highly individualized approach to price determination. While bargaining doesn't preclude the market forces of supply and demand in price-making, still, through bargaining, the price agreed upon can be highly responsive to each person's unique "demand characteristics" as he terms it (especially ability to pay).

There is more to consider than unique demand characteristics to understanding bargaining behavior, because demand characteristics fail to account for the elaborate sensorimotor communication and use of conventionalized signals found in the bargaining process. I find these behaviors similar to Randall Collins's interactive ritual chains described previously, including stereotyped formalities, bodily copresence, mutual focus of attention, shared mood, and rhythmic entrainment. Fuad Khuri (1968), for example, discovered interactive ritual in his study of bargaining behavior in the Middle Eastern suq, where he notes an elaborate expression of obligate market etiquette that "establishes an atmosphere of trust . . . Hence, in a very intricate and sensitive way, bargaining brings order into an otherwise uncontrolled market system" (Khuri 1968: 705).

Similarly, Geertz (1979) notes that in the large, socially complex, and ethnically diverse Moroccan marketplace of Sefrou, the "enormous multiplicity of participants" means that confidence in others cannot be based only on reputation, and yet there is a concern with "the truth of persons" (204–5). One mechanism to establish confidence, he suggests, is through the highly choreographed behavior displayed in the bargaining process signaling that a bargainer, whatever his or her ethnicity or social standing, is familiar with accepted practices in that marketplace. The time committed to the bargaining process is also a factor in the calculus of confidence. An extended time frame of the mutual bargaining entrainment is a potential source of information concerning the degree to which a bargaining partner is willing to pay the price to produce a costly signal of worthiness and to signal commitment to completing the transaction. From Geertz's description, it appears to me that an ability and willingness to engage in shared attention, a key attribute of Theory of Mind ability, is the essential fact of the bargaining ritual. He points out that a proper rhythm of vocalizations ("Sluggishness on one side or the other, or on both, in moving toward consensus—long periods between bid changes and/or small magnitudes of change—indicates agreement will be difficult at best") constitutes a language that allows the interactants to detect "fake signals—an evasive response, an over-ready agreement, an excess of promise—that reveal its presence" (208).

I conclude that bargaining rituals are one important institutional element making possible the democratization of access to marketplace trade and commercial profit. Furthermore, bargaining ritual is a market mechanism that is neutral from the perspective of ethnic identity, wealth status, or gender, and is not an expression of a person's network capital.

"PIGGYBACKING" AND THE SACRED CHARACTER
OF THE TRANSITIONAL MARKETPLACE

"The market is the principal medium for the distribution of economic goods, affording a channel through which the products of farmers, artisans, and craftsmen flow to the ultimate consumer, and through which compensation is returned to the producers. Yet, more than economic significance attaches to this institution, for the marketplace is also a center for social activities and a place where religious rites are held" (Melville Herskovits 1938: 51, describing marketplaces in the vicinity of Kana in the kingdom of Dahomey, West Africa).

Organizational entrepreneurs strategizing to build functional marketplaces often turned to religion and ritual to enhance the potential for cooperative social action, even when official religious dogma condemned merchants and markets. Historical and ethnographic sources often describe how profane and sacred sit side by side in the marketplaces; the success of a marketplace or fair often is attributed to the authority of a religious leader. As well, market days often are concurrent with religious ritual cycles and religious pilgrimages. I would argue that these associations are the outcome of a process by which marketplaces are "piggybacked" on existing religious institutions, sites and persons, as one way to enhance the likelihood that market participants will adhere to the moral demands of marketplace trade. Furthermore, religious figures, as moral exemplars, may be highly suited to serve as marketplace adjudicators. Examples of piggybacking include periodic markets and fairs that took place as part of religious festivals (*panegyreis*) in ancient Greece, and the numerous Medieval European markets that were located near ancient pagan cult centers, Christian churches (which benefitted financially from hosting them), and pilgrimage sites (Figure 6.5). I previously mentioned the Berber holy men whose prestige was enlisted by market-builders to provide for neutral third-party

FIGURE 6.5. *The Fair at Impruneta,* Jacques Callot, 1619. Reproduced with permission of the Fine Arts Museum of San Francisco, San Francisco.

adjudication but whose authority was also thought to enhance market security. In some marketplaces, shrines were built to honor religious authorities renowned for their success in market management. The shrine symbolized that, even in death, market order could be maintained by a "formidable saint" (Benet 1957: 201).

THE MARKETPLACE AS A DISTINCT SOCIAL DOMAIN AND VALUE SPHERE: BORDERLAND STRATEGY AND MARKETPLACE LIMINALITY

"How does one 'think' a marketplace? . . . At the market center . . . we discover
a comingling of categories usually kept separate and opposed: center and
periphery, inside and outside, stranger and local, commerce and festivity,
high and low. In the marketplace pure and simple categories of thought find
themselves perplexed and one-sided. Only hybrid notions are appropriate to such a hybrid place." (Peter Stallybrass and Allon White 1986: 27)

"Thus, the unofficial folk culture of the Middle Ages and even of the
Renaissance has its own territory and its own particular time, the
time of fairs and feasts. This territory . . . was a peculiar second world
within the official medieval order and was ruled by a special kind

of relationship, a free, familiar, marketplace relationship." (Mikhail
Bakhtin 1984: 154, commenting on the literature of Rabelais)

The institutions and ethical codes that provide incentives for commoner participation in open markets must be predicated on an underlying sense that all market participants are understood to possess the requisite moral capacity to understand the difference between self-interest and moral obligation. If this is the case, then marketers are free to engage equitably in transactions as moral equals across the divides of social rank, wealth, ethnicity, and gender. The pervasive social inequalities found in many premodern societies, especially in those tending toward coercive rule, have always presented challenging obstacles to those striving to develop marketplaces. Overcoming social asymmetry requires a radical step, namely, to craft the marketplace as a domain in which there exists what Weber (1978: 637, orig. 1922) described as a state of "absolute depersonalization . . . contrary to all the elementary forms of human relationship . . . [such as those based on] . . . personal fraternization or even blood kinship." Weber realized that a depersonalized market ethic would imply a radical departure from ethical systems that underpin other social domains of society, converting the market environment into what he termed a distinct "value sphere" within the larger compass of society. In his view, this is a domain that stands opposed to social conventions linking status to the privileges of power and wealth found in other spheres.

Weber's idea of a separation of value spheres is a useful path to empirical analysis, which can be brought into play, first, by pointing to a spatial logic requiring the physical separation of contrastive value spheres. Francisco Benet (1957: 212) pointed to the significance of this kind of spatial structuring when he noted that village and market, two key loci of Berber social action, must be separated because "if they were not, these contraries would come to a head-on collision." Similarly, Geertz (1979: 197), in his study of the Moroccan Sefrou marketplace, takes note of how the marketplace is "physically and institutionally insulated from virtually all the other contexts of social life," has its own moral code—the *hisba* ("the covenant of the market") —and its own linguistic culture. The latter refers to the peculiarities of a market lexicon not used in other social settings, including an elaborate terminology pertaining to a person's truthfulness and sincerity; the only linguistic analogs Geertz could identify for this lexicon were terms pertaining to marriage contracts, charity, and religiosity. Other unique lexical domains of the marketplace relate to news, information and its truthfulness, and modes of communication: conversation, talkativeness, and fluency in market transactions and communication skills.

To place marketplaces in marginal locations at the edges of effective political control—a borderland strategy—is commonly used by market-builders to separate a marketplace and its system of governance from the influence of, or control by, any one political center. And marginal borderland populations, whose loyalties may be divided between multiple polities, could be well situated socially and culturally to build market institutions that provide services such as unbiased adjudication. In the marketplaces I studied, there is an additional element of market social and cultural construction that goes beyond the physical, social, and linguistic separation of marketplaces from other social domains. The spatial logic of separation is augmented by the identity-transforming power of what anthropologists refer to as the liminal process. In this case, upon crossing the marketplace threshold, the marketer is transported to a liminal phase in which he or she exits from the social and cultural prejudices and modes of coercive appropriation of goods and services found in the political community, as Bakhtin alludes to in the quote above. As Victor Turner (1969: 131–35) remarks, in a liminal phase social interactions will be more egalitarian, close, and direct than in the political domain, where status distinctions and linguistic categories specify a rigid code of conduct that may result in the physical separation of persons and an inability to effectively communicate or cooperate.

Weber's notion of "absolute depersonalization" is also evident in that the liminal phase has the power to dissolve ethnicity or other possible sources of factionalism and dispute that might interfere with marketplace function, including the relaxing of inequalities found in systems of gender hierarchy. Marketplaces are often noted to be a domain where women's traditional roles are relaxed, allowing them to act to an unusual degree as autonomous economic actors. For example, as Benet (1957: 205) noted in the Berber Highlands, even in that Islamic society women participated in market transactions as independent commercial actors and "the market is a source of feminine private income." In pre-Hispanic Aztec Mexico, for females the "major avenue of social advancement for individuals of non-noble birth was through mercantile activities as a member of the Pochteca [merchant] guild," and women were prominent in the marketplaces as both vendors and market administrators (McCafferty and McCafferty 1988: 48).

Liminality is highlighted by denoting a marketplace's boundary as a socially and symbolically meaningful threshold. Markers, walls, or other threshold-defining features often symbolically demarcate marketplace boundaries. Boundary marking is evident even when marketplace locations are in marginal rural locations with little in the way of built environment or permanent settlement. Shaw, for example, discussing the Berber aswâq, argues that because the marketplaces are so physically ephemeral it is better to understand them in relation to time (market day periodicity) than to physical space, although, even in these rural settings "the participating tribesmen may agree to mark the perimeter of the exchange area with a crude earthen wall topped by a row of cacti of jujube" (Shaw 1981: 40). In addition, aswâq were symbolically bounded by a "holy perimeter" (*haran*) specifying the limits of a zone of safe passage.

Similarly, the famous marketplace of the Ka'ba, in the valley of Mecca, was surrounded by a sacred limit (*haram*) within which no blood could be shed. As Mecca gained in commercial importance, the market managers, the Koreish (Quraysh, Quraish), "self-consciously sought to extend the sacred precinct as a means for increasing the stability of social relations in their trading territory" (Wolf 1951: 337–38).

I noticed many other cases in which physical and symbolic marking of marketplace limits was practiced. In Dahomey, both were important. According to Herskovits (1938: 53): "*Ax'izq*, or the market *aizá*, is the name given to the spirit which protects the market . . . In outward form it is a mound of earth under which are buried definite objects to ensure the guardianship which is required. In marketplaces, this mound is often beside a sacred tree." Among the West African Loango, marketplace entrances "symbolize this 'truce of God'—mounds fenced in with stakes, memorial posts, and structures of poles intertwined with branches of the large-leaved, spreading fig-tree known as *nzandu*" (Thurnwald 1932: 167–68). In ancient Greece, border markets (symbolically associated with the gods Hermes and Dionysus) were signified by stone heaps and markers representing the phallus. By the time the market had been incorporated into the social fabric of urban Athens (after 800 BCE), the boundary (*perirrhanteria*) of the *agora*, the main marketplace (which also then became the center of democratic political activities), was signified by stone markers (*horoi*) (Figure 6.6). Persons deemed to have questionable moral character were not allowed to cross the marketplace (and civic) boundary.

PARAGOVERNMENTAL MANAGEMENT OF THE OPEN MARKET

Interactive ritual chains of bargaining, piggybacking on religious institutions and persons, and liminality provide key foundations for open marketplace cooperation. In more complex cases, these elements are augmented with a formal organizational structure for marketplace governance. Lacking this aspect of institutional capital for cooperation, the maintaining of public order is problematic, potentially making a marketplace a dangerous venue that does not invite participation. In the "explosive markets" of the Berber Highlands, for example, episodes of extreme violence are recorded in a "sudden, panicky 'snapping' which breaks the peace of the *suq*: the *nefra'a*" (Benet 1957: 203). Marketplaces that can manage such violence will thrive and attract large crowds, but violence "will discredit a *suq* and people will stop coming to it" (203; cf. Bridbury 1986: 111).

Market cooperation problems, including the potential for conflict, are mitigated in boundary markets through the development of a form of governance that develops outside the authority structure of the society's political domain. Anthropologists and historians have described various forms of paragovernmental

FIGURE 6.6. Agora boundary stone (*horos*), fifth century BCE, Athens. Courtesy of the American School of Classical Studies at Athens: Agora Excavations.

market management such as "masters of the market" found in some highland Berber markets and among the Loango of West Africa. Similarly, in the "Amin" system in the Moroccan Sefrou marketplace studied by Geertz, pious "reliable witnesses" mediated market disputes. Other examples include the Maghribi trader's coalitions of Medieval North Africa and other merchant guilds; "law merchants," who adjudicated disputes and maintained records on the market dealings of merchants in the European early Middle Ages; and specialized market brokers who facilitated trade between strangers in Hausaland. In Medieval England, market managers employed various kinds of toll gatherers, sweepers, bellmen, and "warranters" who were commodity specialists, for example, the *aulnagers*, who evaluated the quality of cloth.

The Diakhanké, located on the margins of African Malian territory (1600–1850 CE), illustrate a type of market management found in several sub-Saharan African polities influenced by Islam. As Curtin (1971) describes them, the Diakhanké were specialized market managers whose zone of control was technically within Malian territory, but they governed in a fringe area, in some respects independently, as a recognized sanctuary from direct state control. Here, the Diakhanké devoted themselves to religion and market matters, including judicial services and providing caravan protection. Perhaps the most famous Old World example of paragovernmental market managership is the Koreish, sometimes described as a "tribe of traders," who, beginning around 400 CE, managed a major Arabian border market, the Ka'ba, in the environmentally marginal valley of Mecca. The Koreish engaged in commerce, provided protection for caravans, and managed markets with such authority they were able, even in this militarily charged situation, to require market participants to surrender their weapons.

The main marketplace in Aztec Tlatelolco—the most prominent marketplace in all of Mesoamerica during the late pre-Hispanic Period (serving an estimated 50,000 people on major market days)—and other Central Mexican marketplaces provide an interesting Native American version of autonomous market management. The Tlatelolco marketplace was a distinct social domain where the judicial authority of the powerful Aztec Empire was suspended. Market management, including the adjudication of disputes, was entirely in the hands of a group of organizational entrepreneurs, the *Pochteca*. The Pochteca organization consisted of twelve regional subgroups integrated into a hierarchically organized umbrella organization whose central authorities resided in Tenochtitlan, the empire's political capital. The Pochteca organization operated highly autonomously from direct state control but was an important structural component of the imperial system. The leader of the Pochteca was a member of the Aztec Empire's ruling council, and the Pochteca organization independently governed the important commercial city of Tochtepec in what is now the Southern Mexican state of Oaxaca. The Pochteca's judicial neutrality in commercial matters was widely recognized. All recruits were taught to uphold an ethical code peculiar to their organization that emphasized loyalty and solidarity of the Pochteca organization; respect and regard for others, including non-Aztec peoples and their property; and fairness in matters of trade. Their judicial authority included the right to sentence to death Pochteca members who violated the code of marketplace ethics.

CONCLUDING COMMENT

The characteristic features of open marketplaces have been developed across a variety of cultural and social circumstances. I suggest that the successful implementation of open markets has served to challenge traditional forms of power and privilege, allowing common persons greater access to geographically expanded spheres of economic and other social activity. In the concluding chapter, I return to assess the importance of these egalitarianizing processes as social forces that could stimulate the rise of collective action in polity-building. Given their locational marginality beyond zones of direct state control, and their sacred and liminal qualities and self-governance, it was in the marketplaces that people began to imagine the possibility of more egalitarian forms of social intercourse, and new ways to understand what it means to be human, that challenged social asymmetry. In addition, to the degree that open market arrangements enhance a broadly based growth of economic activity, they also may figure into egalitarian political change. Change follows because, in part, as I develop in chapters 7 and 8 (with Lane Fargher), in the fiscal economies of states based on collective action, the growing wealth of commoner sectors elevates their status as important contributors to a state's revenues. Thus they stand in a stronger position to force bargains with state-builders.

7

On the Need to Rethink Theories of State Formation and How Collective Action Theory Will Help

WITH LANE FARGHER (CINVESTAV DEL IPN)

Most theorists of the state embrace an evolutionary scheme that understands the rise of modern democratic states as a new social evolutionary stage and a discontinuity in human history originating uniquely in Mediterranean and European histories. To these theorists, democracy was so progressive and transformative its ideas traveled from "the West to the rest of the world" (Tilly 1975b: 608), enabling humans, finally, to free themselves from the yoke of political oppression. The ultimate source of this progressive development, they argue, was the rise of a uniquely rational mentality that transformed people into willful agents capable of participating in democratic society. Outside of European and Mediterranean experience, by contrast, states formed around the dominating power of a governing elite who ruled over passive subalterns unable to resist despotism.

We think it is important to take a hard look at the progressivist scheme because it is one of the stories humans most often tell about themselves and about the history of society. In this and the following chapter, Lane Fargher and I follow in the footsteps of many historical social scientists who have critically evaluated the traditional view. We centered our critical analysis around collective action theory, an approach, we reasoned, that would allow us to evaluate claims of European and Mediterranean exceptionalism. Correspondingly, the key issue that drove our inquiry was as follows: if our approach aims to understand cooperation as a product of social and cultural process, we need to know whether humans in other historical periods and cultural settings might have turned to cooperative modes of polity-building, not

DOI: 10.5876/9781607325147.c007

necessarily along the same paths as in Mediterranean and European history, perhaps, but similar in analogical and processual senses.

To challenge Western exceptionalism, however, is definitely to go against the
grain. Exceptionalism evidently strikes a positive chord in the minds of many, in
part, perhaps, because it has a venerable history traceable to Greek philosophers
(e.g., from Aristotle: Barbarians and Asians "are more servile . . . hence they endure
despotic rule without protest" [in Anderson 1974: 463]). Greek philosophy was
carried forward without any empirical investigation to be eventually incorporated
in the arguments of influential European authors of the late eighteenth century and
nineteenth century including Charles Montesquieu, Marx, and Friedrich Engels,
who distinguished European history from the "despotisms" of the "Asian" other.
Eurocentrism has persisted until recently in some branches of the social science and
historical literatures as an "asiaticist" or "orientalist" tradition. Examples include
the writings of neo-Marxist and neoevolutionists of mid-twentieth century such as
Polanyi; Karl Wittfogel (author of "Oriental Despotism"); the historical sociologists Charles Tilly and Michael Mann; and the prominent anthropological theoreticians Wolf, Morton Fried, and Elman Service.

THREATS TO THE EUROCENTRIC CONSENSUS

It is time to abandon Eurocentrism if we are to follow up on Tilly's (1975a: 3) suggestion that it is important to weigh theories of state formation "carefully against
experience." Unfortunately, in the question of state-building, the recommended
checking often is absent, yet, in recent decades, we see more tendency to deviate
from the consensus. Archaeologists and historians sensitive to the possibility of
what is called "alternate pathways to complexity" are uncovering evidence pointing
to high levels of cooperation in some premodern, non-Greek, and non-European
complex societies, and even in some of the very earliest states.

These new findings are important because they point to the possibility that cooperation could play a role in state formation in a way that is not well understood or
appreciated. The societies of interest in this regard are those where we find evidence
of social complexity and the state, but often without the expected symbolism of
dominating rulership such as massive burial monuments or other forms of ruler or
dynastic representation. In these polities it appears that the role of monarch, usually thought to be the fulcrum of political process in non-European premodernity,
is either absent or restricted. We include in this group the Bronze Age of Crete,
which was the earliest instance of state formation in Europe, and the Late Neolithic
Period of the Yellow River region of north China, representing the earliest states
or protostates in East Asia (later Bronze Age polities such as the Shang Dynasty,

however, represent a turn to autocracy). Other very early examples of evidence for cooperation include early states in Mesopotamia. Thorkild Jacobsen first proposed (in 1943) that a form of primitive democracy had developed in ancient Sumerian Mesopotamia beginning as early as the fourth millennium BCE, and his insights are supported by subsequent archaeological and ethnohistoric investigations (Jacobsen 1943). Even when a pattern of overt Mesopotamian kingship did make its appearance, beginning during the third millennium, as Daniel Fleming (2004: 237) tells us, "the dominance of individual rule appears to have been constrained by strong counterbalancing forces of the temple and city institutions." Classic Period Teotihuacan, in the Basin of Mexico (200 to 700 CE), and Indus-Sarasvati civilization of South Asia (2600 to 1900 BCE) also exhibit more egalitarian forms of state-building. We have, with Verenice Heredia Espinoza, recently demonstrated that the pre-Columbian Central Mexican polity of Tlaxcallan (1200 to 1500 CE) took the form of a highly egalitarian republic.

The more egalitarian societies I point to were large in scale and socially complex. Yet, in varying ways, they exhibit similarities with modern democracies in the sense that the power of governing officials was strongly circumscribed, and, in some cases we find evidence of public goods, a key element of a collective polity discussed in the following chapter (examples include the massive grain stores and public sewers in Indus-Sarasvati cities). These findings point to the need for an expanded discussion of the nature of early political change that can accommodate both political domination and cooperation, but not necessarily one phrased in terms of Greek or European history. Our task in this and the next chapter is to take a step in that direction by asking: Is it possible that cooperation provided a basis for state-building prior to the emergence of the modern democracies? If so, has that state-building experience had any shaping influence on the rise of those democracies? Is it possible to conclude that the rise of European-inspired political modernity truly represents a leap forward away from autocracy and to the evolution of effective democratic government?

THE RISE OF THE WEST

Traditional theories of state formation argue that the earliest states coalesced when an emergent ruling elite overcame the constraints of egalitarian society to construct centralized polities. They accumulated absolute power through their monopoly of force, their appropriation of powerful symbols (e.g., claiming to be divine "god-kings"), their construction and management of vast irrigation systems, and their direct control over a complex division of labor (the "redistributive economy"). The combination of superior force, divinity, and control of intensive agriculture and economy made possible monarchical domination of a subaltern class of peasant producers and the forced appropriation of their surplus production (the "tributary mode of production" in Wolf's [1982] phraseology). We call this model of social change "oppression theory."

Most of the recent theorizing about the rise of Medieval and Early Modern European states follows the arguments of oppression theory, endorsing the argument that in the premodern condition, cooperation played little role in European political change. Instead, early polities were formed by an emergent ruling elite, variously described as "bandits" (Olson 1993), "racketeers" (Tilly 1985: 171), "coercion-wielders" (Tilly 1990: 20–21), and "coercive and self-seeking entrepreneurs" (Tilly 1985: 169). Not surprisingly, Machiavelli's *The Prince*, in which he advocates for the use of violence to achieve loyalty and political unification, is an important theoretical inspiration for this literature (Machiavelli 2005, orig. 1513).

How is it that Europeans turned the tide against political oppression? Their separate path—according, again, to the consensus position—was made possible by a unique European propensity toward endemic inter-polity warfare, coupled with the emergence of a rational and commercial mentality that brought commercial growth and, with it, a politically influential merchant bourgeoisie class. Monarchs facing high military costs sorely needed resources. One way to enhance revenues was to strike bargains with taxpayers in which monarchs would relinquish some of their political autonomy in exchange for taxpayer compliance. At the same time, growing commerce provided a sound fiscal foundation for building the modern state while also positioning the bourgeoisie to challenge the cultural foundations of aristocratic privilege and replace it with rational forms of democratic governance. These key factors—endemic wars, commercial wealth, and the power of a commercial class—it is argued, were largely absent outside European history. According to the theory, in the despotic condition largely agrarian economies could not produce the tax revenues to support a modern state or foster a commercial bourgeoisie. Thus the agrarian economies were a natural environment for the perpetuation of aristocratic rule over a class of subaltern commoners unable to resist the regimes of power and wealth appropriation imposed on them.

STATE FORMATION: FROM SOCIAL DOMINANCE TO DEMOCRACY

Theories of democracy's origins focus attention on changing systems of taxation. First, monarchs conceded some political autonomy in exchange for increased tax revenues, while at the same time the growth of commerce provided potentially new sources of revenue. Related to the latter factor, we encounter two very different proposals. Gabriel Ardant (1975) argues that the modern state is organizationally complex and costly to sustain and correspondingly could only be supported in a commercially developed economy that presents optimal opportunities for efficient taxation and a commensurate level of wealth production. Agrarian economies, he argues, were poor, with little potential for surplus production at the same time the taxation of individual farm families was inherently inefficient.

Robert Bates and Da-Hsiang Donald Lien propose another fiscal theory. They note how merchants hasten the transition to democracy because their wealth is movable, making it more difficult to tax than the "fixed" resources of an agrarian population. As a result, sovereigns, to collect taxes, will be forced to bargain with those representing commercial interests (Bates and Lien 1985). This kind of fiscal theory has a long history in Europe, and was first proposed by the French economists François Quesnay and comte de Mirabeau in their *Philosophie rurale* (1763). Here they argued that

> No wealth which is immaterial or kept in people's pockets can ever be got hold of by the sovereign power . . . The wealthy merchant, trader, banker, etc., will always be a member of a republic. In whatever place he may live, he will always enjoy the immunity which is inherent in the scattered and unknown character of his property . . . It would be useless for the authorities to try to force him to fulfill the duties of a subject: they are obliged, in order to induce him to fit in with their plans, to treat him as a master, and to make it worth his while to contribute voluntarily to the public revenue. (qtd. in Meek 1962: 63)

In the next chapter we demonstrate that high levels of cooperative state-building did develop apart from European experience, but not necessarily in relation to the rise of a merchant bourgeoisie class. And from data we coded on taxation, we find both fiscal theories to be insufficient because they ignore key classes of information. Yet, the Bates and Lien theory is of most interest to us because it understands egalitarian state-building in relation to a fiscal process in which there is negotiation between state-builders and revenue-producing groups. In the next section we refer to this as a "relational" theory of state-building, a key building block for collective action theory.

THOMAS HOBBES, RATIONAL CHOICE, AND AN ALTERNATIVE TO THE EUROCENTRIC PARADIGM

The writing of Thomas Hobbes often is cited as providing support for monarchical absolutism. The frontispiece of his famous *Leviathan* (Hobbes 1996, orig. 1651) (Figure 7.1) seems to point in that direction. It depicts an out-sized sovereign towering over his territory, his figure portrayed in a way to symbolize what is traditionally understood to comprise the power of the European monarch: the crown, a symbol

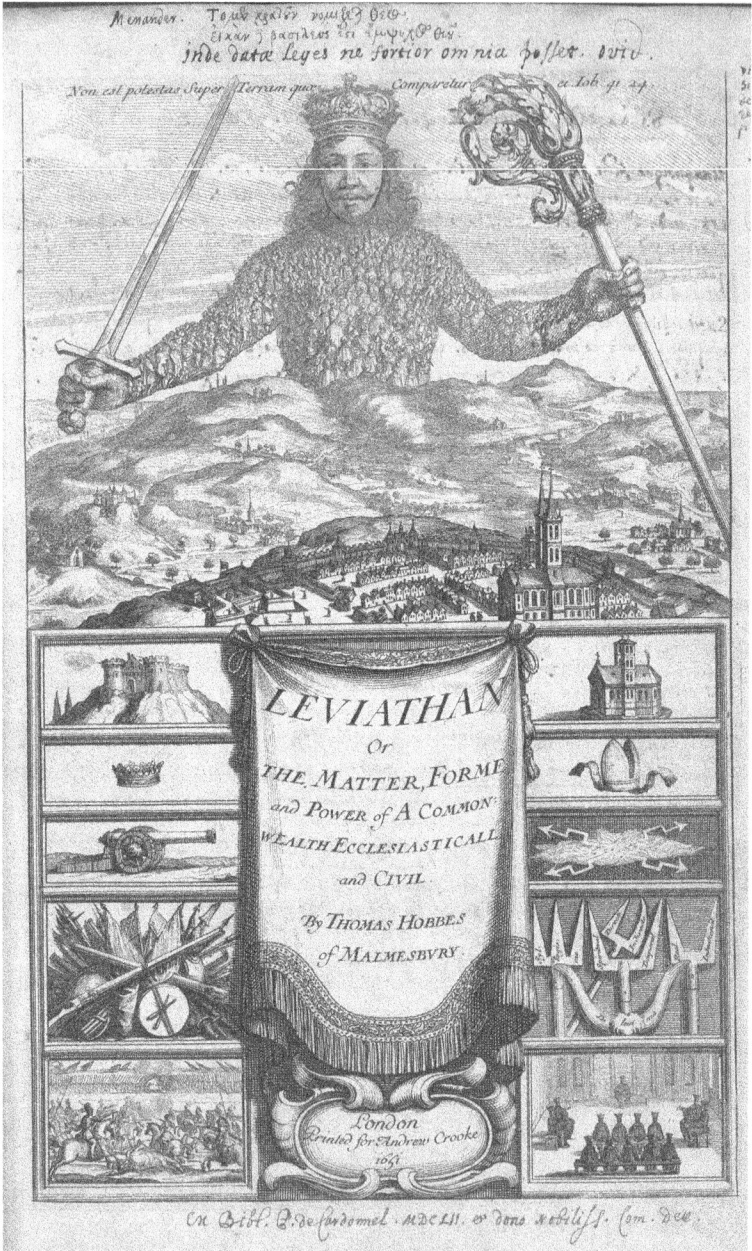

FIGURE 7.1. Illustrated title page to the Head edition of Thomas Hobbes's *Leviathan* (London 1651). Reproduced with permission of the Harry Ransom Center, the University of Texas at Austin.

of aristocratic rule; the sword, a symbol of force; and the bishop's crosier, signifying ecclesiastical legitimation. However, the figure also depicts the monarch's body as made up of a mass of people. This suggests that Hobbes's theory of power consists of more than references to crown, sword, and crosier, because it brings the mass of the people into the discussion. Although Hobbes has been justifiably maligned for his depiction of an inherently conflictive human, and for his legitimization of oppressive government (to Hobbes, any form of the state, however oppressive, is better than none at all), he did at the same time lay down a conceptual foundation on which it is possible to imagine a cooperation-based theory of political change.

Hobbes's key insight that is foundational to a collective action theory might not strike the citizen of a modern democracy as particularly radical, but it is counter to the assumptions of oppression theory. He argued that prior to the advent of states, life was challenging, as families were socially isolated and forced to devote substantial resources to the protection of self and property in a lawless environment. While cooperation could happen—as social contracts between persons—and would provide advantages, still, contracts were fragile in the absence of any means of institutional enforcement. A state, however, can influence this dismal social calculus because it has the authority and power to enforce contracts and to protect property. While persons may prefer the total freedom of life without a state, still, they have the capacity to rationally understand the benefits that accrue from state authority. What is radically different about Hobbes's idea by comparison with earlier European notions of the state is that the latter would not exist except for the rational choices of its subjects. Hobbes's notion implies that the power to govern can be understood, at least in part, as a result of a social relationship between rational subjects and rulers. This was a break from the idea that the power of the state and its rulers resulted solely from ruler attributes of aristocratic rank, control of force, and sacrality.

Hobbes's notion that the choices of common persons could play a role in political evolution is congruent with the idea of the human as a contingent cooperator and as such is worthy of study, within limits. We disagree with Hobbes's assumption, typical of the European Enlightenment literature, that the desire for the protection of property rights would necessarily be a principal force driving people to contract socially with the ruler. As we know from more recent studies of state formation, many polities were not highly collectively oriented and thus lacked the administrative capacity for, or interest in, property protection or the enforcement of personal contracts. We also disagree with the argument that people would be indifferent to the form of state dominion, whether autocratic or otherwise. Also, Hobbes's theory doesn't pay adequate attention to those polities in which there is brutal and often violent oppression by a ruling elite, nor is he aware of the many cases in which intrapolity conflict such as factional disputes between contending members of a governing class often do not enhance either the security or prosperity of commoners. He also fails to address adequately just what would motivate rulers to offer the beneficial but costly services of maintaining public order and upholding contracts. However, his notion that state formation was indeed a product of the choices of common persons was a step in the direction of the theory described and evaluated in this book.

A FISCAL THEORY OF COLLECTIVE ACTION IN STATE-BUILDING

The "fiscal history of a people is above all an essential part
of its general history." (Joseph Schumpeter 1991: 100)

It is not unrealistic to assume that when possible, a head of government (the "principal") will prefer to rule autocratically, controlling the state's resources without interference while ignoring obligations to subjects. However, in spite of a probable preference for autocracy, there are conditions in which autocracy is likely to fail, namely, when there is a relative parity between the power of the principal and taxpayer subjects. Under these circumstances, to achieve a stable political formation and to maximize taxpayer compliance, the principal's actions must be consistent with collective benefit. The principal achieves this by implementing an equitable system of taxation, by providing public goods, by considering citizen voice, and by limiting his or her own behavior and the behavior of the administrative staff. The necessary causal element in the collective scenario is parity between principal and taxpayer: How does that happen?

INTERNAL RESOURCES AND COLLECTIVE FISCAL STRATEGY

Collective strategies for state-building are predicted to occur when a state is strongly dependent on the body of taxpayers as its principal source of revenues or other valuable services (such as military labor), what we term "internal resources." Internal resources, in turn, will develop in tandem with what we term a "collective fiscal strategy." This is a fiscal system in which revenue collection and the management of a state's budget are administratively set apart from the direct personal control of the key principal or principals. It also implies a system of taxation according ability to pay.

Internal revenues and collective fiscal strategy are essential for the development of states based on high levels of collective action. An internal resource fiscal economy will place taxpayers in a relatively strong position to make demands on the governing elite, giving rise to a situation in which rulers and ruled make mutual claims of accountability with respect to each other. But how can taxpayers be confident that a principal will act in a way consistent with collective benefit? The administered aspect of a collective fiscal system is important in confidence-building because it implies limitations over the degree to which a principal will be able to use the state's wealth for personal gain or for political benefit, for example, to subvert demands for reform or avoid punishment for malfeasance in office. And collective action theorists such as Margaret Levi have pointed to the importance of equitable taxation as one strategy to foster high levels of compliance among taxpayers.

We should point out that the concept of collective fiscal strategy and internal revenues are similar to what the economist Schumpeter foregrounds in his notion of a "tax state" or a "fiscal state," in which taxes are collected from the broad population to fund a publically managed state. However, we depart from Schumpeter, whose ideas are grounded in social evolutionary theory, when he argues that modern systems of taxation, in which tax is collected equitably from taxpaying citizens and the revenues managed for public benefit, evolved only with the advent of modern Western-style democracies. Collective action theory abandons social evolution and typology in favor of a processual and comparative approach that aims to identify those causal factors that give rise to collective action in state-building. A typological approach is misleading because any state's revenue sources and fiscal organization will consist of a complex mix of different types of revenues, different degrees of intermingling of the principal's and the state's wealth, and varying degrees of successful implementation of equitable taxation. However, in spite of these kinds of complexities, we assume it will be possible to measure relative degrees of dependence on internal resources and the relative degree of institutional development of collective fiscal strategies, and with these data evaluate the usefulness of a collective action theory of state-building.

COLLECTIVE ACTION AND THE RELATIONAL FORM OF POWER

In a cooperatively based polity the architecture of power is highly "relational." This is a kind of power reflecting the reality of a reciprocal relationship between the state and its taxpayers. This kind of cooperative framework for polity-building has the potential to bring mutual benefits both to persons in positions of state authority and to taxpayers. For example, our data point to an overall higher living standard associated with the more collective polities (discussed in chapter 12), and, as Martin McGuire and Olson (1996) suggest, when rulers depend on taxpayer revenue, taking citizen interest into account will bring higher levels of taxpayer compliance and thus revenue production. However, collectivity in state-building is problematic in part because taxpayers are conditional cooperators who might act in ways counter to group benefit. Similarly, cooperation may fail when authorities charged with managing collective resources behave as rational egoists (the "agency" problem). In large, complex societies, high levels of cooperation will entail even more challenges having to do with the coordination of government functions. These challenges are especially acute, , when a collective state faces the necessity of efficiently collecting taxes from and providing public goods to a large and spatially dispersed population.

Levi, from a survey of Western historical materials presented in *Of Rule and Revenue* (Levi 1988; see also Levi 1997), posits that the central solutions to collective action problems are found in state-building strategies aimed at building a level of confidence among taxpayers that the ruling principals will act in accordance with collective benefit, and that the state's administrative apparatus is suited to realizing collective goals; confidence, in turn, will foster what she refers to as "quasi-voluntary" taxpayer compliance ("contingent consent"). The basic strategies to creating confidence are, first, that the state will divert some of its revenues to the production of public goods. In addition, the state must construct a form of government with the institutional capacity to discover and punish agency among its administrative cadre. The system of administration must also be suited to assigning obligations equitably and to the discovery and punishment of noncompliant taxpayers, in part so that compliant taxpayers feel confident that free-riding will have consequences, and in part because free-riding will be more likely if the risk of punishment is judged to be low. Taxpayer cooperation is also enhanced when there are assurances that principals will observe moral expectations to honor their obligations, and when there is a credible expectation that they can be detected when not doing so and appropriately punished.

THE CONSEQUENCES OF "EXTERNAL" REVENUES: A HYPOTHESIS TO EXPLAIN THE RISE OF AUTOCRATIC STATES

When governing principals have discretionary control over revenue sources not produced by taxpayers, collective action is less likely to be developed. Most commonly, this is seen when a state's main source of income derives from the principal's personal properties ("domain states"), or when principals maintain direct personal control over profits from trade in international commodities. In these cases, governing principals are posited to have less motivation to strike bargains with taxpayers, and, instead, are more likely to rule autocratically without accountability.

Autocracy is evident contemporarily in what political scientists refer to as "rentier states" in which ruling groups have discretionary control over revenues from easily monopolized sources of income such as oil, natural gas, or mineral exports. Political scientists and economists point to the numerous contemporary rentier polities endowed with valuable exportable commodities that generate great wealth yet are lacking in overall economic development and democratic governance (the "resource curse" in Ross [1999]). According to Thad Dunning (2008), the resource curse will be felt more keenly in cases where governing systems are not highly developed and where there is less economic activity in the larger society relative to the value of the principal resource, for example, as we see now in the Arabian Gulf states. In more affluent countries with highly developed institutions for democratic governance, and where there is considerable preexisting economic activity, such as Norway and the Netherlands, however, resource wealth brings less likelihood of authoritarianism.

A METHOD FOR THEORY-TESTING

Lane and I acted on a hunch that collective action theory might provide broadly applicable insights on state formation. But turning a hunch into a plan for research challenged us to identify a method well suited to theory testing. One approach we considered is historical or "time series" analysis, but we soon realized it is not highly feasible in light of our goals. Time series analyses have been used successfully by some authors, for example by R. Bin Wong (1997) and Victoria Tin-bor Hui (2005) in their insightful comparisons of Chinese and European histories with the goal to critique Eurocentric thinking about China. And yet we realized to adopt this approach would limit us to small number of historically well-documented cases.

While historical accounts of particular cases are few, there is an abundance of data on the social and economic makeup of a large number of premodern polities. These data present us with the possibility of a research design based on "cross-cultural comparative research" (sometimes called "cross-sectional research"), a well-developed anthropological methodology we apply to the study of collective action. Rather than the detailed study of a single society, or the comparison of a small number, the goal of cross-cultural research is to analyze data collected from a large sample of societies using systematic methods. This is a useful path to take when the researcher is unsure about the nature of a social phenomenon to be studied, how often it might be expressed, or what variable forms it might take. In our case, we assume that if collective action is to be understood as a social and cultural process that has occurred repeatedly, then, given a suitable methodology for pattern discovery, our best chance to detect it and learn about its variability will come from the study of a large sample of societies. Our methodology will allow us to address the following propositions:

1. If collective action is a problem-generating structure that presents certain kinds of problem-solving entailments wherever it appears, then, irrespective of population size, or local cultural and social setting, there should be some degree of institutional similarity among those polities where cooperation is a goal.

2. As a problem-generating structure, collective action should be evident as an identifiable pattern of associated traits. The successful implementation of collective policies is unlikely, for example, if there is a goal to provide public goods but no corresponding institutionalized controls over the administrative agents who manage those resources. And, given the importance of instilling taxpayer confidence, we expect to find other aspects of collective action as well, including institutional controls over principals. Thus, each theoretically proposed feature is coded separately as a variable and in a manner that is comparable across cases to facilitate analysis of covariance of the variables.

3. If collective action consists of an assemblage of co-occurring traits, by assessing the degree to which the full assemblage of traits is present we will have the ability to measure the degree to which each studied case conforms to or violates theoretical predictions. Societies scoring low on collective action are also expected to exhibit properties of authoritarian regimes where collective action has not been an institutional goal, creating the possibility for comparison of less and more cooperative social formations. For example, our comparative data will allow for an evaluation of the fiscal theory described above linking collective action with internal revenue sources and collective fiscal strategies.

SAMPLE AND DATA REQUIREMENTS

Our first tasks in carrying out the cross-cultural research were to identify a suitable sample of societies and to develop a coding system that would allow us to code data in a consistent manner across a large number of cases and variables. This was not a trivial problem as it was necessary to code for a large number of highly complex variables. For example, we needed to know about all sources of state revenues and the relative importance of each in the overall fiscal system. Our selection criteria started with the requirement that the societies coded meet the minimal organizational criteria for statehood, namely, that they have governments consisting of a governing principal (or principal group such as a ruling council) serving in the capacity of policy-making, and an administrative apparatus organized in at least three levels of administrative hierarchy (this has been shown to be a useful criterion for identifying premodern states versus less socially complex polities termed "chiefdoms").

For each polity, we gathered information limited to a specific focal period for which we found suitable data and during which governing policies were highly stable. For example, rather than describing China in some abstract sense, our coding was specifically for the Early and Middle Ming Dynasty, during which time the basic political strategy envisioned by the dynasty's founder was largely followed.

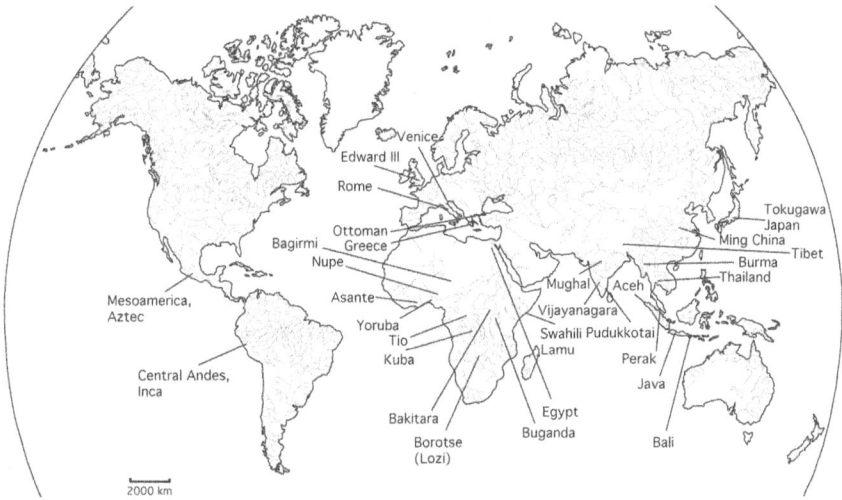

FIGURE 7.2. Locations of the sample of thirty premodern states in the comparative sample.

But we did not extend our coding to include the Late Ming Period, when important policy changes were made and when society was undergoing change in other respects, including a significant phase of economic and political decline.

In China and other cases, we selected a particular focal period because it was the earliest for which the kinds of information we needed were available. We drew our information only from descriptive sources whose quality is widely recognized among area specialists, and we selected societies and particular focal periods for which we could detect little or no influence from European colonial administrations or other forms of recent democratic European influence on governing institutions. We settled on a sample of thirty premodern polities representing most major world areas (East, South, and Southeast Asia; Africa; the Mediterranean and Europe; and the New World) (Figure 7.2). While a larger sample would have been desirable, we were limited by the immensity of a very demanding and time-consuming coding task.

We did not select societies for the comparative sample because they appeared interesting to us from a collective action viewpoint. Instead, to avoid bias we paid no attention to the details of political system, emphasizing instead the availability of suitable and valid data. The data requirements for this project were stringent because our goal was to go beyond simple qualitative observation to develop quantitative measures of key variables that are comparable across societies. This proved to be challenging methodologically, but, with much effort we did arrive at a coding scheme that allowed us to gather comparable data from all of the sample cases and thus to make use of statistical and other methods to identify patterns of correlation or association among variables and across cases. Serendipitously, our method did result in a sample of societies containing a considerable amount of variation in degrees of collective action. Unfortunately, given that very little is known about the relative frequency of more collective polities in the past, we cannot confirm that the sample is representative of the population of all premodern polities.

Ideological Posturing versus Evidence for Social Action

The behavior of persons in a collective group—to enter or exit, to comply or not with obligations—is shaped by the behavior of others: Are others behaving in a manner consistent with group benefit? Given the centrality of behavior to our coding system, we correspondingly focused on what people actually did as opposed to what they should do ideally according to a moral code or other forms of cultural preference. This puts our approach at odds with those branches of political theory in which governance is argued to be most stable when, in the eyes of most people, leaders hold power legitimately, that is, authoritatively. The problem with the notion of legitimate rule is that it is highly subject to ideological manipulation. John Dunn (1988: 73–74), as an example, notes that the absolutists Louis XIV, Joseph Stalin, and Mao Tse-tung all claimed to rule legitimately, but he doubts this was meaningful in situations of "massively inegalitarian political relations" in which it would not be feasible to challenge authority. In nearly all the societies in our sample, we encountered claims about the legitimacy of rule such as those expressed in Classical Islamic thought, where a ruler is expected to overcome "anarchy, confusion, man's selfish nature and the tyranny of the strong" (Hasan 1936: 57; cf. von Grunebaum 1961: 127). In early Hindu and Buddhist political theory, rulers were expected to maintain moral and social order. In the doctrines of the Chinese Confucian literati, the ruler's correct ritual performance and ethical virtue served as persuasive guides to action promoting harmonious relations among the people. And from Alonso de Zorita (1994: 93), an early Spanish commentator on the Aztecs, we learn that rulers were expected to "watch over and punish the wicked, lords as well as commoners, and correct and reform the disobedient."

However, moral theories such as the above did not always align with the behavior of persons in positions of authority. Of the examples just mentioned, a significant expression of behavior consistent with collective action was found only in China and the Aztec polity. Of the societies in our sample, the English polity of the fourteenth century CE was one featuring very low values for our measures of cooperation. In spite of the government's inefficiency, its corruption, and its coercive and autocratic pattern of rule, there is little doubt that most persons believed that the Edward

III ruled legitimately during our focal period. The sense of legitimacy reflected a widely held and passionate belief in the heritability of legitimate power—after all, Edward I, the dynastic founder, was the son of Henry III. Still, people's actions point to the reality that few people, especially commoners, had confidence that the government or its chief officials or associated members of the feudal elite would act in the interest of anyone but themselves. Commoners recognized the severe short-comings of the judiciary, the state's failure to provide public goods, its corrupt and inefficient system of tax collection, and, especially, the royal wastefulness in the use of tax revenues to fight costly and futile wars in France. Dissatisfaction took various forms from antielite narrative-making, such as the poem "Against the King's Taxes," to organized oppositional movements. Eventually, among other causes, this kind of distrust and antistate action resulted in governing reforms, especially the rise of a more powerful Parliament that could weaken the power of kings.

FINAL COMMENTS ON METHOD

Cross-cultural comparative analysis does allow for theory testing, but is sometimes challenging in application. This is not to imply our coding effort was a failure— actually it was quite successful—but the reader needs to be aware that we encoun-tered occasional coding dilemmas. We point to the case of public goods in ancient Egypt (New Kingdom, 1479–1213 BCE), where, in spite of low overall scores on most dimensions of collective action, we found evidence of public goods provision-ing, at least in terms of the state's ability to maintain high levels of public safety across much of the realm; as one pharaoh proclaimed, for women, "no stranger nor any one upon the road molested her. I set each man in his security, in their towns" (in Badawy 1967: 107–8). But was this the result of an intention to provide a public good, or was it unintended, a result of the extreme measures taken by this state to provide for the careful control and protection of the state's and the pharaoh's prop-erties? We suspect the latter but the information available to us was inadequate, so we coded public safety as a well-developed public good.

Another methodological issue pertains to the problem of subjective coder error in the case of highly complex multifaceted variables. To solve this problem, our main variables (public goods, bureaucratization, and control over principals, dis-cussed in the following chapter) were rendered as "constructs" or "scale variables." This method maximizes the possibility of highly replicable coding with minimal effects from coder subjectivity. For example, in the case of public goods we looked separately at the state's ability to maintain public order, to provide water manage-ment, public transportation, and food security, and whether services such as these were made available across the realm or only in selected locations—each of these separate features involved a relatively straightforward coding task (most of the time). The values coded for the component elements are then summed to arrive at a scale measure of degree of public goods overall that can be compared with that of other polities.

In line with the approach taken in this book, our method of measuring degrees of collective action does not have as its major goal the identification of types of states—discrete sets consisting of "cooperative" versus "autocratic" polities—rather, it is to measure degrees of collective action in its various dimensions. It is important to assess degree, not type, for several reasons. First, quantification allows for the use of probability statistics, methods ideally suited for theory testing. We would also point out that there is no such thing as an archetypical collective political regime, nor is there a perfectly autocratic regime. In the case of a state based on cooperation, often we encountered a complex historical dynamic in which state-building is a lengthy and protracted process of overcoming collective action problems and obstacles, such as opposition by traditional elite who will lose privileges, and which may never be fully resolved. Thus a cooperative-leaning state will be a work in progress rather than a completely developed "type." Moreover, strategies contrived to resolve cooperator problems may prove unavailing, requiring new rounds of problem solving. In addition, any state-builder is likely to emphasize one or another of the aspects of collective strategy, reflecting local cultural preferences or prior state-building experience, among other factors. Rather than a type, our coding method gives us something more like a snapshot of a particular polity taken in the midst of this historical dynamic because our frame of reference for data collecting is a specific time span or focal period for which we were able to find data suited to the needs of our coding system and during which there were no major changes in governing policies.

We have been pleasantly surprised at how the method we developed did prove to be sufficiently robust to allow for theory testing as we discuss in the following chapter, a gratifying result, to be sure, especially after devoting more than two years to the coding task (and a year before that identifying a suitable comparative sample). Our study sample of societies varied considerably not only in the degree of collective action but also in the details of how cooperation problems were understood and how they were addressed, a result that allows us to throw new light on the problems encountered in building collective states and to imagine some possibilities for an enhanced collective action theory able to transcend European exceptionalism.

8

Cooperation in State-Building?

An Investigation of Collective Action before and after the Rise of Modern Democracies

WITH LANE FARGHER (CINVESTAV DEL IPN)

In this chapter we use empirical data from our comparative sample to evaluate the utility of collective action theory as applied to state-building. We look especially at the value of a fiscal theory that relates collective action to forms of revenue and to methods of tax collection. In the concluding sections we make additional use of our comparative data by asking the questions: Are premodern states, represented by our sample, fundamentally like or unlike contemporary nation-states? Hypotheses regarding the causes of collective action in state-building will be presented and evaluated in chapter 12. Chapter 13 addresses the question: Have humans taken advantage of their multithousand-year experience at state-building, and the supposedly revolutionary ideas of democratic modernity, to build states based on high levels of cooperation?

To develop a method suited to the study of collective action in state-building, we turned to the work of other theorists who addressed collective action in contexts of social complexity and large social scale. What we noticed in this literature that the three factors of monitoring, punishing, and rewarding—recognized as foundations of cooperation in experimental public goods games—are not an adequate framework for theory building. The ability to monitor is always important, as the contingent cooperator bases his/her cooperation choices in part on the likelihood that amoral action will be detected and punished, but in the context of complexity and large scale other factors emerge as more important to understanding cooperator choice, especially confidence that the leadership is able to effectively bring about beneficial change and to create a system suited to enhancing cooperation.

DOI: 10.5876/9781607325147.c008

Collective action theorists have identified factors that enhance cooperator confidence in an institution's functional capacity. For example, the collective action theorists Karen Cook, Russell Hardin, and Margaret Levi (Cook et al. 2005: 151–65) identify the following key features for state-building: (1) a state must have the capacity to provide for social order but at the same time power must be institutionally constrained; (2) a state must have the capacity to monitor the population and its own administrative cadre to identify taxpayer free-riding and administrative malfeasance, yet monitoring must also be under institutional control to avoid excess intrusion; (3) credible institutions must be developed to monitor the behavior of the principal officials and to allow for removal from office for malfeasance; (4) the benefits and costs of collective action should be equitably distributed; and (5) formalized channels of communication should make relevant information available about the actions of the leadership and the functions of the governing system.

The leadership and organizational properties described by Cook, Hardin, and Levi overlap with the organizational features usually associated with a condition of political modernity, including a rational field administration able to equitably collect taxes and distribute public goods, the ability to equalize access to offices, and the ability to subject the leadership to scrutiny. To assess whether confidence-building collective action programs were developed in the past, we investigated three main variables: public goods (measuring the degree to which a state uses its resources in the public interest and is able to organizationally coordinate a challenging managerial task), bureaucratization (a state's ability to monitor its administrative cadre and punish for malfeasance), and control over principals (limits placed on the independent power of principals, and the capacity of an institutional system to identify and punish malfeasance committed by the principal leadership). Before describing the results of our analysis and our conclusions, we describe the three variables and provide brief descriptions of a few of the societies we studied to illustrate the kinds of information we found useful and to give the reader a sense of the variability we encountered. Appendix A provides key collective action measures for the larger sample of thirty polities. Statistical methods and results are described in Appendix B (a more detailed and technical account of method, results, and data is found in Richard Blanton and Lane Fargher, *Collective Action in the Formation of Pre-Modern States* [Blanton and Fargher 2008]).

PUBLIC GOODS

Recall from chapter 3 that cooperation presents challenging problems when it involves joint interest in the management of resources, whether "common-pool," "public goods," or "club goods." Public goods are most important to consider in the case of collective state-building because they are jointly (collectively) provided, that is, their provision is through the surplus production, profits, or labor of the tax-paying members of the civic unit as a whole. In addition, public goods are important for collective action because they are not subtractive, that is, not excludable, meaning that consumption of services by one person does not subtract from services available to other members of the collectivity. In this sense, public goods are unlike "private goods," commodities distributed through markets, where there will be rivalry for benefits (not everyone can afford a new Audi).

However, it is unreasonable to expect that any public good will necessarily display perfect jointness of provision or perfect nonexcludability—hence the distinction that is sometimes made between "pure" and "impure" public goods. This distinction is needed because, especially at a large social scale, tax collection and the management of jointly produced resources present coordination problems, so that the ideals of joint supply and nonexcludability may be extremely difficult to realize. A case in point is that, typically, while the resources funding military defense are likely to be jointly provided, benefits are likely to be asymmetrical. For example, those occupying border areas, and thus at more risk of suffering from military incursion, benefit more than those more centrally located. We tried to minimize the asymmetry problem by investigating public goods that are likely to be perceived as beneficial across social sectors and geographies. For states, especially premodern ones, public goods also present coordination problems when taxpayer burdens are not appropriately calibrated according to ability to pay. In the premodern condition this problem is particularly challenging because the state typically will find it very difficult to gauge each family's ability to pay—this is, of course, a problem even in modern polities—but advanced administrative technologies offer at least some solutions not available to premodern state-builders. What we have found is that the practical difficulties of realizing true jointness and nonexcludability were challenging but did not always preclude the implementation of collective policies. Instead, coordination problems were confronted in varying ways, although not always as successfully as is seen in some modern states.

DATA-COLLECTING METHODS AND EXAMPLES OF
COLLECTIVE ACTION VARIABLES I: PUBLIC GOODS

Owing to the importance of public goods in the collective action political process, it was important that our method allow us to validly compare the degree to which public goods were provided by each state in our sample. Our method ignores the fleeting actions of particular sovereigns or other principals who may feel a personal obligation to distribute resources, but which would not constitute a firm institutional basis for collective action social process in the long run. Instead, we looked for evidence that the provision of jointly provided public goods was a central feature of a state's policies throughout the focal period and that an appropriate institutional structure was devised to coordinate public goods distribution. Our method also emphasizes those goods that would give us the most potential to evaluate the degree of nonexcludability. We also were interested in the degree to which public goods provided benefits broadly to the civic unit, so we emphasized those goods most likely to have had a day-to-day impact on the economies and well-being of households across social categories.

With these considerations in mind we found that the following public goods best fit our needs: transportation infrastructure (so long as facilities were available for public use); water control (including irrigation management, flood control, and public water for domestic consumption); maintenance of public order; citizen access to impartial judicial services; urban public goods such as fire control; and enhanced food security. We also included variables that measure the degree to which a state offered social and emotional services through endowments to schools or to religious groups and/or the funding of public rituals, so long as these provided benefits to the population as a whole. In the following we briefly summarize the data from a few examples, arranged in order from lowest to highest public goods scores determined from our ten-item public goods coding scheme (with a total potential score of 30) to give the reader a sense of the quite considerable variability in premodern states in this regard (more detailed descriptions and source citations are found in Blanton and Fargher 2008: chap. 7). Each section includes polity name, region, focal period, and public goods score.

DATA SUMMARIES

BAKITARA (OR BUNYORO) (INTERLACUSTRINE
AFRICA, 1860–90 CE, [SCORE]10)

This polity scores very low on public goods. Most notably, there were no publicly funded roads in a situation in which transportation was impeded by dense forest, and we identified weak control of public order. The lack of access to judicial services is indicated by the fact that "private vengeance" was often a way to settle disputes in spite of the fact that district chiefs were charged with keeping the peace, settling disputes, and trying cases. Trial by ordeal, administered by chiefs or the king, often substituted for actual investigation of a crime. And, we noted, typically a first priority of the secondary authorities was to protect the interests of the king, including his extensive cattle herds.

ENGLAND (1327–36 CE, 11)

This polity scored among the lowest in the sample on the provision of public goods. In part the low score results from the fact that the state provided neither funds nor labor for the maintenance of the national infrastructure. For example, the repair of roads and bridges was the responsibility of local families or the individual who constructed them. While a key feature of many agricultural strategies in England of the period involved the use of drainage ditches, there is little evidence of state involvement in the development of this kind of agricultural capital. Local officials, the sheriffs and the bailiffs—along with the keepers of the peace—were charged with controlling crime and punishing criminals. Yet, the system was so corrupt and the monitoring of officials so limited that the state utterly failed to provide for public security or for effective judicial services. According to Theodore Plucknett (1940: 103), "It is not necessary to stress the number of seeming crooks and bandits who were elected [sheriff], for it must be remembered that their generation was one of fierce faction and sometimes of civil war, which will explain most of the assaults, homicides, and house-breakings of which we hear." From Colin Platt (1982: 93) we learn that

> In effect, the government that had set out at the beginning of Edward's reign [Edward I] to restore the law and to reform many acknowledged abuses, had now reversed its policies in the interest of the wars [in France] and was itself pointing the way to a new chaos. Such former outlaws and criminals as returned from the campaigns, hardened in violence by their experience, might have old scores to pay off and would certainly have had problems in re-establishing themselves peacefully in the communities that had been glad to be rid of them. Complaints of disorder, always to be heard in medieval England, rose to a crescendo at the end of the thirteenth century and afterwards took many decades to die down. These were the years, most particularly in the first decades of the fourteenth century, of the criminal gangs and the birth of the legend of Robin Hood.

BALI (THE LATER MENGWI POLITY, NINETEENTH CENTURY CE, 14)

Public goods were few in this polity. Few public roads were built, so that travel between palace centers was difficult in this mountainous terrain unless on the same ridgeline. While irrigated "paddy" (wet-rice) agriculture was the principal system for food production, typically there was only a minimal role for political officials or state resources in the development of irrigation infrastructure or management; instead, an elaborate hierarchically structured system for water management operated largely apart from state control. *Brahmana* priests as well as the governing elite served in the administration of justice, but sometimes community groups had to apprehend offenders themselves. The Mengwi Dynasty of the focal coding period instituted severe penalties for theft, including death for paddy theft, but it is not clear how they could have enforced rules with such limited administrative resources. The state's role, if any, in food security is not clear and appears to have consisted mostly of distributing goods, including food, during the occasional palace rituals. Palaces were recognized as centers of learning and artistic production, and rulers endowed tax-free lands to support artistic endeavors and performances, even in rural areas.

JAPAN (TOKUGAWA PERIOD, MOSTLY EIGHTEENTH CENTURY CE, 16.5)

This state provided some public goods, but commoners in the population were not well served. The immediate hinterland of the capital center at Edo featured a network of roads and canals, but paved roads were found mostly in the higher-status residential areas. Owing to a lack of city planning and road building in some areas, transportation and communication within Edo were inefficient and confusing to outsiders, and the only major roads linked the few largest cities, such as the Tokaido Highway linking Edo and Kyoto. In 1722, an official was placed in charge of agricultural development in the vicinity of the Edo capital, including land reclamation and irrigation, but it is not clear how much work got done other than an extensive canal system that brought water to Edo, mostly destined for palace use. Reclamation and water-control projects often were funded by wealthy households, or wealthy households working in conjunction with local officials. There was some concern with maintaining public order and safety. Yet, in Edo these were mostly in the hands of commoner city dwellers (*chonin*) organized into neighborhood self-help groups of about ten households who comprised their own fire-watch and safety patrols and who paid firemen. In spite of these local efforts, fires in cities such as Edo were a difficult problem owing to inadequate development of citywide fire-control capability. In villages, disputes were usually settled locally, and "famine was not unknown in many parts of the country" (Perez 2002: 27; cf. Toshio 1991: 495). *Terakoya* were small schools where commoners could learn to read and write, but they were supported by local families and communities, not the state.

ASANTE (WEST AFRICA, 1800–1873 CE, 18.5)

This state showed more allocation of resources to widely used public goods. A series of "great roads" connected the capital Kumase to the provinces and included "halting places" where travelers could rest and that served as sites for the exercise of local police authority to guard against thievery. The *akwanmofo* was an administrative agency charged with road maintenance, and appears to have been effective, as we are told that paths were kept open and bridges built. Security in and around the capital Kumase was very tight, and there is some evidence of a policing activity away from the capital, including the previously mentioned halting places along major roads. There was considerable institutional complexity aimed at identifying, trying and punishing offenders; for example, local blood-feud and vendetta were absent in Asante, although some legal action also took place within the matrilineal descent groups. The state was involved in the punishment of criminals, with the central authority maintaining the prerogative of capital punishment. Food was always available in a chief's palace for anyone who wished it, and a drum announced the daily offering of food, but it is not clear how many people benefitted from this redistributive service.

ATHENS (403–322 BCE, 20)

The Athenian government displayed a somewhat mixed picture in terms of public goods. In Athens, one board of magistrates, five in number, was charged with road maintenance, but H. Blümner (1966: 199) writes that "we must not assume that ancient Greece possessed a well-kept complicated network of streets." For example, the important street of the Panathenaia was wide but built only of packed gravel with no formal edges. A superintendent of springs was regarded as an important office, charged with the repair of spring houses and water conduits. Substantial fourth-century projects improved water availability for public buildings and for public fountains, but storm drainage, a persistent problem, was not adequately addressed (later Roman administrators, especially Hadrian, detected serious shortcomings related to water management in Athens and devoted many resources to improving it). While there were many ways to identify and punish corrupt officials, less effort was devoted to the issue of public safety. Magistrates (*astynomia*) were assigned this task (as were the *agoranomoi* in the marketplaces), but their numbers were small and it is not clear how effective they were, for example, crimes were not punished unless an accuser brought the case to the People's Court. According to C. B. Gulick (1973: 20), "there was no regular patrol of the city streets in the interests of the personal safety of private citizens, and the dark alleys and the outskirts of the town were infested with footpads, who clubbed the belated citizen and robbed him of his mantle or purse." There was some concern to address food security. In emergencies, free or cheap grain was distributed to citizens, and magistrate boards monitored grain imports and regulated grain prices. Disabled persons could receive a subsidy from the state, and the state also helped with the costs of raising the sons of soldiers killed in battle. One of the key governing bodies of the polity, the Council of Five Hundred, distributed pensions to deserving disabled persons of low income. We noted that the state was expected to fund public rituals and to pay for and make a large number of ritual animal sacrifices.

Lozi (Southern Africa, late nineteenth century CE, 22)

The Lozi polity exhibited a relatively high level of public goods provisioning. "Canals which score the plain" were dug by order of the kings to facilitate transportation and to improve drainage (Gluckman 1961: 63; cf. Prins 1980: 58–70), although, outside the polity's core zone, there was little state involvement in transportation except that a portage was maintained by the state at the Ngonye Falls. Disputes were expected to be settled locally if possible, but "a well-established and defined system of law, administered by an organized judiciary and executive . . . are alert to protect . . . security" (Gluckman 1961: 63). State gardens were worked with *corvée* labor from nearby villages, but they served, to some extent, as a public good, as did royal cattle herds. Hungry persons could help themselves to the ruler's gardens and fishing sites, and the royal herds and royal storehouses could be drawn from during periods of food stress. Some tribute from conquered groups was distributed in public because "tribute was of the nation" (Gluckman 1943: 79), and some of the goods acquired by rulers in international trade were distributed to "his people" in both the core zone and tributary dependencies (Gluckman 1941: 23, 92, 1943: 80).

Ming Dynasty China (late fourteenth and fifteenth centuries CE, 22)

The polity's Confucian ethic mandated high service levels, but equitability was not always a reality. For example, the most expensive construction was reserved for official roads and canals, but these had only limited allowable commoner use. The famous Grand Canal was a major transportation project, but was used principally, though not entirely, for official business, and no similarly large-scale public transportation projects were undertaken. Road and bridge construction and maintenance were often carried out by local officials but often, as well, were funded by private benefactors, especially after the fifteenth century. The Ministry of Works was charged, in part, with the maintenance of roads and waterways, but did comparatively little to improve transport conditions except as a by-product of state-sponsored flood-control efforts.

A state courier system, a postal system, and transport offices (the latter to handle state-requisitioned goods) were established to manage the growth of official communications and material flows, but were reserved largely for official purposes. State-sponsored expansion of water-control facilities near Beijing was deemed important to lessen the capital's dependence on southern grain, and Ch'ao-ting Chi's (1936: 36) tabulations of official references to water-control works from pro-vincial gazetteers shows a substantial increase in the number of Ming works com-pared with prior dynasties, and these were carried out over a broad geographical area. The first Ming emperor ordered that "all petitions in regard to water benefits, from the people as well as officials, be brought to his attention," and he dispatched officials to the provinces to supervise water control works (Chi 1936: 143–44). A major flood-control project was carried out to inhibit the flooding of Suzhou (Brook 1998: 605). However, in Fujian "as elsewhere, local gentry members played an important role in initiating and financing such repair and construction projects" (Rawski 1972: 12).

Beijing and Nanjing were subdivided into wards in which state officials super-vised police and fire patrols; however, much of north China was troubled by roam-ing bandits. Military officers were sometimes required to quell outlawry and were rewarded for taking action against bandits, though success in war was more highly valued. Local criminal investigation and punishment and the resolution of disputes were in the hands of local state authorities, but also clan institutions, though some legal cases involving commoners received extensive review treatment at the higher levels of the judiciary.

There was considerable concern with food security under Ming governance. Censors were sent to famine areas to supervise relief efforts following floods or locust infestations, while grain from the main state granaries was sold at low prices, loaned, or distributed free in famine areas. The Ming Dynasty promoted the development of civilian or "community preparedness" granaries (the "Ever-Normal Granaries") that were intended to improve food security for the bulk of the population (Figure 8.1). The Ming institution of granaries reflects their adherence to Confucian concerns that a state should provide for the popular welfare, a notion that had influenced prior Chinese states as early as the Han Dynasty. The commu-nity granaries, however, illustrate the dilemma faced by the Ming state in that, while Confucian paternalism was an important driver of policy and government action, government officials also theorized that an effective state governs in a frugal and limited manner allowing for considerable local control. As a result, with its lim-ited regulatory personnel, moral hazards in granary management were a persistent problem. State-subsidized Confucian schools scattered throughout all the prefec-tures trained young men for civil service careers and fed a small number each year into the national universities including the highly regarded Hanlin Academy that prepared superior students for high offices in the civil administration. County-level

FIGURE 8.1. Chinese village granary, from the *Gengzhi Tu* (Plowing and Weaving Illustrated). We thank Francesca Bray for help in identifying the source of this image.

officials of the state (*chih-hsien*) were charged with supervising care of the aged and indigent, and they were expected to be benevolent in their contacts with the public.

MUGHAL (SOUTH ASIA, 1556–1658 CE, 23.5)

This polity diverted considerable resources to public goods. The main arterial roads in large cities were paved by the state, while minor roads remained unpaved or were paved using private funds. Many bridges were built around Delhi, Agra and other imperial cities, and state resources provided for the construction of the main rural roads. For example, the road from Agra to Lahore was planted with trees, and supplied with bridges, but roads were also built "all over north India" (Grover 1994: 239), some with state-funded traveler's lodgings. Drinking water supplies came largely from private wells, but, in the case of a new city foundation, the state would develop infrastructure for water supply and sewage drains. For example, a lengthy canal was dug to serve the new center of Shahjahanabad. It served for agricultural and residential uses as well as for public gardens. In north India, there was some state involvement in the construction of irrigation canals, however, Irfan Habib indicates little overall involvement by the state in promoting or managing canal irrigation (Habib 1963: 256). For example, some irrigation systems that were in use probably preceded the Mughals, and much cultivation was based on rainfall or private well irrigation.

Internal security was a service of the state, in the cities, through the office of the *kotwal*, while rural community policing was done by *chaukidars*, who worked for the village community, not the state; villagers as well as local *zamindars* (local officials) were responsible for their own safety and that of travelers and merchants in their area, and appear to have carried much of the financial burden of crime control. There was "considerable rural banditry," so insurance was required for valuable commodities in transport (Grover 1994: 242), and caravan merchants employed private guards.

Most charity was in private hands, but some minor distributions were made by the state for low-income housing, traveler housing, and famine relief. Grants of land and stipends were given by the office of *sadar* or directly by the ruler, including those given to destitute individuals. The estates of persons dying without heirs and the balance owed from the estates of civil officials were not to be used for ruler's needs or state needs, and instead were designated for charity; similarly, the 2.5 percent tax on income of Muslims was reserved only for "pious works" (Sarkar 1963: 157–59). There is some evidence for state response to famines including food distributions and revenue remissions, but some famines had serious consequences (e.g., Habib 1963: 102–4, 250–51). A postal system was present but was for state use only, leading merchants and others needing postal services to hire messengers. Monasteries received grants from the state in some cases.

METHODS AND EXAMPLES OF COLLECTIVE ACTION
VARIABLES II: BUREAUCRATIZATION

A bureaucratic organization is vested with the responsibility to enact the state's policies, but a bureaucratic system suited to an autocratic regime will differ in many ways from one suited to the management of a collective state. In the interest of our comparative analysis we formulated a measure we call "bureaucratization" with the goal to assess the degree to which a state's administrative system coincides with theoretical predictions from collective action theory. To develop this method we started by mining the insights of the sociologist Weber, as nearly all students of administrative systems do. Weber distinguished what he called the modern legal-rational bureaucracy, associated with the capitalist nation-state, from earlier and more "primitive" or tradition-based systems of administration that reflect patriarchalism (authority derived from models of a master in his household), "patrimonialism" (authority based on the idea that commoners and administrators are personal dependents of the ruler), feudalism (in which rulers make grants to vassals to obligate them), or the routinization of charisma (rule based on the extraordinary powers or sanctity of a ruler). The transformation from these "primitive" forms of administrative systems to legal-rational bureaucracy was achieved in modern nation-states, Weber argued, through the "rationalization of collective activities," which makes possible the "purest type of exercise of legal authority" (Weber 1947: 333).

While we have been inspired by Weber's writings, we depart from his scheme because our goal is to develop a method of comparative measurement rather than a typology of administrative systems. To do that we developed a five-item scale to measure varying degrees of expression of collectively consistent administrative policies and practices. These reflect five main themes: (1) To what degree were there well-developed communicative channels through which commoners could make appeals and complaints concerning taxation, judicial decisions, or other governmental actions? (2) Similarly, to what extent is the judicial system staffed by salaried judges trained in legal theory, and to what extent are judicial decisions monitored by higher authorities to inhibit legal malfeasance? This variable is similar to how we counted citizen access to an effective judiciary as a public good, but in this case we assessed whether the judicial system is highly suited to collective action through its institutional means to provide legal training for judicial officials and it ability to detect and punish official malfeasance. (3) Does a state possess sufficient institutional capital in domains other than the judiciary to detect administrative malfeasance such as misuse of jointly produced goods or excess taxation, and, is it possible to punish officials, including removing even the highest administrative officials from office for failing in their duties? (4) Is officeholder recruitment consistent with collective goals? In the latter we paid special attention to whether recruitment to official positions was "ascripted" (i.e., based on birth or in other ways restricted to an in-group) or open to persons outside of some select group. The latter is preferable from the perspective of collective action because ascripted officeholders may feel more entitled to hold positions and thus are more difficult to remove from office. (5) To what degree are officials salaried? For this variable, we gave higher scores, indicating more conformance with the expectations of collective governance, when officials were salaried rather than awarded some form of local control over a source of income in exchange for administrative or military service. The latter would include variations around *benefice* (where the official would be allowed "appropriation of receipts" in Weber [1947: 312]) and *prebend* (assignment to an official of rent payments, in Weber [1978: 963–64]). *Benefice* and *prebend* reduce administrative costs, but they may devolve into hereditary claims of ownership of office, increasing the difficulty of punishing officials and removing them from office by comparison with salaried officials (Weber 1947: 335–36). We classified *appanage* as an intermediate strategy in which officeholders are reimbursed by awarding them the right to receive rents from some specific locality or type of resource, in the manner of a prebend or benefice, but where the award is made on a contingent basis.

We can put bureaucratization in perspective by noting some of the features of the administrative systems of the less collective polities where bureaucratization was not highly developed such as in what are called "segmentary states." These states have minimal ties between central and subsidiary components of the governing system. They typically feature these elements: weak control over local judicial officials and little institutionalization of a standardized legal theory, the consumption of resources for purposes such as elaborate palaces and court rituals rather than for public goods and administrative costs, the focusing of administrative resources on the management and protection of estates or other resources controlled directly by the state or its principals, and strategies to reduce the workload of central officials by devolving responsibilities onto lower levels (but then losing control over whether lower officials are adhering to official policies). The foremost example of the latter is "tax-farming" (similar to "privatization" of current parlance), a tax-collection option for principals who are lacking an adequate administrative system for equitable tax collection or who are aiming to reduce administrative costs. Tax-farming, in which merchants are given contracts to collect taxes, is a cost-efficient practice for the state but one that opens the door to the potential for overtaxation and other corrupt practices over which the state has little oversight or control.

Below we briefly summarize some aspects of variation in administrative systems in several polities chosen from our comparative sample. More complete descriptions of these societies and data on others in our sample are found in Blanton and Fargher (2008: chap. 8). Each section includes polity, focal period, and the coded value for bureaucratization, a five-variable measure with a potential score of 15.

DATA SUMMARIES

BALI (THE LATER MENGWI POLITY, 1823–1871 CE, 6)

Bali has a low bureaucratization score owing to its weak links between principals and lower officials, and owing to the preponderance of ascription in the recruitment of rulers and secondary officials. Officials were drawn only from two of the three upper castes in the Hindu-inspired cultural code (*brahmanas* are a high caste, but normally were excluded from political offices). Commoners, as a *sudra* caste, could not hold supravillage authority, but sometimes held minor local administrative roles. Heads of royal lineages of lesser status than the ruler operated largely autonomously in their local domains because they inherited their positions rather than being selected by the ruling lord. They even had their own "satellite" lords. The secondary elite were kept within a ruling family's orbit principally through their belief in the symbolic importance of central rulership and the fact that the central power could at times come to the aid of a dependent lord. Also, in what Clifford Geertz refers to as the Balinese theater state, central lords staged impressive funerary and succession ceremonies that confirmed, by the resplendence of the displays, their superior religious sanctity and their superior control over resources and people.

BAKITARA (EAST AFRICA, 1869–1890 CE, 6.5)

This polity scored low on bureaucratization owing to its strongly ascripted administrative system built around the patrilineal clans of both the ruling *Bahuma* pastoralists and the aboriginal *Baheru* horticulturalists. Most palace officials and district and local chiefships were elite members of clans, while what were termed the *batongole* were given estates and gifts by the ruler in exchange for services such as providing servants for the king's household and herding the king's private cattle herds. Taxes were collected by messengers with insignia of the king. They apparently were "paid" from fees they could earn settling disputes or from taking bribes, a type of tax-farming that is not consistent with equitable and corruption-free revenue collection. Any person, "cow-man" (*Bahuma* commoner) or "serf" (*Baheru*) theoretically could appeal a judgment made by a lower chief, even to the king as a last resort, but a ruler's extensive daily ritual round left little time available for official business, and he was usually confined to the royal enclosure. No particular place or time was set aside to accept appeals, so it is unlikely many people could gain access to a ruler.

JAPAN (TOKUGAWA PERIOD, EIGHTEENTH CENTURY CE, 7)

A military administration directed by the Tokugawa family (the *shogunate*), was effectively the main source of governing authority in Japan during the focal period.

This system did not score very high on measures of bureaucratization. The central administration included some salaried officials and included a separate administration governing the vast personal properties of the Tokugawa family. However, the *daimyo* ("feudal warlords") who governed the approximately 270 provincial territories (*han*) were hereditary officials. The *daimyo* had a considerable amount of local autonomy in the conduct of justice, taxation, and administration. They also maintained local military forces, all within limits specified by the *shogun*. Beyond the capital Edo and the *han* administrative centers, rural administration was poorly developed, including taxation; as Louis Perez (2002: 26) puts it: "regional administrators occasionally ventured out into the provinces to 'inspect,' particularly at harvest times, in hopes of garnering a few bribes to turn a blind eye to tax-collection irregularities." During the focal period, *samurai* warriors were moved away from rural areas to live in the castle towns, leaving a vacuum of rural administration and increasing the potential for tax evasion by rural populations. Attempts by the state to gain more control over tax collection and to increase tax revenues resulted in an increase in peasant protests. Although taxes were not collected by private contractors, tax collection was left largely in the hands of local hereditary headmen (*gono*), and there appears to be almost no monitoring of taxpayer compliance or any way to address complaints about tax collection irregularities (a corrupt *gono* "could cheat and embezzle almost at will" [Perez 2002: 33]), although in urban centers complaints from townspeople were more likely to be heard and tax compliance monitored. Appeals for lower-level judicial decisions could be made, in theory, but usually were not, and a revised law code developed in 1742 "was never made public" according to Tsuji Tatsuya (1991: 454). Because rural populations lacked communication channels to make complaints about official corruption, they often engaged in what John Hall (1991a: 24) calls "appeals by force," for example, there were 724 peasant uprisings from 1716 to 1750, involving up to as many as 84,000 persons in one case.

ENGLAND (1327–1336 CE, 8.5)

The governmental structure of early fourteenth-century England was strongly ascripted in the central government, the king's household, and in the feudal hierarchy. However, salaried staffs carried out some administrative functions in all three. Rural administration was in the hands of salaried officials, including the sheriff and his staff, with the assistance of the coroner; some of these positions were locally elected. We also see justices of the peace and keepers of the peace at the local level with duties and responsibilities parallel to the sheriff and his bailiffs, but these officials were controlled and manipulated by the local elite, so the nature of their linkage to the central administration is not always easy to discover. There was a hierarchy of courts but no official judicial branch of the government. The state's revenue administration was poorly developed, not sufficiently monitored, and liable to corrupt practices. Plucknett (1940: 103) found that a number of private landowners served as tax collectors and points out that "as for financial probity, it must likewise be remembered that handling or collecting public funds was a difficult task which often placed the official between the upper and nether millstone. The system was complicated and ineffective, and the crown bore hard upon its agents who in turn had to get the money where they could find it." Similarly, from Joseph Strayer (1947: 4) we find that "there were never enough paid civil servants to collect the king's revenues, and thousands of unpaid assessors and collectors had to be pressed into service. These men were naturally not eager to squeeze the last farthing out of their neighbors and their lack of zeal is reflected in the tax returns." Weak and corrupt administration resulted in the growth of public protest, as described in Scott Waugh (1991: 167): "For the peasantry, local commissioners were no better than central. They complained bitterly about both. Protest poems from the early fourteenth century lament the venality of all royal officials, whether sheriffs . . . judges, bailiffs, or commissioners of array, tax, and purveyance."

Few communication channels were available for commoners to make complaints or appeals, and these were not well organized. Because "over half of the peasant population was juridically servile, subject to *seigneurial* [local elite] jurisdiction and with only rare access to the royal courts" (Hilton 1992: 21), persons judging their cases were not trained in judicial procedures, nor were they official representatives of the state's legal system. Parliament was beginning to take shape and increase its influence during the focal period, but it remained a body of the gentry rather than commoners. Appeals could be made to the king and council but often were ignored even in cases of official malfeasance. As Bertie Wilkinson (1940: 202–3) points out:

> It was the great expression of order and the supremacy of government and law, which stood, and still stands, as a thin barrier between civilization and barbarism; but despite its imposing façade there was inevitably much weakness within. Too often, we may suspect, the office was, as individuals were, a lackey of the great, and oppressor of the poor. It needed a revolution to enable Geoffrey Cotes to bring a successful complaint against Henry Burghersh, and even then his action was attended by a very limited success. On the other hand the power of a great lord could make itself felt in the very antechambers of the king.

This ineffective governing system prompted considerable opposition. According to Platt (1982: 90), during this time the state received a growing number of requests from elite families to allow them to fortify their houses—as protection against rural unrest in their own domains.

ASANTE (WEST AFRICA 1800–1873 CE, 10.5)

Asante scored moderately high on bureaucratization. R. S. Rattray and Ivor Wilks both describe an Asante administrative system that included numerous appointed and salaried officials, but also some ascripted officeholders including the *amanhene*, the divisional paramount chiefs. However, the latter served at the king's pleasure and could be "destooled" (impeached). Clan chiefs played some role in local administration, as did community elders, but salaried "resident commissioners" (*amradofo*) were placed by the *asantehene* (ruler) in the tributary provinces to represent state interests. Minor disputes were adjudicated and punished at the community level, but a decision could be appealed to higher authorities. Positions of authority were not usually held by members of the nobility (descendants of the founders of the Asante state), because in Asante political culture achievement counted for more than noble status. This is clearest in the case of appointed officials who were "pure" servants of the state rather than having significant ties to important matrilineages.

Ivor Wilks (1975: chap. 4) details how the Asante state, after the late eighteenth century, devised new forms of government to increase their range of control (scale), the scope of control (to regulate spheres of activity not previously controlled), and proficiency. These changes allowed the government to transcend the managerial limitations inherent in the hereditary aristocracy of the pre–Imperial Period, and it bears mentioning that these changes brought with them considerable upheaval, especially in their relations with the traditional chiefs. During the nineteenth century, head taxes and inheritance taxes, collected by administrative officials, became important sources of state revenue. Trade was taxed by what appears to have been an elaborate bureaucracy, but revenue collectors were paid a fee based on collections rather than a salary, resulting in some degree of tax-farming, and some other tax-farming was practiced, but only in the comparatively economically marginal tributary areas.

Some nineteenth-century accounts suggest that rulers had access to considerable information about local affairs throughout the empire, and worked long hours to complete administrative work. The Council of Kumase (*asantemanhyiamu*) served as a venue where all kinds of individuals could petition king and council. Some other practices allowed for expression of voice; for example, every subject had the right of appeal to the ruler's court and a call to destool a divisional chief could be brought by any commoner able to mobilize public opinion.

LOZI (1864–1900 CE, 12)

Government by council was an important principle of Lozi administration during the focal period. The main council (*kuta*) was constituted to represent the interests of all the polity's stakeholders: the ruler, representing the administrative system; the traditional aristocracy; and the commoners. Interestingly, the chief councilor of this body (*ngambela*) was always a commoner. Ascripted chiefs of the outer provinces retained considerable local autonomy, but the ruler also had salaried representatives in those locations (*lindumeleti*) concerned primarily with the management of tax collection. Some individuals selected by the ruler for service on the capital's council were awarded temporary ownership of lands (mounded garden and village areas) associated with their specific council title or name, similar to an *appanage*. Village headmen and lineage elders and chiefs of outer provinces as well as ruler's representatives were charged with collecting the basic tax on production and organizing the corvée labor tax. Barotse (citizens) recognized their obligations to the ruler and their local governing elite, but also expected the ruler to heed their voice and to preserve the right of appeal to the ruler.

MUGHAL (1556–1658 CE, 12)

Scholars of the Mughal state—including M. Athar Ali, Jadunath Sarkar, Irfan Habib, and Ibn Hasan—all depict a vast Mughal administration that staffed most positions through open recruitment (i.e., irrespective of social standing, religion, or ethnicity) and in other ways demonstrated a high level of bureaucratization. However, the insistent pressure on lower-ranking officials to provide gifts for higher-ranking officials and the ruler, coupled with the fact of low salaries, were together detrimental to the efficiency of the administrative system.

State officials (*mansabs*) were paid a salary or given a *jagir*, basically an appanage grant of land, from which a specified income could be derived. However, the *jagirdar* "had no rights or privileges apart from those received from the Emperor" (Habib 1963: 319). Taxation was the responsibility of the provincial revenue collection administration (*diwan*) that was accountable to the prime minister of finance. This bureau, kept separate from the provincial governors (*subahdar*), allowed for more direct state management of revenue matters to limit the potential for corruption. Below the diwan there were several kinds of officials (*amin, amil, chaudhuri,* and *karori*) charged with revenue assessment, collection, and accounting.

Outside the core region of northern India, government was more likely to be in the hands of *zamindars* (petty *rajas*), who were local hereditary rulers holding traditional proprietary rights over land and taxes. Although they governed somewhat more autonomously than state-recruited officials in the core area, they were required to pay taxes and provide military services to the state. As well, they were responsible for some aspects of governance in their territories, and many were given a *mansab* grade (i.e., an administrative grade) in the manner of other salaried state administrators.

The official revenue administration extended deeply into the rural communities, including the *qanungo* ("friend of the peasant") and *muqaddam* (who served as state revenue officials at the subregional or village level), although there were also village headmen, councils of village elders, *chaukidars* (village police), and *brahmans* involved in governance at the village level. A massive and costly survey of taxable land by province and village was compiled during Akbar's reign. This and other ongoing surveys were central to the *zabt* administration found primarily in the core regions of Hindustan (the area from Lahore to Bihar). The zabt system aimed to achieve equitable rural taxation by calculating each household's tax obligations from an estimate of crop yield based on farm size. These calculations resulted in a specific tax rate for each household, which was then commuted into a required cash payment amount based on market conditions. This elaborate system allowed for a considerable degree of equitability in estimating tax obligations of individual households, but it was difficult to manage, resulting in some tendency toward self-serving behavior among lower officials who assessed the production potential of households.

In this highly bureaucratized system, tax-farming was officially prohibited, but did occur in some cases. Generally, however, considerable state control was maintained over taxation and tax evasion during the seventeenth century. For example, the *faujdar* was a local territorial agent of the state charged with evaluating the fairness of land-based revenue. Various kinds of taxes and trade practices by officials were declared illegal by both Akbar and his successor, Jahangir, and, some revenue collectors were punished when "complaints reached the emperor's ears" (Sarkar 1963: 69). Governors were charged to "keep all classes of men pleased" by protecting the weak, and diwans were urged to watch for local officials who may collect excessive tax. *Zamindari*-governed areas were more difficult to control than those in the core zone and had higher potential for tax collector agency and corruption, implying considerable administrative costs to identify and punish agency. However, the state claims to have had as much administrative control of zamindari areas as of areas directly administered by the state, and *zamindar* status could be awarded and rescinded by the central officials. Lastly, an extensive bureaucracy of "news reporters" and spies with a variety of titles "honey-combed" the Mughal Empire, charged with "reporting cases of irregularities and oppression" (Habib 1963: 296). Rulers spent much time traveling around the empire, in part for the purpose of collecting information about the state of the provincial administrations.

ATHENS (403–322 BCE, 14)

The theory of democracy embraced in Athens during the focal period exhibited many features of bureaucratization. The key expectations for this social design were to allow voice for citizens, to maintain procedures for the open recruitment of governing agents from the population of male citizens, and to assure the account-ability of government agents, the magistrates (*archontes*). The term for magistrates translates as "rulers," but, unlike the oligarchic rule of some other Greek polities of the period, in Athens these positions were open to all eligible citizens and were normally charged only with administrative tasks, not legislative decision-making. At any one time there were approximately 700 magistrates in office, some elected and the rest selected by lot in cases where special skills were not required, and 500 were councilors (*boule*) serving the People's Assembly (*ekklesia*). Magistrate offices were held for one year, and, ideally, were circulated rather than being held by par-ticular persons. Magistrates were usually paired, based on the assumption that cor-ruption is less likely when persons work side by side. Theoretically, magistrate posi-tions tended to be held by the more affluent citizens. Because most magistrates were not paid, other than those serving on the council, and some magistrate positions entailed costs that were considered part of a citizen's obligation to the state, less wealthy persons probably could not afford to serve in many cases.

The Assembly of the People of Athens was a venue in which a wide range of persons could express voice. The assembly evaluated magistrates as to whether they were "doing their jobs properly" (from Aristotle, qtd. in Hansen 1999: 132). Complaint petitions could be presented there, though there were other channels through which complaints could be made; for example, "Every summer thirty offi-cials sat three entire days in the Agora [the main civic center] to receive written complaints handed in by the citizens" (78). Citizens and foreigners (*metics*) were allowed to bring accusations against magistrates at the end of a term of office, and citizens could bring a private suit against a magistrate they felt had infringed on their rights.

The Athenian system of government required considerable transparency. This was realized in part through the institution of the *metroön*, a state archive where "every public document, written on papyrus, was available to any citizen on request" (Hansen 1999: 11). The People's Court exercised control over magistrates and gen-erals and managed the *euthynai*, the required rendering of accounts at the end of a magistrate's period in office. Courts could also hold magistrates accountable for their behavior during the term of office through public prosecutions. In the *dokimasia*, an evaluative process was used to confirm a magistrate's commitment to democracy and that he met other requirements of office. Annually, a board of ten inspectors, chosen by lot, was selected from the council to inspect the books of all magistrates. Some tax collection was contracted out, for example, the import-export tax was collected by tax-farmers.

MING DYNASTY (LATE FOURTEENTH CENTURY
AND FIFTEENTH CENTURY CE, 14.5)

The Chinese system of the focal period was highly bureaucratized in an elaborate civil service system organized under the emperor and six grand secretariats, the latter consisting of up to thirteen bureaus. In addition there were separate service agencies, including the military administration, which was separate from the civil. The civil service was organized as two separate hierarchical agencies. "General administration" was distinct not only from the military service but also from the Offices of Scrutiny, the Court of Judicial Review, and the "surveillance-judicial" administration (Censorate). The latter three were devoted to identifying official malfeasance. Each provincial administration, with its branch offices (or circuit), was in charge of censuses of population and land, tax assessments and collection, disbursement, personnel, ceremony, construction, water control, and coordination with local agencies. In order to make official communications more effective, so the emperor could learn more about "the affairs of the people," several new administrative branches were established at the beginning of the dynasty including the Office of Transmission. Memorials approved by the emperor and the administration were published in a gazette that provided a record of the activities of the state.

The "surveillance-judicial" administration, or Censorate, "disciplined and rectified all agencies of government," and had "ombudsman-like surveillance and judicial supervision" (Hucker 1998: 72–73, 94). Government censors and inspectors "were expected to make aggressive inquiries and to welcome complaints from anyone who had a grievance, especially about the conduct of an official in local administration" (45, 94); this kind of information could be used in the periodic evaluations of civil service personnel. The various merit evaluation systems took into consideration evidence for avarice, cruelty, frivolity, instability, inadequacy, senility, ill health, weariness, and inattentiveness.

The traditional nobility played little role in the administrative system. Noble titles could be awarded to persons whose service to the state was distinguished, and they were paid stipends; yet, heritability was controlled by the ruler so the nobility "did not constitute an independent power-wielding element" (Hucker 1998: 29). Instead, the "civil service dominated government to an unprecedented degree. It was not seriously challenged by hereditary nobles or military officers" (9). Bureaucratic routines were developed to minimize corruption, for example, related persons could not serve in the same agency and no official served in his home province.

The general population had most contact with the government through the offices of the *chih-hsien*, at the county (*hsien*) level, which had generalized administrative responsibilities of census, taxation, administering justice, providing public services such as care of the aged, keeping the peace, and performing sacrifices. Below the hsien level, nongovernmental agencies at the community level (*li*), each consisting of about 100 households, had certain responsibilities for maintaining order and maintaining local irrigation facilities and schools (the "*lijia* system"). "Tithing groups" of about ten households were subdivisions of each li, one household of which was charged with the local management of tax collection. The li was a small group that would have allowed for efficient monitoring of taxpayer compliance at the local level, and it conformed to the founding emperor's intention that "localities . . . govern themselves as far as possible" (Hucker 1998: 91).

According to Timothy Brook (2005: 46) there was a "persistent evasion of fiscal registration by wealthy households." The response was a "secret police" charged to identify noncompliance (Huang 1998: 109). To establish equitability in rural taxation, and to limit free-riding, the Ming state undertook a massive census of land and population, the latter through the mechanism of the reformed rural *lijia* system, as early as 1381. The land census—a massive project, unsurpassed in any world area at that time—recorded land area and other data by household. These data were recorded in two documents, the "Yellow Registers," which recorded each household's tax obligation, and a corresponding map of taxable properties by district called the "fish-scale registers" (because the plots, mapped side by side, looked like fish scales). The household census was more elaborate than similar surveys done in prior dynasties, categorizing households according to the availability of labor and the amount of land owned, from which their labor and production tax in grain (from men's labor) and cloth (from women's labor) could be calculated. Military households, found mostly in the northern zones, owed the labor service of one able male.

A formal legal code was promulgated as early as 1368, including a vernacular commentary on it that was intended to make the code widely known among the people. The Confucian social theory that informed Ming governance affirmed the importance of "equal educational opportunity for all" (Ho 1962: 255). Public education was key to governance because recruitment into positions in the civil and military administrations was through an examination system, though some boys were tutored privately. Civil service exams had a long history in China prior to the Ming Dynasty, already showing considerable institutional development as early as the T'ang (618 to 907 CE) and Northern Sung (960–1126 CE) Dynasties (the system of open recruitment is discussed in more detail in chapter 11). The examination system was "competitive" and "open," though there were some categories of persons, such as beggars and vagrants, who were ineligible. Successful test-takers were given public acclaim as well as symbolic and material rewards, and they were eligible for the grand competitions that took place in the capital, at which the emperor attended.

Upon entering the civil service, higher-ranking recruits attended the Hanlin Academy to prepare for service in the Grand Secretariat administration. Others were given various lower-ranked positions. Administrators were evaluated for merit ratings at regular intervals and during unscheduled evaluations; promotions were based on favorable evaluations. At the "Great Triennial Court Audiences" a large number of provincial officials were gathered at the palace for an audience with the emperor and high officials, following which a round of promotions and demotions or criminal charges were made. The names of officials found wanting or subject to prosecution were published in a book that is described as having been widely circulated. Punishments administered to wayward officials could be quite harsh and humiliating.

METHODS AND EXAMPLES OF COLLECTIVE ACTION VARIABLES III: CONTROL OVER PRINCIPALS

A principal authority (sovereign or other, such as chief magistrate or ruling council) is central to a state's functioning, symbolically representing the polity as a whole while serving as chief administrator and policy-maker. Thus the principal authority unites "leading ideas . . . together with . . . institutions" (Geertz 1983a: 122). Given a principal's potential to influence events, the potential for self-seeking behavior presents a particularly difficult collective action problem. In the more collective states, in which taxpayer compliance is predicated in part on the confidence that principals will honor obligations to subjects, effective institutions are required to maintain principal power within allowable limits. This includes the ability to limit direct principal control over resources that could be deployed for self-seeking gain. This control applies both to symbolic resources, for example, religious institutions (discussed in more detail in chapter 11), as well as material resources. For example, we looked closely at whether there was intermingling of personal and state wealth.

In addition to restricting independent control over symbolic and material resources, in premodern states, typically, the most effective means for exercising control over principals is to establish a strong institutional counterweight to high office. Typically this will be a governing council or high administrative official possessing sufficient cultural and social capital to authoritatively assess whether or not principals are observing moral codes and possessing the ability to punish them for egoistic behavior. We also reasoned that citizens might value public appearance as a source of information regarding a principal's commitment to cooperative policies. Correspondingly, we looked for evidence of institutions that obligated principals to appear publicly, and this theme is followed up in chapter 11 in a discussion of the artistic portrayal of leading officials in representative art. The following briefly summarizes the data we used to code for control of principals; more complete descriptions and full citation is found in Blanton and Fargher (2008: chap. 9). As usual, the focal period is indicated before the score for control of principals with a high possible score of 18.

DATA SUMMARIES

BAKITARA (EAST AFRICA, 1860–1890 CE, 7)

Bakitara rulers were quite autocratic but at the same time not actively involved in governance. Normally, they were confined to a massive royal enclosure, where an extensive daily ritual round left little time available for official business or public appearances. We could find little evidence for any moral code that would define ideal ruler behavior, except for the obligation to perform frequent rituals. No council or other entity could impeach a ruler, as the "king's power was absolute over all his subjects" (Roscoe 1923: 61), and offending subjects, even his wives, could be "struck down" by a king (63). The hereditary Sacred Guild of Chiefs was consulted on most matters of state, and one mythic tale implies that ruler should listen to the advice of elders, but it is not clear how often others' advice was honored. There is little evidence of restrictions on ruler control of material resources. The rulers' cattle herds were vast and constituted a considerable concentration of resources, and rulers controlled important symbolic systems. Every aspect of kingship was considered sacred. Accordingly, the ruler played an important role in maintaining and enhancing the well-being of the kingdom through his conduct of a complex ritual sequence, most of which were held in the privacy of the palace. These included both formal events and ritualized practices, the latter involving numerous avoidances and scripted sequences of activities, especially surrounding cattle herding, food preparation, eating, human waste, curing/health, reproduction, and death.

BALI (LATER MENGWI POLITY, 1823–1871 CE, 8)

Balinese governance was strongly ruler driven. No high-ranking bureaucratic officials were capable of monitoring, criticizing, or impeaching rulers except in extreme cases (during the focal period, one ruler was deposed because he was insane, but his brother, the new king, was "only dissolute" and was not deposed for it). Brahman priests could not rule but were important to rulers as liturgical experts who could properly "mount the ritual extravaganzas of the theatre state" (Geertz 1980: 37), but there is no mention that they could judge or depose rulers. Sacralization of rulers was a fundamental attribute of Balinese kingship. According to Geertz, hierarchy and status distinctions were central to Balinese social life, extending to royalty whose divine status was an expression of the hierarchical structure of the cosmos. For example, the ruler's palace (*puri*, the palace of a ruling lord) was a sacred symbol and sanctified space designed like a Hindu temple to symbolize the axial structure of the cosmos.

Geertz (1980: 13) characterizes the ritualistic dimensions of Balinese rulership in his idea of the theater state in which "the kings were the impresarios, the priests the directors and the peasants the supporting cast, stage crew and audience." The cremation of a ruler was a spectacle serving to symbolically pave the way for the ascension to the throne of the successor, but the inauguration ceremony was similarly elaborate. However, Balinese ruling families did not control all of the important temples. Cultural integration of the region as a whole was provided in part by annual rituals in the "Six Great Temples" and a "Mother Temple" at Pura Besakih on a sacred volcano that provided a "physical expression of the overall unity of Bali" (Geertz 1980: 40). David Stuart-Fox (1991: 37) refers to these practices as a "separation of religious centre from political centre." And, rulers did not control the important temple of the Goddess of the Lake (Dewi Danu) that played a key role in the nearly islandwide organization of irrigation societies (*subaks*).

JAPAN (TOKUGAWA PERIOD, EIGHTEENTH CENTURY CE, 8)

In this polity, the moral code pertaining to rulership was influenced somewhat by Confucian ideas, but this did not result in a high level of institutional control over principals. Confucian (and Buddhist) ideas were interpreted to imply that each person should behave righteously in a manner corresponding to social status, including rulers who were expected to be the epitome of moral action. Peasants sometimes invoked Confucian and Buddhist ideas of just governance when they made petitions to the government, but moral codes seemed to have little resonance in actual government practice. For example, while the Tokugawa regime was based on a theory of moral rule, no official channels for remonstrance, such as a council, allowed for recall of amoral officials. High officials appear to have served primarily as administrators in the employ of the *shogun*, so were not in any position to criticize him. According to Peter Geoffrey Hall (1991b: 165), "The shogun in theory was a despot, accountable to none but the emperor." This meant little, however, because the shoguns represented the center of political decision-making for the polity, not the emperors. As S. N. Eisenstadt (1996: 195) observed, this represents an interesting situation of "bifurcation between authority and power" because, while the legitimacy of rulership was vested in the traditional emperors, they lacked the power to govern (196).

We were unable to identify any occasions in which a shogun would come before the public or in other ways could be evaluated by a public; instead, rulers remained much of the time in the luxurious quarters of a massive palace/fortress at Edo (now Tokyo). We did not find any restrictions on the shoguns' control of material resources, and they controlled important symbolic resources. For example, even though the Tokugawa house could not claim royal descent, they claimed direct descent from the historically significant Minamoto clan, and they aided in the maintenance of the emperor and court at Kyoto while also gaining symbolic legitimation from marriages into the royal family. In addition, the Tokugawa shoguns made use of religious sanctification to some degree, manifested by the deification of founder Ieyasu as "Great Shining Deity of the East" (Hall 1991b: 149). The *shogunate* exercised powerful control over religious establishments, reducing the wealth and influence of Buddhist monastic orders.

ENGLAND (1327–1336 CE, 8.5)

Kings were obligated to uphold a moral code as outlined in the coronation oath of the Magna Carta. Yet, it is not clear how dutifully this code was obeyed. As Christopher Brooke (1961: 220) points out, one stipulation of the Magna Carta was that there "is or ought to be a recognisable body of law covering all essential operations of royal government and the relations of king and subjects; and that royal government was tolerable only if this body of law was known." This seems to have been problematic in practice, for, as Rodney Hilton (1992: 21) points out, over half the peasant population remained juridically servile, "with only rare access to the royal courts." We could find no context within which the king's demeanor or actions could be publicly evaluated. He did attend meetings of parliament, but only aristocrats and important officials such as the chancellor and the treasurer typically attended parliament and the king's council.

No council or administrative official could legally judge and reprimand the king; while it is true that the nobles removed Edward II from the throne, they did not have the legal authority to do so. As William A. Morris (1940: 4) reminds us, "The king in the fourteenth century . . . was the mainspring of the executive. He exercised an undiminished prerogative in all matters not regulated by statutes," but statutes appear not to have been followed faithfully. As a result, "Government was still in a real and effective way government by the king; the king alone was central and essential to the whole" (Wilkinson 1940: 162). We could find little in the way of restrictions on ruler control of material or symbolic resources. According to Morris (1940: 10), the king maintained strong control over religion: "The two archiepiscopal churches, all the English episcopal churches except one, and a very considerable number of abbeys and priories were under his patronage . . . This meant in general that to the king belonged the custody of the temporalities of these churches during vacancy; that his consent was required before the chapters or convents held new elections, and his approval of the election after it had taken place; and that he exacted the oath of fealty from the new prelate before turning over to him the estates held temporarily in the royal custody."

Kings lived luxuriously, as much or more so than even the wealthiest aristocratic households. As George Holmes (1962: 68) puts it: "government was less concerned with national welfare than it is today and more with the glorification of the king... Royal magnificence, exhibited in a splendid court, in the wearing of jewels, the maintenance of a large retinue, the building of lavish castles such as Edward III's at Windsor, and the waging of expensive wars in support of the claim to France, might sometimes be resented by those who were squeezed to pay for it, but it was generally accepted as a proper object of policy."

MUGHAL (1556–1658 CE, 9.5)

Given the relatively high degree of bureaucratization in the Mughal system, we might expect a correspondingly high degree of control over the behavior of principals. However, there was no "constitutional machinery for controlling or judging" a ruler (Sarkar 1963: 14). While important priests (*ulema*) could issue a decree deposing a ruler as a "violator of Quranic law," rebellion was the only enforcement for such a decree. The *wazir* or *diwan* was the highest government official below the ruler, and appears to have served only as an administrative official under ruler's control. The council of high officials could advise the ruler but not vote on policy.

In addition, in the Mughal polity there were few restrictions on the ruler's control of material resources, though tax revenue from persons dying without heirs and the tax on Muslims was not to be used for the ruler's personal needs. Theoretically, there should have been limitations on ruler control of symbolic resources, especially since in canonical Muslim concepts of rulership, authority was vested by God, but the ruler himself was not consecrated. However, Akbar's concept of rulership went beyond Muslim canon. His success is attributed in part to a "glorification of the emperor's person," including an idea that the ruler was accessible and affable (Richards 1998: 287), but also because he emanated "God's light," a concept adopted from Persian mystic philosophy (298–303). In addition, he traced his ancestry to biblical prophets, to Timur and to nine other Mongol-Turk rulers, and he replaced daily Muslim prayer with sun worship. We add to these features a kind of Weberian "patrimonialism," since high officials were indoctrinated as a ruler's personal disciples based on a master-slave or a patriarchal metaphor. However, in spite of the ability of the rulers to marshal key symbolic resources, they did not have full control over religious institutions. The *mullas* and mosques operated largely separately from the state, and there was some opposition to Mughal ruler ideology among those Muslims who saw Akbar's claims to incarnation as counter to their theology.

These tendencies toward despotism, however, are problematized somewhat by the fact that Mughal rulers did strive to make themselves available in public contexts. They used these venues to shape their presentation of self as accessible and affable. For example, John Richards (1998: 288–89) points out that that the "unremitting public scrutiny" of a ruler's behavior "gave the young emperor [Akbar] an opportunity to create an image of certain, absolute (but not capricious) power." Mughal rulers held daily scheduled meetings in the expansive public audience halls (*diwan-i-am*) (Figure 8.2) in their main palaces and while traveling. Beginning with Akbar, rulers made a daily morning appearance at the eastern wall of the palace fronting a large plain where common people could observe the ruler and make petitions. In a public court of law held once per week, plaintiffs could report grievances, and Jahangir (Akbar's successor) allowed people to tie grievances to a gold chain outside the Agra fort so petitions could reach him directly.

Rulers endeavored to extend their presence over the wide expanse of the empire. Akbar constructed several imperial palaces, including Agra (central Hindustan), Allahabad (eastern Ganga), and at Lahore (Punjab) and moved frequently between these and his main palace at Fatahpur Sikri. Later, he adopted an even more ambulatory strategy reflecting his nomadic "Turco-Mongol ancestry," moving frequently in tent capitals that included public audience halls. It is of interest to note that in paintings depicting public meetings (paintings that are discussed in more detail in chapter 11), Akbar and other rulers of the focal period are shown wearing clothing that while certainly luxurious, was not unlike the attire of officials or other persons in the scenes, and, typically, the ruler is shown at the same scale as others. Akbar also introduced to South Asian political culture the notion of an official chronicle of the reign (the "Akbar Nama"), which he wanted to be an accurate portrayal and to include various topics, including "indigenous customs, private feuds and disputes and moments of personal tragedy and achievement" (Sen 1984: 34).

MING DYNASTY (LATE FOURTEENTH CENTURY AND FIFTEENTH CENTURY CE, 14.5)

During the Early and Middle Ming Period, several social mechanisms allowed for the monitoring of a ruler's actions, not so much in the sense of public appearances, though the emperor's participation was required at certain rites that were public events, and at the "Great Triennial Court Audiences," where a large number of provincial officials gathered at the palace for an audience with the emperor and high officials.

FIGURE 8.2. The Mughal emperor Jahangir at *darbar*, by Abu'l Hasan. Reproduced with permission of the Freer Gallery of Art, Smithsonian Institution, Washington, DC, purchase F1946.28.

For a brief period, special remonstrance officials (*chien-kuan*), among the surveillance administration, were charged with "watching over the conduct of the emperor and denouncing his errors" (Hucker 1998: 92). But, generally, the surveillance administration came to be used primarily to identify and impeach unworthy officials rather than to evaluate and criticize emperors, "contributing to the growth of imperial autocracy" (92). However, there were other communication channels allowing subjects to gauge ruler's actions, especially the Veritable Records. This was an official court gazette that allowed a view into the deliberations of the high councils. The Office of Scrutiny for Personnel could reject memorials such as edicts and other messages coming from the emperor and the palace if they were deemed "inappropriate or unwise" (95).

The central ideological orientation of the Ming emperors was the "vigorous promotion of an ideological orthodoxy based upon neo-Confucianism" (Farmer 1976: 6). In the Confucian system, the rule of a dynasty was certified as legitimate—that is, had the Mandate of Heaven—insofar as the dynasty was able to maintain domestic order and keep the polity secure from external invasion. These ruler services were seen as the basis for taxpayer compliance in what Mark Elvin (1973: 43) characterizes as the "moral unity" of the political community. In addition, the social order was thought to "flourish or perish by its harmonious or disharmonious relations with the encompassing cosmos" (Taylor 1998: 840), and the cosmos was thought to be responsive to human actions including an emperor's sacrifice and prayer. Hence, the official religion was constituted as a specified sequence of public rites, organized by bureaucratic offices including the Bureau of Sacrifices, the Ministry of Rites, and the Court of Imperial Sacrifices. Emperors were not sacralized, but they did participate in some of these rites.

The emperor received his mandate to rule from heaven, but the mandate was confirmed only through sacrifice and "by living as a man of piety"; moreover, the mandate could be revoked for amoral behavior or lack of "demonstrated accomplishments" (Farmer 1976: 98). Correspondingly, high officials of the civil service had the authority to criticize an emperor. Yet, this system was imperfect, as emperors in some cases responded to criticism with "a reign of terror over the civil service" and with public punishments of officials (Hucker 1998: 53). Clearly, the Ming rulers, beginning with the dynastic founder, while largely embracing Confucian ideas, were sometimes at odds with the high Confucian officials. For example, in some cases the Yung-lo emperor assigned important duties to eunuchs of the imperial household thereby bypassing the Confucian officers of the highly bureaucratized civil administration.

There were some restrictions on an emperor's control of material resources. According to Confucian dogma, they should not enrich themselves through commerce or other forms of profit-making. This was thought to be unbecoming of the exalted status of a person who holds power and who should exhibit a "lack of selfishness" and "frugality" (e.g., Elvin 1973: 46). Rulers lacked direct control over the state's wealth; in fact, the treasury provided them with one million *taels* of silver per year for palace expenses such as the pay of army officers in the capital. The standard of living of the emperor was by far higher than anyone else in society. Yet, the first Ming emperor established a policy of "frugality . . . to be practiced by everyone from the monarch down to his lowliest subjects" (Huang 1998: 107). For example, while vast resources were expended to build new capitals and palace complexes at Fengyang and Nanjing, the ruler criticized architects for proposing an excessively decorated palace at the latter site.

LOZI (SOUTHERN AFRICA, 1864–1900 CE, 15)

In Lozi culture, an ideal ruler was "wise, gentle, and soft-tempered" (Gluckman 1961: 54), and while all Barotse (Lozi and subject tribes) owed allegiance to the ruler, subjects were entitled to "claim the king's help and protection," to express voice, and to obtain resources from him, including land (Gluckman 1961: 20, 43). The ruler/subject reciprocity was expressed in patrimonial terms with ruler as "parent." At the same time, ruler was "servant of the nation" (Prins 1980: 71), thus expressing a theme of "symbiosis, of mutual responsibility" (Prins 1980: 118). In addition, Lozi structural history identified an alternating sequence of good and bad rulers, evidently as a kind of moral guide to what constitutes correct rulership. These moral requirements appear to have influenced the institutions of governance. For instance, Lozi rulers claimed descent through males going back to the first king, Mboo. But the operative theory of governance in its totality tempered the power of legitimate rulership with the voice of the people, best represented by the office of *ngambela* (chief councilor). This was a commoner, who was highly regarded in society as a representative of the people and who "[was] expected to constrain and upbraid the king in private" (Gluckman 1961: 45–46).

Few overt restrictions on ruler control of material resources could be identified, but we get a sense that rulers had to be cautious in how they used wealth. They were expected to avoid a display of wealth and instead were expected to show the "quality of generosity" by distributing food and goods, including cloth and cattle (Gluckman 1961: 14). In addition, they were required to attend venues in which a ruler's actions were made public or semipublic; for example, decision-making in governing council meetings required a "full and free discussion" (Gluckman 1961: 41). Ritual events also brought the ruler into the public eye. The ruler was in full view of the political community at the annual movement of all the people, as one, out of the floodplain of the upper drainage of the Zambezi River (to avoid the annual flooding). At this time, elaborate ceremonies preceded the ruler's processional migration from his floodplain capital to his flood season capital, traveling on the royal barge, for which components were assembled from different parts of the polity and during which the "national drums" were played, representing the people.

Through an elaborate installation ritual, the ruler was transformed into a more powerful spiritual being (Prins 1980: 120–21). At a ruler's death, all fires were extinguished until a new fire was ceremonially lit by a priest in every village. Royal burial sites and cenotaphs were sacred sites with deceased rulers even retaining some spiritual potency and offerings made at the burial sites (the "cult of the royal graves," e.g., Gluckman 1961: 26, 30–31; Prins 1980: 123–29). However, there was some separation of ruler from important ritual sites and supernatural forces. The polity's symbolic organization was dualistic, reflected in dual capitals, northern and southern. Greater political power was vested in the north (male) ruler and his capital compared with the south (female) ruler and her capital. The southern capital had more ritualistic and religious than political significance, but the leadership of the south capital could criticize the ruler.

ASANTE (WEST AFRICA, 1800–1873 CE, 15.5)

The *asantehene* (ruler) was subject to control by other officials and a high council. For example, the king's mother had her own stool (a symbol of authority) and she had the power to rebuke the king, his spokesman, and his council "in open court" (Rattray 1923: 82). The king could be arraigned before a national tribunal composed of the *amanhene* (paramount chiefs of administrative provinces) and other officials. The ruler's successor was selected by the high council and the queen mother, and this same group could also destool (impeach) a ruler. A ruler's actions were in full view during sessions of the governing councils, because open debate was required before decisions were made. But it is not clear to what degree the general public could witness such events. However, observation of government in action was possible during the final portion of the polity's main annual ritual: the *Odwira* (yam festival). At this time ritual participants, including the ruler, attended to practical matters of governance. As T. B. Freeman described it in the 1880s, the Odwira "is a kind of annual parliament wherein, towards the latter end of the festival, all matters of political and judicial administration are discussed by the King and chiefs in council . . . and are subjected to the consequences of appeals, from their local Judicial Courts, to the Supreme Court of the King in Council" (qtd. in Wilks 1975: 389).

Interestingly, the "throne" (the "Golden Stool"), symbolizing Asante rulership, was not associated with any particular ruler or matriclan, person, or dynasty. The renowned architects of this African state, Osei Tutu and Okomfo Anokye, envisioned the Golden Stool (*sika dwa kofi*) as a way to signify royal authority but also intended it to serve as a repository of the collective essence of the Asante people. Accordingly, the ruler had no divine or hereditary claim on it. Coincident with this ideology, a theory of moral rulership was developed. For example, a divisional chief was read a list of requirements upon assuming his stool that listed his duties and limitations on his power, and departures from these could lead to destoolment. Such ideas applied to principals as well. At the very end of the focal period, two rulers were destooled, one because he was financially derelict and another because of the "corruption of his personal nature" (McCaskie 1995: 69). Another was destooled in 1803 for failure to preside over the *Odwira* ceremony (136), and one ruler was criticized for retaining fees for his personal use rather than forwarding them to the treasury. If destooled, a ruler was regarded as an ordinary person who could be criticized and punished for actions during his tenure in office.

A ruler's control of material resources was strongly limited. A stool itself did not bring individual wealth to its holder, and even a district's reserve fund was not property of the stool holder. Rulers controlled some important symbolic systems while in office, including important material symbols of rulership consisting of the golden elephant tail—the most important of all elephant tails in the kingdom— and, especially, the Golden Stool. Rulership was to some degree sanctified (but not individual rulers); for example, some clans providing rulers are thought to have emerged from the earth and hence these rulers had a connection to the earth god Ya. However, major ritual sites and temples were located in northern Asante (such as Tekiman), not in the political capital.

ATHENS (403–322 BCE, 18)

In the Athenian democracy, no person or high council constituted what could be called a principal or principals distinct from taxpayers, since taxpayers made up the decision-making and policy-making assemblies and councils. Political authority was vested in assemblies and councils that had separate but overlapping areas of authority, resulting in a system of multiplication of centers of power and separation of powers that could inhibit any attempt by a person or faction to assert centralized control. The main governing councils were as follows:

1. People's Courts (*dikasteria*). People's Courts consisted of panels chosen from among the 6,000 citizens who had been selected by lot at the beginning of each year, who had sworn a citizen's oath (Heliastic Oath), and who were over thirty

years of age. Jurors were selected randomly at the beginning of each court day to "foil any attempt to bribe them" (Hansen 1999: 182). The People's Courts were involved in legally controlling the People's Assembly (see item 2) and prosecuting or denouncing persons accused of crimes against the state. The courts could overturn decrees issued by the assembly and they came to have jurisdiction over political prosecutions, including persons who had proposed illegal decrees to the assembly. The operation of the court and its judgments were by jurors who were always ordinary citizens rather than professional judges, nor were professional advocates used, although professional speechwriters might have been employed.

2. People's Assembly (*ekklesia*). The large citizen assembly was convened four times each thirty-five- or thirty-six-day month of the civic calendar. Out of the 30,000 or so eligible male citizen participants, usually about 6,000 would actually participate in ordinary meetings, a number sometimes required for a quorum. Those in attendance probably included a majority of poorer citizens who benefitted from daily payments made to participants. The chairman of the assembly (*proedroi*) was selected by lot the morning before it began, again, to avoid bribery. During assembly meetings, citizen-speakers (*rhetores*) came forward to present speeches favoring or opposing a proposal. These were usually persons who had received training in public address and rhetoric, and such speakers could become important in the political life of the community. Votes were taken following the speeches, usually with little additional input or discussion from the audience, although interruption might be used as a political tool. The assembly was required to vote, at the first meeting of each year, on the acceptability of the entire corpus of laws; changes could be proposed at this time, and the assembly had to agree to form a board of *nomothetai* to argue a legislative change and to decide whether to ratify it.

3. Boards of Legislators (nomothetai). These boards evaluated proposals to amend the revised law code of 403/2; this council alone had the power to pass laws, though, as mentioned, the assembly also had to vote on the acceptability of the law code once per year. Laws (*nomoi*) were passed concerning important matters such as mining, customs, and external trade. One board was elected by the council and was charged with codifying laws, the other—with members elected at the *deme* (local community) level—was required to certify what the first board had proposed.

4. The *areopagos*. This was a council composed of all former *archons* (highest magistrate officials) that was viewed as a kind of council of elders. It served to

judge homicide trials in cases where the victim was a citizen, but during the fourth century its powers were increased so it could reverse decisions made by the other decision-making bodies.

5. Council of the Five Hundred (*he boule hoi pentakosioi*). This council was composed of fifty persons drawn from the *demes* (local administrative groups) of the ten *phylai* ("tribes," really districts), each selected by lot from citizens nominated by the demes (representatives had to be at least thirty years of age and could serve only twice in their lives). The fifty-person council rotated monthly between the ten tribes. Its business was to prepare items for the Citizen Assembly and the nomothetai and "was at the head of the administration of the state" (Hansen 1999: 388). A council had some rights to fine or imprison or even impose a death penalty in certain kinds of cases involving magistrates. Much of the military, diplomatic, and civil administration of the polity was done by the council; however, genuine debate over policy occurred in the assembly, not just in the council, and legislation was codified and certified by the nomothetai.

6. Tribes (*phylai*) (of which there were ten). Each tribe had a small assembly-place in or close to Athens and sent fifty members to participate in the council. Each tribe maintained a sanctuary in Athens where its eponymous cult hero was honored, where tribe meetings were held, and where information was posted relevant to citizen activities. Tribal divisions organized the council into ten parts, and some magistrate and court positions were chosen according to tribal divisions.

7. Demes (of which there were 139). Each deme had a local assembly, and members participated in it even if they had moved away. These varied in size, and the number of representatives sent by each to the council varied depending on deme size. The *demarcho* (deme leader) was chosen by election or by lot for a one-year term and presided over local government, though most decisions were made by the assembly. Demes certified citizenship (at age eighteen), maintained a register of citizens that was the basis for military call-ups, and identified representatives from their respective tribe for council service.

Several institutional practices contributed to the ability of the Athenians to shape, monitor, and control the actions of magistrates. For one, all resources used by magistrates or other officials were regarded as public property and magistrates' use of them was carefully monitored. Also, a citizen's obligation to the political community was certified in public by oath taking, including the oath required of eighteen-year-olds as they entered obligatory military service, and oaths of office taken upon assuming a magistrate position. Oaths were but one of many social mechanisms designed to avoid what was considered to be the inevitability of free-riding and official agency that was acknowledged in the pessimistic Athenian view of human nature. Pessimism is also indicated by the high frequency of denunciations and prosecutions of officials, especially military leaders. A formal procedure for denunciation existed, including public curses, and officials could be impeached.

The complex institutional arrangements described up to this point were devised as means to enact the Athenian notion of *demokratia*. Demokratia was thought to entail several elements, including rule by the people, liberty (*eleutheria*), the freedom to participate in the political process, and the "private liberty to live as one pleased" without political oppression from one's own government or foreign rule (Hansen 1999: 74) (these liberties applied to "citizens," not to slaves, women, or foreigners). Eleutheria was expressed in freedom of speech, the ideal of due process in law ("no executions without a trial"), the forbidding of torture of citizens, and the protection of private property. Lastly, demokratia implied equality (*isegoria* and similar terms implying equality of opportunity). This equality was conceived of primarily in political terms, including equal rights to address the assemblies and equality before the law irrespective of wealth.

The sense of democracy also included strategies to diminish or downplay the potential political significance of wealth difference. Paul Veyne (1990: 75) points to how a transition from "political gift" to "civic gift" (*euergesai*) corresponded to the emergence of the democratic *polis*. The concept of civic gift served to disconnect wealth from power by restricting the degree to which wealthy patrons could deploy their resources for the construction of client followings to further political aims— instead, civic gifts were intended to benefit the polity as a whole. Other social and cultural mechanisms served to restrict the influence of the wealthy, including gossip and "Old Comedy" theatrical performances that made fun of wealthy families. A new writing style, "plain style," was developed for use on burial monuments and stelae that commemorated war dead. According to Whitley (2001: 366), "A plain style is an effective means for stressing the essential equality of those who died in war" and was consistent with the abandonment of "elaborate marble grave markers . . . that had been so characteristic of late sixth-century Attica." There was also a decline in elaborateness of grave offerings beginning in the fifth century. The construction of "increasingly large and elaborate houses" during the focal period thus sparked critical commentary and debate because the Athenian ideal, espoused by Demosthenes and other prominent figures, was that the leading families should live in modest houses similar to their neighbors'.

Religion could not be manipulated for political gain. State festivals were frequent and costly, promoting polis solidarity and civic devotion through ritual action. But, as Eric Carlton (1977: 235) points out, religion was not "harnessed for the needs of the state." Religious rituals were carried out in the open air largely separate from temples ("very little took place within the temple itself" [Carlton 1977: 239]), and individuals were free to make sacrifices without the aid of priests; in fact, there was no professional priesthood.

CONCLUDING COMMENTS I: QUESTIONING WESTERN EXCEPTIONALISM

We began this chapter by asking if, in a premodern state, the strategies of rulers and subjects could aim for group as well as individual benefit through collective action. The results from our comparative study provide strong support for a "yes" answer to that question. Our thirty-society sample contains within it a wide range of variation from greater degrees of autocracy and bureaucratic ineptitude to greater degrees of expression of collective action. And evidence for collective strategies was found across a wide range of population sizes, environments, and local cultural and social settings. Population size and its relationship to collective action are considered in more detail in chapter 12, but to preface that discussion, we can report that our findings are strongly counter to the expectations of "bottom-up" collective action theorists. Bottom-up (or "polycentric") theory predicts that collective action is more likely to be viable at the local level, in the context of small and socially and cultural uniform populations where mutual monitoring of behavior is feasible. What we found, instead, is a strongly positive correlation between total population size of the polity and the degree of expression of collective action in our sample of thirty polities. This result does not imply that high levels of cooperation are impossible at smaller scales, nor does it imply that all larger polities were highly collective; some of the smaller polities show evidence of collective action, and some larger ones do not. Rather, what we found is a general tendency linking collective action and larger population size.

We also discovered that collective action is a social process in state-building that transcends any particular geographical focus. If we look at the top-scoring and lowest-scoring societies, using a summed score of the three main collective action measures, we find that collective action is represented across diverse areas, environments, and time periods. The highest scorers include societies in tropical sub-Saharan Africa (Asante, Lozi), South Asia (Mughal), East Asia (Ming Dynasty), pre-Hispanic Mesoamerica (Aztec), and the Mediterranean (Rome, Venice, and Athens). The societies scoring lowest include three from Southeast Asia (Aceh, Perak, and Bali), four from sub-Saharan Africa (Bakitara, Nupe, Tio, and Bagirmi), and one European (England).

In the previous chapter we proposed that as a problem-generating structure, collective action should be evident as an identifiable pattern of associated traits. We also found this to be correct, though not in the straightforward manner predicted.

In Appendix B: Table B.1 we report on the results of statistical analysis demonstrating strong positive correlations between the main collective action scale measures of public goods, bureaucratization, and control over principals. Most of the resulting correlation values were high and have statistical probabilities, based on the Spearman's Rank-Order method, of 0.0001 (indicating a result that would happen by chance only one time out of 10,000 trials), indicating very convincing positive results for collective action theory. The only exception to these very high correlations and statistical probabilities is the correlation of the control over principal by public goods variables. This value is positive, and, with a probability value of 0.015, normally would indicate a strong positive correlation. However, that this analysis resulted in lower values than the others is an interesting finding addressed at the end of the chapter and in chapter 13 in a comparison of premodern and modern states.

We are also able to report a strongly positive analytical result in regards to a fiscal hypothesis, namely, that collective action is most likely to unfold when principals are strongly dependent on taxpayers as important providers of a state's revenues, making public goods truly jointly supplied (internal revenues) (our analysis of income sources in relation to collective action is reported in Appendix B: section 1 and Table B.2). These results strongly support the idea that—across different state-building cultures, geographies, and time periods—governing principals will find it worthwhile to strike bargains as a way to gain the confidence and compliance of subjects. The collective fiscal strategies that generate confidence and taxpayer compliance include making themselves accountable and publically accessible, providing public goods, and instituting effective systems of administration for equitable tax collection. Our results also point to the fact that to the extent that principals depend on external revenue sources such as privately held estates, there will be little motivation for them to strike bargains. As a result, they are more likely to rule autocratically with little concern to build taxpayer confidence through institution-building for cooperation, similar to contemporary "rentier states."

MORE ON A FISCAL THEORY OF STATE-BUILDING

What may seem counterintuitive about our results is that the key aspects of the collective polities—accountable leadership, public goods, and rational modes of administration—are usually thought to have emerged only during the historical phase that brought the "modernity" of Western-style democracies. Do our results problematize the notion of a distinct pattern of Western-inspired modernity? We think they do in some respects. What we found from the statistical analysis of our public goods, bureaucratization, and control of principals data strongly supports the notion that in spite of the great diversity of geographical, cultural, historical, and social circumstances represented in our comparative sample, it is possible to identify a process of collective action that embodies many of the elements we associate with modernity but that emerged apart from the historical expansion of democratic modernity. Importantly, we discovered that tax collection procedures varied greatly according to the extent of collective action. Rational tax collection, sensitive to the possibility for corrupt practices and to the need for equitability, is found in the more collective societies in the sample, illustrated in the examples above by Asante, Lozi, Mughal, and Ming China as well as others in our larger sample such as Aztec. Thus, rational strategies for tax collection are not exclusively a feature of political modernity but are, instead, an entailment of collective action viewed broadly.

We also noted that strongly institutionalized tax collection was found in the more collective polities in diverse forms of economy and no matter what kind of good was being taxed. This brings into question the proposal made by Ardant (1975) that the costly modern state could only be supported in a commercially developed economy that presents optimal opportunities for efficient taxation and a commensurate level of wealth production. According to him, agrarian economies could not support modernity, because they were poor while, at the same time, the taxation of individual farm families is inherently inefficient. However, Ardant's Eurocentric hypothesis is not supported from our data. The topic of economic development in relation to collective action is discussed in detail in chapter 12, but at this point it is important to note that we found high levels of collective action in state-building that is statistically associated with growth in both agrarian and commercial economies. Agrarian economies were not always "poor," nor was it impossible to base a tax system on agrarian production.

Recall that Bates and Lien (1985; see also Bates 1991) suggest that when European sovereigns faced a growing commercial economy, they found benefit in taxing the wealth of merchants (moveable goods) as opposed to fixed goods (mostly agrarian production). Democracy arose out of the taxation of moveable goods because merchants, able to easily mask their earnings, would only agree to pay taxes when rulers relinquished some of their power and agreed to be more accountable. In more agrarian-based polities, according to the argument, sovereigns found it easy to tax fixed resources such as land that cannot be hidden from tax collectors. We find the Bates and Lien theory to be misleading because effective and equitable tax collection is always a complex social process requiring considerable institutional development, no matter whether the wealth is fixed or moveable. The key problem is taxing according to ability to pay, for example, when land taxation is based on production capacity, a task that requires the recording of vast amounts of household production data. In general, the less collective polities lacked the administrative wherewithal to tax equitably, as is clear from England and Japan of the focal periods. Both were largely agrarian states, but both were hampered in their tax collection goals by poorly organized, inefficient, and corrupt tax collection systems that did little to endear taxpayers to their state, its rulers, or its administrative cadres and that even incited shirking and peasant oppositional movements.

Taxation according to ability to pay was one strategy we noted in cases of state-builders aiming to increase taxpayer compliance. For example, in the case of Asante, one major source of revenues was a death tax paid (so far as we could tell) especially by wealthy entrepreneurs, and skilled tax collectors were assigned upon a death to carefully assess taxable wealth. In other cases, even in which much of the taxable wealth of a polity was "fixed" (i.e., agrarian), administrative systems were required to collect taxes in a manner consistent with collective action. For example, the administrative reforms of Augustus in the Roman Empire were extended to "establishing . . . uniform standards for measuring and assessing the value of agricultural land" (Hitchner 2005: 211). And we point to the Aztec polity in which officials measured and assessed soil quality and irrigation infrastructure of each rural household's agricultural land and recorded the information in official cadastral registers for purposes of estimating tax obligations as well as to confirm the value of an estate for purposes of sale or inheritance. In the Mughal polity and in the Ming Dynasty, elaborate and costly land surveys assessed the independent production capacities of households in order to equalize tax obligations, and these were among the most ambitious and costly rural-based projects undertaken by either state (the Ming benefitted from a long history of equitable agrarian taxation in China dating to as early as 700 BCE [Deng 2012]). Oddly, Western social science has long claimed that a key foundation of state power in the so-called Oriental Despotisms such as China and Mughal was the construction and management of massive irrigation projects. However, the reality is different: in both Mughal and Ming, while official involvement in irrigation was not extensive, government did carry out massive projects of data recording with the goal to make agrarian tax assessment equitable.

ACCESS TO OFFICES OF THE STATE

Equalization of access to official offices across different sectors of society, which is often associated with political modernity, was also well developed in the more collective societies in our sample. Among the Asante, for example, achievement was noted to count for more than birthright in the selection of administrative officials. In Classical Athens, officeholders were always male citizens, but persons of various social categories—including those who were too poor to be included in taxpayer roles—did participate in citizen assemblies. The Mughal polity practiced open recruitment to official positions, reversing a long history of closed recruitment to high office that was based on the caste system and that had been a signature feature of traditional South Asian political theory and practice. Of the societies in our sample, open recruitment was most elaborately developed in the Ming Dynasty. There, the famous examination system, like the "Ever-Normal Granary," was an institutional resource carried forward into the Ming governance system, building on more than 2,000 years of Chinese state-building experience.

The Chinese civil examination system was a powerful impetus to collective action, minimizing social distinctions and ascripted privilege by allowing for the incorporation of more categories of persons into meaningful participation in official capacities. We think its emergence there should be understood as a signature development in the institutional evolution of cooperation in the human species. In this case, it was in East Asia, not Europe, where a critical social innovation was made that was consistent with collective action and that then underwent extensive institutional improvement, eventually to be implemented in a large and socially heterogeneous polity such as the Ming Dynasty. It was only much later that European state-builders enacted similar recruitment policies, during the Early Modern Period (after the fifteenth century CE), and, when they did, they were influenced by Chinese practices.

CONCLUDING COMMENTS II: MODERN DEMOCRACIES AND PREMODERN STATES

An ideal democracy, according to Robert Dahl (1989), gives leeway for all adults to participate equally as citizens in the political process and to have a say in the government's agenda. Further, it strives for transparency in its governing operation, allows citizens to understand the process of governance, and makes use of competitive elections to fill key positions of authority and to allow citizens a role in making collective decisions. Dahl's scheme is a useful point of departure for comparing highly developed modern democracies with the more collective polities in the sample. However, an important point is that collective action notions demand that more attention be paid to the matter of the fiscal structure of the polity as expressed in its system of taxation and its public goods provision and management.

Otherwise, Dahl's scheme does allow us to identify some points of similarity and difference between modern democracies and premodern polities that were highly collective. Classical Athens, of the study sample, had probably the closest fit with Dahl's ideal, though in this case officials were placed in office more often by lot than by election. In fact, an election-based process that we often think of as the key feature of democracy is not well represented in our sample. In addition to Classical Athens, we encountered forms of electoral processes also in Lamu, an African

Swahili polity of Eastern Africa, where local citizen bodies elected representatives to governing councils. However, democratic elections can be easily incorporated into the conceptual framework of collective action theory. In this sense, elections align with the categories described above for gauging the degree of collective action in a polity's policies. For example, elections may serve to remove amoral elected officials from office, and as such can be fitted into the larger framework of our control over principals and bureaucratization variables. However, rather than taking the form of elections, in the premodern states these forms of control more commonly involved the establishment of institutional counterweights to the power of high-ranking principals in the form of governing councils (e.g. Asante, Lozi), high officials of a civil administration (e.g., Ming China), or threat of legal action for official malfeasance (e.g., Athens). Of course this same principle of institutional counterweighting is found in modern democratic polities with their typical tripartite organization of three branches: executive, legislative, and judicial.

Earlier we alluded to ways in which in the premodern condition state-builders strived to make at least some aspects of the governing process open and accessible, such as public phases of council meetings (e.g. Lozi) and the incorporation of official government business into public ritual, for example in Athens, in connection with the annual Dionysia festival (described in chapter 11), and in the Asante *Odwira* festival. An additional point of overlap between the operation of democratic polities and the kinds of premodern collective polities discussed here pertains to the issue of commoner voice, an aspect of our bureaucratization variable. Again, elections can be a channel for citizen voice in the conduct of government (ideally), and this particular channel is not well represented in the premodern polities. Yet, we encountered other social mechanisms that allowed for the expression of citizen voice, including institutionalized means for commoners to make appeals and complaints concerning taxation or other governmental actions, for example, as described in Asante, Lozi, Mughal, Ming China, and Athens. We also point to the importance of open recruitment of commoners into positions of authority and similar institutional measures that give voice and influence to commoner perspectives in the processes of governing and policy-making.

A notable difference between modern polities and the premodern is evident in the relative frequency of occurrence of monarchy (a monarch is defined as a ruler for life who has inherited the position). While presently only 36 percent of nation-states have some form of monarchy (often serving only as figureheads in otherwise democratic polities), judging from our comparative sample, in the premodern condition monarchy was far more common. In this sample we recorded strong monarchies in nineteen (63 percent) polities, another seven (23 percent) had monarchs but which served side-by-side with other institutions such as governing councils. In only three polities, the chief governing official was other than a monarch: Athens, governed by magistrates; Venice, which had a chief administrative official, the doge, selected by the high governing council; and Swahili Lamu, which regularly rotated chief administrative officials selected from the two main governing councils (Appendix B: Table B.3).

STRONG MONARCHS UNDER CONDITIONS OF COLLECTIVE ACTION

The relatively common occurrence of monarchical rule in premodernity may be related to an interesting pattern we discovered in the analysis of our premodern data that is counter in some ways to the predictions of collective action theory. From a multivariate method called "cluster analysis" we identified three somewhat distinct kinds of states (Appendix B, section 2 and Figure B.1). One we will call the "Low Collective Group" (including Late Medieval England, Bakitara, Tokugawa Japan, and Bali described previously). This group received low scores for public goods (mean = 12.7 out of 30 possible), bureaucratization (mean = 6.9 out of 15 possible), and control over principals (mean = 7.8 out of 18 possible). The other two clusters were more challenging to differentiate because they are similar along the dimensions of public goods (means for public goods are nearly identical, at 18.9 and 19), and close on bureaucratization (with means of 12.8 and 10.5). What the cluster analysis identified, however, are two "faces" of relatively collective polities that differed in one significant respect: One group (including Asante, Lozi, Ming China, Athens, Venice, and Lamu), which we call the "High Collective Group," either lacked monarchies or featured extensive institutional forces equal to the monarch (the mean for our control over principals variable in these cases is 15.7—roughly double the mean score for the Low Collective group). The other group was anomalous in displaying high collectivity in some respects but relatively low scores for control over principals (mean = 9.5). This group, which we label the "Collective with Strong Monarch Group," including Mughal and Rome, featured strong patterns of monarchy in the midst of other attributes consistent with collective action including effective bureaucratization. This anomaly explains the relatively low correlation of the control over Principals and public goods variables noted previously.

We puzzled over what might account for this interesting and unexpected pattern of collective state-building, and we found one possible explanatory variable: revenue sources. While the High Collective Group showed a strong tendency toward internal revenues, as expected from theory (six out of six had predominantly internal revenues), and the Low Collective Group showed the expected tendency to depend extensively on external revenues (nine out of twelve), the Collective with Strong Monarch Group showed a more mixed pattern, albeit one in which most

(67 percent) depended on internal revenues while 33 percent had primarily external revenues. Of the latter, one polity, Egypt, may have developed as a Saudi-like rentier state. The New Kingdom Egyptian state, its associated temple complexes, and its leadership were all vastly wealthy, controlling a large portion of arable land, and they maintained a virtual monopoly over international trade in valuable commodities. We suggest this is a case in which a wealthy state placates its citizens by diverting some of its vast resources in a way that benefitted citizens. We suspect this in the case of the extensive police presence, which rather than intended as a public service, we think was a side effect of the state's goal to protect state property. However, whether intended or not, such services fail the test of public goods because they do not result from joint production, and, as a result, polity formation is not likely to reflect a relational form of power with strategies to maintain the integrity of the governing structure. In fact, Egypt of this period was extremely autocratic, with virtually no accountability of its governing elite, and it lacked avenues for commoner voice.

Another possible causal variable to consider for understanding the Collective with Strong Monarch Group is population size of the polity, with the Low Collective Group tending toward smaller population sizes. Except for Tokugawa Japan, an outlier in this group (estimated at 26 to 30 million for the focal period), the mean population size was roughly 543,000 (it increases to 3.3 million with Japan included). The High Collective Group tended to be more populous. Without Ming China (also an outlier in its group with a population estimated at 130 million) the mean value is 683,400 (with Ming the figure is 22,236,000). The Collective With Strong Monarch Group outpopulated the others with a mean of 6.5 million (and that is without two outliers, Mughal, estimated at 110 million, and the Roman High Empire period, estimated at 61 million)—including these outliers the mean is 17.8 million. These data point to the possibility that in the premodern condition very large and socially heterogeneous populations could coalesce into highly collective polities. When this happened, at the extremes of population size, there was a tendency to build collectivity around an institutionally strong monarchy.

9

Center and Hinterland under Conditions of Collective Action

WITH LANE FARGHER (CINVESTAV DEL IPN)

In traditional views of the premodern condition, the state and its governing structure is viewed as a center that is territorially and socially distinct from a dominated and peripheral hinterland of "primordial" communities. In this chapter we rephrase this terminology, focusing attention on interactions of state and rural social formations to avoid the sense that state and hinterland are, in essence, two separate kinds of social domains. By considering modes of interaction of state and rural social formations, we gain a useful vantage point for the study of collective action, asking the following questions: Does state-building bring advantages or deprivation to commoner elements of society? Are collective states influenced by institutions at the base of society? What role, if any, do persons at the base of society play in civic life? How are rural social formations linked to the state under conditions of collective action?

Historically, the interactions of state and the rural has been understood in two distinct theoretical streams. One is skeptical that states are able to foster cooperation that would incorporate both center and rural. The other position sees that characteristics of the rural may have positive outcomes for collective action at the polity level. Our goal in this chapter is to revisit prior ideas like these in a manner that will be enriched by collective action theory, based on the data we collected as an adjunct to our study of polities. We do that in this chapter's focus on rural communities and institutions, while reserving a similar discussion for the special case of cities and urban neighborhoods in the following chapter.

DOI: 10.5876/9781607325147.c009

THEORIES OF CENTER AND HINTERLAND

Center-hinterland interaction has received abundant theoretical treatment in the historical social science literatures, most often in variations around the perspective of oppression theory. Here a state is seen as a predatory organization that extends its dominance over a primordial substrate of self-governing village-scale communes. By intruding into the domain of traditional communal life, it is argued, the state destroys institutional capital while concentrating power and wealth in the palaces and capitals of the dominant ruling elite. This center of governing power then become increasingly physically, socially, and culturally distant from the dominated hinterland, creating the conditions favoring deprivation and disorganization at the same time as facilitating the growth of despotic rule emanating from the center. Michael Taylor (1982: 57) expresses this argument when he writes that "the state tends to undermine the conditions which make the alternative to it workable, and in this way makes itself more desirable. It does this by weakening or destroying community."

Collective action theorists adopt an antistatist position similar to Taylor's when they argue that cooperation is most likely to be successful when developed from the "bottom up" in small-scale social settings based on personal relationships. According to this theory, any attempt to realize collective action at the scale of polity will fail owing to scale limits on the efficiency of joint supply and distribution of public goods among other scale-limiting factors. Thus, there will be little choice for state-builders other than to institute the command and control abilities of a state as a way to enforce cooperation.

A perspective quite unlike the antistatist views sees the possibility that cooperation expressed at the polity level is shaped by forces emanating from the households and small communities at the base of society. Humans have entertained this question for a long time, most notably as expressed by the Chinese philosopher Kongzi (Confucius, 551–479 BCE). He argued that the kind of moral self-cultivation that is foundational to the ideal society is shaped largely by the experience of family life and filial piety. These values emanating from the domestic domain, he argued further, should play a role shaping the benevolent behavior of rulers and other officials—a theme embraced by the Ming and other Chinese dynasties. Hardin (1982: 43) expresses a similar idea when he argued that cooperative state-builders would have more success if rather than destroying local institutions, they are able to "piggyback" their state system onto preexisting basal social formations that have a history of organization for collective action.

In the following sections, we report on the results of analysis of data collected from our thirty-society sample to evaluate both negative and positive views of state-hinterland interaction in the social development of collective action at the polity level, and we propose some new notions for consideration.

WAS THERE INSTITUTIONAL DECLINE OR
GROWTH AT THE BASE OF SOCIETY?

We noted something like state exploitation of hinterland populations among our least collective polities, but antistatist theories have only limited explanatory potential when considering those polities scoring higher on our collective action measures. In the latter we noted varying degrees of rural transformation, up to and including fundamental restructuring of institutions with the goal to build new forms of institutional capital for cooperation. This included local-scale reorganization as well as the development of direct institutional links between the central offices of the state and rural communities. This finding alerts us to the possibility we will benefit from a new theory that properly addresses collective action process. Most notably in Ming China, Mughal, Athens, and the High Roman Empire, significant and far-reaching transformations of rural organizations and culture reflected state-building policies whose goals were to generate new and more intensive forms of politywide social interaction but also to enhance levels of collective action at the local level. Of interest, judging from the fact that change often was implemented rapidly with little or no local opposition, these policies evidently met with the approval of at least some elements of rural populations who saw benefits in social and culture change.

Generally, the more collective a state was, the more likely it was involved in forging new linkages between the state and local communities and in modifying or building new basal institutions (Appendix B, Table B.4). Direct links from center to the local are needed under conditions of collective action in order to eliminate a powerful intermediary elite who might resist change or prevent the state's policies from being enacted at the local level. We see this in the case of the Mughal polity, whose rulers wished to "shunt aside and neutralize the position of rural aristocrats, to scrape aside the hard resistant shell of local warlord power in order to deal directly with peasant communities" (Richards 2012: 412).

We see institutional change exemplified in the Kleisthenic reforms in Classical Athens, and its associated reorganization of society into 10 "tribes," 30 districts (*trittyes*), and 139 *demes*, as well as in the production of new forms of symbolic representation of the 10 tribes. In Ming China, center and base were conceptually and institutionally linked. Rural policies implemented by the Ming Dynasty founder, the Hung-wu emperor, included the *li-chia* system of administration of units of 10 and 100 households, as well as locally managed public granaries, introduced across the whole of rural China. Each of the li-chia communities was a local tax collection unit and a mandated site of newly implemented cultural practices that promoted community moral discipline. The latter involved community rituals including communal singing, public discussions of filial piety, and a phase in which bad and good deeds were recognized, all in line with Confucianist notions of the community pact (*xiangyue*) that was implemented to enhance the moral quality of village life.

HINTERLAND CHANGE: TRANSACTION COSTS AND "SEMIAUTONOMY"

Rural change in cases such as Classical Athens and Ming China raise the question of cost. How can collective action be implemented while controlling for cost, especially when the scale of society is large? In the cases we coded from the thirty-society sample, we found abundant evidence that state-builders had cost in mind while enhancing basal institutional capital consistent with the needs of a collective state. Often this took the form of increased dependence on local paragovernmental organizations while retaining some degree of official oversight. With this "semiautonomy" strategy, two goals could be realized. First, restructuring was designed to enhance cooperation in local social units, but, at the same time, these entities remained partially self-governing (semiautonomous), thus reducing the state's transaction costs of governance.

The semiautonomy strategy is problematic, however. If central control is too lax, the collective policies of the center will be difficult to sustain, opening the door for corruption and shirking at the local level. We found that to realize a balance between too lax and too tight (and costly) control, links to the higher offices of the state were retained or strengthened in spite of semiautonomy. In China, for instance, local tax collection groupings of the li-chia system were semiautonomous in this sense. They were self-funded (e.g., the voluntary tax-collecting duties assigned to leading families represented an added tax burden to them), as were other forms of paragovernmental organizations headed by local gentry and merchant families who carried out functions such as local-level canal maintenance or river dredging. And the theory of semiautonomy was extended to the household domain, following the Confucian orthodoxy that a family expressing the ideals of unity, righteousness, propriety, and good order would be "regulated" and hence able to function semiautonomously over multiple generations and thus contribute to the proper functioning of the state. As Li-Fu Chen (1972: 409) describes this strategy: "With filial piety, families are regulated, and with the regulation of all families, society is sure to be stabilized."

In Ming China and other cases, however, semiautonomy was nurtured side by side with the establishment of institutions that allowed for periodic monitoring of local organizations and individuals, with a realistic threat of punishment for official or taxpayer malfeasance. In Ming China this was accomplished through various surveillance-judicial bureaus, including a "secret police" (Huang 1998: 109), but, especially, the Censorate, whose members watched over the actions of both officials and persons outside the official structure. This aspect of a semiautonomy strategy is also found in the case of the Roman High Empire focal period, where standardized practices for municipal self-governance were mandated across the ethnically diverse empire based on a charter first developed by Julius Caesar (*Lex Iulia Municipalis*). This charter specified details of municipal structure and function. Yet, when local cases of corruption or other problems arose, the emperor could send a *curatore, correctore, logiste*, or a similar category of official charged with sufficient authority to restore order.

DID COOPERATIVE STATES "PIGGYBACK" ON THE RURAL COMMUNITIES?

Recall Hardin's (1982: 43) suggestion is that cooperative state-builders would have more success if they are able to "piggyback" their state system on collectively organized basal social formations. To better assess the piggybacking idea, for each polity we investigated the characteristic forms of rural communities and from these data developed a coding scheme that allows us to characterize variation in degree of institutional capital for cooperation at the community level. We looked at variables such as the presence or absence of accountable leadership, enforceable rules that can sustain the effective management of communal resources, institutional means for other aspects of governance and recruitment of officials, effective mechanisms for dispute resolution, and evidence for ritual cycles that would enhance community social solidarity (the statistical analyses are reported in Appendix B section 3). From our thirty-society comparative data we discovered a complex and variable picture when collective action is viewed in relation to rural social formations. Generally, the Hardin hypothesis is not strongly supported owing to the many cases scoring high on local community institutional capital but where the communities in question were embedded in polities scoring in the middle or lower values on our collective action measures.

An important cause of deviation from what Hardin hypothesizes is that community systems scoring among the highest for institutional capital are those in which community-scale, or even larger-scale flow-management wet-rice irrigation is a predominant form of agricultural production (as opposed to flood management irrigation or rainfall-based farming). Typically, flood management requires little interhousehold cooperation at the community or larger scales. Often, in cases of flow-management irrigation (e.g., in Bali, Thai, and Burma), high levels of interhousehold cooperation are needed for successful water-sharing and infrastructure maintenance. By contrast we noted that the encompassing Hindu- or Buddhist-inspired political structures of the respective states were highly segmentary. Thus they featured the characteristically weak linkages connecting the central officials of the state to the secondary elite and local communities. In these cases local, or even more expansive, systems of water management operated largely independently with little state involvement.

We did encounter some situations in which piggybacking in the sense of Russell Hardin can be detected. An example is the Aztec *calpultin*, local community formations that were a legacy from prior Central Mexican polities and that contributed social capital to the larger political community. They provided a well-organized organizational base that could then be administratively linked into higher levels of the governing system. Overall, however, across our whole sample, high levels of cooperation in rural communities did not always provide a model for polity-building at the larger scale, nor would states necessarily piggyback on existing systems of institutional capital for cooperation.

FINAL COMMENTS

We conclude that collective polity-building often involved not only a down-to-the-studs rebuilding of rural social formations, but also the enhancement of the social connective tissues linking them to the central offices of the state. Institution-building included new organizational capacities to enhance the administrative self-sufficiency at the local level while maintaining direct administrative links to the high offices of the state to assure local compliance with collective policies (a strategy of semiautonomy). The resulting rural organizations were not a reflection of the kind of primordial "natural" state of humans living in rural communes that is imagined in some social science literature, nor were states always predatory organizations that destroyed the institutional capital of the base. Rather, rural social formations reflect the goals of state-builders who, in cooperation with taxpayers, strived to build collectively organized political systems both at the scale of society and at the local level.

IO

Collective Action and the Shaping of Cities and Their Neighborhoods

WITH LANE F. FARGHER (CINVESTAV DEL IPN)

In traditional theories of premodern state formation, cities are understood to be sites where the supreme power of sovereignty is expressed in material form. This is no doubt correct in the case of the more autocratic regimes. But this approach would seem to have little value when we consider the relational power that characterizes collective action. We suggest that collective polity-building will have its own distinct material, social, and cultural consequences for cities and urbanism and that these consequences demand study as an adjunct to collective action theory. In this chapter our goal is to provide an expanded theoretical framework to address questions of variation and change in cities (as physical settlement sites) and ways of living in cities (urbanism) that takes collective action into consideration.

Our discussion of cities and urbanism has been influenced by the notion that "civic capital" enhances the potential for cooperative problem solving at the scale of the city (Orum 1998). Anthony Orum's approach emphasizes the importance of intracity social interaction, including "alliances among leading sectors" as well as institutionalized "bridges that run between the leading segments of the place and its many citizens" (8) (in the same paper Orum also points to the importance of "a strong vision," and a strong "commitment to the idea of a place"; this symbolic aspect of civic capital is discussed in this chapter and in chapter 11.

The strategy to focus on intracity social interaction proves to be a useful point of departure for the study of collective action in the context of premodern cities (or any cities). To organize for collective action will imply relatively high levels of

DOI: 10.5876/9781607325147.c010

165

interaction and communication among city dwellers. But, when these conditions are absent, city living, by its very nature, tends to produce the opposite results. This is apparent in many premodern cities, such as in the case of Tokugawa Edo, in our sample, where social cleavage was enforced by a combination of moats, walls, and gates that impeded movement and intermingling. The road systems of cities whose roads meander in an "organic," unplanned manner can render cities essentially ungovernable. We would also point to the fact that cities, especially in the premodern condition, were dangerous and unhealthy places to live with their exacerbated potentials for conflict, disease transmission, and fires. In these challenging circumstances we note a tendency for city dwellers to form tightly bounded and insular neighborhood-scale collective action units, such as the "walled ward" systems that inhibit cross-city interaction and information flow, and, thus, civic capital formation.

How is collective action staged in cities when there are physical constraints to movement and a segmented social geography? To better address this question, we collected city data (from our comparative sample) suited to the application of spatial analytical methods borrowed from geographers, to compare the physical properties of cities, especially from street plans. We also noted the structure and function of neighborhood-scale organizations. Were they highly socially bounded, and tending to isolate persons in their local setting, or were they more open and integrated into larger social networks and thus more suited to the integration of persons into the overall social architecture of city life?

We argue that the study of cities will be a valuable adjunct to the study of collective action broadly speaking. Yet, the study of cities and city life presents many practical difficulties. From our comparative study we have a detailed understanding of collective action in polity-building, but in many cases corresponding data on cities and urbanism are difficult to find. For one, we require information pertaining to the focal periods of our sample, but suitable data, especially accurate maps, often are not available; especially in the context of minimal collectivity, there was little interest in or need for maps or the administrative capacity to produce them. Even where we could find city maps or other suitable data sources, we faced a challenge in trying to tease out the effects of collective polity-building in complex urban environments. A city can be a confusing social and physical palimpsest reflecting not only the physical and social residues of prior, and possibly not highly collective, regimes, but also the outcomes of clashes between diverse interest groups with differing preferences in relation to collective action.

In what follows we briefly summarize the results of our search for data from cases that are among the better described from our larger sample. They are arranged in order from least to most collective, with the collective action total values (the sum of public goods, bureaucratization, and principal control, with a possible score of

63) indicated after the focal period. By arranging the cases in this way, we were able to use a largely inductive method in which we looked for patterns of variation in cities in relation to degree of collective action. Our conclusions are outlined following the presentation of descriptive materials.

DATA SUMMARIES

ACEH (INSULAR SOUTHEAST ASIA, 1850–1900 CE, 25)

By 1688 (just prior to the focal period) the main political center at Aceh had a population estimated at 48,700 and a density of forty per hectare. The city was spread out, and consisted of a citadel or walled area containing the main palace and quarters that housed foreign merchants (for a total of .2 square kilometer), but the city's total area, counting the outer residential areas, is roughly 12 square kilometers. This is a typical pattern for Southeast Asian cities in which a large unplanned low-density settlement area surrounds a planned and often walled central zone. Neighborhoods outside the central zone consisted of clusters of client houses surrounding the compounds of wealthy patron families ("person-centered wards" in our terminology); these clusters were widely spaced and separated by areas of meadows and woods within the city limits.

NUPE (WEST AFRICA, 1837–97 CE, 25.5)

Bida, the Nupe capital, extended over an irregularly shaped area of thirty square kilometers and had a population estimated at 60,000. Settlement was highly dispersed and included some unpopulated areas between more densely settled zones. The city's settlement pattern was built around three main royal palaces (each a political faction). Each palace was surrounded by a loosely defined cluster of buildings including a market, a mosque, and the residences of associated crafts workers and other client families who had settled there. Most major and minor roads connected external routes and city gates to the palace complexes; otherwise, few major roads provided for intracity travel.

ENGLAND (1327–1361 CE, 28)

During the focal period, this polity had one of the lowest scores for collective action, in or outside cities. However, there was a vibrant urban culture and highly compact cities, including London, the largest city, with a focal-period population estimated at 45,000 in an area roughly 3.2 square kilometers. Most of the city's population lived inside the limits defined by the old Roman Period defensive walls. But the original Roman orthogonal (gridded) street plan (built during a period relatively high in collectivity) had been largely obliterated and replaced by an unplanned maze of streets reflecting a combination of Roman and Saxon construction, and consisting of "a warren of cross-streets, lanes, passages, and courtyards" (Baker 1970: 18).

JAPAN (TOKUGAWA PERIOD, BUT THE MOST DETAILED DATA PERTAIN TO EIGHTEENTH CENTURY CE, 31.5)

During the focal period the newly founded capital, Edo (now Tokyo), grew to a population estimated at over 1 million, and other castle headquarters of the Japanese secondary governing elite (*daimyo*) also grew in population, spurred in part by the growth of the urban merchant class, the *chonin*. The Tokugawa system scored below the mean value of our sample for collective action, and it provided few public goods in the specific case of the capital, Edo, and our evidence indicates there was a pattern of state neglect also in other cities. Canal construction accompanied urban growth, but canals are not easily interpreted as a public good since they appear to have served principally as moats to maintain separation between social classes. Interestingly, the state did sponsor the construction of aqueducts and underground pipelines that brought water into Edo. However, they could barely be interpreted as public goods because the construction did not equally benefit all social sectors. A system constructed in 1652 brought water first to the *shogun*'s castle and then distributed overflow throughout the city. Moreover, only daimyo and the shogun were allowed to draw water directly from buried pipelines. Commoners could only draw excess water, not consumed by the elite, through official wells.

Road building within the city was limited, and roads were paved only in high-status residential areas. Firefighting, policing, trash, and night soil removal were managed at the local level, either through private contracts or neighborhood organizations (*cho*), or not at all. The state appears to have been especially deficient in firefighting capacity. For example, to assert sumptuary control the state banned the use of roof tiles for commoners, making commoner houses more likely to burn—a rule that was not changed until 1720 CE. William Coaldrake (1981: 252) reports that after a major conflagration in 1657 fire brigades were created, but he is unclear as to how they were staffed or administered. Henry Smith (1978: 50) suggests that the unwillingness of state officials to act to prevent urban fires resulted from the fact that most fires threatened only commoner areas of the city.

Tokugawa architects conceived a city plan for Edo consisting of a hub-and-spoke arrangement with six main roads entering the city to converge at the central

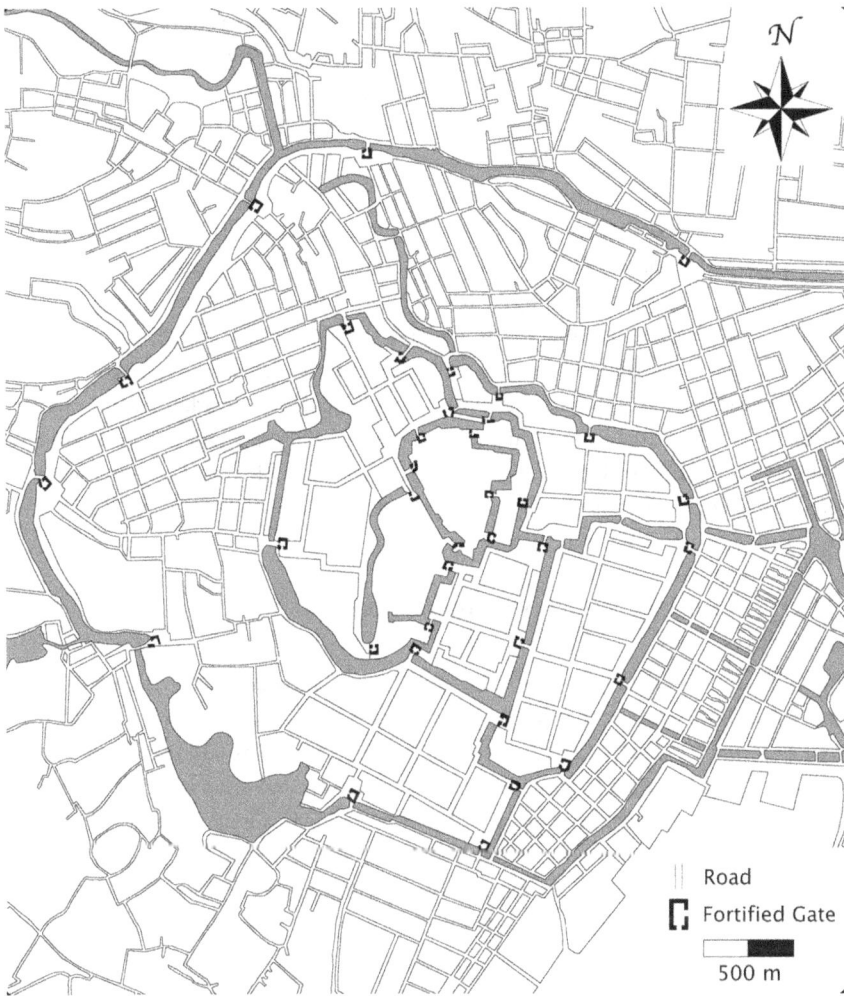

FIGURE 10.1. Central Tokugawa Edo (modified from Coaldrake 1981: fig. 2, with permission). Darkened areas are moats.

palace-fortress complex. Within the hub-and-spoke arrangement, a spiral design resulted in a series of increasingly buffered islandlike zones separated by canals (Figure 10.1). The centralmost and most isolated island was home to the shogun's castle. Daimyo were placed to the northeast and southwest of the shogun's castle, while lower-level samurai formed a belt around the higher-ranking daimyo. Finally, commoners (especially merchants) were located on the southwest edge of the city.

Daimyo were responsible for justice, taxation, administration, and maintaining local military forces within the scope of their respective neighborhood-scale zones, leaving only a minor role for Tokugawa officials in urban governance. The state appears to have taken a very limited role in the social construction of neighborhoods. Commoner districts of the city were divided into "village-sized units responsible for government at the local level" (Hanley 1987: 22). These neighborhoods were governed through the *cho* system, in which landlords and their agents were responsible for local-scale policing and other public services. Neighborhoods were highly bounded both physically and socially (in our terminology, a ward system, implying a neighborhood in which there is special concern with local self-defense, especially from urban crime, requiring walls and guards). No major avenues or urban highways connected different parts of the city; instead, many city streets consisted of blind alleys and dead ends, making intracity movement haphazard and difficult (according to Coaldrake [1981: esp. 246], the historical imprint of these features brings traffic congestion to Tokyo today).

OTTOMAN EMPIRE (EASTERN MEDITERRANEAN AND ANATOLIA, 1300–1600 CE, 34.5)

Ottoman urban administration featured power struggles between local groups and central officials, so that judges, prefect managers, and market supervisors, as well as merchants, guilds, and Janissaries (paramilitary corps), did not always act in concert. Often, administration and public goods were provided by relatively autonomous neighborhoods. State-provided public goods in Ottoman cities were few; for example, in Cairo pious foundations, not the state, funded most public goods (e.g., water supply), and, in the capital, Istanbul, most streets were not paved. State revenues and land were used to construct and endow religious complexes and to construct covered markets. But they appear to have been restricted to the major cities of Istanbul, Aleppo, Bursa, and Damascus. Aptullah Kuran (1996: 130) indicates that most state-funded construction after the ruler Mehmed II focused on royal palaces rather than public works.

According to Suraiya Faroqhi (2000: 147), "Ottoman towns were divided into quarters" (we would say wards, given the concern with physical and social boundedness) that were responsible for policing and fire control. Wards had their own judges, and in Cairo and elsewhere it was commercial guilds that administered tax collection and public goods in some city areas. Each residential quarter in an Ottoman city was closed and appears to have formed a small-scale collective action unit that in some cases collected taxes levied on their inhabitants and were governed by a locally selected head (*shaykh*). These officials had to be confirmed by the Ottoman judge, which provided the state with some, but little, oversight. Sometimes outsiders were admitted into a quarter, but usually quarter inhabitants worked to control the movement of outsiders moving into or through their neighborhoods by building social and sometimes physical boundaries.

Ottoman cities were poorly spatially integrated, and few avenues or urban highways existed because neighborhoods aimed to limit the movement of strangers through their areas. Although Ottoman Istanbul was built over an ancient Roman gridded street plan, during the focal period this road system was built over, resulting in a largely unplanned organic configuration in which street "orientations and widths frequently changed and culs-de-sac were common" (Kubat 1999: 34) (Figure 10.2). The street arrangement of Bursa and Cairo during the Ottoman Period also consisted of mazelike arrangements with many twists and turns, and only a few major avenues were routed across the entire city. Istanbul featured only three main roads that passed along the east-west length of the city. These connected the main city gates to the palace zone; only one major road cut across the grain of these major feeder roads.

ASANTE (WEST AFRICA, 1800–1873 CE, 44.5)

Kumase, a city of about 20,000 during the focal period, was extensively transformed after it had been chosen to serve as the polity's capital in about 1700 CE. The road system of the newly founded center was complex, with main avenues serving to separately connect the palace, on the north edge of town, and the market, on the south edge, to external routes and to suburban residential zones. At the same time a complex network of secondary roads, organized in part as a grid system, provided multiple routes between palace and market and other localities. The capital was established to serve primarily as a center of government, and this is perhaps apparent in the fact that the residences and working quarters of high officials of the polity apparently also served local in-city governing roles in the city's seventy-seven administrative areas. That high officials of the state served in local-scale governance suggests a system akin to administrative districts rather than self-governing neighborhoods or wards (although they are referred to as wards in the local ethnographic terminology).

MUGHAL (1556–1658 CE, 45)

From descriptions of Shahjahanabad (a new Mughal foundation in ca. 1647 CE) (Figure 10.3), we infer an ideal plan for Mughal city organization in which semiautonomous local neighborhoods were incorporated into a citywide administration.

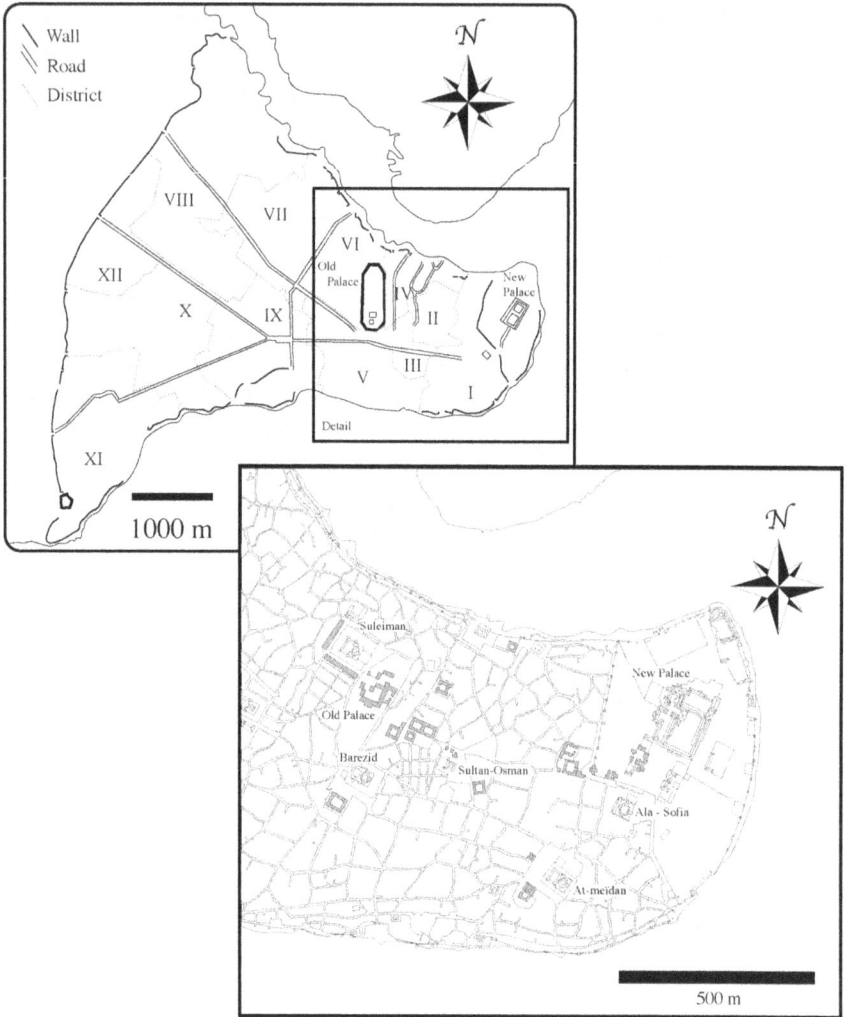

FIGURE 10.2. Istanbul of the focal period (upper image modified from Inalçik 1973: map of Istanbul, with permission; lower image if from the "Map of Constantinople" in Melling, Lacrette, and Barbié 1819).

Cities were governed by appointed officials, including a chief judge (*qazi al-quzat*), a general superintendent (*harasat*), head of the palace-fortress (*qiladari*), a police chief (*faujdari*), and a city magistrate (*kotwali*), along with lower-ranking officials including judges, constables, administrators, and tax collectors. At the same time, self-organized neighborhood organizations played a role in urban governance and

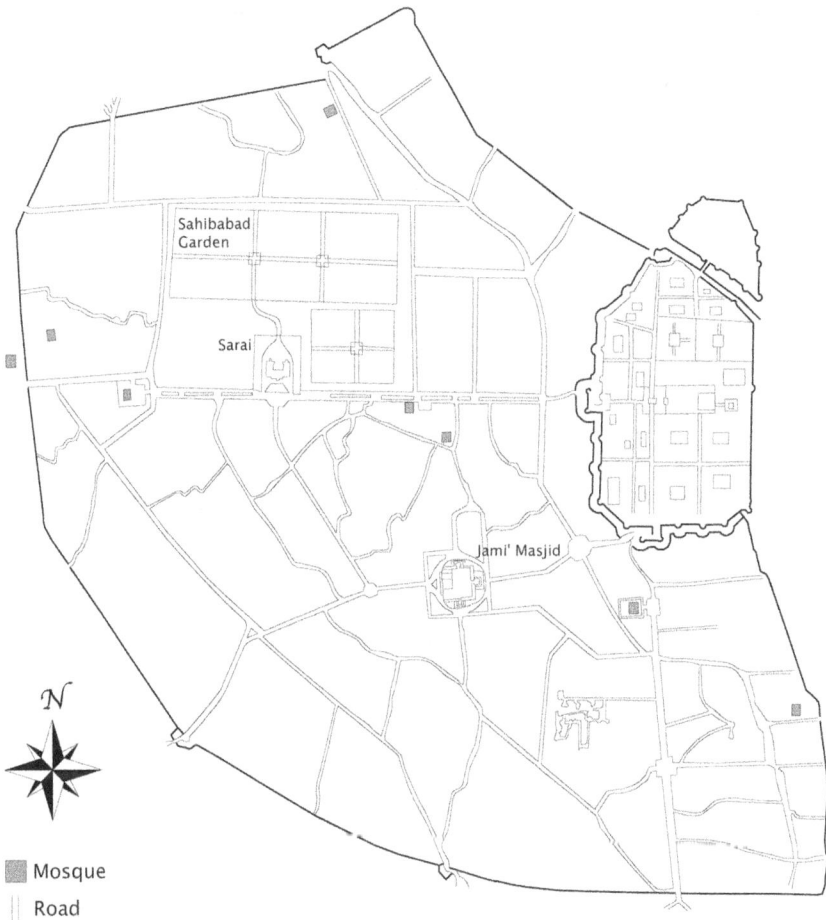

FIGURE 10.3. Mughal Shahjahanabad (modified from the Great Britain India Office 1878, *A Catalogue of Manuscript and Printed Reports, Field Books, Memoirs, Maps, etc., of the Indian Surveys, Deposited in the Map Room of the India Office*, 241).

in some cases wealthy noble families funded the construction and maintenance of baths, mosques, wells, caravansaries, bridges, canals, and gardens. The members of wards (*mahallahs*), surrounded by high walls, shared a caste, craft, or particular social status, or attended the same mosque, and were headed by chiefs (*chaudhuris*) of governing councils (*panchayats*). The latter negotiated taxes with city authorities, arranged security against both internal and external disturbances, and consulted with other chaudhuris on matters of common interest.

This description so far sounds much like cities one might find in a weakly collective polity. Yet, the Mughal state did provide public goods to urban populations, such as canals to bring water for, "drinking, washing, and irrigating to houses, gardens, shops, pools, and baths" (Blake 1991: 64). Typically, in new city foundations, the state would first construct a central sewage drain, then build paved avenues, but leave minor roads unpaved. The Paradise Canal, the longest Mughal canal, brought water to Shahjahanabad, including to a public garden measuring 202,000 square meters, and ending at the palace-fortress on the east side of the city (unlike Tokugawa Edo, in this design the ruler Shahjahan's palace got water only after everyone along its path had taken their fill). And, we point to interesting aspects of change in urban social organization during the Mughal focal period. We know that Mughal administration departed from traditional Hindu practices, and as a result the caste system was weakened, for example, by selecting even high officials from across social sectors and religions. K. N. Chaudhuri (1978: 84) reports that in rapidly growing Mughal cities people purchased house lots where they could get them, and as a result Muslims began to mix with Hindus and rich with poor, suggesting a decline in the importance of mahallah and its associated forms of social segregation.

The ideal of Mughal city planning, judging from the layout chosen for Shahjahanabad, is a highly orthogonal (i.e., gridded) system. This plan provided for numerous avenues that crosscut major sections of the city, providing direct links among quarters and links between quarters and public buildings that would appear to effectively integrate the residential quarters into the city's overall administrative structure. This spatial plan, which does not center the road system on just one central zone or building complex (as the hub-and-spoke plans do), linked a series of city mosques into a network, each acting as a central place where interaction between governing officials and city residents occurred at various spatial scales. The central mosque (Jami' Masjid) acted as the most important gathering place, where people could voice complaints about religious, political, or social policies and where they could come to hear news and information about the state from officials. In addition to this central mosque, there were eight second-level mosques that filled the same role for major city sectors. Finally, a third tier in the system was composed of the ninety-one neighborhood mosques.

AZTEC (1428–1521 CE, 45)

The imperial capital, Tenochtitlan, was a new foundation dating to ca. 1325 CE. Its location in a marginal salty swamp in Lake Mexico–Texcoco (now completely engulfed by modern Mexico City) required that causeways be built for transportation and to control the flow of saline water, as well as aqueducts to bring freshwater into the city from the adjacent mainland. Aztec authorities lavished resources on the new capital, which grew rapidly, eventually reaching a population of some 150,000 to 200,000 by 1519 CE (a total that includes the adjacent commercial city of Tlatelolco, which had been annexed). Hernán Cortés (cited in de Zorita 1994: 157) described a capital "built on the salt lake, and the distance from the mainland to the city is 2 leagues, whatever the direction from which you approach it. It is entered by four artificial causeways, each two lance-lengths in width . . . Its streets (I speak of the principal ones) are very broad and straight; some of these, and all the lesser streets, are half dry land and half water, on which the people go about in canoes. All the streets have openings at regular intervals, to let the water flow from one to the other, and at all these openings, some of which are very broad there are bridges, very large, stone, and well constructed, so that, over many, ten horsemen can ride abreast."

The central civic-ceremonial precinct of Tenochtitlan, a vast walled concourse housing the main temples and other religious institutions of the polity, was located at the intersection of four of the main roads that define the city's quadripartite orthogonal plan (actually, there were two such precincts, the major one in Tenochtitlan, the other serving the annexed Tlatelolco), though additional major roads provided transport links within and between multiple in-city destinations. Major imperial palaces and associated administrative offices, and markets, were arrayed around the civic-ceremonial precinct. Similar complexes of palaces, temples, and markets were centered in each of the four principal quarters created by the east-west and north-south avenues, and these great quarters were a second hierarchical level in city governance. Below this level of organization were neighborhoodlike units, *calpolli* (pl. *calpultin*) (or *tlaxillacallis*) (*barrios* in the local anthropological lexicon). These often were occupational groups with some degree of local functional integrity, for example, each had its own civic-ceremonial complex that included a temple devoted to a patron deity, a market, a school, and the residences and offices of local government under the authority of a headman and a council of elders. However, calpultin were really administrative districts of the state in the sense that their headmen were linked to higher levels of city and imperial government. These headmen assembled each day at the ruler's palace, "where they awaited orders from the king or other high officials and transmitted them to lower officials who supervised their execution" (Calnek 1978: 321). Calpultin also served as local units of tax collection for the central taxation bureau of the state.

Roman High Empire (69–192 CE, 48)

Over its long Republican history (509 to 31 BCE), prior to the focal period, Rome's intracity road system grew in a largely unplanned organic manner, leaving it an "inextricably tangled net" (Carcopino 1968: 45) that resulted in "urban traffic chaos" (van Tilburg 2007: 120). The Republican city even lacked a grand via, a wide and straight showcase street framed by porticos, in the manner of other great Hellenistic cities, until quite late, when, finally, the emperors Nero and Caracalla were able to construct several. Given the well-established physical structure of the old city and its entrenched land-use interests, this inefficient built environment was almost impossible to restructure even by the powerful reform-oriented rulers Julius Caesar and Augustus. Changes brought about under the Augustan program were extensive, but mostly emphasized new construction in the periurban Campus Martius zone outside the main residential areas. By the focal period, major roads did serve to crosscut wards and regions to integrate movement through the city. However, excepting the few via, roads were not named, even informally, which would have further inhibited the legibility of much of the city's road network to travelers. As a result, by comparison with other cities we studied, including new Roman city foundations that had wider streets and grid plans to improve traffic flow, Rome itself largely retained the confusing network of narrow and winding secondary roads from the Republican Period. Only the few major roads were more capacious; Cornelius van Tilburg (2007: 31) estimates there were only four intraurban roads with the status of *viae*, that is, with a minimum width of at least 2.4 meters. In addition, while major highways were paved with stone, secondary streets and alleys often were not paved.

Other than the comparatively limited investment in transportation infrastructure, during the focal period Rome was comparatively rich in urban public goods. Following the Augustan reforms, the state provided for police and fire protection, including a standing police force and courts; by the focal period an estimated 10,000 men provided public security and fire service in the capital. The state invested in public construction meant for use by large numbers of city residents; for example, the Coliseum could hold 50,000 and the Circus Maximus 250,000. There was also investment in large and numerous public baths meant for broad public use, and food security was increased through large-scale redistributions, perhaps feeding as many as 500,000 people on one occasion. At the beginning of the Imperial era, Augustus, in the reforms of 7 CE, implemented a new administrative structure for Rome's city government that remodeled a failed Republican Period system. Republic Period offices concerned with the general welfare of the city were replaced by specialized departments headed by governing boards and staffed by trained professionals, and members of the governing boards were selected by the emperor and were closely monitored. Augustus established the *curatores aquarum* (originally headed by Agrippa) to manage potable water and sewers, *curatores viarum* to manage highways throughout the empire, offices to care for public buildings, *curatelae alvei Tiberis* to care for the Tiber, and an office of municipal police chief (*praefectus urbi*).

The *vici* (neighborhoods) of Rome had a long history during the Republican Period, possibly even dating to the period of the city's earliest origins. Originally, vici appear to have grown in an organic fashion and were highly self-governing, though it is not clear exactly to what degree they also served as administrative districts for the central authorities prior to the Augustan reforms. The latter's design for urban governance maintained some aspects of vici but incorporated them into fourteen administrative regions and a larger number of subdistricts. Older extant vici were incorporated into this new structure with little modification, and new ones were created resulting in approximately 200 local-scale administrative units that in the language of Roman historians are known as wards. Magistrates overseeing the new administrative districts were selected by lot and were responsible for supervising administration and overseeing local vici heads.

MING DYNASTY (ESPECIALLY LATE FOURTEENTH CENTURY AND FIFTEENTH CENTURY CE, 51)

The focal period of the Ming Dynasty was a period of rapid urban growth, a process that challenged Ming policies that had idealized an agrarian-based society and economy. As a consequence, during the dynasty the idea of the city was "re-invented, contested, and re-conceived" (Fei 2009: 1), in part owing to the growth of what Si-Yen Fei (15) calls an "urban public" prone to protests, strikes, and opposition to controversial officials. Ming reforms enhanced the delivery of public goods, including, in Beijing, the material support of bureaus including a governor's office (*fu-yin*) charged to "look after the welfare of the residents, temporal as well as spiritual ... [and the] ... five wardens' offices ... [who provided] ... police patrols, public works and fire watchers" (Chan 1962: 142). To monitor the population's health, to maintain public order, and to identify persons who may be avoiding their *corvée* (labor) obligations, by pretending to be visitors to the city, administrative officials were charged with keeping track of the comings and goings of all visitors to the city, including their illnesses or deaths, and the state provided public cemeteries for deceased indigents. City administrators did this by sending out field officers charged with collecting and analyzing monthly reports from all owners of inns, and other health data were collected monthly from all physicians and fortune-tellers. Houses for the poor were established with mandated service levels that required, for example, that officials in charge of them provide a set number of meals per day (Chan 1962: 142–45).

At the capital, Beijing, which was greatly expanded during the early Ming Period, the state constructed walls, temples, streets, and waterways (Figure 10.4). But similar projects were found in other cities. In the southern areas of the polity, the state

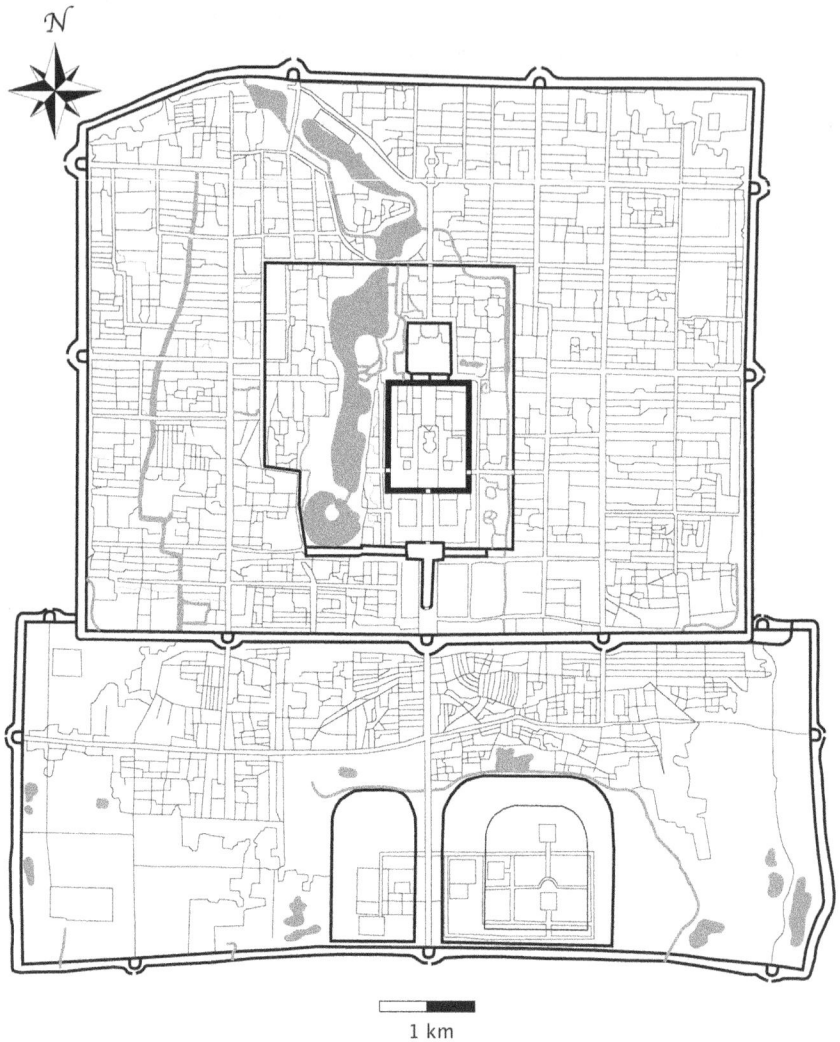

FIGURE 10.4. Ming Beijing (modified from Shatzman Steinhardt 1986: fig. 4, with permission).

contributed to canal construction and the maintenance and repair of channels, ponds, and bridges. City officials were also charged with maintaining the "streets and walls and canals, fighting fires, and caring for the poor" (Naquin 2000: 178). It is interesting to note that, initially, urban public service duties were based on a corvée tax. But this system proved to be inefficient and prone to corrupt practices, and even conflicted with workers' schedules, causing a loss of income or even jobs. Eventually the labor tax was replaced with salaried officials, funded by a monetary tax, in response to demands by city commoners.

Chinese civilization has a long history of highly planned cities featuring gridded street arrangements since at least the first millennium BCE. By the T'ang Dynasty (618–907 CE) cities featured crosscutting avenues that segmented the urban design into walled neighborhood subdivisions (wards). But this highly segmented pattern was largely abandoned during the Ming Period. Outside Beijing, wards were still walled at the beginning of the period, but change is evident; for example, officials in Nanjing voluntarily pulled down the walls, though in other cities such as Hangzhou and Suzhou it took protests and riots to get officials to do the same. This urban social change was due, in part, to taxpayer demands made by the urban poor and middle class for urban reform. As a result, the system of largely self-governing neighborhoods (*baojia*) gave way to more direct state control that made neighborhoods obsolete as social institutions and converted them to administrative zones. It is interesting to note that, evidently, urban dwellers trusted the state's institutional capacity to provide public services over that of the local neighborhood-scale managers. Also, the decline of walled wards reflected a growing Ming economy and its more complex division of labor in production and service industries. Many urbanites were weavers and factory workers who worked long hours extending into the night in parts of the city removed from their residences. When their shifts ended, the gates that closed wards had already been lowered making it difficult or impossible to return home at the end of the workday.

Venice (1290–1600 CE, 51.5)

By the focal period the Venetian polity had become highly collective, with public goods levels comparable to the most collective of the polities in our sample, including improved transportation infrastructure, drainage, flood control, and attention to water quality. Public safety was provided for, and administrative policies and practices were implemented to improve food security. John Norwich (1982: 91) tells us there was even "a rudimentary form of street lighting—making Venice the first city in Europe, with the possible exception of Constantinople, to be regularly and compulsorily lit at night." Further, "Public health was . . . early accepted as a state responsibility, and to the Venetian Republic must go the honour of having founded the first national health service in Europe, if not in the world" (Norwich 1982: 274; cf. Chambers and Pullan 2001: 113).

Prior to the focal period, Venice consisted of roughly seventy local settlement clusters (parishes). Each, according to Dennis Romano (1987: 17), was a "fortified island enclave," a person-centered ward ruled over by a powerful patrician family. In spite of the power of entrenched private interests that often were at odds with the polity (e.g., when private land had to be converted to public land for street widening), as the collective polity was developed parish localism became transformed into a notion of a broadly integrative polity and city that could serve the common interests of the people (*comune Venetiarum*). This was accomplished by converting parishes into administrative districts (*contrata*), each governed by a state official (*capi di contrate*) who managed public goods, evaluated taxpayer compliance, and collected and disseminated information. The seventy contrata were embedded in an administrative system of six districts that could serve as links between the contrata and the central state's governing councils and its chief administrative officer, the doge. District officials also provided for public order. Lastly, the districts were divided into two major administrative segments with the Grand Canal forming the division between them. Beginning especially during the twelfth century, the Piazza San Marco was expanded and architecturally elaborated on to serve as a concourse for the citywide public gatherings and official processions that are discussed in the following chapter.

ATHENS (403–322 BCE, 52)

The Athenian polity was one of the most collective in our sample, owing in part to its citizen participation in governing councils, including the central body (the Council of Five Hundred), the People's Courts, the People's Assembly, and the Boards of Legislators. The high collective action score also reflects the presence of institutions that allowed for the monitoring and control of administrative officials, the magistrates. However, by contrast with other of the more collective states in our sample, Athens received only a moderately high score on public goods. For example, there was frequent flooding and thievery was common. A board of magistrates was charged with road maintenance, yet historical descriptions suggest that most city streets were dirt paths excepting the few that were paved with broken stone.

In chapter 8 we alluded to the construction of a new highly democratic and collective governing system that was accompanied by a changed geography of constituent social groups, the *demes*, *trittyes* (districts), and "tribes." Five of these demes were located in Athens proper: Kerameikos deme and Kolonos Agroraios deme were located in the northern part of the city, Kydathenaion deme (home to the Acropolis) occupied the eastern quarter, Melite deme occupied the western quarter, and Kollytos deme was located to the south. Apart from demes, the social function of neighborhood units in the city is not well understood. Some were based in part on occupational specializations such as Melite and Kollytos that were home to handicraft specialists. Demes, governed by local citizen assemblies, were well integrated into the polity's overall political structure, sending representatives to the Council of Five Hundred and to the Boards of Legislators.

Historical descriptions and maps of early democratic Athens indicate that the city was strongly spatially integrated by a network of major roads providing alternate routes between intracity destinations. The Athenian city plan had been altered to reflect the rise of the democratic political regime beginning during the sixth century BCE, especially in and around the Agora (market and civic center), which was substantially enlarged and transformed to serve as the nerve center and repository of civic symbols for the collective system. Homer Thompson and R. E. Wycherley describe a highly complex urban road system that radiated outward from the Agora and connected large sections of the city to it (Thompson and Wycherley 1972: 192). The most important of these avenues was the Panathenaic Way, which crossed the city from the northwest, passed through the Agora, and continued into the southern part of the city; two major roads branched off of this route to service the northern parts of the city. South of the Agora, the central road branched into two sections, one servicing the southeastern quarter and the other the southwestern quarter of the city, and roads connected the east and west section of the city with the Agora. In addition, there were a number of lateral streets that connected sections of the city directly without passing through the main civic-ceremonial areas; otherwise intracity movement was by way of winding alleys, but these were evidently never far from a major avenue.

CONCLUSIONS, PART I: MOVEMENT EFFICIENCY AND MOBILITY IN THE BUILT ENVIRONMENT OF THE COLLECTIVE CITY

A more collective state must enlarge its capacity to manage the movement of people, information and materials, for example, as the Ming founder did by adding to the governmental administration a courier service, a postal service, and a transport service, and, as in Rome, where Julius Caesar established an official transportation organization, the *vehiculato* or *cursus publicus*. In a city, collectivity will increase what Richard Meier (1962: 79–80) terms a city's "communications load," which we interpret to refer to the amount of communication and transportation required to meet a state's urban public goods and other administrative obligations, and to make possible free movement and intermingling of the population. We suggest that to address a growing need for communication capacity and movement will require modification of the built environment, but urban "renewal" in this sense is particularly costly and subject to opposition, especially from private land owners.

How do polity-builders respond to growing communications load while managing the costs of intracity governance? We found that one possible solution is to discourage settlement dispersion and thus to minimize intracity travel times. We also noted that road planning aimed to increase a city's degree of spatial integration, to provide more and more efficient movement choices between multiple in-city locations. "Organic" (unplanned) growth often is not consistent with high-efficiency movement, nor are road plans that direct the major traffic flows to only a few important locations, usually to the palace/temple city center, thus limiting citywide mobility (a "radial" or "hub-and-spoke" arrangement). In more collective contexts, we found evidence of variations around what are called orthogonal (gridded) road plans, a spatial logic that could realize efficiencies in intracity movement. By orthogonality we refer to spatially integrated street plans that provide the urban traveler alternate routes between locations, and a high density of intersections that would, in the sense of Kevin Lynch (1960), increase a city's "legibility."

COMPACT OR DISPERSED SETTLEMENTS?

Little information on the population densities of cities is available, but what we could find points to the possibility that collective action is consistent with relatively more compact, high-density cities. All of the more collective polities described above featured large, compact cities that had moderately high to high population densities: the estimate for Aztec Tenochtitlan is 130/ha, Rome's is 190/ha (at least), Beijing's is 174/ha, and Venice's is about 100/ha, with Athens weighing in at 170/ha. Of course, high-density compactness could be due to other factors, for example, London's estimated 140/ha was due to the spatial limits represented by Roman defensive walls and the fact that privately owned land outside the city could not be colonized.

Polities scoring lower on collective action display some tendency to exhibit two settlement patterns: one with a near absence of any urban settlements, for example Java and Bali; another with settlements that are referred to as cities but that are highly dispersed, unlike what we usually imagine to be a city. Two of the societies for which maps are available feature such territorially large, sprawling, low-density cities, and are among the least collective polities in our sample: Aceh, with the capital at an estimated forty persons per hectare, and Nupe, with the main center, Bida, at twenty persons per hectare. In Nupe and Aceh, urban settlement density was low in part because open areas lacking settlement were interspersed between residential zones within city limits; Anthony Reid (1980: 241) points out that European visitors to Aceh sometimes found it difficult to distinguish between city and countryside since so many meadows and woods were found within the city limits between clusters of houses surrounding the palaces of noble or wealthy families. The same description would apply to pre-focal-period Venice, with its dispersed parishes, and the capital of focal-period Burma was similarly dispersed.

LEGIBILITY OF SPATIAL STRUCTURE

When collective action is a basis for institution-building it has profound material, social, and cultural consequences for city form and urban lifeways. Among these consequences, our data point to those pertaining to movement, mobility, and the improvement of use efficiency of the cityscape. These processes, we suggest, reflect the strategies of state-builders to accommodate the high levels of social interaction and information flows mandated by collective action. The plans of Bida (Nupe), Istanbul, and, possibly, Vijayanagara and Burma (the latter two judging from descriptions rather than detailed maps), all scoring relatively low on collective action measures, display relatively simple variations of the radial or hub-and-spoke road pattern. In these plans, the major purpose of main roads was to connect the central government / temple complex to destinations external to the city such as secondary centers, resource areas, or distant palaces of the secondary governing elite. In these arrangements, the only direct in-city trips along major roads would be either to or from the city center, with few roads built across the grain of the spokes that would provide for shorter trips between noncenter destinations. In the cases we studied (and in many others known from comparative urban planning research), areas poorly serviced by main roads often were mazes of winding and dead-end streets that inhibited the free flow of citywide traffic. Other factors compounded the movement inefficiencies of radial plans. As we mentioned, movement along Edo's roads, even major ones, was interrupted by moats and fortified gates built to impede the movement and maintain appropriate separation of groups of different levels of social standing in this highly socially stratified society.

Orthogonality, whether "perfect" (formally gridded) or semiorthogonal, is a spatial logic that, at least theoretically, could realize greater efficiencies in intracity movement by comparison with radial plans. While the latter only efficiently moves traffic to and from the main palace / temple complex, orthogonal plans give greater leeway for movement between multiple intracity destinations, and should therefore be consistent with the goals of collective polity-builders by increasing the legibility of urban space and enhancing movement efficiency. However, it bears mentioning that gridded plans are not always reflections of a concern with movement efficiency. For example, standardized grid plans often were used as a system of design standardization for new city foundations in rapidly expanding empires such as in the Spanish imperial cities of the New World. In this and similar cases, it is not always clear to what extent grid plans aimed at movement efficiency.

There are also elements of symbolic meaning attached to highly planned and orderly urban form, namely, the goal to signify a distinction between a rationally ordered domain of "culture" versus a disorderly and defiled domain of "nature." Indeed, as Sybil Moholy-Nagy (1968: 83) argues, "all planned cities are interpreters of social myths." The grid plan as a largely symbolic system may be evident in very early Chinese cities that were built as cosmomagical symbols, but these were not always consistent with high levels of movement efficiency. During the mid-T'ang Dynasty (ca. 800 CE), for example, cities were built in the form of what we call a pseudo grid-plan, because physical (walls and gates) and social barriers to movement were common (this was also true in some grid-planned Japanese cities of the focal period).

Among the societies in our sample, a symbolic basis for grid plans is found in Aceh, Burma, and Pudukkottai, where city centers, though not whole cities, displayed orthogonal (quadripartite) plans; and these, too, had no necessary relation to movement efficiency, instead symbolizing Hindu or Buddhist cosmic schemes. Orthogonality may represent the outcome of yet another spatial logic, judging from the arguments of city planners such as Hippodamus in Classical antiquity. Orthogonal plans were not present until the development of the democratic *poleis*, such as Athens, during the 5th century BCE. Yet, at the time, city planners seemed little concerned with spatial efficiencies. Instead, they argued that orthogonal plans were compatible with their notion of a democratic society in that a grid plan mandates equal-sized house lots and thus promotes the egalitarianism thought to be a central requirement of democracy.

Whatever the purposes are for a grid plan, assuming that movement is unimpeded, a grid has the potential to increase levels of spatial integration that will facilitate intracity mobility. In the less collective polities typically there will be a small number of "integrative points" where major roads intersect, usually at the palace/temple center. In the more collective cases, we noted multiple integrative points such as the intersections of major roads, and/or canals, or where roads converge on a gate, public space, or architectural feature. This dispersed pattern of connected integrative points generates greater in-city movement, that is, greater spatial integration where there are alternate routes connecting diverse locations.

To assess the degree of spatial integration, cultural geographers use a method in which they convert a map of major city roads to a graph showing only the integrative points ("nodes") and the roads ("edges") that connect them. From this kind of graphic representation we can calculate a useful (and simple) measure of the degree to which urban traveler will have alternate routes between multiple points. This is the Beta measure, which is simply the number of edges divided by the number of nodes (integration points). Larger values of Beta, that is, more edges per node, imply more spatial integration and, hence, more movement choices.

The results of the spatial analysis of thirteen cities in our sample strongly point to collective action as a powerful force shaping city road plans (see the details in Appendix B, Table B.5 and section 4). First, the frequency of integration points is strongly influenced by collective action using public goods as a proxy measure. However, it is also possible that the number of integration points is a function of city population size rather than collective action. Yet, when we accounted for city size, the correlation of integration points and collective action remains strong, but there is no statistical correlation between city size and number of integration points. Similarly, Beta, the measure of spatial integration, also shows a positive correlation with public goods, even when controlling for city population size. We conclude that no matter what the size of a city, whether an old city hosting a newly collective polity (where new roads and integration points were added to increase connectivity), or a new city foundation, the staging of collective action in cities brings in its wake relatively more spatially integrated and intelligible road systems.

A city's system of roads is also a more efficient activity system—on a citywide basis—when city travelers feel psychologically at ease as they move through the space. From this perspective, the urban spatial analyst Bill Hillier (1996: chap. 4; 1989) points especially to the importance of a matrix of well-connected integration points, especially if the connections are linear so as to provide for line-of-sight visibility between points (what he calls "isovist points"). Again, collective action is strongly and positively statistically correlated with this aspect of spatial integration and visual intelligibility (see Appendix B, Table B.5 and section 5). The city road systems in the more collective polities such as Aztec Tenochtitlan, Asante Kumase, Mughal (at least the new foundations), Rome (we studied Rome's road system for this analysis but this would be even more marked in the cases of new Roman cities, which were built using a gridded plan), Athens, and Ming exhibit perfect orthogonal or semiorthogonal plans and had relatively higher values of Beta and higher proportions of isovist integration points.

CONCLUSIONS, PART II: PUBLIC VERSUS PRIVATE CONSUMPTION OF URBAN SPACE

"The street began to exist in its own right, not as before a
devious passage grudgingly left over between a more or less
disordered heap of buildings." (Lewis Mumford 1961: 192)

We suggest that in the more collective polities proportionately more of a city's space will be devoted to what Manuel Castells (1978: 15–21, *passim*) refers to as "collective consumption" at the expense of "private consumption" (residences, commercial

spaces, and the like). Collective consumption could include spaces set aside for public goods such as public gardens and water fountains and for the kinds of capacious
and orderly streets Mumford (1961) alludes to above. A capacious transportation
infrastructure makes it possible to accommodate the higher levels of communication inherent in the functional properties of a more collective polity, and the collective consumption of space may also be consistent with the egalitarian goals of a collective polity by encouraging the intermingling of different sectors of a population.
A good example is eighteenth-century Vienna, where Joseph II opened up parks for
public use to encourage intermingling of commoners and aristocrats. Collective
consumption might also include spaces suitable for public appearances of principals and other governing officials designed to, as we put it, "make it possible for a
broad public to assess the decision-making process and the degree of commitment
of principals to the collective enterprise" (Blanton and Fargher 2008: 204). And,
given that in the more collective polities taxpayers are accorded a greater measure
of voice, public spaces may serve as sites for public gatherings. An example is Italy,
where popular movements came to be called *movimenti di piazza*.

   Cities are challenging environments for collective state-building, especially where
there is intense competition for space and long-established patterns of land use. An
entrenched land-owning elite, in particular, often will compete with state-builders
to shape the urban landscape. This was evident in the case of focal-period Venice,
where the growth of the *commune Venetiarum* gradually was able to restructure the
remains of the old patrician-based parish system. But expansion of public consumption was often at the expense of private consumption and this brought opposition,
even lawsuits, from private landowners. Given the potential difficulties involved in
transforming cityscapes, in some cases principals found it beneficial to build a new
city or cities, or to radically transform existing ones. This happened in the cases
of Asante Kumase, Aztec Tenochtitlan, and Beijing described above. The founding of Mughal Shahjahanabad is a useful example where, in spite of the immense
costs, relocation of the capital and construction of a new city were seen as strategies to avoid traffic congestion and other problems in the old capital. According to
Stephen Blake (1991: 27) the Mughal capital at Agra was abandoned in part because
"mansions, shops, and other structures had encroached on lanes and thoroughfares,
rendering safe and orderly transit difficult or impossible."

   In Athens, collective state builders might have benefitted from the city's destruction by the Persians in 479/478 BCE. Damaging as it was, destruction provided an
opportunity to build a substantially new city almost from scratch on the ruins of
the old, although not to the degree that it was possible to fully realize the democratic ideal of the period, namely the orthogonal grid plan (except in the newly
developed port and deme at Piraeus, built in 478 BCE). Changes that were made

in Athens in this period involved the architectural elaboration of the Agora and it environs, including the construction of a new meeting place for the *ekklesia* (citizen's assembly) on the nearby Pynx Hill. Interestingly, the growing requirements for public consumption evidently did result in some reduction of land previously devoted to private consumption, as we know from archaeological finds demonstrating that parts of what became the Agora had been residential and were cleared to make way for the expansion of the public space.

Staging collective action in an existing city may necessitate considerable change in the built environment and the nature of urban space use. Yinong Xu (2000) documents how, in China prior to the mid-T'ang Dynasty (ca. 800 CE), cities had grid-plan design but physical and social barriers to movement were common, so roads served mostly for local traffic. In later periods, including the focal Ming Dynasty, barriers to movement were lifted so that roads became public spaces as they were transformed into "busy streets flanked by shops, restaurants, houses, and the like" (Yinong Xu: 74), and urban legibility was further enhanced by assigning names to roads. Some urban historians have interpreted the absence of urban plaza spaces in premodern China as an indication of a comparatively weakly developed civic life compared with the Greco-Roman and European cultures. Instead, we see only a minor cultural preference in terms of what kinds of public spaces were suited to enhance social connectivity and intermingling. In Ming Dynasty China, rather than plazas, the connective cohesiveness of urban life was achieved through wide, busy streets, while designated plazas were reserved for marketplaces.

Rome is an especially well described instance of a struggle to control public space ensuing as a more collective state was instituted following the Republican Period. Rome had grown enormously during the latter period and, as we described, did so in a largely organic, unplanned and spatially inefficient manner, making it an "undecipherable jumble" in the words of Diane Favro (1993: 230). Administrative reforms brought an increased urban communications load and a response in the form of the *vehiculato* or *cursus publicus*, but this only exacerbated the "urban traffic chaos" (from van Tilburg 2007: 12). Lacking the ability to substantially remake the city physically, owing to private landowner opposition, the state's response was to reform road use, codified as the *Lex Iulia Municipalis*. Of importance, the code asserted that all urban roads were to be considered as public spaces and therefore subject to state control. Once state control had been established, regulations were instituted to relieve traffic congestion by restricting private wagon traffic (e.g., commercial traffic) to nighttime, restricting the degree to which private buildings could block roads, and prohibiting commercial use of streets, for example, for the display of merchants' wares. And, just prior to the beginning of the focal period, Augustus set out on a costly program of urban rejuvenation designed to improve the capital's traffic flow and to increase the amount of public space, for example, for recreational purposes. Diane Favro (1993) argues that the Augustan building program also aimed to visually showcase the city as something more than a random assemblage of buildings and spaces, with the goal to create a coherent narrative of urban greatness for both resident and visitor.

CONCLUSIONS, PART III: NEIGHBORHOODS AND COLLECTIVE ACTION

We define neighborhoods as territorial groups that are bounded, largely self-organizing, and functionally largely autonomous from state authority. In many cities, neighborhoods are basal organizational units that provide an important framework for the city dweller's daily social interactions. Yet, we propose that in collective contexts neighborhoods could be inconsistent with collective action viewed from the perspective of the city as an integrated social whole. We propose that collective benefit will flow from reordering the social properties of basal organizational units in a manner consistent with collective action. This would imply the embedding of neighborhoods more firmly in the social life of the larger urban community with the goal of reducing localized insularity and separation, of encouraging intermingling and social ties across neighborhood boundaries, and of facilitating the coordination of actions between the various territorial segments and the central authorities.

We often think of neighborhoods as a basic component of the urban social fabric, a social space where households are likely to interact most frequently with neighbors to satisfy their most basic needs. Neighborhoods, however, are variable in terms of how institutionalized they are and in terms of how important they are to the social lives of urban dwellers. As is evident from the preceding urban summaries, especially in the more collective polities, neighborhoods often were remodeled internally and restructured as administrative districts of a larger urban institution to enhance the "alliances" and "bridges" essential to civic capital. Thus, at the urban scale, one outcome of collective action will be a decline in the boundedness and independent social functionality of neighborhoods and the rise of a characteristic social geography in which neighborhoods have relatively less operational importance in the daily lives of the urban dweller.

A high degree of neighborhood boundedness is evident when a city ward or block is walled to restrict free movement. A neighborhood also is relatively bounded, even without walls, when members' social ties are stronger within-group than between-group, for example, when neighborhoods are highly self-governing and serve as local public-goods providers. In our sample of societies, the highly bounded and comparatively self-governing city subdivisions are found exclusively in cities of the less or moderately collective political systems. They feature a pattern of "organic" or self-organizing growth, for example, when neighborhoods coalesced around the households of powerful patron families (person-centered wards), as in Aceh, Bida, Edo, Burma, and, prior to the focal period, in Venice. In many of these same cases other largely self-organizing social formations developed side by side with person-centered wards, or instead of them, including the merchant's quarters in Aceh, ethnic and craft workers' enclaves in Bida, *cho* (self-governing walled wards) in Edo, quarters in Ottoman cities, and *mahallahs* in Mughal cities, though the latter declined in importance under Mughal rule.

Tokugawa Edo featured a high degree of physical boundedness of cho, and they served as local organizations that managed multiple tasks such as protection from banditry, fire control, and trash removal. We suggest a process of "introversion of basal social units" is operative in such cases. In this process, because the state is incapable or unwilling to provide needed urban services, people self-organize to provide them at the local level. The result is a city low in overall civic capital and instead is a city with a complex social fabric constituted of a multiplicity of largely unconnected and self-governing neighborhoods. The inefficiency of this form of urban society is obvious. For example, intracity movement may be impeded by the physically and socially fragmented terrain, and there are also impediments to organizational efficiencies, for example, the ability to control a major fire is limited when coordination is lacking between multiple local neighborhood segments.

We find fragmented urban landscapes in Inka and New Kingdom Egyptian polities. In both cases urban space was punctuated with walled spaces and structures, including royal palace complexes as well as workers' quarters or other residential, storage, and work areas. We propose that the bounded nature of city subdivisions in these two cases reflects a high degree of administrative control over state and royal properties, including the warehousing of a state's vast supply of goods set aside for military and other governmental purposes. These functions were carried out in walled structures to isolate activities in them from the surrounding urban population. For example, the layout of the main Inka capital, Cuzco, allowed for the tight control of access to royal palaces and complexes of governmental buildings by enclosing them in walls up to four to five meters high.

Citywide coordination of activities, and other aspects of civic capital, including minimal levels of neighborhood boundedness, are evident in our more collective polities. For example, as we mentioned, during the T'ang Dynasty, at least up to the eighth century CE, Chinese cities featured a highly segmented and gridded urban plan, but the presence of walled wards inhibited citywide movement. By the highly collective Ming Dynasty, walled wards were a declining feature of Chinese urban planning, city subdivisions had become administrative zones, and neighborhoods are only vaguely detectable. In other of the more collective polities, local social formations functioned as basal-level administrative units tied into higher levels of government, even when they retained some aspects of their original neighborhood-like social functions, as in the wards of Asante Kumase, the Aztec calpultin, and the Roman vici. These are examples in which growing collective states did evidently piggyback their organizational structure onto existing social formations, at least to some degree. However, in the majority of collective polities, city subdivisions were primarily administrative entities created by state builders to provide basal-level governance that could be effectively tied into overall city government. Among these, we include subdivisions resulting from the administrative reforms in Rome (while retaining some elements of the prior vici system); county-level and other administrative districts (ward and alley system) in Beijing, Suzhou, and Hangzhou; the seventy contrata and the district structure of Venice; and the deme quarters of Athens after the Kleisthenic reforms that were effectively linked into the civic functions of the Agora. In these more elaborate expressions of collective action in city life, neighborhoods lost some social functions when the state became more directly involved in providing administrative services and public goods at the city scale. As neighborhoods were incorporated into systems of administration, increasingly the social ties of city dwellers tended to expand beyond the neighborhood at the same time that the increasing spatial integration and legibility of road systems increased the efficiency of citywide mobility. In this more open and connected social context, there was more intermingling among a city's occupants and an enhanced potential for coordinated responses to the inherent challenges of urban life.

II

The Cultural Process of Cooperation

Culture, in the commonly expressed anthropological sense, consists of the shared knowledge, values, beliefs, norms, practices, and symbols that members of a group understand to be conventional, proper, and motivating. Here I adopt an approach that is more dynamic and change-oriented, and therefore better suited as an adjunct to collective action theory. A dynamic approach is a better fit between theory and cultural study, I suggest, because a turn to collective action will often entail a disruptive rethinking of that which is conventionally thought to be proper and motivating

To develop a form of cultural study suited to collective action theory, I investigate cultural change in four domains. The first, and most central to the enactment of collective action, pertains to notions about the self in society, expressed in a folk theory of mind. I argue that an appropriate folk theory suited to cooperation is one that acknowledges the psychological nature of the willful contingent cooperator. The second domain pertains to sense perception. Information gathered from the comparative sample of societies and other sources leads me to the conclusion that of the various modes of the sensorium, the institution of collective action provokes change primarily in visual signals and how they are produced, perceived, and analyzed. Third, I argue that collective ideas will exist in relation to multiple different ways of thinking about what should constitute an ideal society, yet, for cooperation to succeed, means must be found to enhance consensus in the face of plurality. In this section I show how the logical structures of duality and opposition have served to enhance consensus in some historical instances and may provide a model for

DOI: 10.5876/9781607325147.c011

consensus-building. Last, I consider the roles of ritual and religion in the institution of collective action.

A SCIENCE OF CULTURE

My goal is to make use of a "science of culture" that is both empirical and comparative and that embraces the goal of identifying cultural patterns and strategies for cultural change that are most consistent with broadly based cooperation. What I found is that in spite of the vast array of cultural differences facing the comparative researcher, in instances where groups form around collective institutions, humans have envisioned similar kinds of cultural constructs to nurture collective goals. Similarities are due, in part, to the fact that collective action is a problem-generating structure, but also to the interplay of cultural production and cognitive properties of the human brain.

My approach to culture recognizes that in ordinary social life people do not often view cultural conventions from critical or change-oriented perspectives. Still, ultimately, culture is contingent and subject to change through ends-oriented social action. In this way I avoid the arguments, common in the social sciences, that an approach emphasizing the conventional and normative will be opposed to a rational choice approach ("values versus interests") or, in anthropology, that inquiry must emphasize the native's perspective rather than attempt to arrive at cross-cultural generalization ("emic" versus "etic"). I avoid these dichotomies by addressing the issue of how collective action, as a social process, typically will entail a rethinking and reconstruction of conventional cultural patterns.

Change is an important dimension of cultural study because the conventions that seemingly unite a cultural group are, in reality, not usually completely shared, at least not in the context of large-scale complex society. In these cases, cultural differences arise from sources including social status, rural versus urban residence, political faction, and ethnic and religious difference, among other sources of heterogeneity. Hence the "culture" of a complex society is likely to be a palimpsest of contending ideas and diverse individual and group preferences that preclude the possibility that any particular way of solving a cooperator problem will be widely viewed as beneficial. To reap what benefits can be realized through collective action will require that notions consistent with it be pushed into a crowded and contentious cultural environment. The challenge for change agents is to find ways to realize consensus in spite of varied preferences and, especially, of the objections of an elite who oppose social change that upends traditional privileges.

That there can be forms of culture consistent with cooperation will seem odd to those social scientists whose argument is that in complex society, culture will serve primarily the interests of particular dominant groups. For those who subscribe to this ideological view there is truth in Marx's claim that culture is only an illusory representation of reality (in Marx's words, "ethereal self-mystification") that serves to legitimate what is in reality not legitimate, namely, the dominance of a particular interest group. Yet, this way of thinking is far from complete, as cultural production consistent with the goals of collective action is predicted to foreground features such as an egalitarian ethic and the importance of truthfulness in communication.

FOLK THEORIES OF MIND CONSISTENT WITH AND INCONSISTENT WITH COOPERATION

"The model of the individual is the animating force that allows
the analyst to generate predictions about likely outcomes
given the structure of the situation." (Ostrom 1986: 18)

It is important to hold on to Ostrom's idea that collective action is impossible without a viable "model of the individual." This is a useful insight that raises the question: Is there a particular notion of the self most consistent with institution-building for cooperation? I suggest there is, and it will be a folk theory that aligns with key aspects of the neurobiological reality of human Theory of Mind capacity and the contingent cooperator.

Folk theories that fail to reflect basic human cognitive capacities will be less consistent with collective institution-building. For example, early Medieval Christian canon did not envision a willful self situated firmly in its social context. Instead, the argument was made that in order to maximize an individual's relationship to God, ideally one should renounce the material world, including social relationships, a metaphysical notion of the person that Louis Dumont (1985: 95) calls the "outworldly individual." In the Medieval Christian scheme, society is conceived of only as an incidental product of God-love, a union of those who share Godly devotion, a framework obviously not well suited to developing a functional society, particularly one able to face the challenges presented by high levels of cooperation. Later Christian concepts, especially those of Calvin, countered the outworldly perspective with the idea that salvation could come in part from a person's good works in the material world, and this brought in its wake possibilities for collective action. In an argument in some ways parallel to Max Weber's famous claim that a protestant ethic facilitated the rise of capitalism, Philip Gorski (2003) makes the compelling argument that the new cultural design for Christianity was politically transformative in the rise of the modern European state in a number of respects. In his example, Dutch Protestant reformers argued for the importance of personal moral accountability, overcame Catholic Church opposition to state involvement in poor relief, and pushed political authorities to institute new systems of social welfare and mass education. The turn away from a metaphysical understanding of the human was further codified by Enlightenment philosophers such as John Locke. He conceptualized the self as a material being capable of rational and potentially moral action based on experience, introspection, and learning.

One entailment of collective action is that contingent cooperators must have the ability to estimate the intentions and possible actions of others. Thus a folk theory of mind that denies any connection between intention and action would not be highly suited to realizing collective action, and cultural designs like this have been noted. The cultural anthropologist Eve Danziger (2006) summarizes ethnographic literature describing societies, including the Mopan Maya she studied, in which understanding a person's mental state—his or her intentions—is not considered a valid or relevant means to explain speech or social action. Robert Paul (1995: 20) suggests that one kind of situation that might be consistent with such a folk theory is in small, closely integrated groups, such as the Sherpa communities he studied, where it is considered a threat to social harmony to speak "plainly about certain aspects of reality." Paul's suggestion begs empirical cross-cultural testing, but, from the evidence he presents, I am skeptical of it. While small group size might be one causal factor, in the Sherpa case I would point out there is an important cultural factor at play, namely, that their Buddhist religious doctrines lack a well-developed notion of a thoughtful self and instead embrace a metaphysical notion, the *sem*. This is an inner person that is "purposed," in the phraseology of Paul (1995: 32), to be inherently good or bad.

CONSEQUENCES OF FOLK THEORY OF MIND FOR JUDICIAL PRACTICE

For cooperation to flourish, it is important to imagine a folk theory of mind that identifies a link between intention and social action, and that even allows for the retrodiction of a person's state of mind that precipitated a past action. Further, the theory has to be applicable in a uniformitarian manner, that is, in a manner that is applicable to all persons in society without regard to social standing or other social or cultural considerations. Obviously, this kind of thinking is not always found. Of the societies Lane Fargher and I studied comparatively, New Kingdom Egypt was a highly politically centralized polity. It endowed the Pharaohs with great power and near-divine status, and in other ways scored quite low on measures of collective action. Its weakly developed judicial institutions subjected accused persons to largely arbitrary decisions because neither judicial theory nor practice entailed any clear procedures to rationally assign fault. The arbitrary nature of this system is evident in the fact that to consult an oracle was an accepted practice for arriving at a verdict of guilt or innocence. Few codified laws existed, so the judicial decisions of Pharaohs, priests, and other authorities (there were no specialized judges) often were arbitrary and tended to favor the elite sectors of society. T. G. H. James (1984: 78) reports, "That the poor and weak could obtain justice was a fundamental object of the legal process in ancient Egypt; but justice for such did not come easily."

Notions of the self consistent with cooperation, including procedures for retrodicting past states of mind, are an important foundational element for the construction of rational modes of judicial practice and theory that can properly assign praise or blame when actions are understood to be voluntary, what Mary Douglas termed the "secular forensic model" of the self (Douglas 1992: 220). The secular forensic model implies that Theory of Mind analytical capacities are mobilized to assess guilt or innocence. This analytical capacity is important in the context of collective action because it is one element of how confidence can be established in a society's governing institutions, especially in the effectiveness of an unbiased judiciary. As Lawrence Rosen (1995: 6) reminds us, the ability to gauge intentional states is an important criterion that marks the difference between assigning guilt based on some randomizing method, such as I described for ancient Egypt, on the one hand, and more rational modes of proof, on the other, in which strategies are available to decipher a possible perpetrator's intentions. According to Leonard Kaplan, "legal theory beginning with the Classical Greeks argued that it was important to understand intention in order to assign fault" (Kaplan 1995: 119).

THE UNIFORMITARIAN FOLK THEORY OF MIND AND OPEN RECRUITMENT TO POSITIONS OF GOVERNING AUTHORITY

A "uniformitarian" folk theory of mind will acknowledge that all adult humans possess an independent, thoughtful mind and, as a result, are capable of cooperation but also defection from obligations. Uniformitarianism is threatened when a folk theory of mind inscribes a particular pattern of thought or cognitive ability according to a system of categories, such as division between elite and subaltern. In these schemes, persons are regarded only as representatives of a social category (the word "person," comes from the Greek word *prosopeion*, referring to a mask—thus the outer person, a recognized social category). By contrast, a concept of the "self" recognizes the inner self-awareness of the rational individual.

I suggest that to distinguish between person and self is useful as a pathway to understanding collective action. Where oppression and autocracy are the central operative principles of an organization, those in power will socially reproduce their privileged position by upholding a notion of a commoner person as a subaltern category. This is an irrational person incapable of social morality or other kinds of analytical reasoning. Hence, the persons most responsible for the governance of society will be restricted to an elite who alone are perceived to possess the requisite moral capacity, training, and experience. A cultural design for cooperation, however, that aims to be inclusive, will embrace a more uniformitarian folk theory of mind that transforms subaltern to citizen. In a uniformitarian folk theory, all adult group members are considered to have the capacity for the moral reasoning of the socially intelligent conditional cooperator. An implication of this idea is that, potentially, recruitment into positions of governing authority can be opened to persons of all social statuses. This is like Robert Dahl's (1989: 105) "Strong Principle of Equality," in which every adult "member of an association is sufficiently well qualified, taken all around, to participate in making binding collective decisions."

It is important to point out that a policy of open recruitment is more than just an expression of a folk theory of mind. When an egalitarian folk theory becomes the basis for a policy of recruitment to positions of authority, the state is sending a palpable signal confirming its embrace of an incorporative and social solidarist strategy for governing. Further, it is doing so in spite of the probable economic inefficiencies that will follow. As most economists, I am sure, would be quick to point out, open recruitment is inefficient owing to the costs entailed in identifying suitable candidates for official positions and in providing training for position service. However, as is true with other aspects of collective action, including public goods, open recruitment should be judged on grounds other than economic efficiency, to instead evaluate its role in building social solidarity and confidence in the institutions of governance. Next I provide four examples—from Europe, China, Hindu and Buddhist states, and Aztec—to illustrate how open recruitment was foundational in major episodes of collective state-building:

OPEN RECRUITMENT AND THE EUROPEAN EXPERIENCE

Donald Brown (1988) documents the arguments of nonuniformitarian, hereditarian theories that denied the possibility for social mobility to some whole sectors of society because the subaltern person was seen as a morally reprehensible being. This pattern is evident in the polities scoring low on collective action in the comparative sample. For example, for Tokugawa Japan, Louis Perez (2002: 26) notes among members of the governing elite a "swaggering contempt for the peasants." A similar degree of contempt was expressed in England of the focal period and in Medieval Europe more broadly (opinions on this issue were somewhat mixed, with a minority of authors of the period seeing peasants as morally exemplary). A common

FIGURE 11.1. Peasant cultivator depicted as a simian. From the Gorleston Psalter ca. 1320. © British Library, London (MS Add 49622, f. 15v).

view was like that described by J. Alexander (1990), who analyzed Medieval Period paintings and found that they often made use of a metaphor of symbolic opposition of the cultured self (the elite) versus a peasantry depicted as a primitive person living close to a state of nature (Figure 11.1). The prevailing Theory of Mind driving a sense of difference was predicated on sharply drawn, castelike boundaries between social classes and whose truthfulness was held to be self-evident and indisputable based on religious doctrine. As Rodney Hilton (1985: 222) puts it, in Medieval social theory "the various orders of society, based on the original tripartite division between those who fight (the nobles), those who pray (the clergy) and those who work (the peasants), were of divine origin and not, therefore, to be changed by the actions of men."

To justify the stratificatory theory of the dominant elite, peasants and others of low social station were understood to live in a perpetual state of idolatry. An early Medieval Christian contempt for the material world, which highlighted the importance of the spiritual life of prayer and other expressions of devotion to God and church, discriminated against those who toiled in manual labor. This included peasants but also others such as cooks and laundrymen, and even merchants, whose work brought them in contact with bodily fluids regarded as sources of spiritual pollution. In England of the focal period, the differentiated folk theory played out in the political arena, where a morally capable gentry and aristocracy alone were given voice in matters of governance. Those remaining elements of the social assemblage—including the rural poor, yeoman farmers and merchants—were denied political voice. This situation gradually changed, as I address later in this chapter and in the following chapter, but elements of it lingered well into the seventeenth century or even later, and the polity's highest offices were restricted to an elite well into the nineteenth century. The prominent author Charles Lamb, for example, following a period of rural agitation, commented in 1886 that "it was never good times in England since the poor began to speculate on their condition. Formerly they jogged on with as little reflection as horses. The whistling ploughman went cheek by jowl with his brother that neighed" (qtd. in Howes and Classen 2014: 76). Even in the twentieth century we see evidence of stratificatory biases. E. P. Thompson (1971) notes that most historical scholars continue to treat the peasant "crowd" as "compulsive, rather than self-conscious or self-activating" (76).

The rise of the Venetian republic provides an early example of changing ideas about social cleavage and the governance of society that influenced Enlightenment thinkers in England and elsewhere in Europe. As early as 1544 the humanist Gasparo Contarini wrote that "as in music the tune is marred when one string maintains a louder tone . . . so by the like reason, if you have a commonwealth perfect and enduring, let not one part be mightier than the other, but let them all (in as much as may be) have equal share in the public authority" (qtd. in De Maria 2010: 5) (admittedly, the republic Contarini wrote about did not have completely open recruitment; persons holding the higher offices were selected from a governing council of roughly 2,000 members). Excepting the pervasive gender bias of the period, philosophers such as John Locke (1975, orig. 1689) laid out the contours of an inclusive folk theory of mind that envisioned the possibility for a rational, self-aware, and socially relational self not morally restricted by low social standing. In the case of Locke and other Enlightenment philosophers, this was not a claim that all humans are rational in all respects, only that, especially in the case of matters pertaining to civil interest, reasoning persons will provide the most potential for reform and a better way of living. Inclusive notions such as this are ripe with possibilities for devising institutions for collective action, including open recruitment. While not adequately acknowledged in the Western historical and social science literatures, which often foreground the importance of participatory elections in their models of modernity and democracy, open recruitment through civil service examinations is one of the most important components of modern democratic societies. As Gregory Blue (1999: 67) points out, prominent eighteenth-century philosophers such as Voltaire and Quesnay promoted a civil service model for European state-building—that is, one based on open recruitment—and saw it as one path to a "constitutionally limited monarchy." These authors also recognized China's historical lead in taking this path. I turn to that example next.

THE CHINESE EXAMPLE OF OPEN RECRUITMENT

> "In ancient times the four orders [the educated gentry, the
> peasant, the artisan, and the merchant] had their distinct
> functions, but in later times the status distinctions among
> scholars, peasants, and merchants have become blurred." (Gui
> Youguang [Ming Dynasty, 1507–71], qtd. in Brook 1998: 143)

In China, open recruitment policies were gradually developed alongside a rethinking of the nature of governance that began during the Zhou Dynasty as early as 1050 BCE. In the revised concept, the legitimacy of a ruler was no longer considered to be only a product of hereditary right or fate. Instead, increasingly, his moral character was considered, including an obligation to forgo personal desire so as to better serve the people. If moral sensibility is not a result of status or fate, this begs the question: How does one acquire it? The most thorough inquiry into the sources of moral virtue was that of Confucius, the first Chinese philosopher to systematize a philosophy of moral self-cultivation and to make the argument that moral growth could be achieved by anyone, not just by rulers. Other of his ideas are highly congruent with the notion of a conditional cooperator and collective action. He argued that it was each person's decision whether or not to strive to be a fully developed human (*junzi*), inspired by devotion and humility. Those who chose the moral path could achieve their goal through learning, self-reflection, and ritual practice in social settings that included diverse activities ranging from formal ritual to etiquette and standards of conduct. Confucius's thinking precipitated a centuries-long conversation among Chinese philosophers concerning the nature of the moral human, ideas that informed the governing policies of many Chinese dynasties.

Just prior to the start of the Ming Dynasty, philosophers such as the Sung Period's Zhu Xi (1030 to 1100 CE) revived Confucianist ideas. His goal was to counter the influence of Buddhism with its metaphysical claim that any notion of an autonomous self is a false consciousness. Zhu Xi's ideas were carried forward and refined during the Ming Period. Neo-Confucianists such as Zhu Xi placed their emphasis on the self and the mind and devised prescriptions for developing a moral mind. This folk theory of mind saw in all humans the potential for analytic thought and, further, argued that training and education, even debate, coupled with introspection, can bring moral self-cultivation. As the philosopher Wang Yang-min expresses it, selfish desires can be overcome if a person strives to achieve a "sincere mind" (e.g., in Munro 1969: 171).

The idea that anyone could, with effort, compose a moral mind is consistent with open recruitment to positions of authority, so it is no surprise that such policies have a long history in China. Already by the fifth century BCE, commoners could be recruited into positions of authority. This is evident in reforms carried out in the

Qin state that removed rule by the traditional hereditary aristocracy and replaced it with a more meritocratic system. Later, open recruitment policies were based on the institutionalization of competitive civil service examinations that were in use by the T'ang Dynasty (618 to 907 CE), and established on a societywide scale during the Northern Sung Dynasty (960–1126 CE) (open recruitment persisted in Chinese political culture until it was abolished in 1905 CE).

By the time of the Ming Dynasty, Buddhism's presence was felt to some degree, but neo-Confucianist and similar theories were more central to Ming governing policies, owing to their emphasis on the importance of moral self-cultivation. During this period the merit-based civil service exam system was elaborated on, and, because students prepared for exams by studying Confucian and other classic texts, there was a corresponding increase in state funding for public schools with the goal of "equal educational opportunity for all" (Ho 1962: 255) ("all" in this case refers to males). The result was a degree of social mobility at that time "probably unparalleled in Chinese history" (261). Also, during the Ming Dynasty, open recruitment was made even more broadly allocative than it had been in prior dynasties. The Ming founder, realizing that wealthy provinces put forward relatively more candidates who had passed the civil service exams, set regional quotas to give poorer regions better access to the valued official positions.

Benjamin Elman (1991) summarizes the many ways the Chinese civil examination system and open recruitment became central cultural pillars of Late Imperial Chinese polities (including the Ming Dynasty): (1) Civil servants trained in Confucian principles "served as a useful countervailing force to the power of entrenched aristocrats in capital politics" (9) and also provided a counterweight to military centers of power; (2) persons who passed the exams were publicly acclaimed, and to pass exams and to then become an official in the government were important criteria of success for the test-taker and his family (even wealthy merchants urged their children to move up socially through this path); and (3) the examination system highlighted the important role played by education in developing moral competency, which, in turn, was a stimulus for the growth of a national school system, as Elman points out, centuries before Europe's.

Hindu-Inspired States and Open Recruitment

By contrast with Confucianist notions that humans have moral choices and are capable of moral self-cultivation, Hindu (and also Buddhist) doctrines that influenced governing policies, especially in South and Southeast Asia, inhibited the development of notions of open recruitment (Hindu-influenced polities in the comparative sample include Vijayanagara, Pudukkottai, Bali, Aceh, and

Java—the latter two influenced by Islam just prior to the focal periods; all of these polities scored lower than many others on the measure of open recruitment, and generally were lower overall in terms of collective action). The cultural designs influencing Hinduism can be traced to first millennium BCE Vedic texts such as the treatise on statecraft referred to as the Arthashastra. In the Vedic *varna* system developed in such texts, all persons are born into the caste (or into the non-Aryan *dasa* status) of their parents, and as a result they become stereotypical caste persons. In this cultural design, a person's *dharma* (one's obligations and privileges to others)—rather than being specified in terms of a broad moral concept that would apply to all persons—is distinct according to caste position. For example, only one pure caste, the *ksatriya*, is considered morally worthy to hold the statuses of ruler, warrior, or high official.

Owing to the emphasis on the dharma of the caste person, in Hindu cultural design an abstract and broadly applicable sense of the self is not well theorized—in fact, self is understood to be an abstract concept and as such cannot be located in the physical body. As Amartya Sen (1987: 5–6) points out, the theory of self that was developed in texts such as the Arthashastra is not highly complex compared with other civilizational traditions including Greek philosophy, and, I would add, Chinese philosophy following Confucius. As Agehananda Bharati (1985: 189) puts it, in Hinduism, "the self as a source of achievement is not considered in philosophical texts." Rather than the moral self-cultivation of Confucianist thought, in Vedic doctrine there is a metaphysical and solitary path to immortality achieved by overcoming normal thought and by renouncing the social and material worlds to eventually arrive at a purely emotional state of mind bliss. And, rather than the self-evaluative inner dialogue that is an important part of moral self-cultivation in Confucianism (and understood by cognitive scientists today as an aspect of Theory of Mind), the meditative religions such as Hinduism and Buddhism, as described by Stephen Tyler (2006: 308), "emphasize a kind of internal silence and impose an end to thought's ceaseless reflection on itself."

Aztec Culture and Open Recruitment

I interpret Aztec notions of the self from a variety of sources that describe the deities and mythic histories of the Aztec peoples as they were recounted in native and Post-Conquest Period codex format. My information is also based on descriptions of ritual cycles recorded after the Conquest by Spanish chroniclers and ethnographers such as Fray Bernardino de Sahagún. That these sources refer to cosmic history, deities, and rituals, however, does not mean that Aztec notions of the person were strongly metaphysical. Instead, I see in these sources evidence for a discourse about the self that in some ways can be compared with other civilizations in highlighting an egalitarian idea of the moral capacity of the person, including the commoner.

Legal systems and modes of governance of the Postclassic Period of the Central Highlands of Mexico (after about 1000 CE), which eventuated in the Aztec Empire, were based on what evidently had been a sea change in folk theory of mind (although prior periods are not well understood in this regard). These new ideas are evident in Postclassic mythic history that can be understood as an extended commentary on how Aztec society and culture resulted from the intermingling of the "primitive" desert peoples (Chichimecs), of the region's northern margins, and the urbanized neo-Toltec Nahua peoples of the region's core zone, the latter governed by hereditary nobility. The mythic histories record the travails of the Chichimec tribes, including the ruling Mexica, who departed from the northern site of Aztlan to migrate south into the wetter and lusher Basin of Mexico and other areas of Central Mexico. As their migrations proceeded, Chichimecs gradually were transformed from marginal desert peoples into civilized sedentary farmers in the Nahua mode. However, the cultural transformation was not complete, as the symbolism of the margin and its key deity—known variously as Tezcatlipoca, Mixcoatl, and Camaxtli—was retained as an important component of Aztec cultural design.

The contrasting nature of Chichimec and Nahua cultural patterns provided a framework for seeing authority and moral capacity in a dualistic sense represented symbolically by deities, who, working side by side, created what the Aztecs thought of as the current world. These were Quetzalcoatl, associated with an ancient and revered Toltec civilization, whose noble descendants held most positions of authority in the empire, on the one hand, and the various expressions of Tezcatlipoca, on the other. In this dual scheme, while the neo-Toltec person is one who enjoys the benefits of civilization such as sedentary farming, material wealth, writing, and urbanism, mythic history indicates that the culturally "primitive" Chichimec peoples are endowed with a well-developed sense of moral purpose and understanding. The symbolism of Tezcatlipoca is key to understanding a highly egalitarian notion of the commoner that was one of the cultural foundations of Aztec state-building. This deity is notable for having the capacity to perceive the potential for virtue in persons regardless of social standing, including the idea that success can be the product of achievement, not just noble birth. This egalitarianizing sensibility provided the cultural foundations for a judicial system structured to assure fair treatment for commoner and noble. For example, Texcoco, traditionally a site of Tezcatlipoca adoration, was also renowned for its progressive judicial theory and practice. Egalitarian notions also paved the way for commoner participation in some aspects of the civic life of the polity, for example, some commoners rose to high office in the imperial system, and commoners served on some ruling councils.

COMMUNICATION AND COLLECTIVE ACTION: A VISUAL
PERCEPTION THEORY FOR CULTURAL ANALYSIS

"The fundamental theoretical problem underlying the question of cooperation is the manner by which individuals attain knowledge of each
others' preferences and likely behavior." (N. Schofield 1985: 218)

To produce cooperative groups "individuals must be highly
visible to one another in order to reduce the severity of the
free-rider and assurance problems." (Hechter 1990b: 21)

Ken Nakayama (2011: v) encourages us to better understand the "interplay of
visual and social process." In this section I address the need for theory-building
in this regard by elaborating on a visual perception approach to collective action.
Schofield's point, from the quote above, that cooperation depends on knowledge of
other's likely behavior, and Hechter's reference to the importance of intervisibility,
are useful starting points for visual-themed theory-building. But the direct intervisibility alluded to by Hechter will be an extremely costly option outside of small-
group contexts, so my focus in this section will be on how knowledge of other's
likely behavior can be gained effectively in spite of large social scale. Examples of
institutions that enhance visual communication have been described earlier in this
book, for example, the cases that Lane Fargher and I describe in chapter 8, in which,
in the more collective polities, leaders were obligated to make public appearances,
and, in some cases government was made more transparent by conducting official
business in public venues. In addition to strategies such as these, I suggest that any
attempt to build collective forms of cooperation in larger groups will place pressure
on change makers to be innovative in developing new forms of visual communication that make use of representative art.

In this section I look more closely at forms of representation and innovative
changes in them that can be characterized as visual aesthetic transitions. In all cultures the various forms of sensory perception—visual, auditory, smell, taste and
touch—will embody meaning and have different social uses. Studies of cultural differences in sensory perception have tended to conclude that uniquely, with the rise
of modernity, visuality emerged as the principal element of the Western-inspired
sensorium, especially in the form of visual media thought to be most suited to communicating complex messages and aesthetic understanding. The growing importance of visuality as early as the European Early Modern Period is evident in the
metaphor John Locke and other philosophers of the period, including David Hume,
used to analyze the introspective capacity of the rational subject's mind. This idea
compared the mind to a dark room, in Locke's terms, "not much unlike a closet

wholly shut from light, with only some little opening left . . . to let in external visual resemblances, or some idea of things without; would the pictures coming into such a dark room but stay there and lie so orderly as to be found upon occasion it would very much resemble the understanding of a man" (Locke 1975: 163).

The visual metaphor in Locke's scheme was a new way to imagine the human mind. But here I argue that it is not entirely unexpected and that, further, an emphasis on the visual dimension of the sensorium is not restricted to the novel thinking of philosophers such as John Locke, or of Western modernity more broadly. Similar ideas are expressed in other civilizational traditions. In Aztec society, for instance, quite unlike Europe and yet scoring high on measures of collective action, an elaborate theory of the self was developed that emphasized the powers of eyes and ears in making a person wise. Rather than a unique historical turn in European cultural history, I see cooperation as a social and cultural force that, to succeed, will require the mobilization of those cognitive systems of the human brain devoted to the acquisition and analysis of visual signals, especially those calibrated to assess states of mind and intention. This is an opportune time to develop such a visual communications theory, given recent discoveries in fields such as the "science of social vision," "affective neuroscience," and the "psychology of art and aesthetic perception."

Excitation, Aesthetic Perception, and Visual Primitives

The perception of visual objects involves multiple and partially distinct modes of sensory processing mediated through various neural substrates in the brain's functional architecture. These distinct modes result in contrasting kinds of cognitive responses to visual signals. Here I distinguish between two main signal-processing patterns—social reasoning and excitation—that are relevant to understanding the cultural foundations of domination and cooperation.

The brain's analysis of visual objects involves multiple neural pathways from eyes to brain and what is called an oculomotor plant that controls eye movements and associated neural machinery. This visual apparatus is especially structured to assess the emotional states and intentions of others through the analysis of facial expression and the analysis of degree of entrainment from gaze, head angle, and other aspects of body proximity and positioning. In many respects these signals provide data for a deliberative process that allows the viewer to evaluate probable states of mind of others and to predict their probable behaviors. In what I refer to as a process of "excitation," by contrast, visual data are processed more passively through the subcortical areas of the brain where responses to visual objects will be more instantaneous and affective than analytical. One aspect of the excitation system analyzes facial expression in a portion of the brain's emotional system, the amygdala. This brain area produces emotional responses to visual stimuli using memory data but also, probably, from innate biases. For example, psychologists and psychological anthropologists have identified universal responses to facial expressions indicating the basic emotions of happiness, anger, sadness, fear, disgust, and surprise.

The viewer experiences affective responses also when visual stimuli are processed in areas of the brain devoted to long-term memory, stimulating what art psychologists refer to as "aesthetic perception." In this process, visual signals generate affective responses in relation to culturally specific notions of aesthetic beauty and symbolic meaning. A related aspect of the excitation system involves what is called a "visual primitive" cognition system. One type of visual primitive processing is to be found in relation to objects with high values of visual sensation from luminance (marked difference in light reflectance). Objects with high luminances will impart a striking sensation of three-dimensionality that is "preconscious and not accessible to intellectual analysis or control" (Livingstone 2002: 109). There appear to be analogous visual primitive responses to the physical shape of objects and spaces, especially those featuring bilateral symmetry. That bilateral symmetry is important in human visual cognition is evident in the fact that, universally, left-right symmetry of the face is noted to be a sign of beauty and sexual attractiveness (although subjects typically are not aware they are responding to that kind of signal). We also know that architects of many cultural traditions have learned to create affectively stimulating built environments by deploying formal and coherent spatial designs that juxtapose equivalent architectural masses along a movement axis. Incidentally, although referred to as a visual primitive by art psychologists, emotional response to bilateral symmetry may not be a particularly "primitive" system. Although it appears to be part of the subcortical circuitry, it is first evident in human material culture in the form of the purposeful manufacture of tear-drop-shaped Late Acheulean hand axes of the Lower Paleolithic Period. These were first produced coincident with a surge in brain size after 600,000 years ago, quite late in hominin neuroevolutionary history.

In the next sections, I build on this visual perception theory to investigate the cultural foundations of domination and cooperation. This subject matter is vast, but my work allows me to suggest that the excitation system—involving visual primitive and symbolically charged aesthetic forms of perception—is most likely to be mobilized as part of the cultural production of societies based on dominance. Visual primitive and aesthetic forms of perception are less likely to be mobilized for cooperation-based cultural design. Instead, cultural construction emphasizes visual stimuli that recruit brain regions of the neocortex that are associated with social reasoning, including simulation of others' intentions. I illustrate the latter by noting a turn to veristic portraiture and other expressions of naturalism to characterize aesthetic transitions associated with the more collective polities.

NATURALISM AND THE QUOTIDIAN IN THE EUROPEAN CASE

> "Good to themselves, and in themselves to all, through grateful
> toil. Even nature lives by toil: beast, bird, air, fire, the heavens, and
> rolling worlds, all live by action: nothing lies at rest but death and
> ruin: man is born to care, fashioned, improved by labor . . . Hence
> utility through all conditions' hence the joys of health; hence
> strength of arm, and clear judicious thought." (from John
> Dyer, "Fleece" (1969 [orig. 1761], 124; author's translation)

Dyer's (1969) poem illustrates a growing appreciation for the quotidian and the common person in Early Modern Europe. This movement is also evident in the works of Denis Diderot, in France, and Henry Alsted, in England, who published innovative encyclopedic works extolling the value of the mechanical arts. Similarly, Adam Smith praised the virtue inherent in agricultural production in his *Wealth of Nations*, for example, when he wrote:

> Not only the art of the farmer, the general direction of the operations of husbandry,
> but many inferior branches of country labour require much more skill and experience
> that the greater part of the mechanik trades . . . the man who ploughs the ground
> with a team of horses or oxen, works with instruments of which the health, strength
> and temper are very different upon different occasions . . . The common ploughman,
> although generally regarded as the pattern of stupidity and ignorance, is seldom
> defective in this judgment and discretion . . . How much the lower ranks of the
> people in the country are really superior to those of the town, is well known to every
> man whom either business or curiosity has led to converse much with both. (Smith
> 1993: 126–27)

While European philosophers were posing new ideas about the rational mind, some innovative authors and artists explored new ways to disturb the Medieval cultural canon by rethinking the nature of the self in society. Artistic production in the canonical mode serves to reaffirm those values shared between artist and viewer, for example, by restricting content to topics considered worthy of representation and by closely adhering to accepted aesthetic standards. Some early modern authors and painters defied the canonical, using their crafts as venues of cultural contestation and change. They did this by highlighting differences between what the artist understands about the psychology of self by contrast and what the viewer understands. This heterodox production signaled a disagreement between artist and viewer that aimed to challenge the viewer's sense of what constitutes the facts of social life.

In recent European history, one direction for heterodox artistic production was toward naturalism. This movement, what art historians refer to as the "picturesque,"

FIGURE 11.2. *The Harvesters,* Pieter Brueghel the Elder, 1565. © The Metropolitan Museum of Art. Image source: Art Resource, NY.

avoids the conventionally beautiful, sublime, or heroic, instead depicting the everyday, the rural, and the peasant. Pieter Brueghel the Elder (ca. 1525/30–69 CE) was an important innovator who, despite criticism from his arts peers (who mocked him with nicknames such as "peasant Brueghel" and "Brueghel the jester") made an artistic turn to represent the quotidian and the commoner subject (Figure 11.2). His heterodox art signaled the beginning of one of the most important themes of later European modernism expressed in Dutch art of the seventeenth century, nineteenth-century naturalists and impressionists (such as Léon Frédéric), late nineteenth-century Russian realism, paintings representing the ideals of republican virtue in the United States Post–Revolutionary Period, New Deal mural paintings, and 1960s and 1970s New Realism.

Since Brueghel, European philosophers, and art historians have struggled to understand the appeal of artistic representations like his, and those of later naturalists, which departed from the canonical depiction of the beautiful, the sublime, and the devotional. Brueghel, a recognized master of the highly technical Italianate style of the period favored by the religious and governing elite, was fully capable of arousing the affective responses of aesthetic perception through his paintings.

Yet, he departed from strictly canonical themes, and, as a result, according to Hugh Honour and John Fleming, "he made this lowest class of the social order stand for all humanity" (Honour and Fleming 1982: 387). By depicting common persons, as in *The Harvesters*, in fine detail and as individual persons who were engaged both individually and socially in various forms of work, relaxation, and community events, Brueghel invited the viewer to imagine an alternative theory of mind of the common person and by doing this helped to advance the commoner subject into society's discussion of moral capacity.

NATURALISM IN PORTRAITURE

According to Donald Brown (2008: 325), realistic portraits are rare in human history, in part because achieving representational fidelity is technically difficult. However, as he points out, in some societies where such skills were present, portraiture was not done or was rare. The Yoruba of West Africa provide one example where skill was present but portraiture was not. Although Yoruba culture of the focal period symptomizes the general absence of realism in African art, this was not always the case. During an earlier period just prior to the focal period, during the fourteenth and fifteenth centuries CE, highly realistic portraits of Yoruba leaders were produced that to this day engage the interest of art historians and collectors. Oddly, by the focal period of the comparative project (late eighteenth century CE), accurate portraits were no longer produced, pointing to the fact of a sometimes complex relationship between collective action and imagery that must be addressed as a prelude to a discussion of the role of portraiture in a study of cooperative institution-building.

Below I describe cases in which veristic portraiture became a part of the culture for cooperation, while in others the visual culture of collective action precluded veristic representation, especially of important governing officials. The latter situations may take the forms of "aniconism" (normative cultural opposition to figural images), but there are other expressions of cultural tension surrounding how leaders are represented, reflecting a process referred to as the "decentering of the self." One example of decentering is the masking of leading officials, a practice thought to submerge the self in a symbol of rulership. This apparently was the preferred mode of public representation of Yoruba rulers during the focal period, as they always appeared masked in formal ritual occasions. But which strategy—aniconism, masking or accurate portraiture—will be a more likely outcome of collective polity-building in any particular instance? Currently no theory exists that can identify the conditions favoring one over the others, but portraiture, of the strategies, has the most potential to deploy the brain's cognitive systems that allow for analysis of intention and trustworthiness. To mobilize these capacities implies an artistic strategy that is, in the words of Norman Bryson (1983: 45) "narrowly cognitive." Narrowly cognitive or "inward" perception (to perceive the invisible mind) implies that a viewer's comprehension of a work is immediate, that is, high in tactile values that are close to universal visual experience and to a lesser degree mediated through the aesthetic perception of locally meaningful history, style, or symbol. To view an accurate portrait of another is to engage Theory of Mind capacity in the sense that it is feasible for the viewer to simulate what kind of person is represented in the figure.

Art historians have noted the evocative powers of portraits that, according to David Freedberg, have the capacity to bring "recurrent . . . psychological and behavioral responses . . . observed throughout history and across cultures . . . [when the viewer] . . . sees living beings, animate, not ones rendered mortal by history, but one which are like him, of . . . the same breath, blood, and flesh" (Freedberg 1989: xix–xx, 200). The power of portrait perception is enabled by two features of the brain's visual-processing system. The first is the way that pictorial cues in artistic representation are able to stand as a supplement to in-person perception. As David Melcher and Patrick Cavanagh put it, humans display a "tolerance to flatness and stasis in images; this relative insensitivity to the dramatic difference between a picture and the real world is one of the foundations of visual art" Melcher and Cavanagh (2013: 360). The other cognitive feature is the way in which even images or sculpted figures, especially if the image or sculpture is physiologically veristic, stimulate the mirror neuron system, thus allowing for the simulation of the actions, emotions, and sensations of others. In this connection it is of interest that the goal of some Western literature of the Early Modern Period was to amplify, in a sense, the inherent human capacities for face analysis by developing a formal theory and method of "physiognomics." These methods claimed to increase an observer's ability to understand a person's character based on outward appearance, particularly through a formal analysis of facial features (analogous face-analysis disciplines were developed in other civilizations, as well).

Accurate portraiture has the power to, as Eric Kandel (2012: 107) puts it, "bring the viewer into the picture" with the goal of stimulating cognitive responses such as empathy and a willingness to be involved. In collective polities, where the ability to govern is counted less in terms of the symbolism of office than in gaining the confidence of citizens, portraiture allows for face analysis as a way for the viewer to theorize what kind of person a leader might be. For example, Oliver Cromwell (1653–59) imagined a form of artistic representation suited to his protectorate. This included a desire to paint official portraits as realistic depictions, to contrast with the traditional canonical mode of representation of British rulers that art historians refer to as "heroic" painting (Figure 11.3). In 1649 CE Cromwell reportedly gave his

FIGURE 11.3. Robert Walker's *Oliver Cromwell*, ca. 1649. © National Portrait Gallery, London.

portrait artist instructions to "use all your skill to paint my picture truly like me and not flatter me at all but remark on this ruffness, pimples, warts, and everything you see, otherwise I will not pay a farthing for it") (qtd. in Bindman 2008: 48) (after Cromwell, heroic representation was resumed when Charles II came to the throne).

MORAL DISCOURSES AND ARTISTIC INNOVATIONS
ANALOGOUS TO THE EUROPEAN ENLIGHTENMENT?

I next describe key elements of cultural discourses and their expressions in artistic representation in societies of the comparative sample. I suggest these highly collective examples are analogous to ideas and forms of representation of the European Enlightenment, especially a turn to naturalistic representation (in Appendix B, section 6, I describe a statistical analysis based on the thirty-society sample, which showed a statistically significant association between higher levels of collective action and naturalistic art).

ATHENS (403–322 BCE)

A phase of rapid culture change accompanied the political reforms of the sixth and fifth centuries BCE that eventuated in the democratic *polis* in Athens. The reconfigured cultural pattern was in part a rethought folk theory of mind that challenged inequality in what had been a sharply stratified society, though signs pointing to egalitarian ways of thinking are present as early as the eighth century. For example, what is called "middling poetry" of this early period was explicitly anti-elite. Hesiod's famous *Works and Days* of the seventh century BCE, for example, was an extended critique of elite privilege while also highlighting the "sacred" tasks of agriculture and husbandry. This is similar to Homer's laudatory treatment of Odysseus's father, Laertes, and his life on the farm. As Victor Davis Hanson (1999: 3) argues, sources such as these represent the "emergence of a new sort of person for whom work was not merely a means of subsistence or profit but an ennobling way of life, a crucible of moral excellence in which pragmatism, moderation, and a search for proportion were the fundamental values."

A cultural design for democracy was further imagined, beginning in the late sixth century, for the democratic *demos*, to which they applied the name *the Athenians*. In the words of Christian Meier (1990: 144), "This meant that the overwhelming majority of the members of the polis, having previously known one another as neighbors, farmers, artisans, and fellow worshippers, now rediscovered one another as citizens and began to act, treat, and collaborate on a new level, with new mutual respect and new mutual expectations." To achieve their unifying goals, the Athenians crafted a popular culture that "supported the liberty and political capability of every citizen" (Pritchard 2010: 2). This change is reflected, perhaps most clearly, by the extension of *parrhesia* (freedom of speech) and *isegoria* (equal opportunity in debate) to the citizen population, including the rural peasantry, who were noted to join other citizens in the *ekklesia* (the people's assembly).

Freedom of speech was critical in the workings of the Athenian democracy. As Josiah Ober (1994: 103) describes it, the polity was "created and re-created through the collective processes of public discussion," a kind of open and egalitarian communication that was a far cry from the "deep horizontal cleavage [that] marked the world of Homeric poems" (Finley 1962: 61). As described by S. C. Humphreys (1978: 233), "the old aristocratic conception of *arete*, in which class attributes, status obligations, and more abstract moral qualities were inextricably mingled, was no longer adequate. Virtue had to be democratic, the same for all men; at the same time it had to be rational, adaptable to all circumstances" ("all men" has to be qualified, as foreigners and slaves were excluded, and women were afforded only limited recognition as active participants in civic life). The new egalitarianism recognized that virtue cannot be read entirely from a person's social standing; rather, virtue is an overtly social phenomenon that evolves from a person's actions in the social community. Further, the self is a conscious individual—a contingent cooperator. Although the overall assessment of human moral quality was generally pessimistic ("impelled by anger, hatred, or appetite . . . to give precedence to his own interests over the interests of others . . . states and individuals alike have a natural inclination to aggrandizement when an opportunity presents itself" in Dover [1974: 81–83]), still, for example, as Plato argued in the Republic, everyone is potentially endowed with the power to understand the nature of social virtue and achieve it, though many will not realize their potential.

Discourses on moral capacity were found in various contexts, including philosophy teaching; funerary orations and speeches; dramatic performances; epitaphs and dedication texts; *encomia* (virtue stories); and biographical narratives that, as A. Momigliano (1985: 88), points out, aimed to interpret the "inner character" of influential persons. Notions of democracy were expressed through a material culture, especially in the rebuilding of the civic space of the *agora*, where paintings glorified the achievements of the democracy in victories against the Persians, and in sculptures symbolizing liberating social change such as that portraying the slayers of the tyrant Hipparchus. At the same time traitors' *stelae* kept the names of miscreants in the public eye. An egalitarian ethic shaped the material world of families as well. As Ian Morris (1997: 102) describes it, after 500 BCE "there are virtually no rich graves or funerary monuments anywhere in Greece, and fifth-century houses hardly vary in size, decoration, plan, or finds."

Karl Marx was surprised to note that even though Classical Athens was an ancient and in some ways, in his eyes, a "primitive" society, nonetheless, its artistic achievements appeal to the modern viewer. Marx's reaction indicates his adherence to a dated and inadequate sequential evolutionist epistemology in which everything is thought to unfold in a determined historical sequence. The processualist epistemology I employ here, however, is not evolutionary, and, instead associates naturalism with collective action, irrespective of time period, technology, or other of the usual indicators of evolutionary "progress." Greek naturalistic art—especially sculpted figural images—is well known among art historians, and it is of interest to note that the turn to naturalism in this respect followed quickly after the mid-sixth-century BCE transition from the Archaic Period (characterized by its stereotypically heroic portrayals of kings), to the democratic *polis*. The turn to naturalism is first evident in the "Severe" or Early Classical style of highly realistic sculpture that depicted details of facial expressions as well as body position. The artistic goal was to communicate what Robin Osborne (2008: 31) describes as "manner and/or a motive" (in this same source he contrasts Greek Classical art with canonical Egyptian art, where the manner of portrayal of the body was "little more than another hieroglyphic sign"). By the fourth-century-BCE focal period in Athens, true portrait sculptures were made of even nonelite persons. The earliest Greek philosophical treatises on physiognomics were written at this same time. That collective action in state-building was processually related to artistic naturalism is evident in the fact that with the decline of the democratic polis, following the Hellenistic Macedonian conquest, ruler portrayals reverted to what James Breckenridge (1968: 130) refers to as the Greek "heroic tradition."

ROME (HIGH EMPIRE PERIOD, 69–192 CE)

Cultural patterns in some ways analogous to democratic Athens emerged beginning during the last century or two of the Roman Republican Period and were elaborated on by the time of the High Empire focal period. Roman cultural design looked back to Greece in spite of a Roman governing system built around the powerful office of *princeps* that would have been unacceptable in Classical Athens. This contradictory situation prompted novel discourses on morality. As Ronald Martin (1981) describes it, for example, the famous historian Tacitus, following in a tradition of other historians such as Cato and Livy, in his various texts asked the same question: "What is to be the public behavior of a Roman under what is nominally a republic, but, is, in fact, an autocracy?"

The life of Tacitus, a foreigner and commoner, illustrates social and cultural change from the prior Republican Period, which had been characterized by a sharp divide between a senatorial class and others, to a social environment featuring a stronger sense of the potential for meritocratic social advancement. In spite of his disadvantages, Tacitus became a famed orator and author and was given a senatorial appointment and consulship as a *novus homo*, or "new man," meaning he was the first in his family to have a senatorial appointment. We see the egalitarian impulse also in the ruler Hadrian's notion of *humanitas*, an argument for equal treatment for all that "paid little attention to the nobility's traditions" (Hannestad 1988: 196).

In spite of the notable political centralization surrounding the princeps, the Roman focal period featured a comparatively high level of collective action, and this corresponded with the growth of discourses surrounding themes of honor, religious piety, revival of custom, and rational analysis of the nature of virtue. A clear instance of the Greek influence in this period is the revival of veristic portraiture. This began under the reign of Augustus, who favored a return to Classical forms of sculptural representation; the practice was followed by later rulers of the focal period as what Breckenridge (1968: 217) calls "Flavian realism." Trajan's column, a monument to his death, sums up the main features of this artistic strategy. The column contains a lengthy panel reflecting a tradition of secular historical documentation in which "Deities hardly ever appear and when they do they do not mingle with mortals . . . The Emperor is portrayed like everyone else: he is the constant focus of the design, but neither of greater stature than, or different from the other" (Hannestad 1988: 167). Plebeian (commoner) themes are apparent in Roman art of the focal period including the burial monuments of freedmen depicting narratives of their life accomplishments, in contrast with the "traditional mythological and allegorizing motifs favored by the ruling classes" (Whitehead 1993: 319).

Venice (1290–1600 CE)

Venice was socially transformed, as were other Italian city-states, during the eleventh and twelfth centuries CE during a period of growing commercial activity—in fact, Venice emerged as one of the most important trade entrepôts, linking the African, European, and Western Asian trade circuits. Trade generated huge merchant fortunes, but the political system that was developed at this time emphasized high levels of cooperation based on a devotion to the values of the *comune Venetiarum*. In part, the collective system was a carryover of elements of Greco-Roman municipal government into Venetian political theory. Yet, many new elements of collective action were added as the polity's leadership struggled to maintain stability and solidarity in the context of a rapidly growing economy and an influx of ethnically and religiously diverse immigrants who were drawn to the advantages of a growing economy and a relatively stable and equitable form of governance.

As immigration increasingly shaped the social system, long-resident families established themselves as an ascripted noble class (the *patriciate*) that monopolized the policy-making privileges of the Gran Consiglio (Great Council), a move that precluded the possibility of open recruitment to many of the highest offices. However, closed recruitment was tempered by the fact that members of the immigrant component of the population (*popolani*) could aspire to become members of a middle social status (*cittadini originari*) through a lengthy process of naturalization, and, in turn, they were afforded opportunities for formal civic involvement in some capacities. The ideal of the comune Venetiarum was extended in some respects to the lower popolani class, as well, though they were barred from civic appointments. The famous Venetian carnival is also a testament to a valorization of equality. This rite of reversal provided commoners with an opportunity to ritualistically imitate and mock the wealthy and governing elite and in other ways invert the prevailing moral order—if only ritualistically for a few days. The governing elite also found it important to accommodate commoner needs, as commoners were prone to mount sometimes destructive oppositional movements.

In Venice, cultural production and institutional change aimed to enhance a widely shared sense of devotion to civic values that prioritized the collectivity over the individual. This practice was viewed as potentially challenging to apply in practice, however, given the Venetian understanding of the self as potentially a selfish being. For example, there was a presumption that officials will be corrupted by wealth, and this prompted the passage of numerous laws carefully defining the privileges and proper actions of the leading authority, the doge, and other officials. During the fourteenth and fifteenth centuries, numerous sumptuary laws were passed limiting overt displays of wealth, even regulating the opulence of private feasting, because in Venetian cultural design this kind of showiness indicated official corruption.

The Venetian state promoted an ethos of *mediocritas* that, as described by Blake de Maria (2010: x), was a dictum "favoring the visual promotion of state and society over individual accomplishment ... Realizing that visual imagery could be (ab)used for personal gain, the Venetian government advocated aesthetic restraint in the private realm." This created a cultural tension between civic devotion and commercial wealth, which is evident in Moretto da Brescia's *Portrait of a Young Man*, analyzed by Blake de Maria (Figure 11.4). Here, a wealthy young man looks directly at the viewer, his eyes and facial expression inviting the viewer to understand his discontent; the reason, is evident in his black velvet cap on which is inscribed, "alas. I desire too much."

A tension between privilege and civic devotion is also evident in the mode of representation of the doge, the chief administrative official, who was expected to act selflessly on behalf of polity. Correspondingly, up to the mid-fifteenth century, even though the northern Italian city-states, including Venice, are noted to have been important innovative centers in the development of portrait painting, the doges were not represented in this way. Eventually, however, portraits of the doges came to be accepted, perhaps because they were seen as an effective way to communicate the stern and forbidding demeanor expected of high governing officials.

FIGURE 11.4. Portrait of Conte Fortunato Martinengo Cesaresco, ca. 1542, Moretto da Brescia. "Alas I desire too much" is written on his cap in Greek. © National Gallery, London / Art Resource, NY.

Art also aimed to enhance the degree of devotion to the city and polity. This was expressed in works highlighting the magnificence and beauty of the city itself. Devotion to city placed pressure on Venetian artists to be innovative in how they depicted the city and its public processions, assemblies, regattas, and religious and

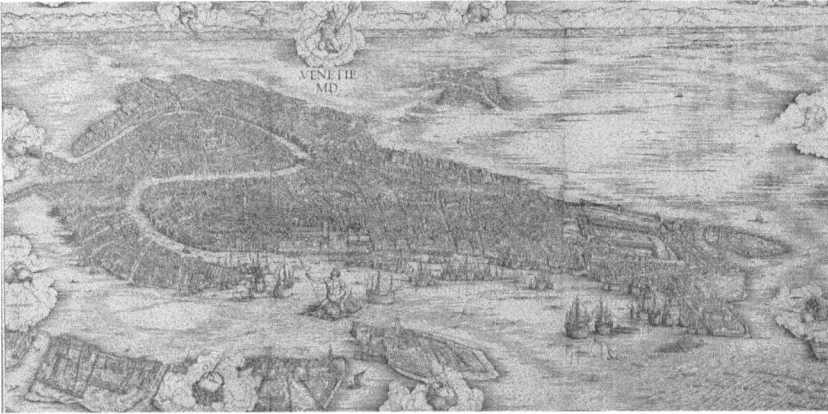

FIGURE 11.5. Jacopo de' Barbari, *View of Venice*, 1500. Copyright the British Museum, Department of Prints and Drawings.

civic rituals, the latter including the procession dedicated to the inauguration of the doges. The ducal precession, as described by Edward Muir (1981: 211) provided a veritable constitution for the polity:

> The sixteenth-century idealization of the Venetian Republic was thus in accord with its processional order . . . This order emphasized a continuity of institutionalized offices transcending any particular office-holder, it trumpeted the sovereignty of the doge . . . [and] . . . More than merely reinforcing the ideology of Venice, the ducal procession helped create that ideology by serving as a conscious, visible, synthesis of the parts of society: each symbol or person in the procession helped create that ideology . . . each symbol or person in the procession corresponded to a specific principle or institution; placed together and set in motion, they were the narrative outline for the myth of Venetian republicanism.

Figure 11.5 illustrates the creativity of artists charged to enhance the sense of the city's beauty and importance. The figure is Jacopo de' Barbari's *View of Venice*, which Naomi Miller (2000: 10) describes as a "stupendous cartographic achievement." Artists were motivated to find novel ways to depict Venetian life not as static portraits, but to capture a dynamic social process of collective action involving the entrainment of hundreds, or even thousands of persons. Figure 11.6 depicts one of these, the Feast of the Sensa, held on Ascension Day, but which had been turned into a largely civic ritual. During this event, the doge sailed in a ceremonial barge, with a large retinue, into the lagoon, where a ritual "reenacted Venice's marriage to the sea" (P. F. Brown 1997: 89). Large-scale gatherings (there were some sixteen

FIGURE 11.6. *The Feast of the Sensa*, by Jost Amman (ca. 1560). Graphische Sammlung der Staatsgalerie, Stuttgart.

annual processionals by the end of the sixteenth century) became an important element of the fabric of Venetian social life that even influenced its physical form. As described by Muir (1981: 209) the "Piazza San Marcos was . . . enlarged and embellished at various times to be more suitable for processions, thereby showing both the power of the republic to redesign the cityscape to suit its own purposes and the central importance of the ducal procession in Venetian public life."

In addition to the depiction of rituals, even prominent artists deviated from traditional forms of expression to devote their abilities to the depiction of the Venetian quotidian (Figure 11.7). For example, according to P. F. Brown (1988: 2), the art history community is in agreement that even one of the city's most renowned artists, Carpaccio, "subordinated the goal of religious story-telling to other concerns: to glorify the city of Venice; to delight the viewer with extravagant and irrelevant detail; to record life as it happened, without editorial intervention."

MUGHAL (1556–1658 CE)

A recent op-ed article in the *New York Times* claims that the turn to democracy in India has broken down what are described as the "primordial" systems of caste, tribe and religion, to open up the possibility that persons could rise up socially through their merits (December 16, 2012, SR1). But these same entailments of collective polity-building were evident centuries earlier during the reign of the Mughal emperors of the focal period. Their polity represents a phase of successful collective state-building in a region that was culturally diverse and that featured ancient cultural traditions not highly consistent with the aims of collective state-building. While Christianity, Buddhism, Jainism, and Judaism were all represented in the polity's

FIGURE 11.7. *The Rialto Bridge in Venice*, Michele Marieschi (1740). The State Hermitage Museum, St. Petersburg. Photograph © The State Hermitage Museum / photo by Vladimir Terebenin, Leonard Kheifets, Yuri Molodkovets.

cultural mix, among other religions, the prevailing political theories in South Asia were influenced by the Vedic texts of Hindu religion. Here key cultural foundations for collective action were lacking; most notably, there were no prescriptions for institutional controls over rulers who, sacralized by the Brahmana priesthood, governed largely unaccountably. The prevalence of hereditary rank in the caste system precluded open recruitment into positions of governing authority. In addition, in Hindu texts the self is not well theorized. Biographical narratives, for example, were rarely produced, and when they were they tended only to stereotype and romanticize. The traditional artistic production of South Asia only rarely included accurate individual portraiture or other forms of naturalism.

Lacking much of a local cultural framework for collective polity-building, Akbar—the grandson of the Mughal founder Babur—and Akbar's son Jahangir were innovative in adapting existing forms of cultural expression and in creating new cultural designs to align their practices with collective strategy. The frequent selection of even high officials from across ranks, classes, and religions points to an egalitarian notion of the self that served to weaken both the traditional aristocracy and the caste system. At the same time, a guiding philosophy was a cosmopolitan religious ecumenism they termed the "universal peace" (*sulh-I kull*), which was consistent with their well-documented propensity for open recruitment, though this policy was pursued in the absence of a Chinese-style civil examination system for which there was no local precedent. Akbar introduced new measures to enhance communication and intermingling among members of the polity's socially and culturally diverse population, even proposing a synthetic calendar (*tarikh-ilahi*) to amalgamate all the diverse calendars in use in South Asia.

Akbar also emphasized the importance of public reasoning to enhance cooperation in a pluralistic society. As Amartya Sen (2005: 16) describes his actions, Akbar supported "dialogues between adherents of different faiths . . . [his] . . . overarching thesis is that 'the pursuit of reason' rather than 'reliance on tradition' is the way to address difficult problems of social harmony . . . [including] . . . a robust celebration of reasoned dialogues." Questions surrounding moral virtues also were topics of interest. In this regard I point to the repurposing of Sufistic poetry to become a medium for the consideration of "mainly . . . ethical . . . [and] . . . philosophical doctrines" (Thackston 2002: 96). An etiquette literature (*akhlag*) was developed that provided moral exemplars for use in the Mughal court, but also was intended to serve as a model for laudable social behavior in the broader society. One new literary genre originating during Akbar's reign has retained its popularity to the present day. The "Akbar and Birbal" stories are interesting moral tales in how they depict Birbal, a Hindu and high official, as a valued confidant of the ruler.

The uniformitarian aspect of Mughal folk theory of mind was expressed in new modes of artistic production sponsored originally by Akbar. One of the most active areas of new cultural design was the introduction of an innovative style of manuscript illustration that art historians regard as one of the most notable phases of artistic change in South Asian history. Akbar himself provided the major impetus for new ideas about the social role of artistic representation, and he and his son Jahangir, especially, became major art patrons and showered prominent painters with cultural honors. Although the new format was a synthesis of elements of Persian and Indian art, it deviated from the prevailing tradition of devotional painting to embrace a highly secular naturalism that art historians refer to as "Mughal Realism," especially in reference to its characteristic "animated expression on faces" (Beach 1987: 17). As Ananda Coomaraswamy (1975: 74) expresses it, "Portraiture is the typical mode of Mughal painting" (and this, as Donald Brown [1988: 31] notes, was in spite of the traditional Muslim opposition to portraiture). According to Andrew Topsfield (2008: 7), "court portraiture began to develop in Akbar's reign. This was a Mughal innovation in India, where kings and courtiers had traditionally been depicted as idealized types rather than as distinct individuals with personal flaws and peculiarities" (Figure 11.8).

Mughal painting also extended naturalism outward from the court in quotidian and egalitarian senses to depict, in the images available to me, variously, holy

FIGURE 11.8. Sketch of Akbar as an old man. © British Library, London, India Office Library, Johnson 57.1.]

men, youths, a gardener, a student and teacher, musicians, and peasants, along with servants and soldiers in palace service, all with individual features of face and garb painted with the same verisimilitude as a high official. In addition to its subject matters and naturalism, Mughal painting also served to foreground kinds of social actions appropriate in a society with a strongly collective political system. It is important that subjects, including the emperors, typically are depicted while entrained, closely sharing attention with others. Even the emperors are shown in animated and attentive discourses with a variety of kinds of people (Figure 11.9). Paintings were also a medium for the telling of moral tales, such as the famous "the slave who fed a starving dog" story (in spite of his own poverty) (Figure 11.10).

It is not always clear whether Mughal art was displayed outside the official palaces, but even if not I suggest it may have played a role in fostering collective action in the state's policies. The manuscript and folio paintings were of small size, probably indicating they were referred to and enjoyed in intimate settings, and, evidently, most were kept in the palace libraries. This tells us that artistic production was not meant for broad appeal or effect among the general population. Yet it might have played a role as a cultural tool in Mughal political strategies, specifically as a way to socialize those persons who were in training for official offices (Figure 11.11). The paintings provided very detailed and subtle visual cues regarding the appropriate kinds of egalitarian attitudes and behaviors, the lifeblood of any collective regime.

MING DYNASTY (MOSTLY LATE FOURTEENTH CENTURY AND FIFTEENTH CENTURY CE)

The source, or meaning, of the Ming dynastic name is uncertain, but Craig Clunas (2007: 10) argues it was the first Chinese dynasty named after a visual quality, namely, "shining," or "bright." Such a name would be apt given that the dynasty's cultural architects gave much attention to developing what Clunas (1997) calls a culture of visuality, "bearing on what to look at, how to look and how to

FIGURE 11.9. *Akbar and a Dervish*, 'Abd al-Samad, Lahore, Mughal, ca. 1586. Image courtesy of the Aga Khan Trust for Culture, AKM141.

FIGURE 11.10. *The Slave Who Fed a Dog*, Kesu Das, Mughal, 1595.
Reproduced with permission of the Bodleian Library, shelf mark: MS.
Elliott 254, fol. 27a.

FIGURE 11.11. *Sansar Chand of Kangra Admiring Pictures with his Courtiers,* attributed to Purkhu, Mughal, ca. 1800. Reproduced with permission of the Museum Rietberg, Zürich, Bequest Balthasar Reinhart © Photo: Rainer Wolfsberger.

conceptualize the act of looking" (138). Innovative practices in this regard included, for example, a new format for official portraits, but is evident in other venues; for example, judicial trials were routinely conducted in public for all to see, and the official court gazette (the Veritable Records) allowed a view onto the deliberations of the high governing councils. The Ming founder specified the choreography of new public rituals, paying close attention to how participants should be entrained. The interest in entrainment is also evident in a category of paintings of the period referred to as "garden gatherings" depicting groups engaged in conversation, and other kinds of narrative scenes were commonly painted.

The Ming Period saw an increase in public writing, including signs, placards, flags, inscribed stelae, public lists of persons who committed shameful acts, and commercial handbills and banners. There was a growing market for paintings, including reprints of classic paintings, even among commoners (Figure 11.12), and painting manuals were widely circulated. One venue for the expression of new visualization perspectives was through printed media, which experienced rapid growth during the fourteenth and fifteenth centuries, including illustrated works. Technological improvements in book production made books more appealing and widely available, including color printing, improvements in woodcut illustrations, copper movable type, and woodcut facsimiles of early editions. Morality books (*shan-shu*) stressed "the internalization of values and moral autonomy" (Rawski 1985: 15). A pictorial biography of Confucius, a Ming innovation, was in wide circulation, and there were illustrated encyclopedias depicting the Ming rulers.

Rural lifeways were culturally valorized during the Ming Dynasty (as Clunas [1996: 55] puts it, "The overwhelming moral authority accorded to agricultural production as the *ben*, the 'roots' of society in the traditional order of political economy is too widely recognized to need further discussion"). This quotidian cultural preference is evident in painting of the focal period (but which is evident also in the last decades of the prior, Yüan Dynasty), which featured the form of naturalism in which commoners and quotidian themes often were represented (Figures 11.13 and 11.14). The turn to the quotidian included encyclopedias and works on agriculture that depicted rural people and work themes. A long-standing Chinese tradition of landscape painting was carried into the dynasty. But, in reviewing this body of work from published sources, I noted that artists interjected quotidian themes into their works more frequently than during prior and less collectively organized dynasties. To evaluate the degree of cultural shift, I systematically analyzed a large number of landscape paintings to compare Ming art with that of the prior Sung and Yüan Dynasties (I report on the method and results of the statistical analysis in Appendix B, section 7). By comparison with Sung and Yüan, I found that Ming artists did more frequently place subjects such as fishermen, peasants, rural houses, and marketplaces in their landscape scenes. This artistic change is of interest because, since few of the artists in question were sponsored by official sources, it illustrates that Ming Period culture change was more than a reflection of official doctrines. Evidently, motivated intellectuals such

FIGURE 11.12. *Village Painter Showing His Wares*, anonymous, sixteenth century. Reproduced with permission of the Freer Gallery of Art, Smithsonian Institution, Washington, DC: Gift of Charles Lang Freer, F1916.554.

FIGURE 11.13. *Gardeners,* Shen Chou (1427–1509). Reprinted with permission of the Nelson-Atkins Museum of Art, Kansas City, Missouri.

FIGURE 11.14. *Street Scenes in a Time of Peace,* Zhu Yu (Zhu Junbi), fourteenth century, ink and colors on paper. Kate S. Buckingham Endowment, 1952.8, The Art Institute of Chicago (image number 00031907–01).

as artists and novelists labored alongside innovative state-builders to promulgate a cultural design consistent with the egalitarian ideals of a collective system. I would also point out that they did so in spite of the elite art theory of the period that was strongly opposed to "mere" representation, because, in its practitioners' view, artistic production should be a largely symbolic system understood only by the highly educated.

The turn to naturalism and the quotidian is consistent with the view of the self that was elaborated on during this period. The Ming founder and others who constructed a highly collective polity benefitted from preexisting Confucianist notions of the self as a contingent cooperator. But state-building involved more than the carrying of traditional ideas and practices into a new dynasty. Recall that just prior to, and during the Early and Middle Ming Dynasty, innovative neo-Confucianist philosophers rejected the spiritual and outworldly notions of Buddhism that had entered China during earlier dynasties, in which salvation requires the renouncing of all that is personally motivating. This metaphysical view was recognized by Ming theoreticians as unsuited to a highly collective polity, and they substituted for it the more secular and materialist cultural design that recognized the rational self and "the moral worth of the everyday world" (Elvin 1985: 172–73), for example, in the claim that one source of the moral being is the physical labor of peasant production.

In addition to representation of the quotidian, another dimension of naturalism evident at this time was the growing influence of realistic portraiture and associated ideas about how to interpret portraits (the Chinese word for portrait, *xiang*, is etymologically related to words denoting physiognomy, fortune-telling, and "fate reading" [from Vinograd 1992: 5–6]). Richard Vinograd (1992) details the lengthy history of Chinese portrait painting, dating it as far back as the Han Dynasty 2,000 years ago. Historically, he notes, prior to the Ming Dynasty, portraiture was a contested issue. Similarly, according to Hui-Shu Lee (2010: 67), historically "imperial portraiture was an intensely guarded and sensitive matter" (in this work, Hui-Shu Lee analyzes a small number of technically competent Sung Dynasty ruler portraits that were intended only for viewing by the ruler's family but that were not an established aspect of Sung political culture). The ambivalence concerning veristic portraiture appears to have dissolved just prior to and during the Ming Dynasty. Correspondingly, the principal Chinese text on physiognomy dates to the fourteenth century, and the first known manual-like text providing technical advice for drawing the face was published at almost exactly the time as the start date for the dynasty. The use of anatomically accurate official portraiture was an important Ming Dynasty innovation, and Clunas (1997: 98–99) argues that ruler images were widely distributed in society. I interpret this new social technology as one intended to depict officials, including emperors, in a rather stark but highly natural fashion to engage the viewer's perceptual ability to read the official's mind and by doing that to provoke a sense of connectedness to him personally. This cultural turn represented a departure from traditional Chinese modes of representation of rulers and of court etiquette, which associated rulership with numerology, geomancy, and the cosmic structure of five elemental phases of nature.

FIGURE 11.15. Portrait of Wen Zhengming, from the S. M. Nickerson Fund, 1957.552. Reproduced with permission of the Art Institute of Chicago.

There are two elements of visual interest in official Ming portraits that, I suggest, reflect a recognition of some aspects of what is now known about the neurophysiology and perceptual psychology of face viewing (Figure 11.15). These portraits make little use of what Alfred Gell (1998: 132) calls "outwardness," by which he means communicating about a subject principally through symbolic expression and opening up possibilities for misrepresentation of a living individual, for example, when leaders are depicted as extraordinarily beautiful. By contrast, most Chinese official portraits are virtually symbol free and highly veristic. The subjects are shown seated in front of a plain background, facing the viewer directly, the face close up, gaze forward, and eyes, especially, shown in considerable detail. The images are not designed to provoke a positive neural response to facial attractiveness—instead, actual persons are depicted, not idealized beautiful people.

Eric Kandel (2012: 337–38) points out that an artist aiming to maximize the viewer's ability to do face analysis will aim for a simplicity of depiction so the viewer's eyes will devote more data-gathering eye scans to crucial features of the face, especially the eyes. Cognitive psychologists are well aware that eye gaze is the most important nonverbal cue that is deployed for mind reading, and direct or dyadic gaze provides the most potential for gaze analysis. Studies of how a human eye perceives a face show that while the eyes make continual scanning passes over the person and associated contextual features (clothing, etc.), for normal persons the most detailed and frequently repeated scans are of the eyes, in particular, and secondarily the mouth and hands. These highly accurate and individualized Ming images place importance on the face and especially on gaze; even the hands typically are not visible or are only a minor element in the image, perhaps to invite the viewer to devote more visual attention to the face.

STRUCTURAL DESIGNS FOR CONSENSUS IN THE FACE OF PLURALITY

> Dualism need not serve to exclude and separate, but rather could be
> thought of as a way to "work together from different angles to help
> us make sense of the world" (Larmore 2004: 52, commenting on the
> anti-dualist sentiments expressed by late nineteenth and early twenti-
> eth-centuries pragmatist philosophers Peirce, James, and Dewey).

> "Expressive behavior which inverts, contradicts, abro-
> gates . . . presents an alternative to commonly held cul-
> tural codes, values, and norms" (Babcock 1978: 14)

Chantal Mouffe (2000), like other political sociologists, addresses a problem facing contemporary democracies: How can a democratic state thrive when there is tension between the need for a consensual understanding of the common good, while, at the same time, respecting the rights of interest groups? A similar paradox surrounding consensus and plurality will arise in any attempt to bring cooperative order in the context of social and cultural heterogeneity. This is true even in the premodern condition in which ideas of individual liberty and the rights of interest groups are not as highly developed as they are in some recent democracies. In the following I draw insights from a modified version of the "structural analysis" pioneered by cultural anthropologists, such as Claude Lévi-Strauss, as a way to identify strategies by which polity-builders addressed the tension between consensus and plurality.

Structural analysis is one way to discover how architects of culture devise schemes in which the subtle and complex variation of a social domain (in the examples below, pertaining to social differentiation) is subsumed into a small number of interrelated but logically opposed (or "symbolically inverted") categories, often expressed as a duality. The categories are then hierarchically structured so as to distinguish groups or categories of persons in relation to concepts such as culture/nature, high/low, pure/impure, or exalted/base. As Douglas (1966) argues, to insinuate meaning into this kind of cultural design sets up possibilities for claims about status and power. An example is when an elite are associated with a spiritually pure domain of "culture" while lower-ranked persons are viewed as living closer to a state of "nature" and thus stand as a potentially transgressive source of spiritual pollution that may threaten the vitality of elite society. In these circumstances transgression must be carefully managed through a system of behavioral rules. Transgression-avoiding rules are evident in the case of the Hindu caste system with its cleavages between higher (pure) and lower (polluted) castes mandated by rules limiting possibilities for intercaste touching or the shared use of space.

Under conditions of collective action, however, I found that cultural architects, in some cases, did create structural-oppositional cultural designs. However, they did it in a way that, unlike the caste system, had the goals of enhancing possibilities for consensual understanding, of mitigating the force of social cleavage, and of expanding opportunities for social intermingling. Through this kind of cultural reasoning it was possible to conceptualize the linked elements of a structural system, such as culture/nature, in terms of complementarity rather than opposition, and in a way that envisions how the interaction of the two could be understood as a source of fertile tension beneficial to the collectivity rather than as a potentially dangerous transgressive force. I illustrate the role of complementarity in cultural design by comparing two of the polities in the comparative sample that featured notable elements of collective action: Athens and Aztec.

DUAL LOGICS: CENTER AND MARGIN, DAY AND NIGHT

"Dionysiac worship . . . inverts, temporarily, the norms and practices of aristocratic society [and makes it possible] . . . to think about an alternative community, one open to all, where status differentiation can be limited or eliminated, and where speech can be truly free." (Connor 1996: 222)

"Tragedy and comedy do not simply reverse the norms of society but inculcate a questioning of the very basis of these norms, the key structures of opposition on which 'norm' and 'transgression' rest." (Goldhill 1990: 127)

In both Aztec and Athenian cultural codes a dual structure of center and margin encoded social and cultural difference, most notably the cleavage between an elite and the mass of the population. In both cases difference was expressed through a logic of spatial order and associated aspects of environment, production, and exchange. Aztec cultural design identified an elite domain of states and its urbanized and literate populations of Nahua peoples. This domain, situated in the wet and lush southern agricultural zones of Central Mexico, was contrasted with the desiccated north that was the habitat of the Chichimec hunters and gatherers thought to live close to a state of nature. In Athenian thought the mountainous zones (*oros*) and their characteristic labors of farmer, shepherd, and even merchant, were set in contrast with the flatter plains and their urbanized and politically structured *poleis*.

The center, in both Athenian and Aztec cultural designs, is identified with the rational logics of elite populations and with their precise calendars, defined geographical spaces, and urban organization. The margin is associated with a mentality that while not necessarily inferior to the center is seen as a different one with more tendency to valorize ecstatic states of being and exhibiting a kind of cunning, guileful, potentially deceptive intelligence that challenges the "truth" of the center's preferred form of highly structured rationality. For example, in an often-repeated mythic tale, Tezcatlipoca, the god most associated with the Chichimecs, brought the collapse of the great Nahua-Toltec civilization by tricking its ruler into debased behaviors not normally associated with the governing elite, including drinking to the point of inebriation and, perhaps, even committing incest with his sister.

In both Athens and Aztec, marginal places and states of being were, to use the phraseology of Jacques Galinier and his coauthors, "translated into the terms of the night" (Galinier et al. 2010: 821). This kind of symbolic system identifies multiple forms of mentality that are presented in terms of an oppositional cultural logic that associates daytime awakeness with a center's structured orderliness, whereas the margin is associated with night and the state of sleeping that are associated with "reversal, destruction . . . reconstruction" (830) and metamorphosis. For example, the principal gods of the margins—the Aztec deity Tezcatlipoca, and the Greek gods Hermes ("the thief") and Dionysus—were "tricksters" whose shifting, elusive persona were seen as challenges to the center's established system of ascribed statuses. However, in both cases, "tricksters" functioned as Barbara Babcock (1978: 29) envisions, not as a way to impose a permanent state of disorder on a well-ordered population. Instead, "clown or trickster . . . never demands that we totally reject the orders of our sociocultural worlds; but neither do these figures simply provide us with a cautionary note as to what would happen should the 'real' world turn into a perpetual circus or festival . . . Rather, they remind us of the arbitrary condition of imposing an order on our environment and experience, even while they enable us to see certain features of that order more clearly."

To an Athenian, the margin was the domain of darkness, the underworld, the left (evil) side of the body, females, wild nature, and ecstatic states of being, while the polis center was symbolically male, rationally ordered, and associated with the celestial rather than underworld domain (the patron god of the center, Apollo, was hostile to ecstatic states of being). To the Aztecs, the margin was associated with the night sky, the moon, the jaguar, and stellar cults as opposed to the solar cults of the urbanized center. Notions of "reversal, destruction and reconstruction" and metamorphosis associated with the marginal peoples align with the egalitarian idea that little about a person can be assumed because the self may transcend existential boundaries, as is evident in one of Tezcatlipoca's avatars, Moyocoyotzin, "he who creates himself" (as translated by Doris Heyden [1991: 189]). In Greek mythology, another of the deities of the margin, the goddess Artemis, was a transcendent figure like Dionysus, a goddess of liminality who exemplified the potential of humans to undergo transformation and transitory states of being.

It bears mentioning that in both Greek and Aztec civilizations, the mentality of the margin came to be associated as well with the behavior of persons in the marketplace, where the potential exists to gain wealth and renown through trade and profit. Norman Brown (1947: 108–12) carries this idea further when he argues that the growth of commerce was the stimulus that brought the margin's cultural design into mainstream Athenian culture and ritual. This is evident in part in the way that Hermes was transported directly into the civic center of the polity, as a deity of the *agora* market zone, which also became the civic center of the new democracy. As Brown (1947: 108) put it, "Hermes' intrusion into the *agora* paralleled his intrusion into the world of culture." Analogously, the intrusion of market-related symbolism into cultural design in Central Mexico is first evident after about 1000 CE at the archaeological site of Tula, Hidalgo, Mexico, thought to be an important site of the ancient Nahua-Toltec civilization. Here, the earliest known representation of Tezcatlipoca is paired with a representation of Topiltzin Quetzalcoatl, symbolically associated with nobility and rulership, who, together with Tezcatlipoca, created the current world. In the same public building a frieze in a colonnaded hall is interpreted by Cynthia Kristan-Graham (1993) as a procession of merchants and evidence for what she calls Tula's "business narrative."

RITUAL AND SOCIAL COORDINATION

In his book *Rational Ritual: Culture, Coordination, and Common Knowledge*, Michael Suk-Young Chwe notes that public ritual is a social practice that "generates common knowledge" (Chwe 2001: 3), and thus contributes to solving the problem of how people in a group are able to coordinate their actions. This is an important insight that contributes to our knowledge of polity-building and collective action, but I depart somewhat from Chwe's interesting presentation by pointing out that to contrast more and less collective polities, which is not part of his discussion, is also to contrast different forms of and purposes for public rituals. To illustrate the importance of understanding this difference, I briefly summarize and then compare three public rituals, one in traditional Bali (a segmentary polity that scored low on collective action), a series of rituals that were part of the annual ritual calendar of the Aztec, and one of the prominent rituals in Classical Athens. From these data I identify two forms of public ritual—spectacle and civic ritual—each of which has different social purposes and whose cultural designs aimed to trigger very different forms of psychobiological response.

Bali (later Mengwi polity, 1823–1871 CE)

Structural analysis of the sort I used to elucidate aspects of Athenian and Aztec cultures is less suited to understanding the cultural design of Bali, where it is emotion, rather than a logical structure of symbolic dualism, that is at the heart of cultural design. In Bali the symbol-rich and stimuli-rich public rituals are best characterized as lavish spectacles that transported participants and observers into what ritual theorists describe as a state of "religious experience" or "numinence" (defined as a strongly "emotional attitude toward counterintuitive representations" [Pyysiäinen 2001: 70]). The purpose of these magnificent, high-arousal spectacles was to reaffirm the central social fact of Balinese political culture, namely, that the privileges and powers accorded to rulers (lords) are rooted in a ruler's centrality to an extramundane and primordial cosmic order. Rulers, thought of as a corporeal gods, were symbolically at the center of the four-cornered universe represented by *padmasana*, or throne or lotus seat of Siva, associated with the potency of *lingga* (phallus of Siva), and with a divinely inspired charisma, *sekti* (religious power). The latter was reflected by the possession of royal regalia ("sacred heirlooms"), including a renowned *kris* (sword) (Geertz 1980: 104–20).

The most elaborate state spectacles confirming ruler divinity took the form of days-long funeral processions of Balinese lords. During the rite's final phase there are, as Geertz (1980: 118) describes it, "three enormous outbreaks of symbolic energy": the procession, the tower, and the fire. The first phase began in the *puri*, the lord's palace, which itself was a sacred symbol and sanctified space featuring a design, like a Hindu temple, that architecturally replicated the cosmic structure. The deceased ruler was removed from the palace and placed atop a massive and elaborately decorated multistoried funeral tower. This structure, whose shape symbolized the structure of the cosmos, was carried in a lengthy procession that riveted the attention of thousands or even tens of thousands of "astonished" spectators. As Geertz (1980: 118–19) describes it,

> The procession was a clamorous and disorderly affair throughout. It began with a mock battle between the men trying to carry the corpse over the palace wall to place it on the tower and the crowd outside seeking to prevent them from doing so. It ended . . . with a series of similar battles as the corpse was brought down from the tower . . . to be set upon the pyre. In between, there was near hysteria: the wild spinning of the tower "to confuse the spirit"; the pushing, shoving, and tumbling in the mud; the laughing scramble for coins and baubles; the relentless clanging of the war music.

The sensuousness and symbolic power of funerary rituals exemplified the character of other Balinese cultural designs that, to again quote Geertz (1980: 103), "cast their most comprehensive ideas of the way things ultimately are, and the way that men should therefore act, into immediately apprehended sensuous symbols—into a lexicon of carvings, flowers, dances, melodies, gestures, chants, ornaments, temples, postures, and masks—rather than into a discursively apprehended, ordered set of explicit 'beliefs.'".

AZTEC (1428–1521 CE)

My discussion focuses on rituals termed Quecholli, staged during late October and early November (at the end of the harvest and beginning of the dry season); Toxcatl, staged during the final month of the dry season; and Etzalcualiztli, which followed Toxcatl and signified the onset of a new agricultural cycle with the arrival of the seasonal rains. Quecholli and the Toxcatl to Etzalcualiztli transition served to commemorate the important role played by the rustic Chichimec peoples of the northern desert regions, and their cultural heritage, within the context of the highly urbanized Nahua-Aztec society. Tezcatlipoca, symbolically associated with the northern desert peoples, was a central player in these events, which were initiated in or took place in relation to a part of the main ceremonial concourse of the imperial capital of Tenochtitlan built to represent a desertlike garden. This faux desert environment situated ritual action in a rustic setting that sharply contrasted with the surrounding architectural opulence of the concourse's public buildings and the nearby palaces of high officials. In the Quecholli rite, the rustic aspect of the ritual was further enhanced when the participants, including the Aztec ruler, made a procession leaving the garden to travel out of the city, along a path strewn with pine needles, to a mountaintop shrine at the edge of the region called Zacatepetl (place of the Zacate Mountain, "where mountain grass is spread" [translation by Johanna

Broda 1991: 83]), which is, again, a reference to origins of the Chichimec peoples in the barren mountains of the region's geographical fringes.

The Toxcatl, occurring at the end of the dry season, transitioned into a fertility and agricultural rite symbolizing the onset of Etzalcualiztli, the period of earthly renewal. Doing this brought a shift from an emphasis on Tezcatlipoca adoration to an emphasis on the deity Huitzilopochtli, whose physical presence was represented by a figure made of a corn-amaranth paste representing the principal grain crop, maize (it is interesting to note that Huitzilopochtli, in many respects the principal deity of the imperial center and the one most strongly associated with its noble rulers, was at the same time recognized as an avatar of Tezcatlipoca). The transition from Toxcatl to the fertility-themed rite centered on Huitzilopochtli is best understood in terms of a spiritual metamorphosis between two states of being of Tezcatlipoca in the same way the ritual is a narrative about the possibilities for achieving a transcendent state of being. As María Elena Bernal-García (2007: 108) puts it, at "the desert garden the Mexica began to retrace their hazardous migration from Aztlan to the Basin of Mexico, albeit through a religious ritual . . . They knew that as the corn-amaranth paste became Huitzilopochtli's own flesh and bones . . . the roaming path taken during their migration had miraculously turned unorganized time and formless space into precise calendars, defined geographical places, and urban organization."

ATHENS (403–322 BCE)

State-sponsored festivals played a critical role in the civic life of the Athenian polis, as indicated by the very full calendar of annual events (at least 120 days of each year). Next to the Panathenaia, which honored Athena Polias—the Athenian patron goddess—the most important rite was the Great Dionysia festival at Athens held during a month named after the goddess Artemis, a deity of the margins whose symbolic references are to metamorphoses and liminality. As described by Paul Cartledge (1985), the festival started by placing a statue of Dionysus at a temple on the road from Athens to Eleutherai to signify the rite's origins in that distant community. In the procession that followed, some participants carried models of erect phalluses, the fertility symbol of Dionysus, but also perhaps alluding to the phallus-like stone markers of rural boundary or border situations, where strangers could come together safely, including border markets, which were symbolically associated with Hermes.

In Athens, the grand procession was an ecumenical affair that included citizens as well as noncitizens; Cartledge (1985: 120) notes that "even prisoners were released from custody on bail." Following the procession, the multiday rite included among its elements parades that celebrated "both military patriotism and a kind of welfare-state democratic paternalism," at the same time that important civic business was conducted in public such as "the renewal of a treaty, perhaps, or the proclamation of honors for individual citizens" (121). Following these events were four days of performances consisting of tragedies and comedies that took place in a vast theater that could hold up to 17,000 persons. The plays addressed moral and political issues of "immediate, contemporary relevance to the Athenian public" (Cartledge 1985: 126). Interestingly, the theater design has been interpreted by scholars to symbolize the agrarian origins of Dionysus, as the performance space was circular in shape and thus similar to a grain-threshing floor. And, the bowl-shaped half-circle design of the theater is interpreted as being highly suited to the civic intentions of the performances. This design, which would have maximized the degree of participant intervisibility, as Ober (2008: 201, following Chwe 2001: 30–33) puts it, was "well suited to the deliberative learning processes of democratic self-governance." Lastly, in the true spirit of Athenian democracy, an assembly was convened at the rite's end in which complaints could be lodged about the conduct of the officials charged with organizing the festival.

SPECTACLE AND CIVIC RITUAL

Any turn to collective action will create a fertile ground both for argumentative discourses about human nature and morality, and for innovative thinking and new cultural production aimed at transforming entrenched cultural designs into new forms of shared understanding. In this situation, Michael Suk-Young Chwe's (2001: 3) point is apt that public ritual "generates common knowledge" and thus facilitates coordination between disparate groups. However, there are varying kinds of rituals and varying kinds of common knowledge and coordination that will be produced through ritual action. While no simple typological scheme can properly capture all the nuances of variation in ritual practices, to add substance to my comparative exercise I follow Stanley Tambiah's (1985: 135) sense that some rituals will fit most clearly in a class he calls "constitutive" acts. These are acts that serve to reaffirm that which is bound by convention and thus not subject to conscious evaluation. Balinese political ritual realizes the constitutive goal of reaffirming the central and unquestionable fact of Balinese kingship, namely, the sanctified status of the corporeal god-kings.

Ritual achieves the constitutive goal by flooding the senses of the "astonished" participants with repeated and redundant messages that limit any possibility or rationally considering alternative understandings of what is being certified. Neurobiologically, this ensues when, overwhelmed by the multiple sensory inputs of spectacle, there is less activity in the exhausted left prefrontal portion of the neocortex, which normally inhibits emotional response in the amygdala. As a result, participants in such a sensory-rich and chaotic scene enter into an emotionally charged state of numinence because, as Daniel Goleman (2013: 35) expresses it, "we're most prone to emotions driving focus when . . . we are distracted, or when we're overwhelmed by information." My suggestion is that spectacle has the power to persuade persons to accede to a social reality predicated on dominance and privilege. It does this by inhibiting the rational appraisal of messages encoded in the ritual, in this case, the centrality of rulers to the cosmic structure and to the governance of society.

By contrast, I would situate the Aztec and Greek rituals I described within the category that Tambiah identifies as regulative acts. These acts, to quote Tambiah (1985: 136) "orient and regulate a practical or technical activity . . . without actually constituting it." In the Aztec and Athenian cases, the rituals do not directly reproduce anything approaching what would be considered the central structural element of their respective political systems; in each case that assemblage of elements is quite complex, residing in the rules governing the behavior of principals, specifying the roles of authorities, accommodating citizen voice, and other related matters. Nor is it likely that the rituals would have "astonished" their participants, as in the Balinese case; certainly a processional path paved with pine needles and a god statue made of corn dough were not designed to trigger powerful emotional responses in the subcortical circuitry of the viewers' brains. Instead, Athenian and Aztec ritual cycles were civic rituals that stimulated thinking about the polity by providing a narrative account of notions that are foundational to the society's collective functionality. In particular, they served to underscore the fact that there are, in a sense, multiple but equally valid readings of the culture.

In Aztec and Athenian societies, important civic ritual cycles situated those representing the margins, the rustic and the rural, into society's mainstream social and cultural fabrics. For example, in both cases the "trickster" gods, Tezcatlipoca and Dionysus, though they were potentially transgressive and marginal figures, and thus potentially sources of evil or spiritual pollution, did not symbolize the irrational "primitive" or "savage" mind. Instead, they are represented as possessing an admirable mentality of the rural person that was perhaps heterodox and guileful but at the same time was recognized to be cunning, adaptive, and quick thinking. Notions like this exemplify how both Athenian and Aztec cultural architects searched for ways to convert hierarchically structured dualities into sources for consensus rather than division.

RELIGION IN THE PROCESS OF COLLECTIVE ACTION

"All the power of civil government relates only to men's civil interests,
is confined to the care of the things of this world, and hath nothing

to do with the world to come ... [and] ... no private person has any
right in any manner to prejudice someone in his civil enjoyments
because he is of another church or religion." (John Locke 1689)

"Akbar laid the foundations of secular legal structure and religious neutrality of the state, which included the duty to ensure
that 'no man be interfered with on account of religion, and anyone is allowed to go over to a religion that pleases him.'" (Amartya
Sen 2005: 18, describing policies of the Mughal ruler Akbar)

The evolutionary psychologist David Sloan Wilson, like other biomathematical researchers, argues that religion has played a role in the evolution of human
cooperation because, as he puts it, "Religions exist primarily for people to achieve
together what they cannot achieve alone" (Wilson 2002: 159). However, I suggest
that in the context of complex societies and, especially in relation to the possibilities for creating a society in the form of a collective civil unit, some forms of religious practice could have negative outcomes. For one, as Roy Rappaport (1978)
argues, social conventions that are sanctified—like the Balinese notion of rulership
discussed above—are not likely to be challenged, potentially limiting the kind of
rational evaluation of persons and institutions that is a central social fact of collective action. By contrast, in the Aztec and Athenian rituals discussed, key concepts
pertaining to social and cultural difference were manifested symbolically, in part, by
references to deities such as Tezcatlipoca and Dionysus. Yet, neither can be seen to
sanctify particular persons or offices. These examples suggest the possibility that the
role of religion and ritual will be different in the case of collective action by contrast
with the more autocratic societies.

Max Weber saw the beginning of Western modernity when people challenged
the idea of a divine and preordained social order. Americans often associate this
kind of secularism with Roger Williams's famous call to separate church and state,
made some 350 years ago in Puritan Massachusetts, which became a cornerstone of
the US Constitution. Yet, similar ideas had been proposed in other times and places,
as the quotes above indicate. In what follows I investigate the interplay between
collective action and religious belief and practice, making the argument that to construct highly cooperative polities, Western or not, will entail a degree of separation
of government from religion, or what is sometimes referred to as a "problematization" of religion and polity-building.

In the social sciences, religious problematization has been associated with the
civilizational traditions of the so-called Axial Age. According to this cultural evolutionist perspective, the path to modernity was first paved by a revolutionary

rethinking of the relationship between religion and politics, most notably by rejecting rule of "god-kings" that had been common in the old-order archaic states. New philosophical and religious ideas of the Axial Age began as early as 500 BCE in such diverse streams of thought as Confucianism and other Chinese philosophical schools, Vedic Hinduism, Buddhism, Classical Greek philosophy, the Hebrew bible, Christianity, and, later, in Islam. I propose that we rethink Axial Age theory as a way to throw new light on the process of religious problematization. Specifically, I suggest, problematization, rather than constituting an evolutionary step toward modernity, is better understood to be one aspect of collective action process.

I base this suggestion on the results of cross-cultural comparative analysis using data from the thirty-society sample. To evaluate the degree to which collective action might be associated with a cultural process analogous to religious problematization, I dichotomized the sample of thirty premodern states by collective action score and developed a variable assessing the degree to which religion was problematized in relation to state or ruler power. The latter measured the degree to which a principal's ability to personally mobilize the cultural forces of religious belief and ritual was institutionally limited. The problematizing of political authority in relation to religion was evident when one or more of the following was noted: ruler and polity were not considered divine, official governing sites were largely secular (often because major ritual centers or shrines were located separately from the main political spaces and activities), and religious cults and orders operated largely separate from state control. Religion as a symbolic source supporting ruler and the state itself, and thus not problematized, was identified when important religious cults or orders were controlled by or were subservient to the ruler or other principals; rulers were strongly sanctified, were thought to have supernatural powers, and/or served as a conduit of supernatural power to the populace; rulers gained power through their control of supernaturally potent objects; or the system of rule was thought to have been established by a creator deity.

From statistical analysis of the resulting data (reported on in Appendix B, section 8), it is clear that there is a strong association between the nonproblematized group and societies scoring lower on collective action. In cases showing one or more strategies of problematization, the polities tended toward higher collective action scores. I conclude that state-builders in a variety of cultural and geographical settings, not just those influenced by Axial Age thinking, enacted policies to separate religion and political power, though, as we might expect, the strategies for accomplishing problematization were cross-culturally variable.

The degree of religion-polity interaction ranged across a wide spectrum of possibilities from societies, such as ancient Egypt and the Inka, in which the principals were like the "god-kings" of Axial Age theory (many people think of ancient

THE CULTURAL PROCESS OF COOPERATION **241**

Egypt as a proxy for all premodern states, very wrongly so), to much more secularized expressions of political process. Some of the latter are mentioned in Axial Age theory. For example, Solon—one of the most important lawgivers of the nascent Athenian democracy—argued that politics be secularized and so should be based on analytical thought, not belief in gods. *Dysnomia* (dysfunction), he argued, was the result of human action, not gods, so it was up to the people to solve social problems. As democracy was developed in later periods, religion, according to Carlton (1977: 235), "was not harnessed for the needs of the state."

Secularization is also evident in ideas associated with the Mandate of Heaven in traditional Chinese political theory, stating that rulers are not sanctified. Secularization is also evident in the Ming Dynasty's neo-Confucianist conception of a rational and thinking self whose moral sensibilities are grounded in the everyday material world rather than in terms of the otherworld spirituality of Buddhism. Religion remained important in Ming China, however; in fact, the emperors, especially the Ming founder, the Hung-wu emperor, were active in specifying new forms of liturgical practice (in the "Great Ming code"). According to these specifications, the ruler was obligated to preside over key rituals thought to be important for "the periodic renewal of the great community of men and spirits" (Taylor 1998: 840). Their actual behavior, however, displays an element of problematization in that, especially after 1540 CE, they often sent delegates to represent them at the rites, even important ones, or sometimes ignored or delayed the rites.

Perhaps the clearest expression of problematization of religion in the sample was in focal-period Venice, where, according to John Norwich (1982: 282),

> The church was kept rigidly in its place, its duties exclusively pastoral, barred from the slightest interference in affairs of state . . . The families of Venetians holding ecclesiastical positions were also suspect. Their members . . . who belonged to the various governing bodies of the state . . . were regularly excluded from all deliberations concerning ecclesiastical matters. Some appointments, such as the coveted embassy to Rome, were closed to these families altogether. No member of the clergy was allowed to serve the Venetian state in any capacity, even as a clerk or notary, or to have access to the public archives.

Other, non-Axial polities also showed evidence of religious problematization in various guises—and in relation to collective action. The Asante polity is a case in point. Here rulers were not sanctified, and further, major ritual sites and temples were located in zones to the north of the polity capital at Kumasi (such as at Tekiman), and priests had little political influence. Problematization was present in the Lozi polity but was complicated. There are some aspects of ruler sanctification; for example, the ruler was transformed, through an installation ritual, into a powerful spiritual being. Royal burial sites and cenotaphs were regarded as sacred sites (the "cult of the royal graves"). However, there is an element of religious problematization in that rulership was expressed in dualistic terms, as is evident in a dual-capital system with northern and southern capitals. While secular power, the basis of Lozi governance, was vested in the northern ruler (and capital), the southern capital and ruler were vested with greater spiritual power, but had little actual governing authority.

SUMMARY

I conclude that collective action prompted rethinking of cultural designs across diverse time periods and cultural settings. In many ways these redesigns shared features in common with Early Modern Europe, including the foregrounding of a materialistic, rational, and egalitarian sense of the self; naturalism in artistic representation; and the separation of religious and civic domains. In both Europe and China there were transitions away from a metaphysical understanding of the ideal self to a notion of the self positioned firmly in nature and society and with a recognized capacity for egoistic social action. It may seem counterintuitive that in societies exhibiting high levels of cooperation, the self is viewed as a highly individualized rational social actor. This would seem odd especially to a person schooled in the ideas of anthropology or evolutionary psychology and who thus equates rationality with selfishness and social chaos. However, folk theories of mind highlighting uniformitarian notions of a socially intelligent human were conceived in the context of high levels of cooperation and show striking parallels across cultural traditions. These ideas also align with what we understand about the general properties of human Theory of Mind capacity.

Of the non-European societies in the comparative sample, sources describing Classical Athens and Ming China provide the most detailed accounting of a willful and individualistic, yet, potentially moral social self in their respective folk theories. A similar self was also theorized to some degree in Aztec, Venice, and Mughal cultures. In all cases the human subject was seen to possess the potential for rational thought that was not differentiated in terms of class position, religion, ethnicity, or center and hinterland (though gender equality was not typically a desideratum, and slaves and other excluded groups were not always viewed in an egalitarian manner). I relate this unifying process, in part, to strategies making possible open recruitment into positions of authority, a key element of any highly collective political economy.

When I suggest that folk theories of mind are culturally constituted, I align myself, but only in part, with relativist twentieth-century philosophers such as Michel Foucault who declared that all notions of self are best understood as culturally specific political myths. I depart from this kind of argument in two respects. First, typically, in these arguments the willful individual in question is found uniquely in Classical antiquity and in the modern Western person. The latter is assumed to result from cultural production that envisioned the detachment of the person from the moral community, ideas that were hastened by Enlightenment Period philosophizing and with the eventual growth of capitalism and democracy. My argument is different. I propose that notions of the willful individual are not just arbitrary elements of a particular cultural pattern. Rather, notions of the self grow out of certain forms of social solidarity; specifically, I suggest, notions of the self that are analogous to the Western person will be—must be—independently developed in all highly cooperative social formations. Second, rather than seeing the willful individual as a purely arbitrary, contingent being, only a cultural construct, I point out that in spite of what is envisioned in a particular folk theory of mind, humans are in reality cognitively complex with the inherent capacity for self-aware social intelligence.

I also took note of new modes of communication associated with a collective emphasis in institution-building. This included Ming China and Early Modern Europe, where there was an explosion of printed media and new or modified forms of visual communication through art. The culture of visualization also shows cross-cultural similarities. While Clunas (1997: 111–12) doubts it will be possible to devise a general "history of looking" because there are so many locally distinct histories to consider, from a cooperation perspective there do appear to be fundamental uniformities in what constitutes representation and looking. In the less collective societies representation more often consists of locally evocative symbols of political power, religious devotion, ritual, and style, while, where collective action is foregrounded, representation turns to naturalism, expressed in various forms. In the artistic traditions of Ming China, Mughal, of Venice, and in Early Modern Europe, naturalism is evident in scenes that depict ethnographic details of ordinary persons at work and play and that extol the virtues of commoners and rural lifeways. Anatomically correct portraiture was an important artistic medium in Athens, Mughal, Venice, Roman High Empire, and Ming China, as well as in Early Modern Europe, while figural images in the less collective polities tended toward depictions of the "heroic" and the symbolic. A case in point is Ottoman political culture of the focal period (scoring relatively low on collective action), which did not make use of veristic ruler portraiture; this form of ruler representation was not adopted until much later, by the eighteenth century CE at the earliest, as reform rulers borrowed elements of political philosophy and cultural design from Europe.

Mughal court painting in some respects represented a novel format among the artistic traditions I studied, in which the impetus toward naturalism emphasized the depiction of rulers and other high officials engaged in animated discoursing and other elements of entrainment in small social groupings that include commoners (similar narrative scenes were also produced by Ming artists). Venice, of the group compared, was also somewhat unique in artistic expression. Venetian artists strived to find ways to glorify the beauty and vibrancy of the city and its people, in maps and paintings of city scenes and in representations of large groups entrained in various civic and religious rituals. In this connection I should point out that this kind of city imaginary, including maps and paintings as well as literature extolling the beauty and satisfactions of city living, were present also in China, somewhat even predating the Ming Dynasty (the Northern Sung, 960–1127 CE), following the decline of the power of aristocratic clans and the beginning of more open and vibrant urban lifeways that Heng Chye Kiang (1999: 202) describes as the emergence of a "popular urban consciousness."

It is important to consider the role of culture as a motive force in the building and sustaining of a collective polity. The cultural vision in question is broadly incorporative and egalitarian, foregrounding a unifying theory of human nature. It also is a vision mandating various forms of public events and forms of naturalistic representation that impart a veracious quality to communication. These features bring an escape from the power of elite symbolism, foregrounding instead a sense of civic consciousness and incorporation.

12

The Causes and Consequences of Collective Action

It is my hope that the empirical and comparative methodology employed in this book's chapters will be seen as a model for future cooperation research. The approach is well suited to placing a cooperation-themed discipline on a firm scientific foundation, not only to discover common notions and practices across diverse social and cultural settings, but also to evaluate theories of causation. For example, with Lane Fargher, I have been able to empirically evaluate the utility of a fiscal theory to explain important aspects of variation in state-building. Yet, there is much more to learn about those conditions that arise in relation to collective action and that may nurture or inhibit it. In this chapter, I address this and other issues pertaining to the question of causation, with the goal to stimulate future discussion and research. I do this with the proviso that to confirm the usefulness of my ideas will require sustained follow-up effort. I call for caution, and more research, because, as typically is the case, causal pathways are complex and difficult to identify with existing methods and data.

LAWS OF HUMAN COOPERATION?

I need to preface this chapter's contents by noting that the causal theories I propose will not approach the positivist ideal of "universal laws." To disavow the possibility for lawlike universality, however, need not imply that my suggestions will have little value for cooperation study. I aim to make a contribution to cooperation

DOI: 10.5876/9781607325147.c012

study but avoid claims of universality because, in social science, to search for laws is to be overly obsessed with the pursuit of complete objectivity. Unfortunately, the contingent character of history rarely presents us with perfectly predictable linear sequences of events that can be called "laws." Collective action process, in fact, may be highly subject to local contingencies given that it will remain only a latent possibility until ways can be found to confront free-riding and agency, to build confidence in governing officials and their programs, to overcome challenges inherent in complex systems management, and to transform autocratic power into relational power—all accomplished within a framework of preexisting institutions, culture, technology, and environment.

Even personalities may shape the details of cooperative arrangements. For example, in some of the studied societies the enactment of collective action might not have been possible without the efforts of a particularly charismatic leadership. These were leaders who sensed the need for change, were in a position to bring about change, and could make change happen. Considering the comparative sample, I would point to influential leaders such as Osei Tutu of the Asante; the Lozi ruler known as Lewanika; the Mughal ruler Akbar; the Athenian reformers Solon and Kleisthenes; Julius Caesar and Augustus of Rome; the Ming Dynasty's founder, the Hung-wu emperor; and Tlacaelel, the primary architect of what Rudolph van Zantwijk (1985) calls the "Aztec arrangement." These individuals were unusually capable motivators who could sustain a devotion to cooperative principles, but at the same time they possessed a practical understanding of how to build workable institutions for cooperation.

But does cooperation always depend on unusually gifted and charismatic leadership? By mentioning the influence of outstanding leaders who were influential in several particular instances, I am not aiming to promote the virtues of what used to be called the "Great Man" theory of history, nor am I discounting the possibility that pressures for social change may emanate from the base of society. For one, although an individual may galvanize change, success is only possible when the underlying conditions are favorable. Also, some episodes of collective action unfolded without the influence of any particularly motivating individual leadership, for instance, in the history of the Venetian Republic. I mention the example of great leaders only to make the point that by ignoring historical contingency, our theories will have limited utility. Correspondingly, the goal here, rather than the discovery of laws, is to develop what are called "explanatory statistical models." These models limit us to the identification of patterns, tendencies, and probabilities, yet, in spite of their limitations, they do constitute a valid source of knowledge. This is true because they identify probable causal factors based on methods that are grounded in empirical observation and comparative analysis, thus freeing us from dependence

on abstract mathematical formulations or exercises in pure deductive logic discon-
nected from the nuances and complexities of actual human experience.

UNDERSTANDING CAUSALITY

The search for an explanatory statistical model begins when the researcher identifies variables that he or she posits might be involved in chains of causality. Often
the variables are chosen on the basis of prior theory, but not necessarily—sometimes it pays to do exploratory fishing for patterns that might reflect causal inter-
connections, or to follow up on hunches that might not fit current theories. The
identified variables must then be rendered "operational," requiring the development
of a method to convert qualitative information (descriptive data from historical,
archaeological, ethnographic, or other sources) into quantitative measures suited
for comparative or diachronic analysis. Statistical analysis of the resulting quantitative data facilitates the identification of interactions among variables, quantitative
characterization of cases (the studied societies), and, with these measures, the pro-
visional evaluation of hypotheses. Thankfully, statisticians have developed methods
for carrying out pattern-searching and theory-testing procedures of the sort I will
refer to below. Some of these methods allow for the evaluation of statistical significance of variable interactions. In this way it is possible to assess the degree to which
an observed pattern might occur frequently by chance alone and without a necessary causal link between variables.

When the researcher feels confident that a causal pattern has been identified, and
that it is not likely to be a chance occurrence, the analyst then proposes the nature
of causality involved—is variable A always prior and causal in relation to variable B
(a simple linear causality), or are A and B mutually interactive (mutually causal), or
are A and B involved in causal chains with other variables (multivariate causality)?
Profound transformations of social or other systems may result, when—in the latter
situations of mutual or multivariate causality—a "kick" ("prime mover") initiates
an episode in which multiple variables interact with each other in a mutually reinforcing pattern—in systems jargon a "deviation-amplifying mutual-causal process."

In this chapter I analyze one such mutually reinforcing pattern, which I name the
"coactive causal process." This is a process involving the mutual causal interactions
among collective action, commercialization, material standard of living, demographic change, and production intensification. I also tentatively identify prime
movers I propose may have provided the initial impetus that sets the coactive process into play. To begin this discussion, my first task is to illustrate the playing out of
the coactive process in the rise of European modernity, then to illustrate similar patterns of change in other venues in which high levels of cooperation can be identified.

THE COACTIVE CAUSAL PROCESS

The presence of elevated real wages (in Neo-Babylonian and
early Achaemenid Mesopotamia and Classical Athens) "defies
any straightforward explanation." (Walter Scheidel 2010: 457)

Scheidel is puzzled about economic growth in Mesopotamia and Classical Athens
because it contradicts prevailing theories of economic change. Gregory Clark
(2007) exemplifies the prevailing theory when he argues that all human societies
prior to the beginnings of industrialization in Europe, around 1800 CE, were caught
in a "Malthusian Trap." Here, low levels of technological innovation, combined
with high fertility, inhibited real economic growth, that is, growth that outpaced
population increase. Uniquely, according to Clark, Western Europeans escaped the
trap with the advent of both innovative production advances of the industrial revolution and declining fertility. Technological and demographic change paved the
way to a "Great Divergence" from the supposed economic malaise and low living
standards that had persisted since the Paleolithic.

There is some truth to this claim, especially if we focus our attention, as Malthusian
Trap theorists often do, on per capita energy consumption. Obviously, with the advent
of fossil fuel and other energy subsidies to production, transport, and other uses, this
metric does show significant change after 1800. However, the notion of a Malthusian
Trap appears to be overstated. Recent investigations of preindustrial complex societies have uncovered historical episodes of marked economic development, unrelated
to industrialization, that included growing commercialization, increased production,
and increased material standard of living—all pointing to real economic growth. For
example, Kenneth Pomeranz (2000) identifies regions of Late Imperial China that
were far more economically developed than European regions of the Early Modern
Period, and Jack Goldstone (2002) identifies episodes of economic "efflorescence"
outside of Europe, including in Classical Athens and the Chinese Qing Dynasty
from 1680 to 1780. Robert Allen (2001) and other economic historians have found
evidence for increased earnings and standard of living in England beginning as early
as the sixteenth century, long before the Great Divergence.

But how is it possible to bring about change from what Robert Lopez (1976:
56) describes as "agrarian balance" to a state of "commercial restlessness," except in
the conditions of technological modernity? In this chapter, I propose one possible
explanatory factor: institution-building for collective action in state-building. I am
able to propose this only because an important goal of the comparative work reported
on in this book was to build an expanded collective action theory that incorporates
multiple contextual variables into the analysis, including geography, demography,
agroecology, and economic variables such as commercial activity and material

standard of living. From these sources of data I am able to link collective action and its varied entailments (public goods, effective governing systems, and a uniformitarian folk theory of mind and associated cultural patterns), to growing commercialization, increased material standard of living, population growth—including a relative increase in urban population—and the intensification of production. These are the elements of the coactive causal process that, I suggest, are simultaneously ignited by collective action (often, it appears, as unanticipated outcomes of it), while at the same time providing a sound fiscal basis to accommodate the considerable costs of building and sustaining institutional capital for cooperation.

THE COACTIVE CAUSAL PROCESS IN EARLY MODERN EUROPE

In chapter 11 I outlined the social and cultural changes that presaged the rise of European modernity: the declining power of the aristocracy and monarchical rule, and the rise of more democratic societies, new theories of a willful self rooted in the material and social worlds, changing ideas about the role of commerce in society, and a growing appreciation for quotidian lifeways and the role of the common person. These changes took place in relation to a coactive causal process that began during the Late Medieval and Early Modern European Periods, especially after about 1500 CE, most notably in what Fernand Braudel (1979, vol. 2: 280) called the "heart of Europe," in its northwestern extremity, especially in the low countries and England, the latter of which I focus on. Other European regions illustrate the coactive process to a lesser degree or much later than the "heart"; for example, in France the feudal manorial system persisted longer, and, correspondingly, the peasantry—whose social status and economic role grew in England remained relatively socially, economically, and culturally marginalized. And, in Eastern Europe the period after 1400 CE saw a strengthening of feudal-like coercive controls over peasant labor in the process referred to as the Second Serfdom.

While those zones of Europe that were within the bounds of the Roman Empire had been highly commercialized, with the collapse of the empire in the west, commercialization ground to a near halt. In England, even basic aspects of occupational specialization fell apart, and some technologies—such as mortared construction and wheel-made pottery—were practically gone by the fifth century CE. Commercial activity began to rebound somewhat between the eighth and tenth centuries, and, though the evidence is often difficult to come by, economic historians have traced the outlines of a slow process of commercial growth after that time. Change can be attributed in part to the fact that after circa 1150 England increasingly was incorporated into the expanding world economy as a supplier of raw wool. Initially, however, this trade benefitted primarily elite sectors of the economy—the manors and abbeys—which were the principal suppliers of raw wool. It also benefitted the foreign, especially Italian and German Hansa, traders, who served as brokers between the large-scale raw wool producers and cloth-producing centers such as those in Flanders.

The period from 1350 to about 1450 was punctuated by wars, social unrest, possible climate fluctuations, and epidemics, especially the Black Death of 1348–49. These factors brought economic and demographic decline, but by the late fifteenth century there was a new round of growth in international trade in which, rather than as a supplier of raw wool, England emerged as a producer of fine wool cloth. This new cloth economy brought benefits across social sectors, including the peasantry, and it is at this point that a coactive causal process came into full swing, featuring population growth, a growing market economy, an increased material standard of living across social sectors, and growing urbanization, especially in the smaller towns that were centers of the export-oriented economy. The causes of these profound changes are not easy to discern, but I point to market evolution as a key— perhaps the key—motor of social and cultural change at that time. I suggest this following on the lead of prominent economic historians such as Rodney Hilton who long ago recognized the importance of market growth as a source of social change that set the stage for European modernity.

Commercial change did not come easily or quickly, reflecting the fact that market-builders faced "a thousand obstacles, many formidable, others tenuous, [that] impeded their activities at every turn" (Bridbury 1986: 117). The social inequality that pervaded the long-standing manorial society and its feudal bonds of personal dependence limited the potential for commoners to participate fully, as independent economic actors, in commercial life. Social change required new notions of property rights to allow property to be "private to individuals and their families, corporations, and other voluntary associations" (Kerridge 1986: 121) (John Locke's influential argument in his *Second Treatise* that private property and ownership over the products of one's labor are basic human rights was published in 1689, long after the changes addressed here were in full swing).

In addition, commoners were not likely to have confidence in the marketplaces until institutions were developed that served to protect their interests there, including moral restrictions on the uses of wealth because, in the European Middle Ages, "anything could be bought," including justice (Bridbury 1986: 83). Other kinds of Medieval cultural values inhibited market development, including Christian dogma that vilified marketplaces and commercial transactions. In spite of social and cultural obstacles to commercial change, Alan Everitt (1967) estimates that already by the thirteenth century there were over 800 marketplaces in England and Wales (in addition to hundreds of commercial fairs), numbers that had increased to between 1,500 and 2,000 by the early fourteenth century.

A growth in numbers doesn't tell the whole story of commercial change, which also saw novel forms of institutional change. Medieval Period commercial systems were not highly developed, tending toward the pattern that I earlier defined as restricted markets. This was true at the local level, where marketplaces often were closed to nonlocal vendors for lack of trust of outsiders. A restricted market pattern also dominated in commercial transactions at the level of the urban or international merchants whose large-scale operations ("private trading," often apart from the marketplaces) reflected their network capital and mastery of complex financial instruments for buying on credit. For example, by circa 1200 CE, Italian bankers had developed systems like modern bills of exchange that allowed them to remit large sums in distant locations. The problem of elite-driven restricted markets was exacerbated by the fiscally stressed English Crown, which struck deals with commercial centers such as Genoa and their alien merchants—German, Lombard, Genoese, Venetian—for loans and military support in exchange for rights to monopoly control over international trade. This tendency toward an elite-oriented commerce contrasts with the plight of commoners, who initially did not benefit from the growing international trade. One reason for this was the near absence of public goods, which extended to the lack of widespread public education. As a result, many commoners were illiterate and thus unable to understand contracts and other financial instruments, so merchants perceived them to be "weak and easy to deceive" (Everitt 1967: 566). In addition, the feudal manors, wishing to profit from growing demand for agricultural products, placed increased pressure on their servile peasants to increase production.

All of these processes seemed destined to end up as an "encysted" system of restricted markets in which increased commercial activity would benefit primarily the elite sectors of society and the alien merchants. Yet, this did not happen for the long run. Alien merchants gradually lost influence; Jewish traders were expelled in 1290, and there was rioting against Italian merchants during the mid-fourteenth century, in part owing to peasant discontent. In this and other respects, change gradually moved the English economy in the direction of higher degrees of commercialization that incorporated commoner households into commercial activities. The causes of this egalitarianizing process are complex, including a growing dissatisfaction with the privileged medieval manorial elite and their claims over their servile *villein* workforces, leading to conflicts that eventuated in the gradual substitution of money payments in lieu of the traditional feudal labor obligations. Villeins thus became tenants working particular plots of land registered in their names, which was a legal benefit in cases of inheritance disputes and the like, or, increasingly, they became freeholders. To obtain the money needed for their manorial overlords, or to purchase land, commoners placed more emphasis on market sales of their surplus production.

Another source of egalitarianizing social and cultural change during the Late Medieval and Early Modern Periods was that in the growing international trade the independent commoner household proved to be an efficient producer, especially in the context of cloth production. The manorial economy, by contrast, was unable to benefit very much from the growing international trade after 1450. Economic historians have identified sources of inefficiency in the manorial system, including a lack of investment in production owing to the lavish spending on glorious houses and estate grounds. In addition, any forced labor on manor land was likely to be grudging and not high in productivity, and attempts to develop bureaucratic management of estates proved ineffective ("Urgent decisions might be shelved because the men on the spot preferred to take no risks, and a top-heavy apparatus of control was needed to oversee the officials in the manors" [in Miller and Hatcher 1978: 196–97]). The Black Death, resulting in an estimated 40 percent to 50 percent population decline, also was a change factor because it put surviving commoner households in an improved bargaining position when the manorial economy had too few workers. And labor shortages were compounded by falling grain prices, which also hurt the manors. At any rate, by the mid-fifteenth century the villein system was essentially gone, and the levies owed to the manors tended to decline.

A new economy of the post-1500 period grew out of the decline of the manorial system, most notably in the southern part of England, where there was growth in the number of and population sizes of towns with commercial functions related to the growing textile industry. The new economy was increasingly commoner driven, but this had earlier origins. As Christopher Dyer (2002: 165), points out, already by the Late Medieval Period peasants produced the bulk of the export wool. The new economy grew slowly, however, and was fraught with conflict including organized commoner uprisings, sometimes against the demands of the manorial system but more often in opposition to the market system itself. However, as E. P. Thompson (1971) argues, these were not movements organized by people who were opposed to a destructive "penetration" of the market into the moral economy of the peasant community; rather, the goal was to create a new moral community—in the marketplaces. This new moral community grew in response to outside merchant-driven commercial forces that commoners perceived as counter to their goal to be active participants in the growing economy. In addition to these directed actions militating for market reforms, the marketplaces also were instrumental in social and cultural change in more indirect, unanticipated ways, because marketplace involvement tended to promote egalitarian sensibilities and the marketplaces provided a venue within which people might imagine the kinds of social actions needed to overcome threats to their desired way of life. As Thompson (1971: 135) expresses it, well into the eighteenth century, "the market was the place where the people, because they were numerous, felt for a moment they were strong."

The growing strength of the commoner-driven market economy is reflected in institutional changes made by the Crown, local officials, and commercial guilds that emphasized, in particular, the following features (summarized from James Davis [2012: 176–77]):

1. Market transactions were required to take place in legally recognized public marketplaces at specified times, goods for sale should be openly displayed, and market transactions should occur openly in the public space of the marketplace. These rules were intended to mitigate what commoners identified as one of the key problems they faced, the practice of "engrossing," the buying of large consignments outside the marketplace, usually by elite urban or foreign merchants. Engrossing was identified as a source of occasional local commodity shortages and also was thought to be potentially fraught with problems of deception and the potential for monopoly pricing. In any commercial system, extramarket transactions pose a problem in that they make it more difficult for the majority of market participants to fully understand how variations in supply and demand are influencing price, because participants are unable to actually see the quantity of goods offered and the amount of human traffic in the marketplace.

2. Market officials such as warranters were employed to certify the quality of products, and witnesses and oaths should accompany the completion of high-value contracts. Bailiffs and constables are required to be present in a marketplace to maintain order and to maintain marketplace sanitation.

3. Market transactions should be based on standardized weights and measures and should make use of official coinage and officially prescribed monetary standards.

Because a marketplace required a Crown-issued franchise in order to operate legally, any infraction of rules could cause loss of franchise and hence loss of the market manager's share of revenues from it.

By the seventeenth and eighteenth centuries the rural economy of England was "rich and diverse" (McCloskey 1976: 130). The engine of economic and social change during the Late Medieval and extending into the Early Modern Period after 1500 was a commercial economy increasingly dominated by commoner producer-vendors, retailers, middlemen and artisans, whose activities brought an increase in the overall material standard of living. Change included a gradual improvement in the quality of housing and clothing and a growing food security that reduced the threat of famine. Agricultural intensification brought substantially higher yields for grain production, in some cases doubling from the sixteenth century to the end of the of the seventeenth / beginning of the eighteenth, but some farms had achieved high levels even earlier according to B. H. Slicher van Bath (1963: 281, table 3). Change was most notable in regions of the south of England, pointing to a degree of "production elasticity" there (the potential to realize gains in production per land unit) never before realized in any prior historical period. Methods of intensification involved decrease in fallowing, the expansion of drainage systems, double cropping, manuring, liming and marling, weeding, the improved care of sheep herds, and other innovative production technologies (Figure 12.1). After the sixteenth century, more rural producers were able to benefit from farm manuals and journals, and increasingly, the growing wool-based export economy came to be dominated by citizens who had gained familiarity with the institutions of international trade. The growth of activity of English merchants is especially notable in the form of a new category of entrepreneurial commoner-producer-vendor, the "clothier." Clothiers not only owned herds but also controlled other phases of production, putting out spinning and weaving tasks to rural and town-based households. They also marketed cloth to intermediaries in London for eventual sale in entrepôts such as Antwerp.

THE COACTIVE PROCESS OUTSIDE THE RISE
OF EARLY EUROPEAN MODERNITY

Using a pattern-discovery method called "Principal Components" analysis (Appendix B, section 9), I found a strong pattern of covariation among the coactive variables coded from the comparative sample (collective action, commercialization, increased material standard of living, growth in degree of urbanization, population growth, and the intensification of production). I infer from these results a process analogous to the coactive process that is evident after 1500 CE in England, but, as the analysis indicates, that played out in diverse social, cultural, and historical contexts. Below I describe the nature of these changes and propose causal explanations for them.

Before I begin that task I should affirm that a coactive process is not a highly structured causal model—in fact, it will remain latent except in certain limited conditions . It is also a statistical model that when subjected to further analysis, reveals several interesting variations around the central coactive theme. From the multivariate analyses described in Appendix B (Figures B.2 and B.3 and Tables B.6 and B.7) I conclude that two related but partially distinct coactive processes can be detected, one driven principally by collective action, the other by urbanism and markets. While collective action and urban/market processes are themselves statistically correlated, still, to some degree, urbanism and markets may develop

FIGURE 12.1. An example of intensification of English rural production during the seventeenth century: "Cider Press," from J. Worlidge, *Vinetum Britannicum: Or a Treatise of Cider*, 1678. Reproduced with permission of the Museum of English Rural Life, University of Reading.

apart from a coactive process involving collective action. In this twin-process model, collective action (using public goods as a proxy) is most strongly correlated with increased living standards, agricultural intensification, and population growth (for reasons I will propose), while market development, though positively correlated with collective action and the other coactive variables, shows a stronger processual association with urban growth.

Market development, however, may also result from other causal factors unrelated to either collective action or high levels of urbanism. Focal-period England (late fourteenth century and early fifteenth) is an example in which, in spite of little in the way of collective action (e.g., Parliament was just beginning to assert control over kings), or high levels of urbanism (most city growth occurred later), some commercial growth can be detected, based on a growing export of raw, then processed, wool into international trade networks. Tokugawa Japan, I suggest, more clearly illustrates a processual connection between urbanism and market growth; eighteenth-century Japan, with four cities exceeding 100,000 people, was more urbanized than England of the same period. While the governing shogunate regime was highly autocratic, featured a weak degree of bureaucratization, and provided only minimal public goods, still, its policy of obligate urbanism—designed especially to control the warrior class (samurai) by moving them from rural to urban areas—contributed to the growth of cities and is associated with a phase of commercial development of rural and urban markets.

Examples such as England and Japan point to the possibility that something like a coactive process may play out to some degree in relation to urbanism and markets even where high levels of collective action in state-building are not found. I suggest, however, that for collective action to develop to its fullest extent, it will do so in relation to the entire coactive process. In those polities scoring among the highest on most measures of collective action—Mughal, Ming China, Classical Athens, the Roman High Empire period, Venice, and Aztec—we see increased living standards, marked population growth, city growth, agricultural intensification, and market development during the focal periods. Only Lozi and Asante, of the polities scoring particularly high on collective action, are missing from this list, because neither showed expansive urban growth or highly developed market systems. In both cases, I suggest, local environmental variables inhibited the full development of the coactive process. The peripatetic settlement pattern of the Lozi, in which most of the population of the polity's core zone, including the governing apparatus, migrated seasonally out of the Upper Zambezi floodplain, may have been one factor retarding city growth and markets. The Asante polity was literally carved out of near-pristine tropical forest just before the focal period. In spite of substantial immigration, Asante's population remained relatively scattered; with a population density of only ten persons per square kilometer, it was among the least dense in the entire sample. A scattered, low-density population may not have been an ideal situation for the development of extensive urban settlements or markets.

COMMERCIALIZATION AND THE COACTIVE CAUSAL PROCESS OUTSIDE OF EUROPE

Historians have often noted the importance of a growing commerce in the rise of modernity in Early Modern Europe, and researchers have noted that in recent history economic development and democratization go hand in hand (though the nature of causality is argued about); as Cheibub and Vreeland (2012: 1) put it, "The correlation between economic development and democracy is probably among the strongest we find in the social sciences." Are there similar correspondences between commercial growth and the rise of more collective states outside European history and recent experience? In the following, I briefly describe market change in three of the sample's more collective polities—Mughal, Ming China, and Aztec—to give the reader a sense of the kinds of data available to the comparative researcher. I then follow up by describing the results of a comparative study of commerce and collective action based on the entire sample.

MUGHAL (1556–1658 CE)

Market evolution has not often been a topic addressed by historical social scientists who study South Asia, making it difficult to place the Mughal Period in comparative perspective. Nonetheless, from what has been done it is evident this period saw profound commercial growth. For example, while copper traditionally served as the major currency metal, an expansion of silver as coinage during the Mughal Period points to a growing monetization and to a need for more rupees in circulation and also is associated with the extension of commercial transactions beyond the "urban-based nobility and merchants" (Subrahmanyam 1998: 218). B. R. Grover (1994: 227) describes Mughal commercial growth in the sixteenth and seventeenth centuries as an "extraordinary expansion of trade and commerce" stimulated in part by the growth of the state and its expanding need for revenues, which came to be collected almost entirely as currency rather than as in-kind. Growing urban populations also brought new levels of economic demand that fostered growth in cash-crop production. In addition, Akbar's annexation of Gujarat, which increased access to important port towns, also figured into the commercial expansion of the period.

MING DYNASTY (MOSTLY LATE FOURTEENTH CENTURY AND FIFTEENTH CENTURY CE)

Markets have a deep history in China. Archaeological and ethnohistoric sources point to considerable institutional development already by the first millennium BCE. Unfortunately, markets have not been a subject addressed in detail by archaeologists or other researchers, but economic historians see the Ming Period as one in which unprecedented levels of commercial activity can be detected. Commerce grew mostly without direct state involvement, as the dynastic founder favored an "ancient agrarian ideal" dominated by a largely self-sufficient village economy. In spite of this official agrarian vision, networks of periodic markets (*shih, chi*), as G. W. Skinner first documented, commercially linked rural households as well as rural and urban populations though interlocking markets, some with only three-day periodicities that reveal high levels of commercial activity. And market conditions are noted to have influenced the agricultural decision-making of most rural households. The number of marketplaces increased, specialized artisanal guilds emerged to organize some aspects of production, and there was also an active land market. Intrapolity trade between regional systems also increased, involving foodstuffs, especially rice, but also cotton and cotton cloth, reflecting a growing agroecological symbiosis between northern regions (cotton) and southern (rice). In addition, there were other interregional markets in timber, tobacco, alcoholic beverages, tea, paper, sugar cane, fruit, and other goods. There was so much growth in the economy that by the Late Ming Dynasty, China already was exerting an influence well beyond its borders; for example, Chinese (and South Asian) goods such as textiles and porcelain were consumed in various parts of Asia including Southeast Asia, and they "became very important to European fashion, even down to a fairly humble level, while no Western good became equally important in East Asia" (Pomeranz 2000: 157).

AZTEC (1428–1521 CE)

The Late Postclassic Period of Central Mexico ("Aztec Period") saw population growth, increased urbanization, and agricultural intensification to unprecedented levels compared with prior archaeological periods and other Mesoamerican regions. The Aztec Period was also notable for its degree of commercial development that also surpassed all other periods and Mesoamerican regions. Especially in the Basin of Mexico and adjacent areas of Central Mexico, a vast periodic market system evolved during the focal period featuring market periodicities typically of five days and an organizational structure including up to five hierarchical levels of marketplaces. These marketplaces linked cash-crop producer households to urban consumers but also to other rural households with complementary production specializations. Imported goods such as chocolate and cotton came from distant tropical regions into the marketplaces. Bernal Díaz del Castillo, a member of Cortés's invasion army, having seeing the main market concourse in Tlatelolco, reflected that "if I describe everything in detail I shall never be done" (Díaz del Castillo 1963: 233). This marketplace served 20,000 to 25,000 persons every day and up to 50,000 every fifth day. Major cities, including the imperial capital Tenochtitlan-Tlatelolco—with a population of 175,000—were provisioned primarily through the commercial system. Wealth increased, even among most rural households, indicated in part by the growing consumer demand for "bulk luxury goods," valuable goods, some imported from distant regions, that were readily available in the marketplaces. These included cotton cloth, green obsidian, fine salt, and cacao (chocolate). The dying of cotton cloth emerged as a major industry for the first time in the Basin's history. The ethnohistorian Patricia Rieff Anawalt (1990: 104) describes clothing, even commoner clothing, as "resplendent in varying colors and designs."

A COMPARATIVE METHOD FOR THE STUDY OF COMMERCIAL GROWTH

Commercial growth is not a topic that anthropologists in past decades would have been likely to address, but as they moved beyond their Polanyi-inspired substantivism, with its concept of a "redistributive" economy, some in the discipline turned their attention to marketplaces and commerce. As a result, while it remains the case that we often lack data on household budgets or the kinds of macroeconomic data that economists take for granted, there is conceptual and methodological progress in this subject. I point especially to the work of G. W. Skinner, Carol Smith, and other students of regional market systems, who have developed comparative methods to evaluate the degree of commercialization based on the study of marketplaces themselves. The key market system variables they identified relevant to assessing the relative development of a commercial economy: (1) the degree to which marketplaces are widespread and accessible to most households, rural and urban; (2) the degree of hierarchy of marketplaces that link the more remote rural areas to major population centers; (3) market-day frequencies (traditional markets usually convene periodically, usually in a regular rotation with between 3 to 7 or even 10 days between scheduled market days); shorter intervals point to higher levels of commercial activity; (4) the degree of production specialization and exchange mediated through market institutions as opposed to those organized through kinship networks, governments, or other nonmarket means of exchange; and (5) the degree of development of "national-scale" markets that link subregions into a politywide system.

When I investigated marketplace variables using data from the thirty-society sample, I found that commercialization is positively statistically correlated with the other coactive variables, including collective action (Appendix B, section 10) This positive correlation comes as a surprise to my anthropology colleagues, who traditionally have distinguished between the redistributive despotisms of the premodern world in which, it is argued, the state basically structured the economy, and modern capitalism, with its strong and highly autonomous bourgeoisie-driven commercial economy. But the parsing out of human economies into two starkly opposed forms is misleading. It is clear from the comparative analysis that collective action process, with its extensive degree of public economy—including the production of public goods—is highly consistent with enhanced levels of commercial activity. In addition, I propose there is a multiplier effect at work here. While traditional theories posit that a premodern state's revenues derive principally from the appropriation of peasant surplus production, it is also the case that a growing commercial economy will provide the state with new revenue sources. This is an important element of the coactive process when market revenues mitigate the high transaction costs of collective action.

I propose there are several mutual-causal pathways connecting collective action and other coactive factors with commercialization. To begin, I suggest that the relative growth of urban populations increases demand for rural production. This brings a corresponding augmentation of market system complexity to connect rural producers to urban consumers, especially in a situation in which there is an overall increase in rural and urban material standard of living for most households. Along with increased urban demand, tax obligations typically are increased and the means of tax collective regularized. Both sources of demand—urban growth and taxes—push households to allocate more time and labor to production, which has consequences for household economies facing production bottlenecks that limit the possibilities for "householding" production (home production of needed goods). This process pushes households toward more production specialization and increased market dependence for goods no longer produced with household labor, bringing a corresponding increase in marketplaces and the number of households engaged in secondary industries and services catering to producer specialists. I discuss the evidence for changes in material standard of living, urban growth, population growth, and intensification of production next.

MATERIAL STANDARD OF LIVING

"The Romans produced goods, including mundane items, to a very high quality, and in huge quantities, and then spread them widely throughout all levels of society." (Bryan Ward-Perkins 2005: 87)

Europe's Great Divergence brought in its wake an increase in material standard of living. But an investigation of the material culture of "pre-Divergence" England, or of other societies and periods, sometimes uncovers historical episodes of substantial change in material richness, even change that was felt across social sectors as we see in the case of the Roman Empire described by Ward-Perkins. As I mentioned, one possible factor we should consider in understanding standard of living and other aspects of economic growth is collective action and its systemic relationship to commercialization. To evaluate this idea, I searched through the sources pertaining to the thirty-society sample and did encounter information relevant to material standard of living, though the data are sometimes spotty. Data pertaining to the usual indicators of living standards—such as per capita real income, savings, or similar variables available for contemporary economic analysis—were typically not available. I substituted for them descriptions made by ethnographers, travelers, merchants, government officials, or similar observers who comment on household consumption of goods including clothing, food, housing, and luxury items. Some archaeologists, also, have been interested in material standard of living, and have measured it based on housing quality and the quality of other material goods as well as biometric measures of health status and mortality from the study of human remains, and in some of my cases these sources were helpful.

To evaluate change in standard of living during a society's focal period, my coding goal was to document stability, decline, or increases in material standard of living during that specific time, emphasizing commoner households. This method focuses attention on change because there is so much cross-cultural difference that makes comparison challenging. A case in point is China, where, since the Han Dynasty, a widely used house plan had been instituted featuring walls and rooms enclosing a private courtyard that accentuated household privacy; construction of wood frame with ceramic roof tiles was common, sometimes incorporating brick and/or mud brick. These houses were comparatively large and well built by any premodern (or modern) comparative standard, and, so far as I could tell, they did not change notably during the focal period (there is very little data on household archaeology for that time). Yet, I did code the Ming Period as a having a positive increase in standard of living, in part because during that time cotton cloth came to be a much more widely consumed good.

Cotton is a useful indicator of material wealth and economic change in Ming Dynasty China and in other situations. In European history it is recognized for its important role in the beginnings of industrial production and, economically, it was the most important commodity of the nineteenth-century capitalist world system. But cotton is a unique good that has figured importantly in other episodes of economic change. Cotton has demanding production requirements, such as a long growing season, that may necessitate production sites far from where it will be consumed, and its lengthy cultivation cycle makes it incompatible with local subsistence farming, crowding it out, both of which events tend to stimulate a complex economy of production specialization and trade. At the consumer end it is a desirable and functional cloth that may assume the status of what my colleagues and I refer to as a "bulk luxury" good (Blanton et al. 2005), that is, a good that is expensive but can be widely consumed when production and distribution systems are able to provide it in large quantities and when incomes are relatively high across social sectors.

In addition to comparative challenges, another issue I faced in studying material standard of living is that European colonialist propaganda has often muddied the waters regarding commoner lifeways, including living standards. The Mughal polity is a good example of how, historically, the analysis of living conditions in India aimed to support arguments about whether the Mughal political system was exploitative, a notion advanced by apologists for British imperialism. Recent scholarship has challenged British propaganda by documenting the demographic decline that followed the imposition of British control and the "economic strangulation of the Indian economy by Britain" (Habib 2002: 280). Irfan Habib and other economic historians have found evidence supporting an overall increase in living standards for the focal period of Mughal state-building, though it probably did decline during the dynasty's final phase, after the focal period. For example, during the focal period there was a widespread increase in consumption of various kinds of garments including shawls from Kashmir and women's saris made of cotton, and, according to Habib (1963: 53–54), cultivators had more cattle and draft animals during the Mughal Period than is true in India today.

Although data pertinent to material standard of living are often sparse and are not always easy to interpret, when I collated what data are available I found a strongly positive statistical association between public goods and other indicators of collective regime-building, on the one hand, and increases in material standard of living during the focal periods, on the other, while the less collective polities tended toward stasis or even decline (Appendix B, section 11). In fact, the analysis showed that for values of public goods of 19 or more (the upper one-third), 75 percent of cases showed an increase in standard of living.

The nature of the causal link between collective action and material standard of living is not easy to discern because, as in other variables discussed in this section, causality is circular and complex, involving multiple variables in addition to collective action. However, it is possible that public goods and collective fiscal strategies did have some causal role. For example, households may have been willing to invest in more costly housing if their situation—rural or urban—is improved in terms of flood control, fire protection, the maintenance of public order, and property registration, which would provoke a land market. In addition, enhanced public order and well-managed marketplaces would also stimulate commercial participation and so generate new sources of wealth and opportunities to consume more categories of goods. It is of interest to note an additional set of positive correlation values, those connecting collective action and material standard of living with larger population size, growing urbanization, and population growth. I turn to the latter variables next.

POPULATION SIZE, POPULATION GROWTH, AND CITIES

The idea that collective action will be more successful in small-group contexts is a widely accepted but is an infrequently investigated assertion. Classical Athens is often cited as an example of the advantages of small scale for achieving high levels of cooperation in a premodern polity where it was possible for citizens to participate directly in a participatory democratic process. However, the analysis of data from the comparative sample produced an unanticipated result that there is a strong positive correlation between collective action, total population size of polity, and population growth during the focal period (Appendix B, section 12) . These results are particularly strong when population size is correlated with public goods as a proxy for collective action.

To interpret these interesting and perhaps counterintuitive statistical results, I begin by pointing out that while the Athenian polity of the focal period was below the mean population values for the sample, it by no means was the smallest, with a population of 100,000 (citizens and their families) and a total of about 290,000 (counting noncitizens) in an area of 2,500 square kilometers for Attica. Can the rel atively small size account for Athens's high score on the collective action measures? I suggest that no, scale will not be a complete explanation, because there are many polities in the sample of about the same size or smaller with less expression of collective action. In fact, and also counter to the hypothesis linking collective action to small scale, with few exceptions the smallest polities tend to score below the mean values on measures of cooperativity. Moreover, many of them featured segmentary forms of organization in which the central elite were only weakly linked to secondary officials and local communities, in spite of small scale. Although there is variation within this small-sized subsample, generally in the polities making up the bottom quartile of population total, which is below roughly 170,000 persons, I found that (1) measures of collective action are lower, with a mean value of collective action total of 12.4, while the mean value for polities in the upper quartile is 21; (2) five out of the eight smaller-scale societies had serious intraperiod political disruptions with negative consequences for commoners, usually involving dynastic successional disputes or wars between factions competing for power (Appendix B, section 13); and (3) there is little evidence for increased material standard of living for commoners during the focal periods. The latter was true even though some of these polities were periphery outliers connected into larger world-system networks as commercial providers of raw materials consumed in distant core areas in Europe or elsewhere. These world-system ties brought increased economic activity but tended to inhibit collective action because they provided opportunities for the governing elite to control or tax trade as an external revenue source. Moreover, external ties often differentially enhanced the wealth of powerful merchant groups, including, in some cases, foreign or "alien" merchants, and landowners, as in the examples of Bali and in the pre-1500 period in England described previously.

Another demographic challenge I noted in the smaller polities is a tendency toward high rates of exit (commoners "voting with their feet"), which is understandable if commoner households lacked economic opportunities and voice, had low social status in an autocratic political system, and endured frequent political disruptions or other sources of social disorder. The tendency to exit may well be indicated by the fact that in six out of the eight smaller-scale societies, the leadership was concerned about labor shortages; in some cases, perceived shortages led to wars against other polities aimed at labor capture. Perceived labor shortages also brought a pattern of social and cultural change inconsistent with the entailments of collective action. I refer to what economic anthropologists describe as "wealth in people" political economies. In these societies, most notably found in parts of sub-Saharan Africa and Southeast Asia, overall population density remained relatively low while land was relatively abundant. As a result, polity-building was predicated on the control of people as much as the control of land, and, correspondingly, wealth tended to be counted in persons. This situation resulted in the development of various local social conventions specifying the nature of rights in persons and their labor such as tenantry, serfdom, patron-client relationships, and slavery.

In addition to overall larger sizes and population growth associated with the more collective polities, there is also a statistical association between collective action and the relative growth of urban populations. The latter was comparatively measured by looking at the population sizes of main centers and the development of a hierarchy of populous cities and towns connecting rural areas to the main political and commercial centers (Appendix B, section 14). The causal forces fostering episodes of urban growth are multiple and complex, but a case can be made that collective action is implicated in the coactive causal process. I should point out that in analyzing this variable I emphasize those societies where urban growth reflected principally the residential decisions of individual households, unlike the obligate urbanism in which cities were planned, built, and populated through the policies of highly centralized states. Cities of the latter type were established in Inka Peru, in ancient Egypt, and, to some extent, in focal-period Japan, all of which scored relatively low on collective action.

CAUSAL FACTORS IN DEMOGRAPHIC CHANGE

Lane Fargher and I (Blanton and Fargher 2008: 275–80) propose several hypotheses that might clarify the causal relationships between collective action and larger population size, the tendency toward population growth, and relatively more urbanized populations. These proposals remain speculative because typically the data are lacking regarding the nature of change in birthrate, mortality, and migration. I summarize the causal proposals also with the caveat that, again, all of these variables are influenced by multiple chains of causality in the larger coactive process.

PROPENSITY TO EXIT

I mentioned previously that the smaller polities generally featured less well-developed systems of collective action, often featured systems of constrained labor, and often suffered from labor shortages, some of which was due to high rates of exit from the polity. While exit was not found to be an important social force in collective action in general (Blanton and Fargher 2008: 272–75), it did pose problems for the leadership in many of the smaller polities and in some of the other less collective societies. An example is New Kingdom Egypt, also near the middle of collective action measures (and exhibiting little or no population growth during the focal period). According to Stuart Smith (1995: 3), "Egyptian political renegades and deserters from the labor *corvée* . . . [migrating to Nubia] . . . provided both a drain on Egyptian state resources and a potential threat in the service of potential rivals like Kerma."

POPULATION GROWTH

Generally there is a positive correlation between collective action and population growth, though this is a statistical result with some exceptions. Venice, a major international trade center, featured many public goods but lacked much overall population growth owing to the many epidemics that inhibited growth. Overall, however, the data available to me suggest that the more collective polities provided the advantage of comparatively fewer social disruptions such as violent episodes associated with successional disputes or antistate social movements (Appendix B, section 13), the absence of which might have allowed for more consistent population growth. In addition to this aspect of enhanced security, the relatively greater impact of public goods in highly collective polities could provide life-extending and fertility-improving material and emotional benefits, not only making exit from the polity less likely, but also bringing higher birthrates and longer life spans. At the same time, migrants might choose to move from less to more collective polities. For example, in Lozi (Barotseland), one of the most collective polities in our sample, rulers brought in followers from distant provinces who became "loyal dependents" (Gluckman 1941: 32; 1943: 21), and Elizabeth Colson (1969: 30) notes that large numbers of refugees came into the region to seek safety. Other polities in the sample were similarly noted to be magnets for immigration, including Athens, Venice, and Aztec.

Low Cost of Empire

More collective polities may be able to expand territorially at comparably lower military cost if commoner subjects see advantages in new political alignments that promise public goods and the other benefits of a collective system; it would be primarily the local governing elite who would lose power and would correspondingly oppose incorporation. For the same reason, annexed provinces may have less tendency to struggle for autonomy.

Collective Action, Urban Public Goods, and Civic Capital

Cities grow in population size in part because the collective governments require relatively more developed administrative apparatuses, some of which, along with their personnel, will be sited in and around cities, but other factors could serve to augment city growth, including increased commercial functions of cities in a growing economy. Sources pertaining to the comparative sample described the benefits provided to city dwellers by public goods such as improved water quality, fire protection, and maintenance of public order, among others, that not only would make cities more attractive migration destinations but also would mitigate the well-known health hazards encountered in premodern cities (the "urban graveyard effect"). Cities might also be viewed in a comparatively positive light, both for residents and potential immigrants, because, in the more collective polities city road networks were configured to enhance geographic legibility and, in some cases, cities were reimagined symbolically as desirable places to live or visit. At the same time, in the more socially open and spatially well integrated cities there was increased potential for comingling of persons representing different social and cultural orientations, perhaps also making cities more congenial environments for potential immigrants and for rural visitors to city markets and other attractions.

PRODUCTION INTENSIFICATION

The degree of production intensification is another variable influenced by the multiple causal forces of the coactive process. To develop a measure of intensification I emphasize agricultural production and, in this category, mostly grain production; most of the societies in the comparative sample featured largely agrarian economies with grain agriculture as a leading sector (Athens and Venice were different in that they depended extensively on imported foodstuffs rather than local agricultural intensification). I also emphasized agricultural intensification because economic anthropologists and economic historians have devoted considerable attention to this aspect of production; their work has resulted in useful yardsticks to measure it, at least in terms of methods for assessing how production output can be increased per land unit rather than per capita (which is more difficult to estimate). While climate, topography, and other environmental factors influence production per land unit, there are also nearly universal human factors to consider. Low intensification values are indicated when most households devote little time or effort to field tasks such as plowing or weeding, make little use of biotechnologies such as fertilizing, and invest little in land capital such as irrigation facilities and terracing. In societies at the higher end of the intensification scale most rural households managed multiple crop cycles each year, devoted considerable effort and time to field tasks including weeding and fertilizing, and invested in land capital.

There is a strong positive statistical correlation between degree of production intensification and the public goods measure (Appendix B, section 15). This is true even though, as I mentioned, in two of the highly collective societies—Classical Athens and Venice—the agricultural supply zone was increased in scale to include distant periphery areas. The correlation value is high also despite that some societies featured high levels of production intensification but not the other aspects of coactive causality. These are mostly societies in Southeast Asia (in the sample, Thailand, Burma, Bali, Java) in which wet-rice agriculture involved (and still involves today) highly complex flow-management irrigation as well as terracing and other labor-intensive practices. Yet, these are societies that generally did not exhibit high levels of collective action in polity-building. In these few cases intensive agricultural practices often reflect the workings of local community-scale institutions that foster shared-resource cooperative management, typically with little direct involvement by a central government. Bali's irrigation system, for example, described in great detail by the ethnographer Stephen Lansing (1987), is interesting in the way its operation transcended local community and polity scales and operated largely apart from the governing elite.

ADDITIONAL FACTORS CONTRIBUTING TO
PRODUCTION INTENSIFICATION

I hypothesize that the main connection between production intensification and collective governing policies is to be found in how rural households make decisions in response to a variety of external factors. These factors include urban demand, pressure to produce more to meet tax obligations and a willingness to meet those obligations, the degree of growth of functional and accessible market systems, and favorable governing policies, including equitable taxation. I follow up on the latter aspect by comparing the taxation policies of one of the least collective polities in the sample, fourteenth-century England, followed by descriptions of two polities that scored well above average for the collective action measure, Aztec and Ming China.

ENGLAND (1327–1336 CE)

Very low agricultural productivity is evident at this time, especially in *demesne* land of the large estates worked by the *villein* populations, though in areas of weak control by the nobility and the king (e.g., the Fens), free peasants intensified production through land capital, labor, and biotechnologies. Considering the whole, however, using wheat production as a proxy for agricultural productivity, some estimates for 1300 CE are very low indeed, averaging ten bushels per acre per year (600 kilograms/hectare/year), similar to estimates for Roman Period productivity of 1,000 years earlier. This low figure remained unchanged until about 1500 but had nearly doubled in some areas by 1700. Low and stationary production values around the time of the focal period were due in part to the minimal incentives provided by the state that could foster production intensification. As is typical for a less collective polity, the English government of the focal period provided few public goods and had a weakly developed taxation administration. As I described previously, the latter depended extensively on tax collectors who had no official status, leading to corrupt practices and inefficiency, including the inequalities that result when tax collectors were less willing to press close acquaintances and relatives for compliance as much as persons outside their social network. In addition, lords and the wealthy landowning gentry often were given immunities from taxation. As a result, taxation was often not proportionate to household wealth, and this increased the levels of frustration of commoners who resented being taxed at all, especially given their lack of voice in government, the virtual absence of public goods, and the fact that revenues requested by the kings in some cases were squandered on distant and unproductive wars.

Because the state lacked any detailed census of land or productivity by agricultural plot, taxes were assessed on household wealth measurable by easily identifiable household goods. This is an administratively low-cost approach to taxation, but one that probably would have inhibited motivations to increase production and to accumulate material wealth. In addition, taxes were assessed and tax policies were decided ad hoc, whenever parliament chose to approve a levy, so taxpayers could not be certain as to what the tax rate would be, when it would be levied, or who would be subject to taxes. In 1334, for example, the poverty exemption was suddenly eliminated to shift more tax burden onto poorer families.

Aztec (1428–1521 CE)

England's chaotic and unfair taxation system of the thirteenth and fourteenth centuries contained few incentives for households to increase production, and, in fact, agricultural productivity per unit of land remained unchanged during the period in question. By contrast, the Aztec focal period featured a transition to intensive agricultural production methods that achieved levels of per hectare production that are among the highest anywhere in the premodern world, only being surpassed in the modern world after the mid-twentieth century. This is most evident in the shallow lakes of the Basin of Mexico, where low artificial islands (*chinampas*) were constructed that allowed for accurate control of water availability to crops all year, though other areas in the same region saw the development of flow-management irrigation systems and slope terracing. Through water management, fertilizing, and year-round cropping of up to three crop cycles per year, chinampa production of maize achieved as much as 3,000 to 4,000 kilograms/hectare/year.

No doubt the region's growing urban population and market system were incentives to intensification, but, following the arguments of my colleagues Lane Fargher and Verenice Heredia Espinoza, I suggest that collective action, particularly as expressed in taxation policies, may also have spurred agricultural change (Fargher and Heredia Espinoza 2012). The key to this process was the careful documentation by the official tax collection administration and its local representatives of the size and productivity of each household's land holdings. From these data, assessments could be made that assured that taxpayers would be taxed at a constant, known, and fair rate based on production potential. To fairly assess productive potential necessitated the development of standardized measurement instruments and methods of calculating the areas of irregularly sized agricultural fields, and the resulting data were recorded on painted cadastral registers that were continually updated. These methods not only established a predictable basis for tax assessment, but they also constituted a documented association between a particular household and its land and other properties, including houses, that is tantamount to a system of private property registration and property law. It was also a well-established social convention of Aztec society that the household wealth of free families could not be appropriated by members of the nobility or the state. This kind of predictability of taxation and ownership, I suggest, were incentives to increase production and also were foundational to an active market in land. When it is possible to estimate future returns to hard work and land improvements, because land value was assessed through standardized methods and officially recorded, households may be more likely to invest in their properties.

Ming Dynasty (mostly late fourteenth and fifteenth centuries CE)

Production intensification during the Ming Dynasty was so vast that the Chinese economy became a major force stimulating the rise of the Early Modern world economy. This phenomenal growth, I suggest, was an extreme example of a coactive process that was spurred, in part, through collectively consistent taxation policies. In China, all of the more collectively oriented dynasties—including the Ming— pursued policies consistent with a free and landowning peasantry. This was viewed by state-builders as a key revenue source and also an important bulwark against the political influence of aristocratic and estate-owning landlord families. Although taxation policies began to change toward the end of the Ming focal period, the key element for most of the period in question was a massive land and population registration program, the Yellow Registers, that recorded each household's tax obligation in terms of grain from male labor and cloth from women's labor, and a corresponding map of taxable properties, the Fish-Scale Registers. These registers comprised a cadastral survey so ambitious it was equaled only one other time in the premodern world, in the massive Mughal *zabt* survey of taxable land, carried out under the reign of Akbar over most of the area of northern India from Lahore to Bihar.

Eventually the Ming system was beset with many administrative difficulties; for example, careful up-to-date land surveys or measures of actual production were difficult to sustain given the Ming policy of very light government—there were only three to five functionaries in each county-level (*hsien*) administrative unit responsible for on average 90,000 persons (the comparable Aztec value would have been closer, on average, to 1,000 to 2,000 persons per local governing unit). Additional administrative problems can be attributed to the period's notable commercial growth bringing a more complex division of labor. These factors problematized the traditional view of rural household economy in which the basis for the taxation system was male agriculture and female weaving. Also, many households migrated away from their registration communities, in part to avoid tax obligations, but also in response to new economic opportunities, so over time the original surveys had declining utility.

Nonetheless, I propose that land registration made possible something approximating fair and predictable taxation levels and a form of ownership akin to private property. Particular households were administratively associated with particular plots of land, which, as in the Aztec case, would have provided incentives for agricultural intensification and other forms of investment. Certainly, there is abundant evidence for Ming Period intensification to levels even exceeding earlier periods in China, for example, especially in south China, some rice production levels reached 3,000 to 6,000 kilograms/hectare/year, while cotton production spread into the lower Yangtze, especially in areas not suited to rice, after 1350, and became a major Ming crop in that area. The main crop in south China was rice, usually cultivated as paddy, and often double-cropped (further south), or intercropped with wheat or other crops (further north in south China). Irrigated rice cultivation was intensive, involving land reclamation, weeding, fertilizing, transplanting, and water management. In particular, rice production in the south often required terracing, canal construction, and other facilities to maintain acceptable levels of field inundation at critical times, for example, through dike construction to limit flooding in some low-lying fields (poldered fields). The Ming Period saw improvements in the quality of Southeast Asian Champa (double-cropping) rice, and increased fertilizer use, and these brought additional production increases. The state also commissioned, printed, and distributed agricultural manuals to help farmers increase their per unit land production. Southern irrigation techniques included both flow and flood management, though water capture in small farmer-owned tanks was more common than gravity-flow canal distribution systems. As a result, while some large irrigation works were constructed, irrigation normally was locally managed by households on small plots (roughly 1 *mu* per cultivator, or 700 square meters). In this respect China was unlike the community and multicommunity flow-management irrigation cooperatives of Southeast Asian regions such as Bali, Java, Thailand, and Burma. I suggest that this difference resulted from China's household-based tax registration system that aimed to achieve equitable levels of taxation and a strong connection of households to particular landed resources.

COMMENT

The Aztec and Ming examples (and Mughal, which I briefly mentioned) illustrate the kind of rational field administration of taxation that Western researchers have attributed to European modernity but ignored in relation to non-European societies. Polities such as Mughal, Aztec, and China have been characterized in European literatures since the late eighteenth century as despotisms whose centralized power was attributed in large part to state control over large-scale irrigation agriculture. However, recent scholarly research has confirmed some, but not extensive, state involvement in irrigation management in these cases; certainly it was not a major element of political economy. In Ming China, according to Francesca Bray (1984: 109–10), even the highly productive irrigated rice production of the southern regions involved mostly water capture in small farmer-owned tanks, and the latter were usually built and managed by households or small cooperative groups, not the state. Similarly, in the Mughal polity the state was rarely directly involved in irrigation management; for example, the Indus flowed largely "uncontrolled" (Habib 1963: 29–30). In the Aztec case, the current consensus among archaeologists is that while the state was involved to some degree in water-management projects for agriculture, there was considerable locally based construction and management as well.

THE COACTIVE CAUSAL PROCESS: A COMPARISON OF AZTEC AND INKA

The statistical analyses described above, based on a large sample of well-described polities, show that collective action in polity-building is an essential part of the coactive causal process. We can gain another perspective on coactive process by investigating similarities and differences between societies that are in many ways comparable, but show difference in the degree of collective action. To illustrate, I briefly compare two pre-Hispanic New World civilizations—Inka and Aztec—whose populations made use of similar technologies emphasizing lithic, copper and bronze tools, and of course pottery, and which also shared important crops, especially maize. In both areas, there was intensification of maize production, illustrating similar potentials for production elasticity. However, Inka and Aztec societies had developed quite dissimilar modes of governance during the respective focal periods. The Inka polity scored below the Aztec in terms of overall collective action, mostly owing to the Inka's highly autocratic form of governing, while the Aztec system included a number of features consistent with collective action such as governing councils with commoner representation and a highly bureaucratized judicial system.

Corresponding to the different degrees of collective action, while key aspects of the coactive causal process are not evident in the Inka case, the period of growth of the Aztec polity displays all of its elements. For example, while there were Inka Period cities, this society was not rated high on overall degree of urbanization. Cities remained relatively small, possibly because families were forbidden to migrate, though the state itself did forcibly move many people, as *mitimac* colonists, to provide labor for various state-sponsored or elite productive enterprises. The capital at Cuzco was highly specialized for political functions and was an important repository of state symbols, but it housed relatively few people, only 15,000 to 20,000. The state suppressed the commercial economy, especially in the empire's core zone, and as a result institutions for paragovernmental market management were not important factors in the institutional construction of society. The state's record-keeping technologies were highly developed, yet they served principally to provide information about "the number of corvée-liable citizens in any given area, the number of llamas grazing on each state pasture, the hoard of maize and wool and cloth in a given [state] warehouse or anything likely to interest the policymakers" (Murra 1980: 110).

By comparison, during the Postclassic focal period, Central Mexico was by far the most highly commercialized region of the pre-Hispanic New World, with a major marketplace that served up to 50,000 people per day and numerous lower-ranking marketplaces. And, Aztec cities were massive, by premodern standards, including an estimated population of 175,000 for the capital and marketing center of Tenochtitlan-Tlatelolco, but many other cities with populations in the tens of thousands dotted the landscape. The total population of the imperial core, estimated at well over 1 million in the Basin of Mexico alone (in part owing to immigration), was much higher than all prior archaeological periods, and, as I alluded to previously, the overall material standard of living improved in many respects. The state developed methods for assessing the wealth of families and recorded the information, thus associating particular households with their productive resources. A politically influential paragovernmental organization, the Pochteca, managed the marketplaces and was highly regarded in society for its devotion to moral principles of market behavior and fair adjudication of marketplace disputes.

A CONSEQUENCE OF ORDERLY TAX COLLECTION: ADVANCES IN GEOMETRY AND MATHEMATICAL NOTATION

Land surveys under conditions of collective action promoted the independent development of methods of surveying, mathematical notation, and geometrical calculations used to estimate the area of irregular fields in the Aztec case and in Ming Dynasty China. Similarly, the Greeks attributed the beginnings of their mathematical culture to the necessity of measuring the areas of irregular surfaces, which did correspond with the rise of the democratic polity (sixth century BCE).

CAUSES OF AND CONDITIONS FAVORING THE COACTIVE CAUSAL PROCESS

Earlier I alluded to the difficulties inherent in any attempt to describe a situation of mutual and multiple causation, because the particular conditions that initiate the chain of events will be difficult to identify and because data suited to hypothesis testing are difficult to come by. My sense, however, is that there are grounds to make reasonable proposals about the nature of causality, and in what follows I describe four conditions that may have been conducive to setting in motion the coactive process: production elasticity, growing wealth inequality, urban biosocial challenges, and marketplace social evolution.

Production Elasticity

The benefits accruing from collective action and the coactive process are, in a sense, a luxury that exacts a high price. While state-builders strategize to minimize cost, still, collective action and corollary features of the coactive process ignite change, social complexity, and a demand for labor power. They demand that people be able to move, to intermingle, and to be visible to one another. Change is mandated in administrative complexity and in social technologies for measuring land areas and census-taking. Increased flows of information and goods place strain on communication, storage, and transportation technologies and infrastructures, and on the built environment of urban space-use. The costs inherent in a turn to collective action are borne by new wealth production. But wealth and collective action will be stymied unless systems of production are sufficiently elastic enabling most households to respond to new demands and opportunities.

To a degree, production elasticity will be inherent in the natural environmental setting. Especially in a largely agrarian economy, a region with deep fertile soils and dependable water sources will have more production elasticity than a rugged mountainous terrain or a desert. Yet, by pointing to environmental potential, I risk proposing an environmental determinist argument. A deterministic argument is misleading in part because, unless other social and cultural conditions are met, even a potentially rich environmental setting highly suited to intensification will not necessarily host collective action and the coactive process. Economic anthropologists learned long ago that households will intensify production only when they see good reasons to do so, not just because they can.

The weakness of an environmental determinist argument is also evident in the case of sub-Saharan Africa. At first glance, it would seem to be a region in which limited production elasticity would have inhibited collective action and the coactive process. Traditionally, over much of this tropical area food and fiber production was horticultural, making extensive use of perennial crops more suited to local environmental conditions than cereal-based agriculture. Irrigation of crops is almost absent, and generally it is accepted that the perennial crops such as yam and plantains are not highly suited to intensification strategies by comparison with the domesticated grasses such as wheat, rice, and maize. As a result, the rotating field systems characteristic of horticultural regimes ("slash and burn") are comparatively low in per hectare productivity. Yet, in spite of these inherent limits, evidence for intensification abounds in the sustaining areas of the two most highly collective polities in the sub-Saharan sample, Asante and Lozi. Both T. C. McCaskie (1995: 31) and Ivor Wilks (1993: 47) note that in the vicinity of the Asante capital, Kumase, there is evidence for an unusual degree of agricultural intensification (for Africa) involving pig "nurseries" and continuous, two-crop-per-year cultivation of root crops. The main agricultural zone of the Lozi polity was the vast floodplain of the Upper Zambezi River, which had been improved for agricultural use by constructing an extensive system of canals that "score the plain" (Gluckman 1961: 63; cf. Prins 1980: 58–70). These canals served both to increase the cultivable area by draining swamps while providing for transportation infrastructure.

That the natural environment alone is not a causal factor is also indicated by societies such as those in parts of South and Southeast Asia where wet-rice production was practiced. These environments were highly consistent with production intensification based on labor-intensive flow-management irrigation, fertilizing, and terracing. High levels of cooperative water management are needed to achieve intensification, and this typically took place at the community level or at larger spatial scales, as in Bali. Yet, these developments had nothing to do with the development of highly collective forms of government or of coactive process—cooperation was expressed only in one institutional domain, the irrigation cooperative, while polities themselves tended toward political segmentation and autocracy. Large urban centers were rare, and markets tended toward restricted forms where the governing elite and alien traders controlled the profitable long-distance trade. This system exacerbated social differentiation and inhibited the development of local paragovernmental forms of marketplace management.

The incompleteness of an environmental theory is also indicated by examples of collective action and the coactive process thriving even when the potential for local agricultural intensification was minimal. For example, there was little potential for agricultural intensification in the vicinity of Classical Athens (wheat productivity was similar to Medieval England, averaging only 650 kilograms/hectare/year during the focal period). The Athenian democracy thrived by combining local and imported food, depending extensively on supply zones in the Black Sea region. Another case of an import economy is Venice, which, during the focal period, imported much of its food supply and other goods rather than investing in agricultural development in its local domain. Terra Firma supply zones of the Venetian empire such as Astria, Aquileia, and Triest provided Venice with timber, charcoal, stone, wheat, and pigs, among other products. The wealth that Venice depended on to support its costly apparatus of collective action and its imported food supply came from its position as a major entrepôt in world-system trade. This strategy proved tenuous after the sixteenth century, however, when there was a reorganization of world-system exchange networks that deprived Venetians and other Mediterranean trade centers of much of their profits; at this point, the Venetians did shift their attention to local agricultural development.

Similarly, Pomeranz (2000: chap. 6) shows how in early modern England economic growth stemmed in part from local agricultural intensification, but additional production was shifted to external peripheries in the manner of Athens and Venice. However, by comparison with those two, England's periphery exchange network encompassed a much larger spatial scale and depended to a much greater degree on production by slave labor in its circum-Caribbean supply region. By establishing colonies and plantations, England gained what Pomeranz calls a "New World windfall" in food energy and other imports, which he estimates by 1800 represented the equivalent of over 10 million acres of average production on English farms. For example, by 1800, sugar imports alone provided ninety calories a day of average caloric consumption, or roughly 4 percent, and by 1901 they amounted to 20 percent of calories. The system of energy subsidy for the English case violates one of the predictions of collective action theory, namely, that collective action will bring in its wake a general lessening of social inequality by building a form of social solidarity that cuts across social divides. Instead, while there was some degree of weakening in social differentiation in the core zone from late feudalism to early modernity, that social change was funded in part by the forced labor of slaves in the periphery supply zones.

WEALTH INEQUALITY

Of the comparative sample, nearly a third of the societies had commercial connections to large-scale trade networks, most serving as periphery suppliers of raw materials or other goods into core-zone economies. In a few cases, such as Venice and Swahili Lamu, profits were realized from long-distance trade in their role of trade entrepôt. The data point to how both raw-material supply and entrepôt economies brought increased economic inequality. Often, too, as important sources of state wealth, the control and taxation of foreign trade brought with them the predicted forms of autocratic governance based on an external revenue economy similar to the "resource curse" of the contemporary rentier states. Recall, however, that a resource curse is likely to be most keenly felt when local governing systems are not highly developed and where revenues from foreign trade and exporting are large in relation to the scale of the local economy. By contrast, a "Norway effect" is found where the local economy is large in relation to export revenues and where effective governing systems are in place prior to the advent of large export-economy revenues.

The data from the comparative sample suggest that something like the Norway effect was in play in some of the societies Lane Fargher and I investigated. An influx of wealth from an export economy appears not to have had the usual effect where the majority of the population recognized wealth as a source of political instability and corruption. In these cases wealth spurred efforts to create new institutions aiming to maintain acceptable levels of governing efficiency and stability. We see this process in the case of Athenian democracy where, according to Robert Wallace (1998: 17), the people of Athens engaged in a struggle against a "wealthy upper class." And, according to Veyne (1990: 75), one aspect of the resultant institution-building was a system of required civic gifting that restricted the ability of wealthy patrons to build networks of clientage that could unduly influence the political process. At the same time, a multitude of rules were in place to reduce the possibilities for official corruption.

Similarly, in Swahili Lamu, the dual ward organization (*mitaa*) served as a mechanism for power-sharing between the "old" money of the northern ward's population and the less affluent, often immigrant population of the southern ward. This system featured citizen participation in ward councils, elected officials, and power sharing by rotation of elected *diarchs* (principals), who represented the two wards. According to James de Vere Allen (1993: 224) and A.H.J. Prins (1971: 48), this governing system accommodated the interests of diverse constituencies and minimized the degree to which wealthy families could dominate the political process.

Like Athens and Swahili Lamu, in Venice, wealth was abundant but was recognized as a challenge to the social fabric. Correspondingly, the system of governance maintained extensive controls over officials, especially the chief administrative officer, the doge. He was expected to strive to be loved by the people, to favor the poor, to ensure justice, to supply public goods, and to give an ear to the people's voice. This officer was carefully monitored, could be impeached at any time, and was not allowed to own properties outside Venetian territory. At the end of each term of office, he was investigated by the state attorneys and his estate was subject to fines and confiscation for malfeasance.

Urban Biosocial Challenges

In cities, intense and frequent social interactions enable novel social alliances among persons and groups, while compactness brings movement efficiencies that spur the growth of commerce. Yet, inevitably, in the premodern condition, cities will require creative institutional problem-solving to manage an influx of immigrants and to mitigate threats to health and safety including fire danger, disease, ethnic and sectarian conflict, and intense competition for high-value spaces. I propose that these kinds of urban biosocial challenges will be generative forces for social, technological, and cultural innovation and change in the direction of collective action; only the more collective governments will have the required institutional capacity to relieve urban maladies. City dwellers not only would welcome political change but also may provide an important impetus for change (I would point out that the sociologist Castells [1978] makes this argument for contemporary European cities). A case in point is the Ming Dynasty, a period when the system of self-governing wards (the *baojia* system) was transformed into a structure of administrative zones governed by salaried officials of the central state. This reformed pattern of city governance was installed, in part, as a response to demands made by the urban poor and middle class who proclaimed, "we want taxes" in exchange for state services to replace the corrupt and ineffective local neighborhood-scale organizations.

BORDERLAND SOCIAL PROCESS: MARKETPLACES AS SITES
OF SOCIAL FOMENT AND EGALITARIAN IMAGINATION

"The [ancient Greek] economy is constantly asserting itself
and threatening to escape from the normative frame thrown
around it by the polity." (James Redfield 1986: 52)

The Gandhian anticolonial Noncooperation Movement in India "staked out its presence in the "extraterritorial" space of
the market ... [a] ... choice locale for integrating the imagined greater community." (Anand Yang 1998: 164)

For Berbers of the Bled es Siba (the "Land of Insolence") "it is no exaggeration to say that the life of the tribe almost in its entirety happens in the market. It is the place where the natives meet; not only do they provide for their daily needs through sales but also it is the spot where ideas are exchanged, political information is passed on, the announcements of the authorities are made and the reaction to these are formed ... political conspiracies started, public outcries raised, broadminded proposals mooted and crimes hatched." (from E. Doutte, *Merrakech, Comité du Maroc*, 1905, quoted in Benet 1957: 193)

"The market remained a social as well as an economic nexus. It was the place where one-hundred-and-one social and personal transactions went on; where news was passed, rumour and gossip flew around, politics was (if ever) discussed in the inns or wine-shops round the market square. The market was the place where the people, because they were numerous, felt for a moment they were strong." (E. P. Thompson 1971: 135)

I propose that we take into consideration another possible generative force for social, technological, and cultural change, namely, that an important starting point for collective action can be found in marketplaces. By proposing this originating source for collective action, I am not taking the position of contemporary market fundamentalists who argue that markets alone will provide optimal solutions for social problems. Instead, I point to geographic marginality, sacrality and liminality, and self-governance as forces that were conducive to the imagining of new modes of cultural understanding and forms of social intercourse and organization that spilled over into other domains, including the political.

To propose a causal connection between marketplace and social change in the direction of egalitarianism is by no means a novel idea. For example, Albert Hirschman (1977, 1982) documented the arguments of Adam Smith, Thomas Chalmers, and others who saw the growth of commerce as a stimulus to the development of rational thinking and moral conduct that could serve as a foil to patrician interests. During the nineteenth century, the economist David Ricardo proposed that the state itself evolved to provide governing services for markets. More recently, Rodney Hilton and other historians argue for a central role of the marketplaces in social and cultural change in the rise of Early Modern England. Similarly, scholars following in the tradition of Bakhtin's writing on the popular culture of the carnival and the marketplaces point to how the venues' oppositional and liminal qualities made them incubators of an egalitarian rethinking. In their summary of this literature, Stallybrass and White (1986: 27) suggest that to "think" a marketplace is to imagine how it unsettles identity and how it brings "a commingling of categories usually kept separate and opposed: centre and periphery, inside and outside, stranger and local . . . high and low . . . In the marketplaces pure and simple categories of thought find themselves perplexed and one-sided. Only hybrid notions are appropriate to such a hybrid place." What is novel in my proposal is to argue that marketplaces had the power to provoke culture change and a turn to collective action outside the context of the history of Western modernity.

In chapter 6 I discussed the evolution of marketplace institutions from a cooperation perspective, and I revisit some aspects of that discussion as a source of ideas about the possible role of marketplaces as originating sites for collective action. My approach need not imply that somehow people necessarily envisioned a future of benefit from collective action and then undertook the creation of marketplaces to achieve it. Instead, the historical process at play was probably something more akin to what we refer to as "Romer's Rule," in which an initial change aimed only to solve a particular narrow problem, in this case the kinds of cooperation problems associated with open markets. Only later did such narrowly contrived problem-solving exercises in the marketplaces prove to have broader social change implications.

I suggest that marketplaces were the primary venues for the resolution of cooperation problem-solving in large and socially and culturally heterogeneous groups. Initially, at least, these marketplaces were located in weakly governed boundaries and frontier regions at the limits of state authority. Here social and physical marginality rendered marketplaces ripe with opportunities for social and cultural novelty and what Weber identified as a "charismatic" fervor that endowed marketplaces with the power to bring social and cultural change. Given their extraterritorial context, proper marketplace function was not likely to result from traditional governing authority. Rather, novel institutions for paragovernance were developed by marketplace entrepreneurs with the goal of devising operationally effective institutions to provide for safety, cleanliness, order, and, importantly, the equitable adjudication of disputes. The necessity for managerial effectiveness is amplified because such marketplaces must be functionally competitive if they are to attract the marketing crowds and thus generate revenues for market managers. As I alluded to previously, marketers will prefer to patronize a better-managed market, and one where a market's tolls and taxes properly reflect the value of services rendered. This paragovernmental process, I suggest, had eventual social change implications for the development of modes of cooperation in the political domain. In the marketplaces, people came to imagine the possibility that a form of governance could be problem solving and efficient, with the goal of providing management services commensurate with what is demanded of those it serves and to do so on a socially equitable basis.

In later historical periods, when collective action institutions for polity governance are evident, marketplaces were incorporated into the institutional structures of the central political institutions and often became significant sources of state revenues. However, for markets to function effectively as commercial venues and as revenue sources, the center elite will be obligated to incorporate the marketplace's egalitarian ethic and functional efficiency into their designs for state-building. We saw this earlier in the way that ideas and institutions of the Greek marginal peoples were brought into the cultural and social mainstream with the rise of the democratic polis. Recall how the trickster god Hermes was transported into the civic center of the polity as a deity of the *agora* market zone, which became the center of Athenian civic life; as Norman Brown (1947: 108) put it, "Hermes' intrusion into the *agora* paralleled his intrusion into the world of culture." Rituals such as the Great Dionysia Festival preserved the vitality of cultural concepts associated with the marketplaces—marginality, liminality and metamorphosis—and as such reaffirmed the importance of the commoner and the commercial in the social fabric of the polity.

13

Final Thoughts

Insights Gained from an Expanded Collective Action Theory

Cooperation in large and complex societies is a social and cultural process that has been fashioned out of diverse social and cultural settings. By considering cooperation as a process, I propose, not only provides an appropriate design for research, but it also is a path to effective policy-making. To illustrate this latter possibility, in what follows I point to several current ideas about society and human nature that I propose require re-evaluation with a processual cooperation theory in mind. My suggestions are in three sections. First, I argue that Western academic theories that posit an altruistic or compassionate human pay too little attention to the importance of institution-building. Second, I also question the influence of promarket economic theory and ideology that tends to paint collective action as "socialism," and its public goods as an inefficient economy. Third, I argue that, however commendable in theory, democratic ideals may not be as transformative as generally thought. Although the advent of democracy is understood as a transformative moment in human history, carrying with it the promise of a world free from the yoke of autocratic rule, when we look at the aftermath of the democratic revolution we see an uneven distribution of democratic governance among the world's polities and even the backsliding of once democratic regimes to autocracy, but why?

DOI: 10.5876/9781607325147.c013

POLITICAL IMPLICATIONS OF AN ALTRUISTIC
OR COMPASSIONATE HUMAN NATURE

Effective problem-solving and policy-making ultimately depend on a well-developed theory of the human social actor. Yet, with regards to the question of cooperation, there is little overlap between the human altruist imagined in evolutionary psychology theory and the rational social actor of collective action theory. In this book I have laid out an empirically based critique of altruist thinking and its biomathematical methodology that I see as not only inadequately grounded in anthropological knowledge but also excessively dependent on formal mathematical models that vastly simplify a complex human psychology.

But there is more to consider than the scientific validity of evolutionary psychology. To truly understand why a particular notion of human nature might garner attention among social scientists, and the public, it is also reasonable to think about its relevance to contemporary ideological discourses. I suggest the altruist human is an idea that should be subject to this kind of scrutiny. This need not imply that all biomathematical researchers can be assumed to be inspired by ulterior political motives, though some, such as Jonathan Haidt, clearly are (Jost 2012). Yet, by considering the political implications of the human altruist we might have a better way to understand the current popularity of evolutionary psychology's arguments that, to loosely paraphrase Claude Lévi-Strauss, in the minds of many are good to think, good to write, good to publish, and good to read.

Some critics of sociobiology and evolutionary psychology (mentioned in the bibliographic essay) point to one possible attraction of this line of theorizing. I refer to the fact that some authors see consistencies between evolutionary psychological theories and contemporary neoliberal economic ideas. And, as Susan McKinnon (2005: 70) argues, when such ideas are couched in scientific language they appear as "natural universals" that better serve to validate ideology. In the particular case of the altruist human, I agree that neoliberal ideas are supported when we imagine that it is altruism, not institutions, that drive cooperation. A key argument of neoliberal theory promoted by many economists, conservative politicians, and development agencies such as the World Bank, is that public services are not most efficiently provided by the state. Instead, services are ideally privatized but also complemented by the actions of volunteer organizations or persons whose efforts constitute altruistic acts of charity. The role of of altruism is also highlighted by framers of the "new economies," such as Airbnb and Uber, who make use of a "sharing economy" terminology. To Natasha Singer, their language "frames technology-enabled transactions as if they were altruistic or community endeavors" (*New York Times* Sunday Business, August 8, 2015, 3).

Neoliberal thinking is implicit in Sussman and Chapman (2004: 16) and Lee Cronk and Beth Leech, who provide what they see as support for the claim of altruistic ubiquity by citing the aftermath of the 9/11 tragedy. Here they see an example of the pervasiveness of altruistic motivation, given that "thousands of people volunteered at Ground Zero ... [and] ... Many thousands more around the world responded to calls for donations and relief supplies, with cash donations by individuals totaling more than $1.5 billion" (Cronk and Leech 2013, ix). Of course this outpouring was touching in how it showed many people's sympathy for those who lost their lives and for Americans more generally. My wife, Cindy, and I were touched also by a letter we received from Turkish acquaintances we knew from having done fieldwork there some years before, apologizing for what the attackers did and hoping we were coping well.

From the perspective of a policy-maker, however, it is not clear what conclusions could be reached from the 9/11 experience. First, if cooperation is "all around us," why would such a thing happen in the first place? Also, the theory of altruistic ubiquity seems to imply that we should passively wait for catastrophe, then assume the negative consequences will be ameliorated through an upwelling of altruistic response. The perspective of collective action theory and its focus on institutions, I suggest, is better able to provide a realistic assessment of an incident like 9/11 and to find ways to use our knowledge of it to minimize the possibility of future occurrences. For example, rather than confirming that cooperation is "all around us," 9/11 exposed avoidable cooperation failures both prior to and following the event, failures we can learn from. For example, Jason Ryan and Theresa Cook, in their ABC News report (September 18, 2007) quoted the head of US spy operations in his admission that the tragedy could have been prevented had there been more willingness by federal agencies to share information ("It was an issue of connecting information that was available") (Ryan and Cook 2007). I would also point out the apparent institutional failures of insurance companies and New York pension plans when they allowed millions in excess pension and insurance claims from faked 9/11-caused injuries (www.cnn.com/2014/02/24/justice/new-york-ptsd-9-11-scam/).

COMPASSIONIST THEORIES OF THE "AUTHENTIC" HUMAN

It is important to note that human altruist theory is highly consistent with a tradition of social science thinking that many find ideologically motivated in a manner analogous to evolutionary psychology. I refer to what Michael Thompson, Richard Ellis, and Aaron Wildavsky refer to as "compassionist" theories, which, in the recent social science tradition, are derived from sources including Jean-Jacques Rousseau, Émile Durkheim, and Karl Marx (Thompson et al. 1990). These authors promoted idealistic views of what humanity is like in its supposed "natural" state. Marx's communist theory, for example, posited an "authentic" communitarian human who once existed in the small communities of the past and may still be found in a few societies not influenced by capitalism and the state. In Marx's scheme, it was the advent of private property, the market, and the state that aroused a competitive and self-seeking human prone to antagonistic individualism, a state of being that is overcome only when private property, the commercial bourgeoisie, and the state are destroyed. Out of destruction a communistic society will naturally emerge, he argued, and be driven by spontaneous cooperation among members of, in Marx's terms, a "free association" of equals. Because spontaneous cooperation alone would sustain society, little or no institutional structure for cooperation will be required.

The mid-twentieth century application of Marxist theory in China provides an example of institutional planning failure resulting from an excessively optimistic notion of an underlying cooperation-prone human nature. Communist planners, following Marx, assumed that it was the marketplaces that abetted competitive and self-seeking behavior, bringing conflict and wealth inequality. According to G. W. Skinner (1985: 24), in the communist view, "Price-setting markets mean haggling and haggling means contention; furthermore, they thought, markets disrupt solidarity by introducing competition and envy through stimulating the mobility aspirations of all and fulfilling them only for some."

Beginning in 1959–61, following on the state's antimarket theory, Chinese planners pursued policies aiming to dismantle the market system and to sever commercial ties between rural and urban populations. Yet, because they assumed that market decline would bring spontaneous cooperation, planners failed to anticipate that an institutional system would be needed to replace the commercial economy. The Chinese people suffered from this miscalculation when, rather than an emergence of spontaneous cooperation, the loss of markets brought a massive disruption of commodity flows, a decline of agricultural production, economic depression, an increase in poverty, and the starvation of an estimated 20 million persons.

ARE PUBLIC GOODS A SOCIALIST ECONOMY?

Altruist theory appears to be consistent with neoliberalism, but is it possible to conclude that collective action theory also aligns with a particular ideological position? My Purdue University students seem to think so, often making the inference that when I refer to cooperation, collective action, and public goods I promote a "socialist" agenda. But this thinking is a mistaken logic fueled by ideological confusion. For one, by definition, socialism implies a state possessing primary ownership of the means of production, implying that key revenue streams will fit into the category Lane Fargher and I call "external" (i.e., external to the body of taxpayers). As a result, it is unlikely the state's power will be relational in the sense of collective action. In fact, historical and contemporary socialist states have shown a propensity toward coercion, autocracy, and comparatively poor public goods provisioning.

The "socialist" label is also problematic in light of the fact that, as I demonstrated, collective action and market development are highly correlated. This finding suggests that public goods economies and market economies in many cases are complementary and even mutually reinforcing economies (with exceptions I allude to below). By contrast, both autocracy and economic inefficiency have been noted in many of the planned and state-controlled economies of socialist states.

I would also point to the fact that any perception that public goods and collective action imply "socialism" is one mired in the questionable conceptual divide common in Western thought that a "good society" is built either from social engineering and high levels of state interference in economy (the socialist argument), or is built from the beneficial "spontaneous order" that develops out of unregulated economic action (the market fundamentalist/capitalist/libertarian argument). I see this kind of dualistic thinking as only one more example of an excessively simplistic typological and binary logic that plagues Western thinking. From the comparative research reported here, I see possibilities of framing a more nuanced view that problematizes the divide between socialism and capitalism.

ARE PUBLIC GOODS BEST EVALUATED AS A FORM OF ECONOMIC DISTRIBUTION OR AS A SOCIAL FORCE ESSENTIAL TO COLLECTIVE ACTION IN STATE-BUILDING?

Through our endeavor to adapt collective theory to state-building outside of Western experience, Lane Fargher and I were made aware of the value of a fiscal theory to explain variation in forms of the state. Our data demonstrate that taxpayer-produced internal revenues have a powerful effect creating conditions favorable for relational forms of power, public goods, and accountable leadership. By contrast, statistical analysis points to how principal-controlled resource regimes are consistent with authoritarianism much like the contemporary "rentier" states.

While fiscal theories gained recognition through the writings of prominent economists such as Joseph Schumpeter, over the last century many economists and conservative politicians turned to the idea that state-managed public goods are a comparatively inefficient means of economic distribution and should be resorted to only in cases of market failure. Yet, to understand collective action in state formation, public goods must be regarded as far more than simply one optional form of distributive economy. Instead, they are crucial to the operation of cooperative state-building, for several reasons. While the fiscal argument does not preclude the possibility of state failure in the provisioning of public goods—any such system will

fail in the absence of effective institutions to manage potential cooperator problems—when such a system is effective, public goods are a difficult-to-fake signal
that the operative principles of a state are consistent with collective benefit. At the
same time, when principals distribute public goods they are not able to claim credit
for the creation of benefits, because they have been jointly produced. Thus public
goods truly reflect the relational quality of a state's power, positioning the citizenry
as a vital player in the civic unit.

How does the fiscal theory apply in the case of a "rentier state" such as Saudi
Arabia? Here sovereigns maintain control over the state's immense wealth, some of
which is allocated for public benefit. This appears to violate the proposed connection between type of revenue source and the relative degree of collective action, as
in this case the state provides services in spite of its external revenue sources and its
concentration of political power in the hands of a few. However, it remains the case
that the services in question are not genuinely public goods because they are not
jointly provided. As a result, while their distribution may confer a kind of legitimacy to the state and its rulers, they are not predicted to engender relational power
and ruler accountability in the sense described by collective action theory—and, in
fact, in Saudi Arabia the leadership has been able to ignore most calls for reform.
Instead, the provision of services most likely represents a strategy to stave off opposition to autocratic rule.

HOW DIFFERENT ARE PREMODERN AND MODERN STATES?

"What were the first governments like? Archaeologists and historians
tell us they were extraordinarily unfree. Basically, all the first centralized
governments were led by despots . . . [but now] . . . Modernity is increasing the forces that tend historically to push human rights along—communications, education, and reason . . . If history is any guide, these trends
militate toward long-term expansion of freedom and rights." (quote from
Steven Pinker, who was speaking at the 2014 Oslo Freedom Forum, in
Danny Hakim, the *New York Times Sunday Review*, October 26, 2014, 5)

Malfunctioning governments "remain a widespread phenomena across the globe." (Adserà et al. 2003: 445)

Given that humans have a lengthy history of state-building, up to 5,000 years in
some regions, is it possible to conclude that through lengthy periods of state-building
experience humans have learned how to enforce the integrity of the governing elite,
make public goods available, and give voice to commoners? Evidently, not, in spite

of Pinker's optimistic view, as Alicia Adserà and her coauthors conclude (Adserà et al. 2003). Here I address the issue of malfunctioning states through a comparative consideration of the nature of state-building in premodernity and modernity.

I base my comparison on the premodern sample and on cross-sectional data for contemporary states made available through the offices of the World Bank, United Nations, and Organization for Economic Cooperation and Development (OECD), among other sources. Much of this kind of information pertains to measures of economic growth and the suitability of governing systems to manage and encourage growth, while other sources emphasize cultural preferences or psychological or health-related variables such as subjective well-being. Few sources provide information that closely parallel the categories coded in the comparative premodern sample; comparative assessments of public goods, in particular, are poorly represented in the data tabulations for contemporary nation-states. With the goal of comparing a sample of contemporary polities with our premodern sample, I did locate a source that provides at least some measures comparable to the ones Lane Fargher and I developed, the "Global Integrity Report" (https://www.globalintegrity.org). This is, coincidentally, a sample of thirty societies at the time of our analysis (their intention is to add more cases).

Lacking any public goods measures, to compare the two 30-society samples, I emphasized governmentality measures, including one Global Integrity variable that roughly equates with our measure of control over principals. This is their "Conflicts of Interest Safeguards and Checks and Balances: Executive Branch." I developed a proxy for bureaucratization by summing the values of four Global Integrity measures that address effectiveness of administrative systems: "Public Requests for Government Information"; "Election Integrity"; "Civil Service: Conflicts of Interest Safeguards and Political Independence"; and "Law Enforcement: Conflicts of Interest Safeguards and Professionalism" (I evaluate the statistical validity of the Global Integrity data in Appendix B, section 16; a list of societies included in the sample is found in Appendix B, Figure B.4).

The statistical analysis of the Global Integrity data identified interesting similarities between the contemporary and premodern polities, and suggests only a glimmer of overall progress in building states that would exemplify the best practices of collective action. Similarity is evident in that I found positive correlations between the two proxies for bureaucratization and control over principals, and the statistical values are similar for the two samples (for the premodern sample $r = 0.75, p = <$ 0.0001, while for the contemporary states $r = 0.66, p = <$ 0.0001). These very high and statistically significant results indicate that whether past or present, institutions related to principal control and bureaucratization tend to develop hand-in-hand as part of a process of institutional development for cooperation.

It is also of interest to note that a cluster analysis of the Global Integrity data produced a tripartite grouping analogous in some ways to the premodern clusters reported in chapter 8 and in Appendix B, Figure B.1 (the dendrogram and associated statistics are reported in Appendix B, Figure B.4). Like the premodern clusters, this analysis clearly shows one group analogous to "High Collective" group (27 percent of the total, compared with 20 percent for the premodern). Like the premodern High Collective group, these polities featured overall high levels of the principal control and bureaucratization variables. Another group is similar to the Low Collective cluster in having uniformly low scores on all variables (43 percent of the contemporary polities compared with 40 percent for the premodern). In both samples, a middle group is identifiable from the cluster analysis, though, in the case of the contemporary polities this is not analogous to the "Collective with Strong Monarch" pattern found in the premodern sample, in which moderate to high measures of collective action coexisted with a powerful monarch. Instead, these were cases that simply showed more of a mixed pattern in variable scores.

The Global Integrity data also allowed me to evaluate the fiscal theory of collective action with contemporary polities. From data sources including World Bank and others I subjectively categorized each of the Global Integrity polities in terms of a predominance of external or internal revenues in a way that roughly matches the coding for the premodern sample. This exercise was challenging because in a large number of cases, contemporary states are in the process of privatizing previously state-owned industries and in some cases it was difficult to determine just how far the process had been carried out. However, if state's revenues derive in large part from its control of oil or other exportable wealth, if major industries are controlled by the state, or if privatizing is in process while key industries maintain strong ties to offices of the government (e.g., in Russia, where state representatives sit on boards of directors and firms and their owners are subject to arbitrary confiscations), then the polity was coded as having a strong orientation toward external fiscal economy.

In Appendix B, Table B.8, I report on the results of a t-Test of comparison of mean values for measures of governmentality from the Global Integrity Report, dividing the sample by predominantly internal or predominantly external revenues. The results are nearly identical to the results of analysis of the premodern sample reported in Appendix B, Table B.2, namely, that governmentality scores are significantly higher where there is a predominance of internal revenue. This exercise points again to the vitality of a fiscal theory and to how it is taxpayer-produced revenue—whether in premodernity or in modernity—that is a central causal factor in whether a state's power will be truly relational and, hence, to a greater degree based on cooperation, or will tend toward autocracy when the main revenue streams are external.

This comparative exercise, though based on a small sample of premodern and modern states, suggests that Pinker's assessment of the role of "modernity" as a force for progressive state-building is overly optimistic. While modernization has been a powerful force (recall Charles Tilly's claim that European democratic institutions have "moved from the West to the rest of the world" [Tilly 1975a: 608]), I suggest an alternative scenario that, informed by collective action theory, is attentive how important institution-building and internal revenues are to the construction of workable collective states.

Premodern state-builders were confronted with numerous challenges in building collective states, in most cases owing to opposition by an elite who stood to lose traditional privileges coupled with a lack of adequate communication, transportation, and data-management technologies. However, in some respects there were actually fewer impediments to building state capacity in the past than state-builders face at present. I say this because, while the idea of democracy is a powerful one, it does not always carry much weight when we consider the similarly powerful economic forces unleashed by the advent of a muscular globalization process that, especially since the 1970s, often has diminished possibilities for democratic reform.

In premodernity there was nothing comparable to the international tax competition that forces states to keep taxes low to attract highly mobile capital, and that thus inhibits the possibilities for sustaining a collective state. And while premodern autocrats controlled assets such as private estates, today's autocrats have many new sources of revenue they may draw from that allow them to ignore demands for reform. For example, we see multinational corporations bribing state leaders and exporting profits to low-tax havens, strategies that maximize corporate profit but also nurture despots while robbing citizens and the state of needed revenues. In our study of premodern states we did not encounter the equivalent of today's propensity toward worker-impoverishing capital flight from developing countries. There were no international agencies such as the International Monetary Fund, whose neoliberal policies of fiscal austerity, privatization, and trade liberalization often have had negative economic and political outcomes for developing countries. Countries such as the United States and agencies like the IMF also distribute foreign aid and sovereign loans, which augment resources that autocrats may use to maintain power and also result in high debt-servicing costs that detract from a state's abilities to build governing capacity. And the premodern societies we studied did not feature anything like today's exaggerated "resource curse" (the dilemma that great wealth often does not bring democracy), brought especially by the profits from petroleum-export economies that finance corrupt and autocratic regimes.

In spite of the democratic ideal, humans remain mired in a steady-state phenomenon, evidently with a deep past, in which good governance is always a possibility but is unevenly distributed. However, we can learn from the long human experience in state-building to find an alternate path. First, while the policies of agencies like the World Bank have recently focused more attention on the need for democratic reform, more can be done to mitigate the effects of international capital markets and other entailments of capitalist globalization that prop up autocratic regimes. At the same time, both state-builders and citizens at the local level and the international community must push for broadly beneficial economic development while building fiscal economies in which citizen-paid taxes are a major source of state wealth.

Bibliographic Essays

CHAPTER 1: INTRODUCTION

The difficulties involved in cooperation in public goods games is illustrated in Sefton et al. (2007). Cooperation in such games was enhanced with possibilities for monitoring and for agreeing about punishment in Ostrom et al. (1992). Charles Erasmus (1977: 50), following Morton Deutsch, summarizes factors favoring enhanced cooperation in experimental games: the ability to have knowledge of what others have done; the ability to exercise mutual control of outcomes, for example, by devising rules for handling violations; and the ability to depend on third-person intervention.

CHAPTER 2: WHAT DOES EVOLUTIONARY PSYCHOLOGY TELL US ABOUT HUMAN COOPERATION?

Sussman and Chapman (2004) and Sussman and Paul Garber (Sussman and Garber 2004) note the late twentieth-century change from earlier Darwin-inspired research by sociobiologists that emphasized competition and conflict among animals (e.g., Lorenz 1963)—Lorenz, in fact, won a Nobel Prize for his work—to a more recent concern with cooperation among what are now called evolutionary psychologists. Stephen Pope (2004: 317) notes that sociobiologists who envisioned an "atomistic" and competitive human actually depart from Darwin, who pointed to the advantages of naturally cooperative humans. Sahlins (1976) writes a critique

DOI: 10.5876/9781607325147.c014

of the earlier sociobiological theories from an anthropological perspective. Philip Kitcher (1985) provides an in-depth critique of the claims of sociobiology, as do the authors in Hilary Rose and Steven Rose (Rose and Rose 2000).

Important early contributors to the new cooperation direction for animal research include Wynne-Edwards (1962) and Wilson (1975), the latter based in part on research with eusocial insects. Recent primate research (e.g., Sussman and Chapman 2004; Sussman and Garber 2004) has been one factor forcing earlier sociobiologists to reconsider how to apply Darwinian ideas, specifically, away from an emphasis on competition and conflict and toward theories of cooperative social action. Biological determinist theories derive principally from Darwinian ideas but can trace their thinking (e.g., Miller 2008) also to eighteenth-century British philosophers who argued that although society to some extent reflects the outcomes of individual experience and rational action, at the same time rationality is tempered by capacities that are prior to experience, including the innate senses of compassion and an understanding of right and wrong.

The "dilemma" of cooperation is discussed in all the major biomathematical sources listed below; as Nowak (2006: 1560) puts it, "Natural selection...needs help for establishing cooperation." Cross-cultural variation in beneficence and justice obligations is discussed in Joan Miller (1994). Jon Elster (1989: 35) doubts that altruism plays an important role in human cooperation. Jonathan Parry (1986) notes the relatively recent history of notions of charitable giving in human culture history. Boyd and Richerson (1985: 19–31) describe the costs and benefits of computer simulation methods.

Major sources for the evolution of human psychology are Barkow et al. (1992) and Peter Carruthers (2006). "Mental modules" are described as "minicomputers" in David Buller and Valerie Hardcastle (Buller and Hardcastle 2006). Nowak and Highfield's (2011) *SuperCooperators: Altruism, Evolution, and Why We Need Each Other to Succeed* is one of the most recent books in the biomathematical vein. Other useful sources include Boyd and Richerson (1990, 2005), Boyd , Gintis, Bowles, and Richerson (2005), Boyd and Sarah Mathew (Boyd and Mathew 2007), Boyd et al. (2005a, 2005b), Joseph Henrich (2004), Henrich and Natalie Henrich (Henrich and Henrich 2007), Peter Turchin (2006: chap. 5); see also Mario Mikulincer and Philip Sharer (Mikulincer and Sharer 2010). Many of us might take issue with the claim of Gintis (2012: 433) that humans are predisposed to character virtues including honesty, trustworthiness, promise-keeping, and obedience. The moral intuition idea, which is accepted by some psychologists (e.g., Feinberg et al. 2012), is from Jonathan Haidt (2001).

What I am calling a biomathematical paradigm is critiqued recently in Rose and Rose (2000); more critiques are found in Scott Atran (2002), Buller and

Hardcastle (2006), Gould (1980), West (et al. 2011), and Blanton and Fargher (2013) (there termed Darwinian Anthropology).

The current status of research on inclusive fitness, reciprocal altruism, altruistic punishment, and group selection are summarized in Nowak (2006) and Nowak and Highfield (2011) and the other biomathematical sources cited above. A discussion panel of prominent evolutionary psychologists responded to Pinker's (2012) critique of the group selection theory in http://edge.org/conversation/the-false-allure-of-group-selection/. Price (2012) also finds group selection theory to be lacking. Laura Betzig (2014) illustrates how insect eusociality has influenced evolutionary psychologists.

Sarah Hrdy (2009) highlights the importance of cooperative breeding in human bioevolutionary history, but empirical work by Beverly Strassmann (2011) leads her to critique the notion that cooperative breeding has always been a key aspect of human reproductive strategy. Jeffrey Simpson and Lane Beckes (Simpson and Beckes 2010: 44–45) provide a summary of sources dealing with the possible biological roots of nepotistic bias, and they point to disagreements about biological causality among evolutionary psychologists. Anthropologists have not found firm evidence for kin selection or for biologically based kin preference (e.g., Jones 2000; Kaplan and Hill 1985: 227); Keith Hart (1988) found that in the marketplaces he studied in northeast Ghana, merchants find it easier to cooperate with nonkin trading partners rather than kin. Intrafamilial conflict is discussed by economic anthropologists including Blanton (1995), Hart (1992), and Wang Sung-hsing (1985). A biological theory of parent-offspring and offspring-offspring conflict is first proposed by Robert Trivers (1974). Donald Pfaff (2015: 122) summarizes current thinking about the role of hormones in prosocial maternal behavior.

Sahlins (1965) points to the many instances of one-way sharing where reciprocation is not expected. He also (1972: Appendix A) demonstrated the evidence for generosity in food-sharing among foragers, but recent studies of contemporary foragers point to a more complex situation, as reported in sources such as Hillard Kaplan and Kim Hill (Kaplan and Hill 1985), Nobuhiro Kishigami (2004), Frank Marlowe (2004), Nicolas Peterson (1993), and Christopher Boehm (2004). Kristen Hawkes (1993) points out that forager food-sharing is often a strategy aiming to maximize prestige rather than as a response to food insecurity. That cooperation will evolve biologically as mental modules, so long as punishment is coordinated, is argued in Boyd, Richerson, and Soltis (2005: 216), and in Boyd et al. (2010). The ultimatum game research that showed differing propensities to punish in different cultural groups is Henrich et al. (2004). The mention of "do-gooder derogation" is from Benedikt Herrmann and colleagues (Herrmann et al. 2008: 1366).

Group selection ideas are developed in David Sloan Wilson (2002). Nowak and Highfield (2011: 265) point out that biological group selection works only when there is positive assortment, that is, when persons with cooperator instincts interact mostly with genetically similar others (cf. Henrich 2004: 16), making group selection an example of inclusive fitness (West et al. 2011). The claims that human prosociality is driven in part by social instincts that evolve through a process of gene-culture coevolution is found in many sources, notably Boyd and Richerson (1985, 2005), Herbert Gintis et al. (2005), Richerson and Boyd (1999), Joseph Henrich (2004), and Henrich and Henrich (2007).

The anthropological notion of internally uniform and closed local systems of the human past is critiqued in Frederik Barth (2000) and Wolf (1982: 4–7); this same topic is addressed for South and Southeast Asian forager-traders in Kathleen Morrison and Laura Junker (Morrison and Junker 2002) and in Edwin Wilmsen and James Denbow (Wilmsen and Denbow 1990), who present arguments favoring the "revisionist" perspective that places foragers in large social fields beyond the local. Catherine Cameron (2008, 2011, 2013) documents the abundant evidence pointing to the fluidity of group boundaries and processes of interaction such as captive taking and slave trading in small-scale societies across the world. The dynamic processes of group dissolution and coalescence are discussed in Stephen Kowalewski (2006). An example of linguistic exogamy is found in Jean Jackson (1983). Tim Ingold (1999) points to the importance of what he calls "adhesive" social relations, by which he refers to the ad hoc and pragmatic joining together of families or individuals for shared activities not necessarily based on either bonds of kinship or reciprocity. Claude Lévi-Strauss (1974: 195) describes what he calls "inverted racialism" in the form of "systematic adoption of enemies or foreigners" among the Caduveo of Brazil. Harold Driver (1969: e.g., 324, 335, passim) summarizes the vast literature on adoption and marriage of war captives in native North American societies (see also Jorgensen 1980: 247 and Maps CU-187 and CU-188). Robert Bailey (1988) documented the tendency of forager women to marry across ethnic boundaries. Aram Yengoyan (1968) shows how the aboriginal Australian marriage section system, with its rigid specifications for exogamy, forced families to maintain spatially expansive social networks to find suitable marriage partners for their children. The abundant evidence for human migration in the past is discussed in Baker and Tsuda (2015), Bolnick (2011), and Snow (2009).

Jung-Kyoo Choi and Samuel Bowles (Choi and Bowles 2007) argue that competition between local populations would promote the evolution of prosocial behavior. Evidence counter to this notion comes from Chagnon (1988) and Marc Howard Ross's (1992) cross-cultural research on conflict and child socialization. The interaction of endemic war and socialization for violent aggressive males was also found by William Divale and Marvin Harris (Divale and Harris 1976). Pinker (2011: chap. 2) summarizes the literature documenting the high rates of violence found in small-scale human societies.

I cited Iannaccone (1992) in relation to cooperation problems in religious groups; similar results are reported in Richard Sosis and Candace Alcorta (Sosis and Alcorta 2003) and Sosis and Eric Bressler (Sosis and Bressler 2003). Anthropologists have frequently encountered intragroup competition and conflict (factionalism) (e.g., Siegel and Beals 1962; Silverman and Salisbury 1977). The results of a comparative study of highland New Guinea societies by Blanton and Jody Taylor (Blanton and Taylor 1995) are similar to those of D. K. Feil (1987). Their method contrasted the more closed and egalitarian groups as against Big Man groups where competition for prestige occurred in the context of large and open social networks. Like Feil, we found evidence that the latter may have been more biologically successful, with an average population density of 82.3 persons per square kilometer, while the average for the more cooperative groups is 20.5 per square kilometer.

Pope (2004: 317) notes that sociobiologists who envisioned an "atomistic" and competitive human actually depart in some ways from Darwin. Although Darwin's theory of natural selection emphasizes the importance of competition for resources, he also suggested that human cooperation might provide advantages in some circumstances. Recent primate research (e.g., Sussman and Chapman 2004; Sussman and Garber 2004) has been one factor influencing earlier sociobiologists as they rethought ways to apply Darwinian ideas, specifically away from an emphasis on competition and conflict and toward theories of cooperative social action.

Carl Degler (1991) traces the history of Darwinian thought in social science and other disciplines during the twentieth century. Nowak and Highfield (2011) provide a brief overview of the history of experimental game research. Mayr (1982: chap. 12) discusses the early history of mathematical genetics. Howard Margolis (1993) discusses the role of habits of mind in scientific thinking. Evidentiary problems inherent in studies of biological evolution have led distinguished biological researchers to argue that a Darwinian-based research design might not fit easily into the empirical sciences; Lucien Conway and Mark Schaller (Conway and Schaller 2002: 159), for example, describe the "inevitably spotty, inevitably imperfect clues about that very distant past" that problematize the testing of theories about evolutionary change. John Cartwright (2008: chap. 4) identifies what he sees as pitfalls in the research direction of evolutionary psychology.

The Paul Krugman quote is from the *New York Times Magazine*, September 6, 2009.

CHAPTER 3: THE PATH TO COOPERATION THROUGH
COLLECTIVE ACTION AND INSTITUTIONS

Olson (1965) was among the first social scientists to point out that rational individuals have difficulty acting in the common interest. In addition to Olson, the following collective action theorists have been particularly helpful as I developed the sections on cooperation especially as it relates to rationality, collective action, and institution-building: Dennis Chong (1991), John Elster (2000), Russell Hardin (1982, 1991), Michael Hechter (1983, 1987, 1990b), Margaret Levi (1988, 1997), Mark Lichbach (e.g., Lichbach 1996), Elinor Ostrom (1986, 1990, 1998, 2007), and Samuel Popkin (1979, 1988). Common-pool resource management is discussed in sources such as Ostrom (1990).

Unlike biomathematical theory, in collective action theory the self is not viewed as displaying any inherent propensity toward either cooperation (or punishment of noncooperators) or defection from obligations, because their social actions represent the outcome of conscious choice. However, I should point out that even some collective action theorists, such as Ostrom (2005), identify "types" of potential cooperators such as "preferential cooperators" or "preferential rational egoists"—but, in my opinion, this carryover from biomathematical (and economic) theory is not needed or useful. I benefitted from Dennis Chong's (2000: 4) discussion of how culture change involves "a large element of rationality"; see also his comparative study of the United States civil rights movement, where he concludes that "there will be strong incentives for individuals to participate when collective action is carefully planned and executed and has the power to improve the lot of the group" (Chong 1991: 11).

Herbert Simon (1969: 63–65) summarizes his notion of "satisficing" in which decision methods result in satisfactory rather than optimal solutions. The "extreme" notion of rational choice theory found in economic thinking (*Homo economicus*) is characterized by Lina Eriksson (2011: 101) as a self-interested person who "objectively perceives the world around her," so that "symbols and culture have no meaning," "she has no emotions," does "not identify with any group," and "collective meanings are irrelevant." Economists such as Carl Lyttkens (2013: 5) argue that rationality implies a striving for "power, wealth, and status," an idea that is not all useful for the rational choice theory of collective action.

Elster (2000) provides a useful critique of rational choice theory. Critics of rational choice theory, such as in the book edited by Margaret Archer and Jonathan Tritter are alluding primarily to the economists' highly individualizing perspective (Archer and Tritter 2000). The notion that self-interest may be gained through benefitting others, as argued by Becker (1976; cf. Amartya Sen 2002: 33–37) has some aspects in common with what is called a "sociological rational choice theory" (Kiser and Bauldry 2005: 172) and "group solidarity theory" (e.g., Hechter 1987). The sociological approach closely follows the lead of Max Weber in envisioning a self whose choices are influenced by cultural values ("value rationality") (e.g., Gorski 2003), but, at the same time, has the capacity to behave as a willful social actor. Chong (2000) also provides a useful overview of how cultural norms, values, and identity shape social action, but points to how cooperation is contingent (Chong 2000: 16) because it also involves a reflective, rational component. Kiser (1999) provides a recent review of agency theory in political science and sociology.

Bo Rothstein (2005) provides useful insights on the "social trap" problem.

I benefitted from the discussion of trust and confidence written by Keith Hart (1988: 187; cf. Cook et al. 2005). Eric Uslaner (2000) suggests a dichotomy between "moralistic trust," based on a cultural value, and "strategic trust" based on experience, but I prefer the term "confidence" to the more cumbersome "strategic trust."

Mark Lichbach (1996: 217) point to the disadvantages of trying to enforce cooperation through coercion. The chapters in the work edited by James Acheson (1994) attest to the value of a new institutional economic approach for economic anthropology. The anthropologist Bronislaw Malinowski (1944) argued for the value of an institutional approach for anthropological study. I also consulted Ostrom (2000, 2010), Kiser and Ostrom (2000), Ostrom and James Walker (Ostrom and Walker 2000), and Greif (2006) for insights about institution-building. Many aspects of the work represented in this book reflect the influence of Weber, especially, from *Economy and Society* (Weber 1978, orig. 1922); for example, behavior of governing agents (264), equitable taxation (1024–25), recruitment of governing agents (983–987, 1043), and transportation and communication infrastructure (1051–55) among other subjects.

CHAPTER 4: CULTURAL ANTHROPOLOGY: THE MISSING VOICE IN THE CONVERSATION ABOUT COOPERATION

Leda Cosmides, John Tooby, and Jerome Barkow argue that Darwinian theory will provide a sound scientific basis for human study and will allow for the unification of the natural and social sciences (Barkow, Cosmides, and Tooby 1992). Cronk and Leech (2013) make a similar plea for consilience of biological and social sciences (see also Mesoudi 2011). Mary Midgley (2000: 84) recognizes the sometimes ideology-ridden nature of social science, but argues this is not an acceptable reason to recast social science in principally biological terms by inflating Darwinism "into a universal system."

Karl Popper wrote about socially constructed forms of knowledge in *The Open Society and Its Enemies*, vol. 2 (Popper 1962, orig. 1945). Louis Dumont (1977) traces the history of Western concepts of the self. Additional sources for the discussion of rational choice and individualism include Raymond Boudon (2003), Mary Farmer (1992), Stephen Holmes (1990), Albert Hirschman (1992), Daniel Little (1991), Steven Lukes (1973), Amartya Sen (1977, 1987), William Sewell (1992), Bryan Turner (1983), and Milan Zafirovski (1999).

That human society is based in part on an innate sense of compassion and an understanding of right and wrong is expressed in the writings of David Hume (1978, orig. 1739), *A Treatise on Human Nature*, and in Adam Smith's (1969) first book *The Theory of Moral Sentiments*. Dumont (1977: chap. 5 and chap. 6) describes Mandeville's influence in Adam Smith's 1776 book on the wealth of nations (1993). Economic rational choice theory was fully developed during the latter nineteenth century and into the twentieth century (Eriksson 2011 provides a recent summary of history and ideas).

That *Homo economicus* is a problematic concept is evident from recent ethnographic research applying the Ultimatum and Dictator experimental games in diverse cultural settings. These researchers found that rather than competitive egoists, in highly commercialized societies there were comparatively high levels of fairness and willingness to punish for unfairness; these same features were not often found in smaller-scale societies where there is little commercialization (Henrich et al. 2004; Henrich, Ensminger, et al. 2010).

Other critics of traditional economic theory include Jerry Evensky (2005: 245, passim), Granovetter (1990, 1992), and Neil Smelser and Richard Swedberg (Smelser and Swedberg 2005). Although Adam Smith is an acknowledged source of utilitarian theory, he also was fully aware that emotion drove much of human behavior, as did the Enlightenment philosophers such as Hume (e.g., see the discussion in Gay 1954 and Holmes 1990).

One anthropologist, caught between the two ideas that anthropologists normally abhor—namely, a rational choice understanding of human nature and biological "innateness"—illustrates her preference when she argues that rational choice thinking is definitely wrong while, she argues, there is value in the claims of "evolutionarily minded psychologists, economists, and neuroscientists" (Hrdy 2009: 6–7). In fact, she regards as "revolutionary stuff" their conclusion that humans are not rational (in her sense, therefore selfish), and, instead, "are born predisposed to care how they relate to others" (6).

Albert Hirschman (1992: 35–55) details how nineteenth-century theorists, including Romanticists and Marxists, strongly rejected seventeenth- and eighteenth-century notions that rational individualism is consistent with social harmony. German Romanticism is derived from sources such as Johann Gottfried von Herder (1978, orig. 1774) (cf. Reill 1975). Its impact on anthropology is examined in Adam Kuper (2002). Marvin Harris (1968) coined the phrase "historical particu-larism" to describe the antitheoretical and antireductionist anthropology of Franz Boas and his followers (cf. Stocking 2001: 40–42). Maurice Bloch (2012) traces the history of anthropology's skepticism about the role of psychological study.

Emile Durkheim wrote about the role of religion in social life in *The Elementary Forms of the Religious Life* (Durkheim 1965, orig. 1915). Mauss's famous work on reciprocal exchange is *The Gift: The Form and Reason for Exchange in Archaic Societies* (Mauss 1967, orig. 1925). His article "A Category of the Human Mind: The Notion of Person, the Notion of Self" (Mauss 1985), reprinted in M. Carrithers, discusses his and Durkheim's ideas about the traditional and modern concepts of self (Carrithers et al. 1985). Chapters in the latter volume analyze the notions of self and person expressed by Durkheim and Mauss. Jonathan Turner and Alexandra Maryanski (Turner and Maryanski 1979) trace the history and content of function-alist thought.

Blanton and Fargher (2008: chap. 2) discuss the adoption of elements of Marxist theory by neoevolutionists of the mid-twentieth century. Marxist ideas about the "primitive collectivities" of Asiatic societies (e.g., Marx 1973: 473) are critically evaluated in Eric Hobsbaum (1964: 24, 33–35), Maurice Godelier (1978: 212, 220–25), Barry Isaac (1993: 434), and Mikhail Vitkin (1981: 445) among many other sources.

Polanyi's (1944) critique of Western economies, the starting point for what is called "substantivist" economic anthropology, shares much with Marx's similar research program (Isaac 2005: 21). The influence of Marx and socialist thought on Polanyi and other substantivists such as the historian Finley is documented by Kari Polanyi-Levitt (1990) and Mohammad Nafissi (2005). Anthropology's embrace of Marxist ideas during the tumultuous 1960s is also described by Sherry Ortner (1984: 138) and D'Andrade (2000). A critique of substantivism is found in Blanton and Fargher (2010).

Samuel Popkin (1979) critiques the romanticized view of the moral economy of the peasant community promoted by authors such as Wolf (1957) and James Scott (1976), which, as Donald Attwood (1997: 147) expresses it, is an anthropo-logical view that sees human subjects "as helpless victims rather than active agents."

That humans are not always good cooperators, even in small groups, is abun-dantly evident in ethnographic sources. Gregory Johnson (1983) finds that nomadic pastoralist group size is limited by the incidence of interfamily conflict as scale increases. The causes and sometimes violent consequences of village fissioning in a tribal society in lowland South America is documented in one case by Chagnon (1983). A. R. Holmberg's (1969) ethnography of the Siriono highlights the minimal degree of cooperative behavior such as food-sharing; see also the Mundugumor, first studied by Margaret Mead (1935) and restudied by Nancy McDowell (1991). James Greenberg (1981, 1989) investigated a peasant village in Mexico, that, from moral economy theory, should exhibit a high degree of social cohesion, but he makes note of the violent consequences of the "monstrous face" of factionalism (Greenberg 1989: 13). Factional disputes are the main cause of a homicide rate there, ten times the US rate, even in the period before the introduction of commercial coffee farming (which brought a further increase in homicide) (Greenberg 1981: table 30).

The idea of an anthropological imagination here and in later chapters draws inspiration from those few anthropologists who have seen the value of understanding cooperation, most notably Douglas (1986 especially) and Popkin (1979), although the material presented here does not follow their ideas completely. That the Western person is relatively individualistic is widely accepted (e.g., Cannell 2010), but some anthropologists now consider the dichotomy of Western and other mentalities to be overly simplistic (e.g., Attwood 1997; Goody 1996: 165–204; Hollan 1992; Kusserow 1999; and Spiro 1993).

Evidence for a growing interest in cooperation among anthropologists is seen in my and Lane Fargher's *Collective Action in the Formation of Pre-Modern States* (Blanton and Fargher 2008), in David Carballo's (2013a) edited volume titled *Cooperation and Collective Action: Archaeological Perspectives*, and in volumes devoted to cooperation and related topics published by the Society for Economic Anthropology (Acheson 1994; Marshall 2010). The challenges and promises of an anthropological discipline imagined here—which bridges science and humanism, biology and social science—are discussed in John Bock et al. (2008), Richard Feinberg (2009), and James Jones (2009). My notion of an anthropological imagination also was influenced by two earlier works with similar aims, one written for sociologists by C. Wright Mills (1959) and one for an anthropological audience of the 1970s by Muriel Dimen-Schein (1977).

CHAPTER 5: THE CONTINGENT COOPERATOR AS SEEN FROM THE PERSPECTIVES OF NEUROBIOLOGY AND BIOEVOLUTION

Katherine MacKinnon and Augustín Fuentes demonstrate a growing interest in finding ways to integrate anthropology with brain science (MacKinnon and Fuentes 2012). The cooperation theorist Chwe (2013) is one of the few institutionalists to recognize the importance of Theory of Mind ideas. That epigenetic processes result in what is variously termed "neural plasticity," "phenotypic plasticity" or "cortical plasticity" in human (and great ape) neural structure is argued in Buller and Hardcastle (2006), in Steven Mithen (2010), and in Kathleen Gibson (2005: 29–33) (cf. Karmiloff-Smith 2000; MacKinnon and Fuentes 2012). Smith

(1996) points to how learning and experience enhances ape Theory of Mind skills; enhanced deception in language-using versus non-language-using captive apes is mentioned in Robert W. Mitchell (1999: 303). Douglas Raybeck and Paul Y. L. Ngo (Raybeck and Ngo 2011) draw from cross-cultural data to assess the relationship between childhood experience and adult skills.

The advantages of an approach that considers biological roots of the potential cooperative behavior is discussed in Randolph Nesse (2001) and Steven Rose (2000: 303). Neurobiologists have known for some time that damage to the neocortex brings a decline in an individual's capacity for productive social interactions (e.g., Deacon 1997: 254–78). Daniel Wegner (2009) and Goleman (2013) discuss the role of the neocortex in the control of the subcortical functions. Leslie C. Aiello and R. I. M. Dunbar (Aiello and Dunbar 1993) and Dunbar and S. Schultz (Dunbar and Schultz 2007) propose a relationship between primate brain development (especially relative neocortex volume) and the size of groups that interact in socially complex ways, especially when individuals are dependent on bonded social relationships (cf. Roberts 2010). Gary Feinman (2011) discusses organizational threshold sizes of human groups. On social memory, see Leslie Brothers (1997: 41). David Begun (2010) traces the early phylogenetic history of our branch of the Hominoidea, though various forms of social intelligence are distributed more broadly among other primates.

Robert Seyfarth and Dorothy Cheney compare the social behavioral complexity of monkeys and apes (Seyfarth and Cheney 2012: 634). Recent research relevant to Theory of Mind and related matters on ape cognition is reported on in Sue Taylor Parker et al. (1999), and in Matsuzawa et al. (2006); however, there is not complete agreement as to whether ape cognition is the same as human Theory of Mind (e.g., Call and Santos 2012). A limited variant of state attribution in Eurasian jays is described in Ljerka Ostojic et al. (2013; cf. Emery and Clayton 2004). Byrne (1995) documents instances of deception by monkeys. Jane Goodall (1971) was the first to note tactical deception in chimpanzees. Mitchell (1999) compares ape and human abilities for tactical deception, which is thought to be a key indicator of Theory of Mind abilities (Hirata 2006).

The evolution of primate social intelligence is summarized in several sources including Dunbar (2003, 2007) and Dunbar and Schultz (2007). Aiello and Peter Wheeler (Aiello and Wheeler 1995) propose an "expensive tissue" theory for the behavioral modernity of genus *Homo*. Katarzyna Bozek et al. (2014) propose a relative loss of muscle tissue (by comparison with other primates) in the evolution of genus *Homo*. Evidence for cooking as early as 800,000 years ago is reported in Naama Goren-Inbar et al. (2004). Lewis Binford (1989), based on ethnographic and archaeological data, points to the kinds of problem-solving cognitive requirements of lithic technologies. A special issue of the journal *Current Anthropology* (Aiello 2010) is devoted to recent research on the role of expanded social memory in the evolution of behavioral modernity, including that implied by chipped-stone tool-making (e.g., the chapters in Nowell and Davidson 2010; Malafouris 2013). Byrne (1995) discusses the technical intelligence of apes.

Additional sources for Theory of Mind research include Carruthers and Smith (1996b), Whiten and Byrne (1997), Byrne and Andrew Whiten (Byrne and Whiten 1997), Rebecca Saxe and Simon Baron-Cohen (Saxe and Baron-Cohen 2007), and Kandel (2012). Gibson (2005: 35) points to the greater human capacity for Theory of Mind reasoning compared with apes; Dunbar (2007) documents how humans are able to understand multilevel intentionality to five levels.

Vittorio Gallese and Alvin Goldman first proposed that mirror neurons might play a role in mind reading through simulation in humans (Gallese and Goldman 1998; see also Gallese and Sinigaglia 2011). Cognitive neuroscience research on how primates analyze facial expressions has expanded in recent decades (e.g., Little et al. 2011).

Moreso than other animals, primate social interactions involve facial expressions and gaze tracking (Emery 2000). Gaze tracking and the gauging of emotion from facial expression is discussed in Reginald Adams (Adams et al. 2011), Robert Frank (1988), Kandel (2012), Karen Schmidt and Jeffrey Cohn (Schmidt and Cohn 2001: 20), and Valerie Stone (2006). The role of joint visual attention in Theory of Mind capacity is discussed in Simon Baron-Cohen and John Swettenham (Baron-Cohen and Swettenham 1996), Daniel Povinelli (1996), Robert Gordon (1996). Patterned interactional practices in human social life are discussed by Emanuel Schegloff (2006). Peter Smith (1996) points to the role of language in mind-reading ability, and language as a form of mental rehearsal of action is discussed in Carruthers (2006: 307–12, passim), and in Peter Smith (1996). David Premack (2004) points to the role of representational understanding in imitation and teaching.

CHAPTER 6: COOPERATION OR COMPETITION IN THE MARKETPLACE?

Evidence for premodern markets has been noted for the eighth century BCE Eastern Zhou Dynasty (Shen 2003), the third millennium BCE in Mesopotamia (Silver 1983), in premodern South Asia (Chaudhuri 1985; Chaudhuri 1982 and Subrahmanyam 1998), and pre-Hispanic Mesoamerica (Berdan 1986; Blanton 1996; Smith and Berdan 2003). Market exchange in the relatively small-scale societies of aboriginal Melanesian societies is documented in Theodore Schwartz (1963), in Thomas Harding (1967), and in Malinowski's (1932: 189) description of *gimwali* trade in the Trobriand Islands. Martin Lewis (1989) finds commercial transactions in the "village-scale" society of the Buguias region of Northern Luzon, Philippines. Commercial exchange connected the agricultural Pueblo Indian groups of the American Southwest with forager Plains tribes during the Colonial Period, for example, at the annual Taos Fair (Levine 1991), and this pattern was a continuation of a pre-Hispanic pattern (e.g., Wilcox 1991). The archaeological study of markets is undergoing rapid methodological development, as is evident in Bruce Dahlin et al. (2007), Feinman and Christopher Garraty (Feinman and Garraty 2010), Garraty and Barbara Stark (Garraty and Stark 2010), and Kenneth Hirth and Joanne Pillsbury (Hirth and Pillsbury 2013).

In Blanton (2013) I make use of some of the concepts developed in this chapter to compare market evolution in the Maya, Oaxacan, and Central Mexican regions of late pre-Hispanic Mesoamerica (1000 to 1520 CE). Economists who have turned to an approach similar to cooperation researchers include Gintis et al. (2005) and Paul Milgrom et al. (1990); unfortunately, in some cases they accept the claims of biomathematical researchers about the innateness of human cooperativity.

Gift and commodity (including barter) are discussed in sources such as C. A. Gregory (1982) and in Caroline Humphrey and Stephen Hugh-Jones (Humphrey and Hugh-Jones 1992). Sahlins (1972) developed a scheme of reciprocities in the chapter titled "On the Sociology of Primitive Exchange" in his substantivist *Stone Age Economics*. Institutional economics now has a vast literature summarized in sources such as Bates (e.g., Bates 1994), North (1981, 1990), Acheson (1994), and Oliver Williamson (1975). Roger Friedland and A. F. Robertson situated anthropology within the twentieth-century social sciences, and discuss its separation from economic theory (Friedland and Robertson 1990).

Hirschman (1982) provides a useful summary of the history of rival ideological claims in Western history that markets have been either civilizing, destructive, or feeble. The market as a site of perceived amoral behavior as expressed in Greek philosophy is discussed in William James Booth (1993), Roy Dilley (1992), Finley (1974), Nafissi (2005: 3–10), Parry and Bloch (1989), and Redfield (1986: 30); in Chinese Confucianist political thought (e.g., Duyvendak 1928: 49–55); in Tokugawa Japan (Hall 1991a: 3); and in Medieval Europe; and the African Christian Church of the post–Roman Period (Bridbury 1986: 84; Le Goff 1980: 59–65; Parry 1989: 78; and Shaw 1981: 69). Hirschman (1977, 1982, 1992), Stephen Holmes (1990), and Gabriel Almond (1991: 468) describe the douceur effect and other favorable notions of the market expressed during the seventeenth and eighteenth centuries in Europe. As stated by Adam Smith (1993: 260) "Commerce and manufacture gradually introduced order and good government, and with them, the liberty and security of individuals."

The Classical Greek idea of moral economy in the autarchic household and community, and its history in recent Western thought, is traced by Booth (1993) and in Nafissi (2005). Polanyi (1944) laid out his argument about the rise of market-based societies in *The Great Transformation: The Political and Economic Origins of Our Times*; for a critical appraisal of his work, see Isaac (2005) and Blanton and Fargher (2010). Finley (1973) argues that Classical Athens lacked a well-integrated commercial economy and Murra (1980) idealizes the Inka economy as a premodern example of socialism. His claim resonated for many decades in anthropological thinking, but recently it has been challenged (e.g., Burger 2013; Mayer 2013). Yang (1998: 6–16) identifies the ideologically motivated and thus mistaken nineteenth-century views of village India and its persistent influence on anthropological studies in India and elsewhere (see also Attwood 1997). Peregrine Horden and Nicholas Purcell critique "primitivist" antimarket thinking as it has been applied in Mediterranean history (Horden and Purcell 2000: 146–52). An example of the moral economy approach in contemporary peasant study is found in Scott (1976) and critiqued by Popkin (1979).

The history of commercial change in Europe is traced by Braudel (1979) in his three-volume *Civilization and Capitalism, 15th–18th Century*. I also drew from the work edited by B. L. Anderson and A. J. H. Latham (Anderson and Latham 1986) and Joan Thirsk (1967). G. W. Skinner's (1964, 1965a, 1965b, 1985) three-part essay on Late Imperial Chinese markets influenced anthropological market study (see also Blanton 1976 and Smith 1976). The theory of retail location (Central Place Theory) is adapted for traditional market systems in many sources; anthropological examples include Blanton (1996), Skinner (1964), and Carol Smith (1976). Recent summaries of market studies in anthropology are found in Blanton and Fargher (2010), Fargher (2009), Feinman and Garraty (2010), Garraty and Stark (2010), and Carol Smith (1974). Blanton (2001) summarizes characteristic features of traditional markets. Detailed ethnographic studies of marketplaces and market systems, done by anthropologists, are few and far between, but I would cite, in particular, Geertz (1979), various publications of Polly Hill (e.g., Hill 1966, 1970, 1971), Gracia Clark (1994), Scott Cook and Martin Diskin (Cook and Diskin 1976), Ralph Beals (1975), Benet (1957), Theodore Bestor (2004) and Tuulikki Pietilä (2007).

Benet (1957) follows C. S. Coon in using the terms *Bled el Makhzen* ("Land of Government") and *Bled es Siba* ("Land of Insolence"). My major source for North African markets is Brent Shaw (1981), but see also Walter Fogg (1932, 1936, 1942), Geertz (1979) and especially Benet (1957). Ernest Gellner (1972) contrasted Berber Holy Men of the intertribal sphere with tribal chiefs. The concept of the "total" institution was first proposed by Mauss (1967, orig. 1925) to capture how reciprocal gift exchange engenders alliances and personal dependencies and thus has to be understood as more than just an economic system. The marketplace as a total institution is often expressed. For example, as described by D. P. Sinha (1963: 172–73), the marketplaces in Central India are important for recreation, festivals, meeting with kin, conflict resolution, and negotiation of marriages, and they were the most important sites of intervillage communication (cf. Herbert Eder 1976; E. Skinner 1962; G. W. Skinner 1964). Yang (1998: 16) sees a similar role for the rural markets of Bihar, India, as "units of social, cultural, and political organization—units within which power was dispersed and exercised and within which people increasingly developed and acquired notions of identity and community."

Colin Renfrew (1975) develops an "early state module" in which elementary units of political control are separated by less directly governed interstitial zones. As Scott (2009: chap. 2) points out for Southeast Asia, "the friction of terrain set up sharp, inflexible limits to the effective reach of the traditional agrarian state" (43), and provides some metrics for the nineteenth century indicating zones of direct sovereignty of only between 160 to 240 kilometers in diameter. The very earliest polities were even smaller as indicated in the data for Mesoamerica and the Mediterranean summarized in Blanton (2004). Boundary zones separating pre-Hispanic Postclassic polities of the Mixteca region of Mexico represented a "hostile sociopolitical setting," but where various border institutions could be found such as sacred sites and border markets (Pohl et al. 1997).

Polanyi (1944: 62–63) described local markets similar to the Geertz's (1980) Balinese example described in the text. Milgrom et al. (1990) point to the institutions of trade in the Champagne Fairs.

Smelser and Swedberg (2005: 5) contrast economic and sociological approaches to power. Theoretical and comparative sources for ethnic trading groups (trade diaspora) include Yoram Ben-Porath (1980), Curtin (1984), Ensminger (1992 and 1997), Janet Landa (1981), and Rahul Oka and Augustin Fuentes (Oka and Fuentes 2010: 15–18). Examples include Chinese merchant groups in Southeast Asia (Davis 1973: 170–72; Dewey 1962: 44–49; T'ien 1953); and Arab, Swahili, and other foreign trader groups in sub-Saharan Africa (e.g., Cohen 1969; Miracle 1962: 699; Perinbaum 1980; Tosh 1970; cf. Forman and Riegelhaupt 1970: 206). The concept of trader network capital is developed in Marcel Fafchamps (2004: chap. 16). Disadvantages abound for commoners when they lack comparable sources of network capital that an elite or merchant groups can make use of to dominate interpolity trade and its profits and that allows them to earn what Fafchamps (2004: chap. 16) refers to as "network rents" (cf., Roberts 1970). That economists should better acknowledge the embeddedness of economy in social relations is argued in Granovetter (1985, 1992) and in Santhi Hejeebu and Deirdre McCloskey (Hejeebu and McCloskey1999). However, pursuing this approach requires an appreciation of the potential for social asymmetries inherent in restricted markets and embeddedness.

Cassady (1968), Humphreys (1978), Khuri (1968), and Pietilä (2007) provide useful information on marketplace bargaining; Geertz (1979: 221–29) analyzes bargaining behavior and etiquette in the marketplace in Sefrou, Morocco, and points to the high transaction costs found in traditional marketplaces (see also Geertz 1978). Collins (2004) summarizes the literature of symbolic interactionism and related sociological theories as the backdrop to the study of interaction ritual chains; see also Stephen Levinson (2006). Mitchell (1999) uses the phrase "strategic social scripts" to imply the kind of entrainment discussed by Collins. Future bargaining research will benefit from understanding how Theory of Mind abilities enhance the capacity for discerning valid signals of truthfulness from verbal cues, gaze, and facial expression. While humans and apes can be skillfully deceptive, some aspects of nonverbal communication are less subject to cheating, for example, the unconscious smile response referred to as the "Duchenne smile," and other unconscious behaviors such as blushing and a shame signal consisting of glancing around and lowering the head (Schmidt and Cohn [2001] provide a useful summary of human facial expressions).

Much of the information on piggybacking comes from *The Market in History*, edited by edited by Anderson and Latham (1986). Greek religious festivals are described in Antony Spawforth (1996: 926). Thomas Dexter (1930) points to how pre-Christian Pagan fairs were associated with religious sites and rituals. The literature on North African Berber markets, previously cited, is also useful, especially Benet (1957). That the authority of religious figures allows them to manage markets and adjudicate disputes in a neutral manner is discussed in Polly Hill (1966: 296). Religious organizations or specialists can benefit from the increased traffic in a well-managed market (e.g., Sawyer 1986: 62–64), but in early Christian culture this created a dilemma because by associating with markets and commerce church officials were in violation of church canon emanating from the papal offices (Bridbury 1986: 86; Le Goff 1980: 63–65; cf. Shaw 1981: 69).

The economic sociologist Weber (1978: 637, orig. 1922) described the market as a state of "absolute depersonalization" and a distinct "value sphere" governed by its own rationality (e.g., Weber 1946: 331–33). The concept of liminality is well known in the anthropological literature, beginning with Arnold van Gennep (1909) and through the various publications of Victor Turner (especially Turner 1969) and Victor Turner and Edith Turner (Turner and Turner 1978). Jean-Christophe Agnew (1979) applied the notions of liminality and threshold to market study. Max Weber proposed a similar social process he termed "charismatic authority" that "repudiates the past and is in this sense is a specifically revolutionary force" (Weber 1947: 362). Scott (1990: 122) described what I am calling the liminal character of the Medieval European market when he points out that in the marketplace "privilege was suspended." Scott Hutson (2000) found evidence for pre-Hispanic market behaviors (liminal in the terminology used here) similar to those noted by Rabelais in Medieval Europe. Numerous sources describe women's market participation and the gender emancipation that follows from market growth (e.g., Babb 1989; Benet 1957: 205; Boserup 1970: 87–95;Clark 1994; Cohen 1992: 79; Hill 1971; Hilton 1985: chap.16; Hodder 1962; House-Midamba and Ekechi 1995; Kaphan 1996; Mintz 1971; van Aert 2006; Wycherley 1978: 94). Ober (1995) and R. E. Wycherley (1978: 62) discuss the *horoi* of Classical Athens. The Koreish and their market at Mecca are discussed in Wolf (1951).

Masters of the highland Berber market are described in Benet (1957: 201–3). Loango market management is from Thurnwald (1932: 168). Maghribi trader's coalitions are analyzed in Greif (2006), and European "law merchants" by Milgrom, North, and Weingast (1990). Specialized market brokers in Hausaland are mentioned in Polly Hill (1971: 315). The Diakhanké were studied by Curtin (1971).

Information on the Aztec specialized market managers and merchant group, the Pochteca, is from Frances Berdan (1986), van Zantwijk (1985: chap. 7), Jerome Offner (1983: 156), and Fray Sahagún (1950–69, vol. 8: 69, vol. 9: 24). The alliances between alien traders and aristocrats and rulers in European late Medieval history is described in many sources (e.g., see the comments in Hilton 1985: 289).

CHAPTER 7: ON THE NEED TO RETHINK THEORIES OF STATE FORMATION AND HOW COLLECTIVE ACTION THEORY WILL HELP

Brian Nelson (2006) summarizes traditional sources pertaining to the rise of the modern state. The sociologist Pierre Bourdieu (e.g., Bourdieu 1977: 164) illustrates the point we make about how some prefer characterizations of a premodern "other" very much unlike "us" when he explains that in the premodern condition commoners were unable to distinguish between reality and the view of nature and society manufactured by the governing elite that served to legitimate authoritarian regimes. Similarly, the anthropologist Morton Fried (1967: 226) argues that a subaltern class will internalize norms that justify inequality, making the beginnings of coercion possible "without the conscious awareness of the members of the affected societies." According to Marx, it was only in later European history that the "herd mentality" of the subaltern was transcended with the emergence of the "fully social" human and the corresponding "human society" that "would in time subordinate the whole world" (Vitkin 1981: 445; cf. Engels 1972: 216).

"Orientalist" notions are alive and well, even in recent and much lauded works, for example, see Francis Fukuyama (2011: 290), which makes uninformed claims about premodern Chinese "despotism," as he sees it, that reflect the Western consensus more than empirical reality (compare with Charles Hucker [1978], who discusses the role of a powerful Chinese civil service administration that served as a counterweight to the tyranny of rulers). Orientalist notions are critiqued in many sources including Jack Goody (1996: chap. 6), Perry Anderson (1974: 489–95), Barry Isaac (1993), Edward Said (1978), and Romila Thapar (1992).

Several researchers have addressed the more egalitarian forms of premodern polity-building or alternate pathways to complexity, among which are Christopher Beekman (2008) (pre-Columbian West Mexico), Blanton et al. (1996) (Mesoamerica), Matthew Coon (2009) (pre-European Eastern Woodlands), George Cowgill (1997) (Teotihuacan), Stephen Dueppen (2012) (West Africa), Joshua Englehardt and Donna Nagle (Englehardt and Nagle 2011) (Mycenaean and Mesoamerica), Fargher et al. (2011) (Tlaxcallan, Mexico), Gary Feinman (2001) (Mesoamerica, Feinman 2000) (aboriginal societies of the American Southwest), Fleming (2004) (early Mesopotamia), Adam King (2003) (Mississippian chiefdom), Nikolay Kradin (2011) (early Mongolian Nomads), Li Liu (2004) (Late Neolithic China), Susan McIntosh (1999) (sub-Saharan Africa), Barbara Mills (2000) (aboriginal societies of the American Southwest), William Parkinson and Michael Galaty (Parkinson and Galaty 2007) (Crete), Timothy Pauketat (2007) (pre-European Eastern Woodlands), Peter Robertshaw (2003) (East Africa), David Small (2009) (Classical Greece), Elizabeth Stone (2008) (early Mesopotamia), Tina Thurston (2001) (early Iron Age Europe), and Mary Beth Trubitt (2000) (Cahokia). See also Blanton (1998), Blanton and Fargher (2008, 2009), Timothy Earle (2002), Robert Ehrenreich et al. (1995), Fargher and Blanton (2007, 2012), Fargher and Verenice Y. Heredia-Espinoza (Fargher and Heredia-Espinoza 2016), Feinman (1995), Leonid E. Grinin and Andrey Korotayev (Grinin and Korotayev 2011), and Douglas Price and Feinman (Price and Feinman 2010).

Some researchers who adhere to the European consensus have had to face the reality that there is evidence pointing to high levels of cooperation in some complex societies in past times, and, to overcome their cognitive dissonance, have conjured up bizarre arguments to defend their position. One typical response in these cases is to simply deny that the societies in question actually were states, as Moshe Berent (2004: 371) does when he concludes that the Classical Athenian democratic *polis* wasn't a state at all but rather was only an "association or partnership" (other early polities showing evidence for high levels of collective action, especially Indus-Sarasvati civilization, have received similar analytical treatment, for example, Gregory Possehl [1998]). Indeed, in a sense, Berent is correct, in that a highly cooperative state is a kind of "association," yet, this and other cooperative polities did have complex governing systems that are easily identified as states as defined here.

Thurston (2010: 195) makes the argument that in the post–World War II Period, scholars were fascinated by the absolute power, especially the examples of Adolf Hitler and Benito Mussolini, and allowed these instances to influence their theories of state formation. She also points to the influence of the soured political climate in the United States of the 1960s and '70s Vietnam war era, which "fomented an obsession with control and central authority" (2010: 199). According to Roy D'Andrade (1995), in anthropology the oppression model (claiming there is no such thing as "good power") passed directly from the radical Left into postmodern anthropology.

Oppression theory is found in recent works such as in *Violence and Social Orders* by Douglass North, John Joseph Wallis, and Barry Weingast (North, Wallis, and Weingast 2009). Charles Tilly's (1990) *Coercion, Capital, and European States, AD 990–1990* illustrates the main themes of oppression theory as applied to European history. Tilly (1975a, 1985, and 1990) discusses the role of warfare in European state formation. Oppression theories for premodern state formation are well represented in the writing of Bruce Trigger (2003, e.g., 47, 443). This line of argument is summarized and critiqued in Blanton and Fargher (2008: chap. 2). Thomas Ertman (1997) critiques the oppression theories of early European state-building. Recent critiques of Eurocentric views are found in Andre Gunder Frank (1998), Ian Morris (2010), Kenneth Pomeranz (2000), and Wong (1997).

In the twentieth century, the idea that power stems from social relations rather than from attributes of a person or group was first developed by social exchange theorists such as Richard Emerson (1962) (also see Mustafa Emirbayer 1997),and similar ideas were adopted by some political scientists (e.g., Ahlquist and Levi 2011). We quote Schumpeter (1991), who foregrounded a "fiscal sociology" theory during the early decades of the twentieth century as a way to unite economic and social research, although his approach is different from ours in taking an evolutionist perspective that associated the rise of "fiscal" regimes (with reciprocal obligations of taxpayers and the state) only with modern democracies. Fiscal sociology died out after the 1920s as economists turned their attention away from social factors and to quantitative analyses of the economic consequences of taxes for market functioning, but there is now a revival, for example, as seen in volumes edited by Deborah Bräutigam, Odd-Helge Fjelstad, and Mick Moore (Bräutigam et al. 2008), Isaac Martin, Ajay Mehrota, and Monica Prasad (Martin et al. 2009), Andrew Monson and Walter Scheidel (Monson and Scheidel 2015), and B. Yun-Casalilla and Patrick K. O'Brien (Yun-Casalilla and O'Brien 2012). The latter book makes it clear that fiscal strategies and internal revenues are found in various areas and time periods in Eurasia (and we would add, in the case of the Aztec polity described in the following chapter and in African cases such as Asante), not just as an entailment of European political modernity (see also Monson and Scheidel 2015).

Internal and external revenue sources are described in Blanton and Fargher (2008: chap. 6). Martin McGuire and Mancur Olson argue that rulers will act in the interest of taxpayers, assuming they depend on the latter for revenues, but argue there will be little difference between autocratic and democratic regimes in this regard (McGuire and Olson 1996). Their argument departs from the predictions of collective action theory, which predicts that "internal" (taxpayer-produced) revenues are not likely to be associated with autocratic regimes, which is what we confirmed from our cross-sectional analysis of premodern states and our comparison of modern polities as described in chapter 8. A fiscal theory focuses most attention on tax revenues, but other sources of value produced by taxpayers must be considered, for example, in the growth of the Athenian democracy where commoners assumed more importance in military formations and naval warfare. The contribution of commoner soldiers to Athenian society, and its consequences for broadly based citizen participation in the political process, are discussed in Snodgrass (1981: 102).

Michael Ross (1999) reviews theories for why contemporary "rentier states" tend to have little democratization or economic progress (see also Jensen and Wantchekon 2004). Our collective action research has been inspired by Margaret Levi's (1988) *Of Rule and Revenue*. Other more generalized collective action sources we consulted include Mancur Olson (1965), Mark Lichbach (1994, 1995), Robert Bates (1983), Bates and Lien (Bates and Lien 1985), Russell Hardin (1982), Michael Hechter (1983), and Ostrom (e.g., Ostrom 1998, 2007). Levi (1997) and Cook et al. (2005: 151–65) outline the conditions for confidence-building in the governing institutions of states.

Robert Dahl and Bruce Stinebrickner discuss the nature of legitimate leadership (Dahl and Stinebrickner 2003: 60–61). Sources for Islamic, Hindu, Buddhist, and Chinese moral codes are Ibn Hasan (1936: 57), G. E. von Grunebaum (1961: 127), J. C. Heesterman (1998: 14), Stanley Tambiah (1976: chap. 5), Frederick Mote (1968: 398), and de Zorita (1994: 93).

Our comparative method was influenced by sources such as Michael Coppedge (1999), Carol Ember and Melvin Ember (Ember and Ember 2001), Ember, Ember, and Bruce Russett (Ember, Ember, and Russett 1992), Ember et al. (1991), and Sanford Labovitz (1967, 1970). See also Blanton and Fargher (2008: 25–32, 113–14).

CHAPTER 8: COOPERATION IN STATE-BUILDING? AN INVESTIGATION OF COLLECTIVE ACTION BEFORE AND AFTER THE RISE OF MODERN DEMOCRACIES

Olson (1965) describes the unique properties of public goods; that they are considered only a substitute means of provision of social wants in cases of market failure was proposed in Richard Musgrave (1959). Additional sources we consulted for public goods include Russell Hardin (1982: 17–20), Levi (1988), and Gerald Marwell and Pamela Oliver (Marwell and Oliver 1993). Citations for the data reported in the sections on public goods, bureaucratization, principal control, and taxation are in Blanton and Fargher (2008). Additional sources not cited there include a history of granaries and food security in Chinese history by Wong (1991); Ming public schools are documented by Sarah Schneewind (2006). Evelyn Rawski (1972: 22) notes that the Ming state was well aware of the moral hazards associated with the community grain stores. Deng (2012: table 14.2) identifies fiscal states in China (with private landholding rights and taxes based on production abilities) as early as about 700 BCE, and Wong (2012) identifies the Ming Dynasty as an example of a premodern fiscal state, as does Richards (2012) for the Mughal polity.

The theory linking water management to the evolution of "Oriental Despotisms" (e.g., Wittfogel 1957) has found little empirical support (e.g., Robert Hunt 1988), but has persisted in Western social science; as Karl Butzer (1996: 200) puts it, the theory, "like Elvis, refuses to die."

Benjamin Elman (1991) provides a useful summary of the Chinese civil examination system; see also Ho Ping-ti (1962). Hucker (1978: 49–50) describes Ming improvements in the examination practices. Herrlee Creel (1970: 15–27) points to Europe's late adoption of a civil examination system that was based on Chinese precedent (see also Brook 2005: 189). As our work does, Victoria Hui (2005: 1) challenges the notions that recent European political history is seen in terms of "checks and balances" while for China, ethnocentric European historians see only a "coercive universal empire."

General speaking, theories of democracy have not developed in relation to collective action theory. Instead, the theoretical arguments in the democracy literature more often surround the issue of what should constitute the ideal form of democracy, especially the debate between those who argue in favor of "protective" democracy that limits itself to the minimal functions of providing for order and protecting property rights, versus "developmental" democracy, in which it is argued that democratically elected leaders should pursue additional goals such as promoting social and economic equality (e.g., Cunningham 2002).

CHAPTER 9: CENTER AND HINTERLAND UNDER CONDITIONS OF COLLECTIVE ACTION

Edward Shils (1961) and Geertz (1983a: 122) comment on the importance of studies of center and base (or margin) in the analysis of complex society. Sources on state-hinterland interaction that influenced our thinking include Catherine

Boone (2003) and Michael Hechter and William Brustein (Hechter and Brustein 1980), though we disagree with the latter's assumption that states can be understood to develop in relation to a preexisting substrate of "natural" and primordial rural communities. Any notion of the primordial rural commune is challenged by research that shows the contingent and historically variable nature of village communities. As G. William Skinner (1971: 280) notes about Chinese history, for example, during the interregnums between strong dynasties, "the . . . progressive closure of villages . . . represented the culmination of rational responses to an increasingly unstable and threatening external environment." When conditions were more stable, according to Skinner, village social solidarity tended to decline, while the primary social field of the peasant household was expanded to include the "standard market community." Popkin (1979) critiques naive moral economy views of the peasant village.

Andrey Korotayev (1995) restates the hypothesis linking a state's territorial growth with the rise of despotism, an idea first proposed in the eighteenth century by Charles de Secondat Montesquieu (1989). While more autocratic states no doubt typically are exploitative in relation to communities, Scott (1976), Taylor (1982), and Ostrom (1990) all exemplify an antistatist position that fails to recognize the possibilities for collective action in state-building. Their antistatist arguments are critically evaluated in Levi (2002).

Boone (2003: 326–27) argues that in Africa, local-scale institutional capital facilitates collective state formation. Richard O'Connor (1995: 974) proposes that wet-rice flow-management irrigation among Thai, Burmese, and Vietnamese became the "nucleus of their states and the mold for their culture." But our data point to relatively low or moderate scores on collective action, at the scale of polities, in Southeast Asian societies and in other cases where we find flow-management wet-rice production (Blanton and Fargher 2008: 283–85).

Philip Ivanhoe (2000) traces the history of ideas about moral self-cultivation in Chinese philosophy. Chen (1972: 409) and Creel (1964: 170; 1970: 376–78) discuss the Confucian notion that familistic values of filial piety informed the expected behavior of rulers and other officials.

Anthropologists have explored the relationships between scale and social complexity, for example, in Ember (1963), Feinman (1998), and Johnson (1978 and 1983). But these earlier sources did not account for collective action as discussed in Blanton and Fargher (2008: 275–80; cf. Feinman 2011). The prominent cooperation researcher Olson (1965) argues that cooperation is less likely at larger societal scale because as size increases, people will be less willing to jointly supply public goods (as each person's contribution increasingly is a smaller proportion of the total). More recent work amends his argument somewhat by arguing that the limiting factor of group size in collective action is the high cost of providing public goods while joint-ness of supply is not likely to be limiting. This will be true especially if at least some group members are willing to supply the good even while others contribute less (Hardin 1982: 67–89)—assuming this "critical mass" of high-contributing persons is able to coordinate their actions (Marwell and Oliver 1993: 53), which itself would be a challenging cooperation problem. And we agree with Marwell and Oliver that this kind of argument, requiring cooperation among a small group of significant contributors, represents a reversion to a "small group" solution to a "large group" collective action problem (Marwell and Oliver 1993: 54). We should point out that Hardin's hypotheses result from formal mathematical analysis rather than empirical observation, while all of our results are based on empirical data and analysis.

Osborne (1985) provides a readable summary of the *deme* structure of Attica that was introduced as part of the Kleisthenic reforms of 507 BCE. That Chinese *li-chia* organizations and public granaries were locally managed is from Francesca Bray (1984: 422), but the potential for free-riding and agency were recognized, as Rawski (1972: 22) points out. The newly instituted Ming community rituals are described in Martin Heijdra (1998: 469–70) and in Joseph McDermott (1999: 299–304). Monitoring of basal groups was accomplished in part through surveil-lance-judicial bureaus, including a "secret police" described by Ray Huang (1998: 109) and the Censorate, in Hucker (1998: 73, 91–99). As Chinese notions about the functionality of household were developed, they were encoded in domestic habitus, including formalized architecture, everyday practices, and ritual (e.g., Bray 1997: chap. 3; cf. Heijdra 1998: 468–70). The municipal charter of Julius Caesar, *Lex Iulia Municipalis*, is described by Frank Abbott (1963: 452). Descriptions of *curatore, correctore, logiste*, and similar categories of officials are from Harmut Galsterer (2000: 359). Recent summaries of the Aztec *calpolli* (pl. *calpultin*) are found in Offner (1983: chap. 5) and M. E. Smith (2003: 132–34).

CHAPTER 10: COLLECTIVE ACTION AND THE SHAPING OF CITIES AND THEIR NEIGHBORHOODS

The chapter title is modified from the title of the first of Spiro Kostof's monumental two-volume work on urban patterns through history (Kostof 1991 and 1992). In addition to Kostof, this chapter benefits from a vast and rich literature on cities old and new (e.g., Blanton 1976; Cowgill 2004; Fletcher 1995; Fox 1977; Sjoberg 1960; M. E. Smith 2007, 2011; Skinner 1977; Storey 2006b; Wheatley 1971). The work reported here summarizes the results of a quantitative analysis of neighborhood and collective action found in Blanton and Fargher, "Neighborhoods and the Civic Constitutions of Pre-Modern Cities as Seen from the Perspective of Collective

Action," in *The Neighborhood as a Social and Spatial Unit in Mesoamerican Cities*, edited by Charlotte Arnauld, Linda R. Manzanilla, and Michael Smith (Blanton and Fargher 2012). A brief report, aimed at an archaeological audience, on the spatial structure of cities is found in our "The Collective Logic of Premodern Cities," *World Archaeology* (Blanton and Fargher 2011).

Sources used for the data summaries include, for Aceh, Reid (1993: tables 7 and 8) (see also Brakel 1975: 64). Reid (1980) discusses the general pattern of Southeast Asian early modern cities. The Nupe data are from S. F. Nadel (1942: 40–43, plan 1). The Balinese Mengwi polity is described by Geertz (1980: 46–47; cf. Schulte-Nordholt 1996: map 8). Timothy Baker (1970) provides a useful perspective on focal-period London. The focal-period population for Edo is from Nakai Nobuhiko and James McClain (Nobuhiko and McClain 1991: 564–68; on populations of castle-towns, see John Hall 1991a: 6). Wakita Haruko (1997) points to a pattern in Kyoto in which *chonin* guilds, rather than the state, provided public goods at a local neighborhood-scale level. On Tokugawa Period urban public goods, see Coaldrake (1981), Susan Hanley (1987), Perez (2002: 28, 125), Constantine Vaporis (1997: 40), Nobuhiko and McClain (1991: 535–37), and Henry Smith (1978: 50). The urban morphology of Edo is described in Coaldrake (1981; cf. Vaporis 1997: 40). The role of the daimyo in governance is discussed in Perez (2002: chap. 3); that there was only a minor role for Tokugawa officials in urban governance is discussed in Nobuhiko and McClain (1991: 534), Hanley (1987: 22), and Henry Smith (1978: 50–52), and the *cho* system in Henry Smith (1978: 51–52), Hanley (1987: 13), Nobuhiko and McClain (1991: 535–37), Perez (2002: 28), and Henry Smith (1978: 50). Spatial separation between social classes is described in Coaldrake (1981: 248, 249) and Hanley (1987: 22).

Ottoman urban administration is described by Faroqhi (1994: 584–93) and André Raymond (1995: 32, 33). On public goods, see Raymond (1995: 33, 35–37), Çigdem Kafescioglu (1999: 70–71), Faroqhi (1994: 587; 2000: 147), and Kuran (1996: 116, 126, 130). For Cairo neighborhoods, see Raymond (1995: 33, 35–41). The restrictive road networks of Ottoman cities are described in Faroqhi (1994: 578). Istanbul's road network is mapped by Halil Inalçik (1973: 232) and discussed by Ayse Kubat (1999).

The founding and growth of Asante Kumase is summarized by Wilks (1975: 111, 375–79, figs. vi and vii). Blake (1991) provides much of our information on Shahjahanabad and Mughal city governance, but see also Jadunath Sarkar (1963: 12, 211, 212) and Abul Farooque (1977: 63). M. Athar Ali (1995: 271–72) describes Mughal governing policies while Chaudhuri (1978: 84) reports on the decline of urban neighborhoods under Mughal control. Blake (1991: 54–55, 84) discusses the order and function of mosques in Shahjahanabad.

Sources we used for our discussion of the Aztec capital of Tenochtitlan, in addition to early descriptions by Hernán Cortés (our cite is from de Zorita 1994: 157) and Diego Durán (1994: 110–11), include van Zantwijk (1985: 107), Edward Calnek (1978, 2003), Ross Hassig (1985: 60), and William Sanders (2003). Our understanding of the Augustan reworking of the Roman urban administration derives from Favro (1992) and J. Bert Lott (2004). Roads in Rome are discussed by Jérôme Carcopino (1968: 45), Valerie Hope (2000: 77), F. Scagnetti and G. Grande (Scagnetti and Grande1978), Alan Kaiser (2011), and van Tilburg (2007). For urban public goods, we followed, besides Favro (1992), Mark Hassall (2000: 321) and James Packer (1967). Histories of Chinese city planning are found in Nancy Steinhardt (1990) and in Paul Wheatley (1971). T'ang Dynasty walled-ward cities are described in Alison Dray-Novey (1993) and in Ho Ping-ti (1966). We followed Susamu Fuma (1993), Hucker (1998: 15), and Xu (2000) on the history of the Ming Dynasty baojia system. The administrative structures of urban zones are discussed by Susan Naquin (2000: 171–73). Residential mobility and neighborhoods are described also by Fuma (1993: 53, 76), Naquin (2000: 197, 198), Xu (2000: 163), and Richard Belsky (2000). Our information on Ming urban public goods is from Belsky (2000: 56), Albert Chan (1962), Fuma (1993: 49–52), Naquin (2000: 177–78), Hucker (1998: 15, 89), and Richard von Glahn (1991: 281); for Suzhou, Michael Marmé (1993: 31; 2005: 150; cf. Xu 2000: 136). The transition from corvée labor tax to a tax in currency is discussed in Fei (2009: 29–75), Fuma (1993), Naquin (2000: 178), and von Glahn (1991).

The early Venetian parish system is described by Romano (1987: 17); for the idea of the comune Venetiarum and its administrative structure, see Romano (1987: 18–19, 22). The struggle between private and public interests in the rise of this highly collective polity is commented on by Romano (1987: 25–26). Public goods included transportation infrastructure (e.g., Chambers and Pullan 2001: 6, 136; Norwich 1982: 202; and Romano 1987: 18, 22). Drainage, flood control, and water quality are discussed in Norwich (1982: 26), Frederic Lane (1973: 16), and Romano (1987: 25–26); public safety in Romano (1987: 9), Chambers and Pullan (2001: 20, 88–89), and Guido Ruggiero (1980: 5–6, 12, 14, 15). Commodity price controls and grain distributions for emergencies are discussed in Lane (1973: 14) and Romano (1987: 18), street lighting in Norwich (1982: 91), public health measures in Norwich (1982: 274) and Chambers and Pullan (2001: 113).

Charles Gulick (1973: 20) describes public safety in focal-period Athens. Water control infrastructure is assessed in Thompson and Wycherley (1972: 195–200; cf. Wycherley 1978: 249–50). For maintenance of city streets we consulted Blümner (1966: 199), John Camp (1986: 45), Peter Hall (1988: 40), and Thompson and Wycherley (1972: 193, 194). That a board of magistrates was charged with road maintenance is found in Gulick (1973: 303) and Mogens Hansen (1999: 243). The Kleisthenic administrative reforms of administrative divisions and the urban demes are described in Hansen (1999: 34) and in Rodney Young (1951: 138–39, 140–42). Demes are linked into the central governing institutions as is evident in sources such as Hansen (1999: 34) and Whitley (2001: 340). The changing urban morphology of Athens after 600 BCE is summarized in Camp (2001: 82–83, *passim*), Thompson and Wycherley (1972: 192), Norman Pounds (1969: 139), Ian Morris (2006), and Charles Gates (2003: 254). Tonio Hölscher (1991: 371) discusses the new civic functions of the Agora.

The population density estimate for Aceh is from Reid (1988: tables 7 and 8) and for Nupe is from Nadel (1942: plan 1, pp. 40–43). For density estimates of the other cities, we used Calnek (1976: 287–302) for Aztec Tenochtitlan-Tlatelolco; for Rome, Favro (1992: fig. 7), Palmer (1990: plan 1), Scagnetti and Grande (1978: fig. 2), and Glenn Storey (1997: 975, 2002); for Beijing, Nancy Shatzman-Steinhardt (1986: fig. 4); for Venice, David Chambers and Brian Pullan (Chambers and Pullan 2001: 4), and Dennis Romano (1987: 28); and for Athens, Ian F. Morris (2006: 42).

Jill Grant (2001) points out that grid plans may serve to "symbolize control" rather than provide for movement efficiency. The argument for a primarily symbolic role for planned urban form is made by Moholy-Nagy (1968: 83). Wheatley (1971: chap. 5) traces the history of gridded city form in China (cf. Steinhardt 1990). The central zone of Ava, the Burmese capital, and its cosmic design are described by Reid (1993: 80–81). Orthogonal city planning in Classical antiquity is discussed in Ferdinando Castagnoli (1971); the importance of economic egalitarianism in Greek democracy is discussed in the same source and in Whitley (2001: 359).

Graph analysis of road networks is discussed in sources such as Roger Robinson (1976) and Ronald Abler (Abler et al. 1971). Lynch (1960) and Hillier (1989, 1996) provide useful insights on city form and usability. We were influenced by the work of Barbara Stark (e.g., Stark 2014), a pioneer in the comparative study of early urban open spaces such as parks and gardens.

Rapoport (1980–81) highlights the importance of neighborhoods in city living. The section on neighborhoods benefitted from our reading of Abigail York et al. (2010), Arnauld et al. (2012), and M. E. Smith (2010). Modern urban planners encourage neighborhood development as a way to increase pedestrian movement at the expense of intraurban motorized transport (e.g., Peter Neal 2003). But recent trends in the United States, especially in the cities of the Southwestern states, suggest that neighborhoods, as gated compounds, are primarily a means to maintain property values, to enhance segregation by race and economic status, and to privatize policy-making and governance to avoid public accountability (e.g., in Evan McKenzie 1994).

The bounded official structures in New Kingdom Egyptian cities are noted by Peter Lacovara (1997). Inka cities reflect a highly bureaucratized and politically centralized polity as is evident in the descriptions provided by Terence D'Altroy (2002: 91), Catherine Julien (1982: 123), and Murra (1980: 75, 91, 128). For details on the main capital at Cuzco, we relied on D'Altroy (2002: 109, 114, 115) and Brian Bauer (2004: 137).

CHAPTER 11: THE CULTURAL PROCESS OF COOPERATION

The phrase "science of culture" is borrowed from the anthropologist Leslie White (1949). Ortner (1984: 134) describes the struggle between those who embrace "emic" or "etic" approaches to anthropological inquiry.

It has often been noted that culture may play a role in the development of modern organizations. In a study of organizational change, IBM Global Business Services (www.ibm.com/gbs/makingchangework) found that monetary and non-monetary rewards ranked low as causal factors in explaining successful change episodes, and the use of sanctions was even less important. Key factors explaining successful change included a sense that the leadership was effective, especially in its ability to honestly communicate what the change process would entail; a demonstrated passion for change; and the creation of a shared vision uniting management and other stakeholders.

The Marxist notion that the rational and willful individual is a product of bourgeois ideology is traced in F. Allan Hanson (2004). I first encountered the idea that cultural production may be consistent with the goals of collective action from my reading of Sewell (1985) and Carlton (1977). The latter distinguished "interest ideology," which typically reproduces elite dominance, from "civic ideology," which I associate with collective action. The latter emphasizes the importance of coordination of information needed to build consensus in the face of social cleavage (cf. Cronk and Leech 2013: 124–50).

In addition to Ostrom's 1986 article I benefitted from the insights of T. K. Ahn, Marco Janssen, and Elinor Ostrom on institution-building and cultural notions of the self (Ahn et al. 2004). The book edited by N. J. Enfield and Stephen C. Levinson provides examples of Theory of Mind thinking in different cultures (Enfield and Levinson 2006). William Edgerton (1947) commented on the nature of judicial process in New Kingdom Egypt.

Waugh (1991: 158) described bias against commoners in focal-period England, and Freedman (1999) analyzes images of the European Medieval peasant. Jacques Le Goff (1980: 59–61, 90) discusses the Medieval European concepts of "contemptible" persons and professions, and Mary Douglas (1966) views notions of impurity in cultural systems as social boundary-maintaining mechanisms (her example is the Hindu caste system). Dumont (1985) provides an extended discussion of the history of the Western self that includes a comparison with Hindu and Buddhist concepts (see also his 1977 book). I also drew from Alexis Sanderson (1985) for Hindu concepts, and followed Ivanhoe's (2000) useful summary of Chinese theories of moral self-cultivation. See also Munro (1969) on early Chinese concepts of the human.

Markku Peltonen (2002) mentions the influence of Italian sources such as Gasparo Contarini (1599) on emerging English notions of what constitutes a republic and citizenship. Reforms in the Chinese Qin state that introduced a meritocratic system of recruitment are described in Gideon Shelach and Yuri Pines (Shelach and Pines 2008: 219–20). Ho (1962) was my basic source on the history of the Chinese civil examination system, and I summarize Elman's useful 1991 paper. Creel (1970: 15–27) documents how early modern European state-builders borrowed Chinese ideas for open recruitment into civil positions (Brook 2005: 189 makes a similar point); in spite of Chinese influence, in England, according to Jack Goody, senior posts in the civil administration and military were largely the province of an elite until the nineteenth century (Goody 1996: 202). Hucker (1978: 49–50) describes Ming improvements in the examination practices. Donald Brown (1988: 33–41) discusses social mobility in Hindu South Asia and in premodern China (61–69).

Aztec (Nahua language and culture) mythic history is analyzed in Fargher et al. (2010), which draws from numerous sources, including Boone (1991: 148), Susan Gillespie (1989), Harold Nicholson (2001), van Zantwijk (1985: 96–97), Heyden (1991: 189), Sahagún (1950–82, II: 5), and Offner (1983).

David Howes (1991) and in Howes and Constance Classen (Howes and Classen 2014) provide wide-ranging commentaries on the diversity of human sensoria. Alfredo López Austin (1988) discusses the Aztec theory of the self. My principal sources from art psychology are Robert Solso (2003) and Margaret Livingstone (2002); Anjan Chatterjee (2010) provides a summary of recent advances in the field of neuroaesthetics. Universal responses to facial expression of emotion are described in the collection edited by Adams et al. (2011); see also Chatterjee (2010: 56–57), Frank (1988), Kandel (2012), Schmidt and Cohn (2001: 20), and Stone (2006). Freedberg (1989: 200) writes about how portraits evoke emotional responses (cf. Bryson 1983; Gell 1998: 132, 136; Porter 2005); Freedberg and Gallese (2007) link this to how the brain responds to representation through the mirror neuron system. The neurophysiology of vision in relation to artistic depiction of the mental states of subjects is also discussed in Eric Kandel (2012) and in Adams et al. (2011). Thomas Wynn (1995) comments on the meaning of the Acheulean hand axe tradition.

On naturalism in relation to collective action, see Blanton (2011). Jonathan Crary (1990) writes about Enlightenment philosophers' use of visual imagery in their theories of human intellect. The tendency to depict the folkloric details of the everyday life of common persons beginning in the Early Modern Period is discussed in Andrew Ballantyne (2002); additional art historical sources are David Bjelajac (2005: chap. 4), Alison Hilton (1978), Nochlin (1989: chaps. 2 and 8), and Jakob Rosenberg, Seymour Slive, and Engelbert ter Kuile (Rosenberg et al. 1966). Many art historians assume that naturalism in non-Western art is evidence of Western cultural influence rather than as a sociocultural and neuroaesthetic process as is argued here, for example, in relation to Japanese painting of the late Edo Period and early Meiji Periods as argued in Penelope Mason (2005: 319–46).

The moral philosophical content of David Hume's and Adam Smith's writings is discussed in Gertrude Himmelfarb (2001), who also provides a comparison of British and French Enlightenment literatures. Paolo Rossi (1970) documents the growing interest in the dignity of ordinary labor and the mechanical arts in Early Modern Europe.

The general absence of realism in African art is discussed in Douglas Fraser and Herbert Cole (Fraser and Cole 1972). Frank Willett (1972) discusses an early pre-focal-period (fourteenth and fifteenth century CE) of the Yoruba during which highly realistic portraits of Yoruba leaders were produced. Christopher Steiner (1990) points out that in some collective polities, the governing elite are not represented as autonomous subjects in art or in ritual occasions (cf. Feinman 2001: 167–68). Donald Brown (2008) develops a theory of portraiture that is in some ways similar to my argument, but he associates it with weaker systems of social stratification rather than collective action. The growth of physiognomics in Euro-American literature is described by Breckenridge (1968: 4) and Christopher Lukasik (2004, 2011). Martin Porter (2005) documents the role of physiognomics in European culture but mentions other cultural traditions in this regard in ancient Greece, Rome, and China.

The role of art in Greek democracy is discussed in David Castriota (1998). Changes in the direction of naturalization in Greek art are discussed in Osborne (2008) and Breckenridge (1968: 101); Greek physiognomic theory is described in Porter (2005: 49–50). The communication of moral discourses in Classical Greece is discussed in K. J. Dover (1974) and Momigliano (1985). The negative Greek view of humans is described in Ober (1998). I benefitted from the useful summary of the Athenian sense of self in Humphreys (1978). Plato's argument is made in *The Republic* (Sterling and Scott 1985: section 518). Victor Ehrenberg (1951) provides a useful summary of the sociological content of the plays of Aristophanes.

Donald Brown (1988: 162–70) summarizes sources describing change in degrees of social stratification from the Roman Republican Period to the High Empire Period, and notes a reversion to a "caste-like" pattern of social stratification by Late Antiquity (170–75). Paul Zanker (1988: 98–100) writes about Roman art including figural representation.

Venetian cultural production aiming to enhance a widely shared sense of devotion to the civic values of the comune Venetiarum is discussed in Romano (1987: 25), ducal processions in Muir (1981), and carnival in Peter Burke (1987: chap. 13). De Maria (2010) discusses the relationship between art and concepts of the self in society. The emergence of Venetian cityscapes and civic processional scenes is evident in Patricia Fortini Brown (1988). M. Margaret Newett (1907) describes the extensive imposition of sumptuary laws in the fourteenth and fifteenth centuries. Donald Brown (2008: 334) discusses the struggle over the role of official portraiture in Venice.

Thomas L. Friedman's opinion piece in the *New York Times*, titled "Egypt: The Next India or the Next Pakistan" was published on December 17, 2012. Mughal open recruitment policies were described by Hasan (1936: 350, 356); see also Amartya Sen (2005: 18–19). Change in the function of Sufistic poetry under the Mughals is discussed in Wheeler M. Thackston (2002: 96), and the development of an etiquette literature to provide moral exempla is from H. Mukhia (2004: chap. 2). Mughal court painting, including illuminated historical narratives, was a new form of political communication in South Asia (G. Sen 1984; cf. Guy and Britschgi 2011, Topsfield 2008), as was "Mughal Realism," including portraiture, as discussed in Milo Beach (1987: 17) and Coomaraswamy (1975: 74). While military, royal hunting, and court scenes were most common, commoners and quotidian scenes were also produced, such as those found in Beach (1987: figs. 5, 6, 9, and 30) and Verma (1994: plates III, XIV, XVI, and L) that depict youths, a gardener, a student and teacher, musicians, and a peasant.

Concepts of self in Late Imperial China are drawn from Tu Wei-ming (1985), Elvin (1985), and Munro (1969); the idea that the moral being grows from the physical labor of peasant production is discussed in Bray (1997: 41). Technological improvements in book production and other communicative media during the Ming Period, during and after the late fourteenth century, are discussed in Laurence Sickman and Alexander Soper (Sickman and Soper 1960: 164) and in Rawski (1985: 15); this took place earlier than in Europe, where an analogous jump-up in numbers of book titles began during the seventeenth century (e.g., Porter 2005: fig. 3). Ming Dynasty painting of the focal period also featured the form of naturalism in which commoners and quotidian themes were represented in encyclopedias and works on agriculture that depicted rural people and work themes (e.g., in Bray 1997). A comparative analysis of Ming landscape painting with prior dynasties is found in Blanton (2011), which points to an increase in the use of quotidian themes in Ming painting. During the Ming Dynasty, the art of physiognomy was revitalized (Porter 2005: 48), and this development was accompanied by the advent of individual official portraiture, a

Ming Dynasty innovation within the context of the history of art in China (M. K. Hearn 2008: 130). The limited-use Sung Dynasty official portraits are analyzed in Lee (2010). Chinese schools, private academies, and tutors are discussed in Hucker (1998: 31, 39) and in Schneewind (2006). In the same source Hucker describes the published lists of discredited officials (Hucker 1998: 44–45). The vernacular commentary on the Ming law code is mentioned in John Langlois (1998: 172, 179–80).

On Bali, see Geertz (1980); I also made use of insights from his "Centers, Kings, and Charisma: Reflections on the Symbolics of Power" (Geertz 1983b). Bloch's (1974) suggestion that in the premodern condition ritual serves to uphold autocratic forms of authority applies in some cases, such as Bali, but is mistaken when he identifies this as an aspect of all "traditional" forms of authority.

Many of the original insights for an understanding of the role of symbolic dualism in human culture are from Claude Lévi-Strauss (e.g., Lévi-Strauss 1963). I gained additional insights on duality ("symbolic inversion") from Babcock (1978).

For the section on Aztec ritual I depended mostly on the chapters in David Carrasco (1991), especially those by Broda and Heyden; I also greatly benefited from Bernal-García (2007). An analysis of the role of Tezcatlipoca in pre-Hispanic polity-building, in Tlaxcala, is provided in Fargher et al. (2010). Emily Umberger (2014) documents the close relationship of the Aztec deities Tezcatlipoca and Huitzilopochtli.

Hellenic scholars differ as to whether Dionysian ritual, including the theatrical performances, played a civic role in the democratic polis in Athens (e.g., Rhodes 2003), but from this literature a number of scholars have taken the position that Athenians did use these cultural forms to enhance the possibilities for consensus in the face of cleavage; I especially benefitted from Robert Connor (1996), Simon Goldhill (1990), Ober and Strauss (1990), and Cartledge (1997). Cartledge (1985) provides a useful summary of the Athenian city Dionysia, and Dagmar Weston (2012) discusses the cultural meaning of the form of the Greek theater. Friedrich Nietzsche was the first Western philosopher to argue that a synthesis of two dimensions of human nature, the Apollonian (highlighting the cultured and rational) and the Dionysian (highlighting the irrational and instinctive), was a spur to the creativity of Greek dramatic art (e.g., Sweet 1999). Ober (2006) points to other aspects of public performance in the civic life of Classical Athens.

The section on Greek notions of margin and center was derived from Norman Brown (1947), E. R. Dodds (1951), Pierre Vidal-Naquet (1981), and R.G.A. Buxton (1992). Ober (1995: 111–12) comments on the liminal properties of the disputed boundary zones between Greek *poleis*.

That borderlands may be symbolically translated into "terms of the night" is developed in Dodds (1951: 102, 136, 140) and Galinier et al. (2010). Markets and the symbolism of the night are conflated in some other cultural settings, though this association deserves more comparative investigation. For instance, Dexter (1930: 32–33) notes the "odd," probably pre-Christian, nighttime *mercats* (markets) in England; he also notes that women presided over night markets in Malacca, though I was unable to confirm that.

Cooperation researchers have often noted the importance of communal ritual in fostering human cooperation (see the summary in Carballo 2013b: 257–61). I expand on the topic of ritual in relation to cooperation in Blanton (2016). Ritual and numinence are discussed in Rappaport (1979); see also Ilka Pyysiäinen (2001). Wegner (2009) and Richard Davidson and Sharon Begley (Davidson and Begley 2012) are additional sources besides Goleman (2013) that discuss how mental exhaustion may limit the brain's ability to control emotional responses. My argument is not that spectacle inhibits deliberative appraisal of an instinctive moral sensibility to want to obey authority, in the sense of the moral intuitionist Haidt (2001). Instead, I argue that spectacle makes it likely that persons will be less likely to objectively evaluate dubious social conventions.

A more detailed analysis of the process of religious problematization in relation to collective action is found in Blanton and Fargher (2008: 291–94; 2013). "Axial Age" thinking is summarized by Karen Armstrong (2006). Some authors identify the Axial Age as a social and cultural evolutionary stage that paved the way for modern societies and modes of government that were superior to the earlier theocracies (e.g., in Eisenstadt 1986; cf. Morris 2010).

Chinese cityscapes and maps are discussed in Kiang (1999). Joseph Rykwert (1998) writes how city form and ritual evokes a sense of civic identity.

CHAPTER 12: THE CAUSES AND CONSEQUENCES OF COLLECTIVE ACTION

The rise of Osei Tutu is described in Wilks (1975: 111, *passim*) and in R. S. Rattray (1929: 219, *passim*), Lewanika in A.H.J. Prins (1980: 30–31). Akbar's rise is documented in many sources including Ali (1985, 1995). The law-making of the Athenians Solon and Kleisthenes is described in Hansen (1999). The law-making of Julius Caesar appears in many sources including Abbott (1963: 138, 452) and Elizabeth Rawson (1994), that of Augustus also in many sources including Abbott (1963: 266–85). Many sources describe the history of the rise of the Ming founder (e.g., Farmer 1976: 30–37 and Hucker 1998: 70–73). Van Zantwijk (1985) writes about the Aztec arrangement and the state-builder Tlacaelel.

Carol Ember and Melvin Ember summarize the statistical methods for cross-cultural comparison used in this study (Ember and Ember 2001). Appendixes 2 and

3 in Blanton and Fargher (2008) provide data and sources on population, urbanism, commercialization, production, and material standard of living I used to develop codes from the comparative sample and to develop the descriptive sections, and for the comparison of Aztec and Inka.

Recent evaluations of the Malthusian Trap idea and similar arguments claiming European exceptionalism are found in Pomeranz (2000), Wong (1997), Frank (1998), and Ian Morris (2010). Mark Elvin (1972) proposes a similar "High-Level Equilibrium Trap" for Chinese history after 1300 CE. Institutional economists such as North (1981) and Greif (2006) connect economic growth to institutional development, but do not emphasize collective action as I do here.

Deng (2012: table 14.1) poses a change process in Chinese fiscal states, that began as early as 685 BCE, linking economic growth, tax capacity, government revenue, and public goods, in a mutually reinforcing causal pattern similar to my notion of a coactive causal process.

In addition to sources cited in the text, my discussion of the Medieval to Early Modern European coactive causal process, especially as it occurred in England, is based on Robert Allen (2001), Anderson and Latham (1986), Alice Beardwood (1931), Kathleen Biddick (1985), Richard Britnell (2004), James Davis (2012), Spencer Dimmock (2007), Dyer (1989, 2000, 2002, 2007), Everitt (1967), Fargher (2009: 358–61), Rodney Hilton (1985), Lopez (1976), Edward Miller and John Hatcher (Miller and Hatcher 1978), Josiah Russell (1948), Margaret Spufford (1984), Thirsk (1967), and E. P. Thompson (1971). Jan Luiten Van Zanden (2009: fig. 33, chap. 8) documents economic growth in Europe, especially in England, from 1300 to 1800. The estimates for increases in grain yields are from Slicher van Bath (1963: table 3).

Janet Abu-Lughod (1989) documents the growing scale of world-system exchanges, anchored in China and South Asia, that gradually incorporated previously marginal zones such as Western Europe, including England. Methods for the comparative study of periodic markets and degree of commercialization are found in Carol Smith (1985), G. W. Skinner (1964), and Blanton and Fargher (2010: 214–15). Causal theories of market evolution are presented in Blanton (1983 and 1985), and that question is also raised in Blanton and Fargher (2010).

The rejection of traditional substantivist economic theory by many anthropologists has ushered in new ways of thinking that have made it possible for me to imagine the workings of the coactive causal process. The paper by Feinman and Garraty (2010) and the chapters in Garraty and Stark (2010) and Hirth and Pillsbury (2013) summarize recent thinking about premodern markets. I also benefitted from recent research on the economic histories of Classical Greece, especially Athens, and High Empire Rome written by authors including L. de Ligt (1993),

B. W. Frier (1999), R. Bruce Hitchner (2005), Keith Hopkins (1980, 1995–1996), D. J. Mattingly (1988), Ian Morris (2004, 2005, 2006), Ober (2010), Peter Temin (2013), and Ward-Perkins (2005).

Mughal Period economic development and demographic change (up to the last few reigns of the dynasty, at which time the economy went into decline) are described in Satish Chandra (1982), Chaudhuri (1985), B. R. Grover (1994), Habib (1963: 77–78), and Hasan (1936).

The summary of intensification, commerce, population, and standard of living in China followed Bray (1984, 1997), Brook (1998), Heijdra (1998), Rawski (1972), G. William Skinner (1964), and Kathy Walker (1999). Harriet Zurndorfer (2011) describes the thriving Ming cotton industry, and the associated growth of market towns; he comments that most of the cotton produced was consumed by commoners (see also the summary in Fargher 2009: 373–75). Walker (1999: 31) points out that cotton became the basic clothing material for nonelite. Frank (1998) and Pomeranz (2000) document China's growing world-scale economic influence during the Ming Dynasty. Ronald Knapp (1986) traces the history of the Han-style house form in China.

Ancient Mesoamerica has also been a site of much new research on commercialization, as can be seen in recent summary works by Feinman and Linda Nicholas (Feinman and Nicholas 2012) and Kowalewski (2012). Aztec commercialization and standard of living are becoming better understood from archaeological and ethnohistoric work reported in sources such as M. E. Smith (2003: 90) and Blanton (1996), bulk luxury goods consumption is discussed in Blanton, Fargher, and Heredia Espinoza (2005), and population growth is summarized in Blanton (2004); see also the summary of economic and demographic change in Fargher (2009: 362–69). M. E. Smith (1987) summarizes archaeological indicators of wealth in agrarian states.

Hirschman (1970) proposes a theory linking the potential for exit from a polity to the behavior of leaders. Igor Kopytoff (1987) writes about African "wealth in people" societies (cf. Kopytoff and Miers 1977; Robertshaw 1999).

The book edited by Tina Thurston and Christopher Fisher (Thurston and Fisher 2007) provides a recent perspective on the causes and consequences of agricultural intensification. Stephen Lansing (1987) is my major source on Balinese wet-rice agriculture (see also Christie [1992] and Geertz [1980]). The estimate of ten bushels per acre (600 kilograms/hectare/year) average for England of about 1300 CE is from Robert Allen (2009: 62). Blanton (2004: table 15.2) summarizes and compares agricultural productivity estimates for Mediterranean Roman Empire and Late Postclassic Mesoamerica. Michael Whitby (1998) confirms the need for Athenian food imports, mostly coming from the Black Sea, during the fourth century BCE. The Venetian network of food suppliers extended from as far as the Black Sea region (Lane 1973: 69) to closer sources such as Veneto and Friuli (Pullan 1971: 28). Sources for English tax administration included Platt (1982: 92–93), Plucknett (1940: 103), and Waugh (1991: 157–59). The Aztec *chinampa* productivity estimate is from William Sanders and Barbara Price (Sanders and Price 1968: 148).

Fargher and Heredia Espinoza (2012) point to how land surveys and cadastral record-keeping are consistent with a concept of land ownership (see also Lockhart [1992: chap. 5] and H. R. Harvey [1991]). Mi Chu Wiens (1988) and Clunas (1996) describe Ming Dynasty cadastral and census surveys. Scott's (1998: chap. 1) discussion of cadastral surveying assumes that it is one aspect of how states make society more "legible" as a way to enhance their degree of centralized control. However, he fails to distinguish between more and less collective polities, which, obviously, have different kinds of political goals. According to Bray (1984: 109–10), in Ming China even the highly productive irrigated rice production of the southern regions involved mostly water capture in small farmer-owned tanks.

Aztec land ownership, survey methods, and records are documented in James Lockhart (1992: 149–55) and Barbara Williams and Herbert Harvey (e.g., Williams and Harvey 1988). An active Aztec land market is described by Offner (1981).

Land surveys under conditions of collective action appear to have promoted independent development of methods of surveying, mathematical notation, and geometrical calculations used to estimate the area of irregular fields in the Aztec case (Harvey 1991; Williams and Jorge y Jorge 2008) as in Ming Dynasty China (Clunas 1996: 193–94). The Greeks attributed the beginnings of their mathematical culture to the necessity of measuring the areas of irregular surfaces (Neugebauer 1952: 145), which did correspond with the rise of the democratic polity (sixth century BCE).

Major sources for the Aztec-Inka comparison (other than Aztec sources already mentioned) include D'Altroy (2002), D'Altroy and Timothy Earle (D'Altroy and Earle 1992), Craig Morris (1982), and Murra (1980).

When I allude to how "most" households must be able to intensify their wealth production, I allude to the fact that coactive process will be inhibited when many households are unable to bear their share of costs. Hardin (1982: 67–89), however, suggests that collective action may develop even when not everyone is in a position to (or willing to) contribute if a minority is able to organize to provide the needed resources. There is little evidence for this minority-support theory in the comparative sample, with the possible exceptions of Classical Athens—where much taxation fell to wealthier families (though the military contribution of commoner soldiers was evidently a major factor in the rise of Greek democracy)—and, possibly, Asante, where inheritance taxes were an important source of revenues. A deeper problem with Hardin's suggestion, in the case of jointly provided public goods managed by a state, is that taxpayers gain power vis-à-vis the state because they are the main source of revenues—a key claim of collective action theory. When there is a minority of wealthy taxpayers willing to support the state's institutions, they are predicted to gain outsized influence, potentially pushing the governing system toward elite-driven autocracy.

Venice's dependence on an external supply zone was threatened by its loss of world-system trade centrality. As Abu-Lughod (1989: 131) puts it, for Venice decline came because of "the inability of the Italian mariner states to determine what would happen in regions far beyond their control"; and, more specifically (Abu-Lughod (1989: 638), "when northern Europe moved out into the Atlantic . . . [it left] . . . the Mediterranean a backwater."

The consequences of participation in the growing world-system scale economies, in the case of the comparative sample, is discussed in Blanton and Fargher (2008: 266–72). Growing trade between Athens and Near Eastern polities, including Egypt, began after about 900 BCE (e.g., Morris 1999: 77; Runciman 1982: 367). Hansen (1999: 285) describes the importance of silver exports in this new economy that exacerbated social inequality. Venice emerged as a key semiperiphery player in the context of a Eurasiatic world system that grew after 1250 CE (Abu-Lughod 1989). For circa 1,000 years, long-distance trade through the Swahili area has connected interior African regions to the Arabian Gulf and Indian Ocean trade routes (Abungu and Mutoro 1993), and by the focal period Swahili Lamu was a major entrepôt in this part of east coastal Africa (Ylvisaker 1979: chap. 7).

It is well recognized that preindustrial cities could be dangerous places to live (the "urban graveyard effect"), for example, from G. Storey (2006a: 5–9; cf. R. Storey 1992), with a high potential for social conflict (Kostof 1992: 102–10), especially under conditions of weak or nonexistent city management. That Ming Dynasty urban reorganization was in part a response to demand for services by commoner residents is documented by Fuma (1993), Naquin (2000: 178), and von Glahn (1991).

Bates (1983) evaluates David Ricardo's theory linking markets to state formation. The main sources for liminal process are Victor Turner (1969) and Victor Turner and Edith Turner (Turner and Turner 1978), but see also Agnew (1979). Kopytoff (1987) writes about the social consequences of the relative institutional vacuum of frontier regions. Redfield (1986) documents the importance of the market in the rise of Classical Greek society, though, as he points out, it was never considered "ethically reputable." Hansen (1996: 96) argues that the Greek idea of freedom has its roots in commerce.

CHAPTER 13: FINAL THOUGHTS: INSIGHTS GAINED
FROM AN EXPANDED COLLECTIVE ACTION THEORY

Several authors find hidden political agendas in the writings of recent evolutionary psychologists (e.g., McKinnon 2005) and in the writings of its precursor, sociobiology (Kitcher 1985: 3–11) (though see a counterargument made by Lyle and Smith [2012]). Margaret Archer and Jonathan Tritter comment on how neoliberal policy finds economic efficiency in voluntary organizations that provide public goods services through "altruistic acts of charity" (Archer and Tritter 2000: 1). M. Thompson, R. Ellis, and A. Wildavsky (Thompson et al. 1990: 155–58) comment on the policy implications of Marxist theory and identify other "compassionist" theories proposing an authentic human nature that is naturally cooperative.

The characteristics of twentieth-century socialist societies are described by János Kornai (1992) and Katherine Verdery (1991). Acemoglu, Verdier, and Robinson (2004) allude to the role sometimes played by foreign aid in the sustaining of autocratic rule. Joseph Stiglitz (2002) details the negative outcomes of neoliberal policies in organizations such as the World Bank and the International Monetary Fund. Mick Moore (2008: 57–62) summarizes how globalization negatively affects tax collection in developing countries.

Appendix A

Values of collective action scale variables, the summed values of the three variables, and the main revenue source ("external" = 1, "internal" = 2).

	Public Goods	Bureaucratization	Principal Control	Collective Action Total	Resource
Nupe	10.0	7.5	8.0	25.5	1
Yoruba	16.0	9.5	11.0	36.5	1
Asante	18.5	10.5	15.5	44.5	2
Bagirmi	13.0	8.5	6.0	27.5	1
Kuba	13.5	10.0	8.5	32.0	1
Tio	12.5	6.0	8.5	27.0	1
Buganda	15.5	11.0	10.5	37.0	2
Bakitara	10.0	6.5	7.0	23.5	1
Lozi	22.0	12.0	15.0	49.0	2
Swahili Lamu	10.0	11.5	14.5	36.0	1
Thailand	18.5	8.0	9.5	36.0	2
Burma	20.0	12.0	9.0	41.0	2
Bali	14.0	6.0	8.0	28.0	1
Aceh	10.0	6.0	9.0	25.0	1

continued on next page

DOI: 10.5876/9781607325147.c015

	Public Goods	Bureaucratization	Principal Control	Collective Action Total	Resource
Perak	12.5	5.5	7.5	25.5	1
Java	18.5	10.0	9.5	38.0	2
Vijayanagara	18.0	9.5	9.5	37.0	2
Pudukkottai	17.0	7.0	7.5	31.5	2
Mughal	23.5	12.0	9.5	45.0	2
China	22.0	14.5	14.5	51.0	2
Japan	16.5	7.0	8.0	31.5	1
Tibet	19.5	8.5	6.0	34.0	2
Egypt	20.0	10.0	8.0	38.0	1
Athens	20.0	14.0	18.0	52.0	2
Rome	24.0	12.0	12.0	48.0	2
Venice	21.0	14.0	16.5	51.5	2
England	11.0	8.5.0	8.5	28.0	1
Ottoman	16.0	9.5	9.0	34.5	1
Aztec	21.0	11.5	12.5	45.0	2
Inka	22.0	10.0	8.0	40.0	2

Appendix B

TABLE B.1. Values on the right side of the diagonal are the zero-order r and Spearman rank order correlations (the latter in brackets). Values to the left of the diagonal indicate statistical significance of the two correlation measures.

	Public Goods	Bureaucratization	Control over Ruler
Public Goods	—	0.68 [0.7]	0.4 [0.44]
Bureaucratization	<0.0001 [<0.0001]	—	0.76 [0.75]
Control over Ruler	0.08 [0.015]	<0.0001 [<0.0001]	—

SECTION 1

Collective action theory posits that a relational form of power will link principals and taxpayers to the degree that taxpayers have the ability to bargain with principals. This is likely to happen when taxpayers provide many of the resources needed by the state (our "internal" revenue sources). In our coding we included the following as internal: (a) taxation of market transactions; (b) taxation of basic agricultural and craft production; (c) labor tax; (d) taxation of other production (e.g., mines); and (e) other internal levies, including inheritance tax, poll tax, land tax, and estate tax. Principals are predicted to be less inclined to bargain with taxpayers when they are able to depend on resources largely apart from what taxpayers produce (our "external" revenues) such as (a) revenue from land (including mines) directly controlled by principal or the state (this included only categories such as

DOI: 10.5876/9781607325147.c016

feudal estates, palace lands, and lands that were administered separately from other taxed land); (b) revenues from external warfare and/or empire, directly controlled by ruler, and managed apart from the normal taxation administration; (c) revenues from monopoly control by the ruler or the state of internal and trade; (d) state taxation of international trade, again, where the proceeds are controlled directly by the ruler; (e) degree of direct control of the labor of categories of persons distinct from the ordinary labor levies of taxpayers, for example, tenants working state land or state-owned slaves. All the coded states had both internal and external revenue streams, but data provided for the coded cases allowed us to assign priority to one or the other in most cases. Our analysis showed that polities tilted toward collective action when revenues were either strongly internal or when there was a rough equality between internal and external. The less collective polities exhibited a strong tendency toward external revenues (discussion of the data and methods for coding are provided in Blanton and Fargher 2008: chap. 6). The following table provides data on mean values of public goods, bureaucratization, and control over ruler split by resource emphasis (external and internal) with t-Test results. These very strong statistical results provide an important test case for a key element of collective action theory:

TABLE B.2. The main collective actions scale variables compared by type of revenue.

	External Revenues $n = 14$	Internal Revenues $n = 16$	t-Test for difference of means (2-tailed)
Public Goods	13.5	19.5	$p = {<}0.0001$
Bureaucratization	7.7	11.1	$p = {<}0.0001$
Control over Principals	8.2	11.6	$p = 0.0024$

TABLE B.3. Tabulation of monarchical and other forms of principal governance in the premodern sample (with selected sources).

	CA Total	Monarch-Based	Other Governing Institutions	No Monarch
Bakitara late 19th century	23.5	Roscoe 1923: chap. 4		
Aceh 1850–1900	25.0		Reid 1975: 55	
Nupe mid-19th century	25.5	Nadel 1942: 47, 89–117		
Perak 1800–1870	25.5	Gullick 1958: 44–45		

continued on next page

	CA Total	Monarch-Based	Other Governing Institutions	No Monarch
Tio 19th century	27.0	Vansina 1973: 386–87		
Bagirmi 1800–1900	27.5	Reyna 1990: 59, 92		
Bali 1823–71	28.0	Geertz 1980: 104–6		
England 14th century	28.0	William Morris 1940: 4		
Pudukkottai 1700–1800	31.5	Dirks 1987: 130, 156		
Japan shogunate 18th century	31.5	Hall 1991b: 150, 160–61		
Kuba late 19th century	32.0	Vasina 1978: chap. 11		
Tibet 1792–1951	34.0	Carrasco 1959: 80		
Ottoman 1300–1600	34.5	Lybyer 1966		
Swahili Lamu 1800–1870	36.0			Prins 1967
Thailand 1782–1873	36.0	Rabibhadana 1969: chap. 3		
Yoruba 1750–1800	36.5		Law 1977: 62–67	
Buganda late 19th century	37.0	Wrigley 1996: 64		
Vijayanagara 1350–1564	37.0		Saletore 1934: 254	
Java 1700–1900	38.0	Moertono 1981: 16–17, 61–72		
Egypt 1479–1213 BCE	38.0	O'Connor 1983		
Inka 1438–1532	40.0	D'Altroy 2002: 91		
Burma 1752–1800	41.0	Koenig 1990: chap. 3		
Asante 1800–1873 CE	44.5		Wilks 1975: chap. 10	
Mughal 1556–1658	45.0	Sarkar 1963: chap. 8		
Aztec 1428–1521	45.0		van Zantwijk 1985	
Rome 69–192	48.0		Abbott 1963	

continued on next page

	CA Total	Monarch-Based	*Other Governing Institutions*	*No Monarch*
Lozi late 19th century	49.0		Gluckman 1961: 47	
China 1368–ca. 1600	51.0		Hucker 1998	
Venice 1290–1600	51.5			Lane 1973: 96–97
Athens 403–322 BCE	52.0			Hansen 1999

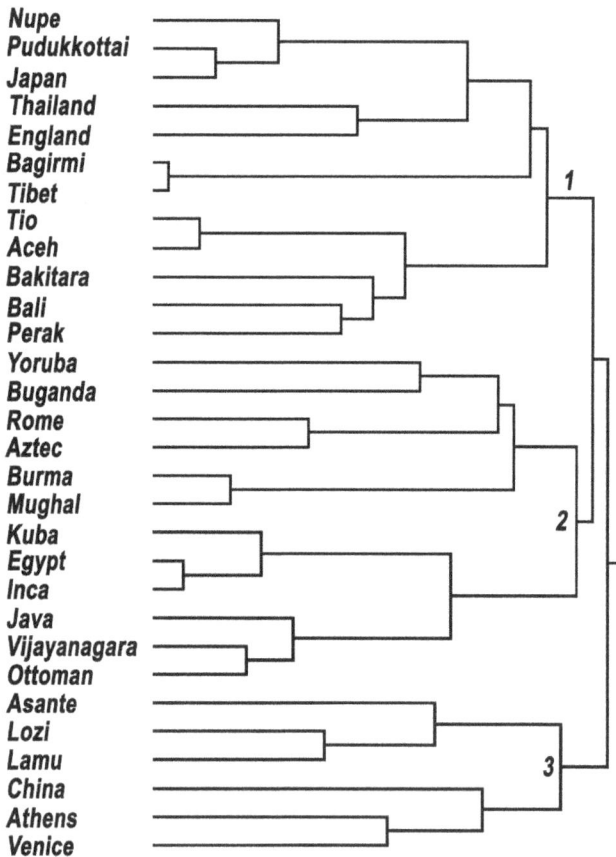

FIGURE B.1. Cluster dendrogram illustrating three types of polities measured by our main collective action variables of public goods, bureaucratization, and control over rulers.

SECTION 2

Hierarchical cluster analysis is a useful exploratory method for finding clumping of similar cases when each case is described by multiple variables (e.g., Shennan [1988: 212–40]). The method used here (Ward's) is an agglomerative approach that first identifies the most similar pairs of cases sharing similar values across multiple variables. It then treats each of the first "generation" of paired cases as a new cluster unit, which it then pairs with each cluster's most similar other cluster, and this process is continued until all cases have been clustered together.

TABLE B.4. Data for degree of official intervention in building institutional capital in rural communities in four categories (with main sources), with the mean of public goods for each category. From the four categories, numerical values of 1 to 4 were used to represent degree of state involvement (1 least to 4 highest). The resulting correlation coefficient for public goods by state involvement, using Kendall's tau, is 0.5 (p = 0.008). For bureaucratization by state involvement Kendall's tau = 0.5 (p = 0.007).

I. Little direct official intervention at the local scale:

  Japan (Hall 1991a: 7; Naohiro 1991: 51–53)

  Mean for public goods =16.5

II. Only specific categories of rural households or communities were under direct state control:

  Buganda (Kottack 1972: 362; Wrigley 1996: 63–64), Bakitara (Roscoe 1923: 56, 83–86, 116), Lozi (Gluckman 1941: 32, 1943: 21, 1961: 22, 62), Pudukkottai (Dirks 1987: 189), Egypt (O'Connor 1990: 17)

  Mean for public goods =16.9

III. Particular communities, provinces, or subregions were reorganized or populated with state intervention:

  Asante (McCaskie 1995: 89; Wilks 1975: 52), Thailand (Vella 1957: 26), Burma (Koenig 1990: 54, 107–8), Java (Moertono 1981: 68, 113, 133–35; Schrieke 1957: 146–49), Vijayanagara (Morrison 2001: 265; Sinopoli 1994: 234), Mughal (Habib 1963: 178, 290; Sarkar 1963: 12), Ottoman (Inalçik 1994: 72–73, 145, 176–77), Aztec (e.g., Blanton 1996: 67)

  Mean for public goods = 19.25

IV. Direct state intervention in the restructuring of communities and other rural institutions:

  China (Heijdra 1998: 461, 468–71; Wiens 1988), Athens (Hansen 1999: 34; Whitley 2001: 340), Rome (Birley 2000: 139; Galsterer 2000), Venice (Norwich 1982: 208–9, 284), Inka (Julien 1982: 123; Murra 1980: 75)

  Mean for public goods = 21.8

SECTION 3

The coded data for the measure of local institutional capital is found in Blanton and Fargher (2008: appendix 3, variable h). The results of the analysis are mixed, with only public goods, of our measures of collective action, showing a positive correlation with community institutional capital ($r = 0.66, p = 0.0001$).

TABLE B.5. Spatial integration data for selected cities. Map Sources: Bida (Nadel 1942: Plan1); Edo (Coaldrake 1981: fig. 2); Istanbul (Inalçik 1973: 232); Bursa (Kuran 1996); Cairo (Raymond 1984: fig. 1); Buganda (Roscoe 1965: Plan 1); Asante Kumase (Wilks 1975: map vii); Shahjahanabad (1878, Great Britain India Office), Tenochtitlan (Calnek 1976); Rome (Shepherd 1911: 22–23, and Favro 1992: fig. 7); Ming Beijing (Shatzman Steinhardt 1986: fig. 4); Ming Suzhou (Xu 2000: fig. 6.10); Athens (Morris 2006, Tomlinson 1992).

	Population	Beta Edges/ Nodes	Single Isovist Points (percent)	Complex Isovist (percent)	Public Goods	Integration Points
Bida (Nupe)	60,000	0.92	25	5	10.0	21
Edo	1.3 million	N/A	16	3	16.5	38
Istanbul	400,000	1.16	63	25	16.0	8
Bursa	300,000	1.15	65	29	16.0	34
Cairo	250,000	1.32	64	3	16.0	33
Buganda	77,000	1.20	100	52	15.5	27
Kumase	20,000	1.23	100	80	18.5	15
Shahjahanabad	400,000	1.38	86	46	23.5	28
Tenochtitlan	175,000	1.35	77	47	21.0	44
Rome	350,000	1.19	92	71	24.0	48
Beijing (Ming)	500,000	1.16	91	57	22.0	47
Suzhou (Ming)	300,000	1.52	73	60	22.0	45
Athens	150,000	1.16	64	33	20.0	36

SECTION 4

The bivariate fit of number of integration points by public goods is strongly positive ($r = 0.58, p = 0.036, n = 13$). A partial correlation analysis that accounts for the effects of population size produced a similar correlation between integration points and public goods ($r = 0.58$), while the correlation value of integration points by population is $r = 0.26$. The bivariate fit of Beta by public goods gives $r = 0.64$, $p = 0.025$ ($n = 12$). When we did partial correlation of Beta, public goods, and population, the *r* of integration points by public goods remains 0.665, while the *r* for population by public goods is negative (−0.3179); in the Beta calculations, Tokugawa Edo is omitted because it was difficult to interpret how major roads were connected to integration points.

SECTION 5

We estimated this aspect of spatial intelligibility, first, by counting the number of "single isovist" integration points from our city maps (points connected linearly to at least one other integration point) (e.g., Hillier 1996: 153) (Table B.5). The bivariate fit of single isovist points by public goods (as a proxy for collective action) is $r = 0.59, p = 0.033$ ($n = 12$). We assessed the degree of global patterning of a city's road plan by counting the number of what we call "complex isovist" points that have linear paths to two or more other integration points. The bivariate fit of complex isovist points by public goods is $r = 0.68, p = 0.011$ ($n = 13$).

SECTION 6

Using data summarized in Blanton (2011: table 2) I compared mean of the total score for collective action of societies that had a mostly symbolic emphasis in official artistic production with those societies that had more evidence of veristic portraits and depictions of the quotidian (though I was not able to discover the nature of artistic production in many cases). The results of the t-Test (2-tailed) indicated a difference between the means (with the symbolic emphasis much lower) significant at $p − 0.001$ level ($n −15$).

SECTION 7

To investigate whether Ming Dynasty landscape painters were comparatively more attentive to the quotidian, I coded 148 scenes for presence/absence of such themes from collections of landscape paintings available in two collections (Sickman and Soper 1960; Watson 2000). The coded images dated from the prior (and less collective) Sung and Yüan Dynasties (e.g., Elvin 1973: chap. 6), as one group, and the Ming Dynasty images (up to the mid-seventeenth century, the end of the coded focal period) as the other. From this coding I did find a statistically significant association of commoner and quotidian themes and Ming paintings (Chi-square 43.7, two degrees of freedom, $p = 0.001$).

SECTION 8

When I cross-tabulated "evidence for problematization of religion and power" by the dichotomized collective action total score, the result showed a strong association between problematization and higher levels of collective action (Fisher's Exact Test, 2-tail, $p = 0.0183$, $n = 28$; the coding scheme and citations are found in Blanton and Fargher 2013: 103–13).

SECTION 9

The purpose of Principal Components analysis (similar to "Factor Analysis"; see Comrey 1992) is to identify a structure of relationships among multiple variables. The analysis results in a series of mathematical constructs (principal components) that become, in essence, a new set of variables with which to correlate the variables (the coactive variables in this case). The analysis illustrates a central causal structure ("first principal component"), which is the coactive process, given that all of the coactive variables correlate ("load") positively with it (see the "loading matrix," Table B.7), and this component explains a large proportion (48.78 percent) of the pooled variance (the percent calculated from the "eigenvalue" of each principal component) (Table B.6).

TABLE B.6.

Principal Component Number	Eigenvalue	Percent
1	2.9270	48.78
2	1.20	20.12
3	0.90	14.97
4	0.50	8.65
5	0.29	4.80
6	0.16	2.70

TABLE B.7. Loading Matrix

	PC 1	PC 2	PC 3	PC 4	PC 5	PC 6
Public Goods	.8	.33	−.24	−.29	.27	−.18
Market Measure	.75	−.56	.05	.12	−.24	−.23
Intensification	.61	.04	−.73	.27	−.06	.15
Urbanization	.69	−.56	.32	.07	.29	.16
Living Standard	.81	.26	.23	−.36	−.27	.16
Pop Growth	.48	.63	.4	.46	.01	−.04

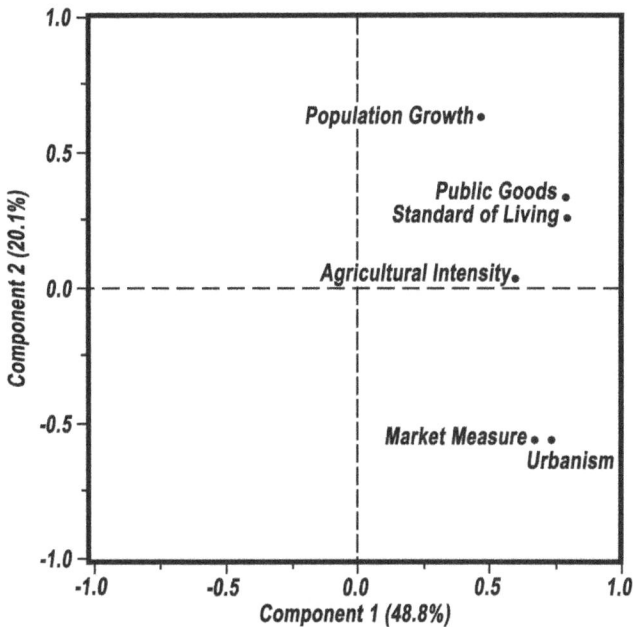

FIGURE B.2. Cross plot of the correlation values for the coactive variables with the second Principal Component (the Y axis) by the first Principal Component (the X axis) (which, combined, explain 69 percent of the pooled variance). This plot shows how all variables are positively correlated with the first Principal Component (i.e., they have values above 0 for the axis), yet, considering the second Principal Component, it is evident that population growth, public goods, standard of living, and agricultural intensification (positive with Principal Component 2), are processually distinct from the market measure and urbanism (negative with Principal Component 2).

SECTION 10

The nonparametric correlation of degree of commercialization by the collective action total measure produced a positive value that is strongly statistically significant (Kendall's tau = 0.37, $p = 0.0098$; commercialization by public goods, Kendall's tau = 0.3, $p = 0.04$).

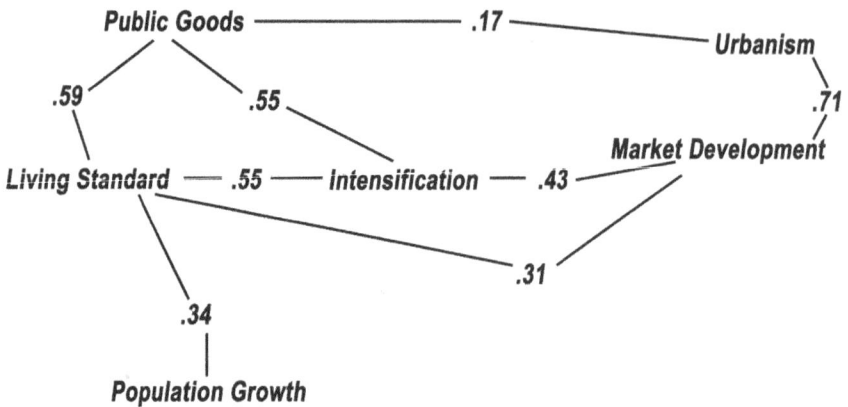

FIGURE B.3. Partial correlation values of the coactive variables. The partial correlation method aims to identify spurious correlations, for example, when variables A and B have a positive correlation, but when their correlation is due to the influence of a variable C rather than any real processual tie between A and B. Partial correlation is a mathematical procedure used to remove the effects of a C variable to discover the true correlation of A and B. The following model shows the highest positive partial correlation values of variables in the coactive process, with each variable partialed with respect to each other variable, and illustrates how coactive process based on collective action is related to but somewhat apart from a coactive process based on markets and urbanism.

SECTION 11

The material standard of living data were coded so as to distinguish between cases of little or no change (or even decline) and cases of notable increases evident during the focal period. Using public goods as a proxy for collective action, I find that the cases with evidence for increased living standards, the mean value of public goods is 19.8 ($n = 15$) while for the other societies it is 14.6 ($n = 13$). The means are statistically significantly different based on a 2-tailed t-Test ($p = 0.0002$).

SECTION 12

Total population size is correlated with collective action (using public goods as a proxy for collective action) ($r = 0.48, p = 0.0067$). This analysis is rendered questionable by very large outliers with populations in the tens or hundreds of millions, such as Ming China. When I removed these (including Mughal, Ming, Rome, Japan, Vijayanagara, Ottoman, and Inka) the correlation of population by public goods is still positive and significant though weaker ($r = 0.46, p = 0.027$). I repeated the analyses by partitioning the data into four quartiles of population size (including all cases) as a way to evaluate how population and collective action might be processually related at various scale ranges. Correlation values were again positive for all but the third quartile, where the slope of the regression line was flat (from lowest to highest quartile, Pearson rs are 0.47, 0.42, 0.04, 0.62). Territory size of the polity is also positively correlated with collective action (again using public goods as a proxy, $r = 0.54$, $p = 0.002$). Again, this result is potentially distorted by polities with territorially exceptionally large scales (Mughal, Ming, Rome, and Ottoman), but even without these cases, $r = 0.56$, $p = 0.003$.

The mean value of public goods for the polities with population growth during the focal period (18.5, $n = 15$) is statistically significantly higher than the value for polities lacking growth or where there is little evidence for growth (15.2, $n = 15$, $p = <$ 0.05, 2-tailed, based on a t-Test of differences of means), even though the range of public goods values in the two groups is similar (12.5–23.5, 10–24, respectively) (cf. Blanton and Fargher 2008: 275–80).

SECTION 13

I found that my sources described relatively more episodes of intra-focal-period social disruptions (i.e., social disruptions that authors found to be worth commenting on but that were not direct causes of systemic collapse) in the relatively less collective polities. The correlation of frequency of social disruption by collective action summary variable gives a value of Kendall's tau of 0.3035, $p = 0.0389$, $n = 30$ (the coding methods are described in Blanton 2010).

SECTION 14

Multiple causes for city growth are evident in the thirty-society sample, including commercialization, such as in London and Tokugawa Edo during their respective focal periods (although England of that period was not highly urbanized overall), but collective action likely played a causal role owing to a growth in the functional complexity of primary governing centers and in the lower-ranking centers that connected the central offices of the state to rural areas. This is evident when societies in the sample are coded as less urban (i.e., with proportionately smaller cites and more attenuated growth of secondary centers) and moderate-to-high urban. Using public goods as a proxy for collective action, while there is a difference between less and more urbanized cases (the mean for public goods for the less urban is 15.6, $n = 16$, and for the more urban is 18.3, $n = 14$), this is significant, based on a 2-tailed t-Test, but at only the 0.09 level. However, if we substitute the bureaucratization variable to get at the coordination aspect of collective action, the difference is more marked (for the more urban, the mean for bureaucratization is 10.9, while for the less urban the mean is 8.5). These means are significantly different using a 2-tailed t-Test ($p = 0.0073$).

SECTION 15

With Lane Fargher, I coded agricultural intensification comparatively based on the production strategies of the great majority of rural households. In our measure, a value of 1 signifies less labor-intensive cultivation methods (based on the prevalence of fallow cycles, weeding, double cropping, intercropping), biotechnology (e.g., fertilizing, new seed varieties), or land-oriented capital investment (e.g., drainage, irrigation, terracing of sloping ground, flood control). Our high value of 3 indicates the widespread use of such methods, whereas a score of 2 usually indicates that not all households practiced intensive methods (see Blanton and Fargher 2008: appendix 2 for additional information on agriculture; cf. Blanton and Fargher 2010). There is a strong positive relationship between public goods and the measure of production intensification, with a correlation value of Kendall's tau = 0.43, $p = 0.0026$.

SECTION 16

The Global Integrity Report assigns scores ranging from 0 (least evidence for governance integrity) to a high of 100 for each variable. To evaluate the validity of the Global Integrity measures, I correlated the GI summary score with a measure of governmentality for 2000/2001 from the World Bank and Stanford University (Kaufman et al. 2002), using their voice and accountability comparative measures (how government is selected, monitored, and replaced, and the degree to which citizens are allowed to participate in the selection of governing officials). The fit of the governance matters measure by the Global Integrity overall measure is $r = 0.57$, $p = 0.002$, showing a high level of consistency of the two sources.

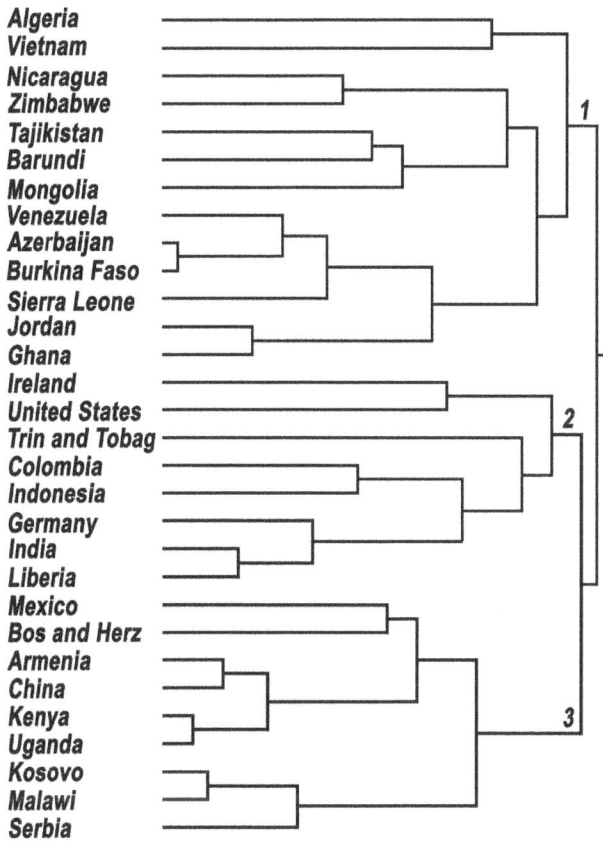

FIGURE B.4. Cluster dendrogram of polities included in the "Global Integrity Report" (https://www.globalintegrity.org).

TABLE B.8. A t-Test comparison of Global Integrity polities sorted by primarily external and internal revenue (the coding of major revenue sources made use of the CIA World Factbook (https://www.cia.gov/library/publications/the-world-factbook/) and the US Department of State Background Notes.

	External Revenues (mean)	*Internal Revenues (mean)*	*t-Test for difference of means (2-tailed)*
Global Integrity Summary Score	61.9 $(n = 13)$	72.1 $(n = 15)$	$p = 0.004$
Proxy for Bureaucratization	215.2 $(n = 13)$	285.5 $(n = 15)$	$p = 0.0006$
Proxy for Control over Principals	48.7 $(n = 13)$	60.9 $(n = 15)$	$p = 0.024$

References

Abbott, F. F. 1963. *A History and Description of Roman Political Institutions*. 3rd ed. New York: Biblo and Tannen.

Abler, Ronald, John S. Adams, and Peter Gould. 1971. *Spatial Organization: The Geographer's View of the World*. New York: Prentice-Hall.

Abu-Lughod, Janet L. 1989. *Before European Hegemony: The World-System in A. D. 1250–1350*. Oxford: Oxford University Press.

Abungu, George H. O., and Henry W. Mutoro. 1993. "Coast-Interior Settlements and Social Relations in the Kenya Coastal Hinterland." In *The Archaeology of Africa: Food, Metals, and Towns*, ed. T. Shaw, P. Sinclair, B. Andah, and A. Okpoco, 694–704. London: Routledge.

Acemoglu, Daron, Thierry Verdier, and James A. Robinson. 2004. "Kleptocracy and Divide-and-Rule: A Model of Personal Rule." *Journal of the European Economic Association* 2 (2–3): 162–92.

Acheson, James M., ed. 1994. *Anthropology and Institutional Economics. Society for Economic Anthropology. Monographs in Economic Anthropology 12*. Lanham, MD: University Press of America.

Adams, Reginald B., Jr., Nalini Ambady, Ken Nakayama, and Shinsuke Shimojo, eds. 2011. *The Science of Social Vision*. Oxford: Oxford University Press.

Adserà, Alicia, Carles Boix, and Mark Payne. 2003. "Are You Being Served? Political Accountability and Quality of Government." *Journal of Law Economics and Organization* 19:445–90.

DOI: 10.5876/9781607325147.c017

Agnew, Jean-Christophe. 1979. "The Threshold of Exchange: Speculations on the Market." *Radical History Review* 21:99–118.

Ahlquist, John S., and Margaret Levi. 2011. "Leadership: What It Means, What It Does, and What We Want to Know about It." *Annual Review of Political Science* 14:1–24.

Ahn, T. K., A. Marco Janssen, and Elinor Ostrom. 2004. "Signals, Symbols, and Human Cooperation." In *The Origins and Nature of Sociality*, edited by Robert W. Sussman and Audrey R. Chapman, 122–39. New York: Aldine de Gruyter.

Aiello, Leslie, ed. 2010. *Working Memory: Beyond Language and Symbolism*. Special edition 51, Current Anthropology.

Aiello, Leslie C., and R. I. M. Dunbar. 1993. "Neocortex Size, Group Size, and the Evolution of Language." *Current Anthropology* 34:184–93.

Aiello, Leslie C., and Peter Wheeler. 1995. "The Expensive Tissue Hypothesis: The Brain and the Digestive System in Human and Primate Evolution." *Current Anthropology* 36:199–221.

Alexander, J. 1990. "Labeur and Paresse: Ideological Representations of Medieval Peasant Labor." *Art Bulletin* 62:436–52.

Ali, M. Athar. 1985. *The Apparatus of Empire: Awards of Ranks, Offices, and Titles to the Mughal Nobility (1574–1658)*. Oxford: Oxford University Press.

Ali, M. Athar. 1995. "Towards an Interpretation of the Mughal Empire." In *The State in India, 1000–1700*, edited by H. Kulke, 263–77. Delhi: Oxford University Press.

Allen, James de Vere. 1993. *Swahili Origins: Swahili Culture and the Shungwaya Phenomenon*. Athens: Ohio University Press.

Allen, Robert C. 2001. "The Great Divergence in European Wages and Prices from the Middle Ages to the First World War." *Explorations in Economic History* 38:411–47.

Allen, Robert C. 2009. *The British Industrial Revolution in Global Perspective*. Cambridge: Cambridge University Press.

Almond, Gabriel A. 1991. "Capitalism and Democracy." *PS, Political Science & Politics* 24:467–74.

Anawalt, Patricia Rieff. 1990. "A Comparative Analysis of the Costumes and Accoutrements of the Codex Mendoza." In *Codex Mendoza, Volume 1: Interpretation of the Codex Mendoza*, edited by Frances F. Berdan and Patricia R. Anawalt, 103–50. Berkeley: University of California Press.

Anderson, B. L., and A.J.H. Latham, eds. 1986. *The Market in History*. London: Croom Helm.

Anderson, Perry. 1974. *Lineages of the Absolutist State*. London: NLB.

Archer, Margaret S., and Jonathan Q. Tritter, eds. 2000. *Rational Choice Theory: Resisting Colonization*. London: Routledge.

Ardant, Gabriel. 1975. "Financial Policy and Economic Infrastructure of Modern States and Nations." In *The Formation of National States in Western Europe*, edited by Charles Tilly, 164–242. Princeton: Princeton University Press.

Armstrong, Karen. 2006. *The Great Transformation: The Beginnings of Our Religious Traditions*. New York: Alfred A. Knopf.

Arnauld, M. Charlotte, Linda Manzanilla, and Michael E. Smith, eds. 2012. *The Neighborhood as a Social and Spatial Unit in Mesoamerican Cities*. Tucson: University of Arizona Press

Atran, Scott. 2002. *In Gods We Trust: The Evolutionary Landscape of Religion*. Oxford: Oxford University.

Attwood, Donald W. 1997. "The Invisible Peasant." In *Economic Analysis beyond the Local Level*, edited by Richard E. Blanton, Peter N. Peregrine, Deborah Winslow, and Thomas D. Hall, 147–69. Society for Economic Anthropology, Monographs in Economic Anthropology 13. Lanham, MD: University Press of the Americas.

Axelrod, Robert. 1984. *The Evolution of Cooperation*. London: Penguin Books.

Babb, Florence. 1989. *Between Field and Cooking Pot: The Political Economy of Marketwomen in Peru*. Austin: The University of Texas Press.

Babcock, Barbara A. 1978. "Introduction." In *The Reversible World: Symbolic Inversion in Art and Society*, edited by Barbara A. Babcock, 13–38. Ithaca: Cornell University Press.

Badawy, Alexander. 1967. "The Civic Sense of the Pharaoh and Urban Development in Ancient Egypt." *Journal of the American Research Center in Egypt* 6:103–9.

Bailey, Robert C. 1988. "The Significance of Hypergyny for Understanding Subsistence Behavior among Contemporary Hunter and Gatherers." In *Diet and Subsistence: Current Archaeological Perspectives*, edited by Brenda V. Kennedy and G. M. LeMoine, 57–65. Calgary: University of Calgary, Department of Anthropology.

Baker, Brenda J., and Takeyuki Tsuda. 2015. *Migration and Disruptions: Toward a Unifying Theory of Ancient and Contemporary Migrations*. Gainesville: University Press of Florida.

Baker, Timothy. 1970. *Medieval London*. New York: Praeger.

Bakhtin, Mikhail. 1984. *Rabelais and His World*. Trans. Hélèn Iswolsky. Bloomington: Indiana University Press.

Ballantyne, Andrew. 2002. "The Picturesque and Its Development." In *A Companion to Art History*, edited by Paul Smith and Carolyn Wilde, 116–24. Oxford: Blackwell.

Banfield, Edward C. 1958. *The Moral Basis of a Backward Society*. Glencoe, IL: Free Press.

Barkow, Jerome H., Leda Cosmides, and John Tooby, eds. 1992. *The Adapted Mind: Evolutionary Psychology and the Generation of Culture*. New York: Oxford University Press.

Baron-Cohen, Simon, and John Swettenham. 1996. "The Relationship between SAM and ToMM: Two Hypotheses." In *Theories of Theories of Mind*, edited by Peter Carruthers and Peter K. Smith, 158–68. Cambridge: Cambridge University Press.

Barth, Frederik. 2000. "Boundaries and Connections." In *Signifying Identities: Anthropological Perspectives on Boundaries and Contested Values*, edited by Andrew P. Cohen, 15–36. London: Routledge.

Bates, Robert H. 1983. *Essays on the Political Economy of Rural Africa*. Cambridge: Cambridge University Press.

Bates, Robert H. 1991. "The Economics of Transitions to Democracy." *PS, Political Science & Politics* 24:24–27.

Bates, Robert H. 1994. "Social Dilemmas and Rational Individuals: An Essay on the New Institutionalism." In *Anthropology and Institutional Economics*, edited by James M. Acheson, 43–66. Society for Economic Anthropology Monographs in Economic Anthropology 12. Lanham, MD: University Press of America.

Bates, Robert H., and Da-Hsiang Donald Lien. 1985. "A Note on Taxation, Development, and Representative Government." *Politics & Society* 14:53–70.

Bauer, Brian S. 2004. *Ancient Cuzco: Heartland of the Inca*. Austin: University of Texas Press.

Baumard, Nicolas. 2010. "Has Punishment Played a Role in the Evolution of Cooperation?" *Mind & Society* 9:171–92.

Beach, Milo Cleveland. 1987. *Early Mughal Painting*. Cambridge: Harvard University Press.

Beals, Ralph L. 1975. *The Peasant Marketing System of Oaxaca, Mexico*. Berkeley: University of California Press.

Beardwood, Alice. 1931. *Alien Merchants in England, 1350 to 1377: The Legal and Economic Position*. Cambridge: The Mediaeval Academy of America.

Becker, Gary S. 1976. *The Economic Approach to Human Behavior*. Chicago: University of Chicago Press.

Becker, Gary S. 1981. *A Treatise on the Family*. Cambridge: Harvard University Press.

Beekman, Christopher S. 2008. "Corporate Power Strategies in the Late Formative to Early Classic Tequila Valleys of Central Jalisco." *Latin American Antiquity* 19:414–34.

Begun, David R. 2010. "Miocene Hominids and the Origins of the African Apes." *Annual Review of Anthropology* 39:67–84.

Belsky, Richard. 2000. "Urban Ecology of Late Imperial Beijing Reconsidered: The Transformation of Social Space in China's Late Imperial Capital City." *Journal of Urban History* 27:54–74.

Benet, Francisco. 1957. "Explosive Markets: The Berber Highlands." In *Trade and Markets in the Early Empires: Economies in History and Theory*, edited by Karl Polanyi, Conrad M. Arensberg, and Harry W. Pearson, 188–217. New York: Free Press.

Ben-Porath, Yoram. 1980. "The F-Connection: Families, Friends, and Firms in the Organization of Exchange." *Population and Development Review* 6:1–30.

Berdan, Frances. 1986. "Enterprise and Empire in Aztec and Early Colonial Mexico." *Research in Economic Anthropology* Supplement 2:281–302.

Berent, Moshe. 2004. "Greece: The Stateless Polis (11th–4th Centuries BC)." In *The Early State, Its Alternatives and Analogues*, edited by Leonid E. Grinin, Robert L. Carneiro,

Dmitri M. Bondarenko, Nikolay N. Kradin, and Andrey V. Korotayev, 364–87. Volgo-grad: Uchitel.

Bernal-García, María Elena. 2007. "The Dance of Time, the Procession of Space at Mexico-Tenochtitlan's Desert Garden." In *Sacred Gardens and Landscapes: Ritual and Agency*, edited by Michel Conan, 69–112. Washington, DC: Dumbarton Oaks Research Library and Collection.

Bestor, Theodore C. 2004. *Tsukiji: The Fish Market at the Center of the World*. Berkeley: University of California Press.

Betzig, Laura. 2014. "Eusociality: From the First Foragers to the First States." *Human Nature (Hawthorne, N.Y.)* 25:1–5.

Bharati, Agehananda. 1985. "The Self in Hindu Thought and Action." In *Culture and the Self: Asian and Western Perspectives*, edited by Anthony J. Marsella, George DeVos, and Francis L. K. Hsu, 185–230. New York: Tavistock Publications.

Biddick, Kathleen. 1985. "Medieval English Peasants and Market Involvement." *Journal of Economic History* 45:823–31.

Bindman, David. 2008. "Ideas and Images of Britain c. 1570-c. 1870." In *The History of British Art, 1600–1870*, ed. David Bindman, 19–53. New Haven: Yale University Press.

Binford, Lewis R. 1989. "Isolating the Transition to Cultural Adaptation: An Organizational Approach." In *The Emergence of Modern Humans: Biocultural Adaptations in the Later Pleistocene*, edited by Eric Trinkaus, 18–41. Cambridge: Cambridge University Press.

Birch, Jennifer. 2012. "Coalescent Communities: Settlement Aggregation and Social Integration in Iroquoian Ontario." *American Antiquity* 77:646–71.

Birley, Anthony R. 2000. "Hadrian to the Antonines." In *The Cambridge Ancient History, Second Edition*, vol. 2: *The High Empire, A. D. 70 to 192*, edited by A. K. Bowman, P. Garnsey, and D. Rathbone, 132–94. Cambridge: Cambridge University Press.

Bjelajac, David. 2005. *American Art: A Cultural History*. New York: Harry N. Abrams.

Blake, Stephen P. 1991. *Shahjahanabad: The Sovereign City in Mughal India, 1639–1739*. New York: Cambridge University Press.

Blanton, Richard E. 1976. "Anthropological Studies of Cities." *Annual Review of Anthropology* 5:249–64.

Blanton, Richard E. 1983. "Factors Underlying the Origin and Evolution of Markets Systems." In *Economic Anthropology: Topics and Theories*, edited by Sutti Ortiz, 51–66. Society for Economic Anthropology, Monographs in Economic Anthropology 1. Lanham, MD: University Press of America.

Blanton, Richard E. 1985. "A Comparison of Early Market Systems." In *Markets and Marketing*, edited by Stuart Plattner, 399–416. Society for Economic Anthropology, Monographs in Economic Anthropology 4. Lanham, MD: University Press of America.

Blanton, Richard E. 1995. "The Cultural Foundations of Inequality in Households." In *Foundations of Social Inequality*, edited by T. Douglas Price and Gary M. Feinman, 105–27. New York: Plenum Press.

Blanton, Richard E. 1996. "The Basin of Mexico Market System and the Growth of Empire." In *Aztec Imperial Strategies*, by Frances F. Berdan, Richard E. Blanton, Elizabeth Hill Boone, Mary G. Hodge, Michael E. Smith, and Emily Umberger, 47–84. Washington, DC: Dumbarton Oaks Research Library and Collection.

Blanton, Richard E. 1998. "Beyond Centralization: Steps toward a Theory of Egalitarian Behavior in Archaic States." In *Archaic States*, edited by Gary M. Feinman and Joyce Marcus, 135–72. Santa Fe: School of American Research Press.

Blanton, Richard E. 2001. "Markets." In *The Oxford Encyclopedia of Mesoamerican Cultures*, vol. 2, edited by Davíd Carrasco, 168–71. Oxford: Oxford University Press.

Blanton, Richard E. 2004. "A Comparative Perspective on Settlement Pattern and Population Change in Mesoamerican and Mediterranean Civilizations." In *Side-By-Side Survey: Comparative Regional Studies in the Mediterranean World*, edited by Susan E. Alcock and John F. Cherry, 206–42. Oxford: Oxbow Books.

Blanton, Richard E. 2010. "Collective Action and Adaptive Socioecological Cycles in Premodern States." *Cross-Cultural Research* 44:41–59.

Blanton, Richard E. 2011. "Cultural Transformation, Art, and Collective Action in Polity-Building." *Cross-Cultural Research* 45:106–27.

Blanton, Richard E. 2013. "Cooperation and the Moral Economy of the Marketplace." In *Merchants, Markets, and Exchange in the Pre-Columbian World*, edited by Kenneth Hirth and Joanne Pillsbury, 23–48. Washington, DC: Dumbarton Oaks Research Library and Collection.

Blanton, Richard E. 2016. "The Varieties of Ritual Experience in Archaic States." In *Ritual and Archaic States*, edited by Joanne Murphy, 23–49 Gainesville: The University Press of Florida.

Blanton, Richard, and Lane Fargher. 2008. *Collective Action in the Formation of Pre-Modern States*. New York: Springer.

Blanton, Richard, and Lane Fargher. 2009. "Collective Action in the Evolution of Pre-Modern States." *Social Evolution & History* 8:133–66.

Blanton, Richard, and Lane Fargher. 2010. "Evaluating Causal Factors in Market Development in Premodern States: A Comparative Study, with Critical Comments on the History of Ideas about Markets." In *Archaeological Approaches to Market Exchange in Ancient Societies*, edited by Christopher P. Garraty and Barbara L. Stark, 207–26. Boulder: University of Colorado Press.

Blanton, Richard, and Lane Fargher. 2011. "The Collective Logic of Pre-Modern Cities." *World Archaeology* 43:505–22.

Blanton, Richard, and Lane Fargher. 2012. "Neighborhoods and the Civic Constitutions of Premodern Cities as Seen from the Perspective of Collective Action." In *The Neighborhood as a Social and Spatial Unit in Mesoamerican Cities*, edited by M. Charlotte Arnauld, Linda Manzanilla, and Michael E. Smith, 27–52. Tucson: University of Arizona Press.

Blanton, Richard, and Lane Fargher. 2013. "Reconsidering Darwinian Anthropology: With Suggestions for a Revised Agenda for Cooperation Research." In *Cooperation and Collective Action: Archaeological Perspectives*, edited by David M. Carballo, 93–127. Boulder: University Press of Colorado.

Blanton, Richard E., Lane F. Fargher, and Verenice Y. Heredia Espinoza. 2005. "The Mesoamerican World of Goods and Its Transformations." In *Settlement, Subsistence, and Social Complexity: Essays Honoring the Legacy of Jeffrey R. Parsons*, edited by Richard E. Blanton, 260–94. Los Angeles: Cotsen Institute of Archaeology and the University of California Press.

Blanton, Richard E., Gary M. Feinman, Stephen A. Kowalewski, and Peter N. Peregrine. 1996. "A Dual-Processual Theory for the Evolution of Mesoamerican Civilization." *Current Anthropology* 37:1–14, 65–68.

Blanton, Richard E., and Jody Taylor. 1995. "Patterns of Exchange and the Social Production of Pigs in Highland New Guinea: Their Relevance to Questions about the Origins and Evolution of Agriculture." *Journal of Archaeological Research* 3:113–45.

Bloch, Maurice. 1974. "Symbols, Song, Dance and Features of Articulation: Is Religion an Extreme Form of Traditional Authority?" *Archives Européennes de Sociologie* 15:55–81.

Bloch, Maurice. 2012. *Anthropology and the Cognitive Challenge*. Cambridge: Cambridge University Press.

Blue, Gregory. 1999. "China and Western Social Thought in the Modern Period." In *China and Historical Capitalism: Genealogies of Sinological Knowledge*, edited by Timothy Brook and Gregory Blue, 57–109. Cambridge: Cambridge University Press.

Blümner, H. 1966. *The Home Life of the Ancient Greeks*. New York: Cooper Square Publishers.

Bock, John, Suzanne Gaskins, and David F. Lancy. 2008. "A Four-Field Anthropology of Childhood." *Anthropology News* 49:4–5.

Boehm, Christopher. 2004. "Large-Scale Game Hunting and the Evolution of Human Sociality." In *The Origins and Nature of Sociality*, edited by Robert W. Sussman and Audrey R. Chapman, 270–87. New York: Aldine de Gruyter.

Bolnick, Deborah A. 2011. "Continuity and Change in Anthropological Perspectives on Migration: Insights from Molecular Anthropology." In *Rethinking Anthropological Perspectives on Migration*, ed. Graciela S. Caban and Jeffrey J. Clark, 263–77. Gainesville: The University Press of Florida.

Boone, Catherine. 2003. *Political Topographies of the African State*. Cambridge: Cambridge University Press.

Boone, Elizabeth Hill. 1991. "Migration Histories as Ritual Performance." In *Aztec Ceremonial Landscapes*, edited by David Carrasco, 121–51. Boulder: University Press of Colorado.

Booth, William James. 1993. *Households: On the Moral Architecture of the Economy*. Ithaca: Cornell University Press.

Boserup, Ester. 1970. *Woman's Role in Economic Development*. New York: St. Martin's Press.

Boudon, Raymond. 2003. "Beyond Rational Choice Theory." *Annual Review of Sociology* 29:1–21.

Bourdieu, Pierre. 1977. *Outline of a Theory of Practice*. Translated by Richard Nice. Cambridge: Cambridge University Press.

Bowles, Samuel, and Herbert Gintis. 2003. "Origins of Human Cooperation." In *Genetic and Cultural Evolution of Cooperation*, edited by Peter Hammerstein, 429–43. Cambridge: MIT Press.

Bowles, Samuel, and Herbert Gintis. 2011. *A Cooperative Species: Human Reciprocity and Its Evolution*. Princeton: Princeton University Press.

Boyd, Robert, Herbert Gintis, and Samuel Bowles. 2010. "Coordinated Punishment of Defectors Sustains Cooperation and Can Proliferate When Rare." *Science* 328:617–20.

Boyd, Robert, Herbert Gintis, Samuel Bowles, and Peter J. Richerson. 2005. "The Evolution of Altruistic Punishment." In *Moral Sentiments and Material Interests: The Foundations of Cooperation in Economic Life*, edited by Herbert Gintis, Samuel Bowles, Robert Boyd, and Ernst Fehr, 215–27. Cambridge: MIT Press.

Boyd, Robert, and Sarah Mathew. 2007. "A Narrow Road to Cooperation." *Science* 316:1858–59.

Boyd, Robert, and Peter J. Richerson. 1985. *Culture and the Evolutionary Process*. Chicago: University of Chicago.

Boyd, Robert, and Peter J. Richerson. 1990. "Culture and Cooperation." In *Beyond Self-Interest*, edited by Jane J. Mansbridge, 111–32. Chicago: University of Chicago Press.

Boyd, Robert, and Peter J. Richerson. 2005. *The Origin and Evolution of Cultures*. Oxford: Oxford University.

Boyd, Robert, and Peter J. Richerson. 2006. "Culture and the Evolution of Human Social Instincts." In *Roots of Human Sociality: Culture, Cognition, and Interaction*, edited by N. J. Enfield and Steven Levinson, 453–77. Oxford: Berg.

Boyd, Robert, Peter J. Richerson, and Joseph Henrich. 2005a. "Cultural Evolution of Human Cooperation." In *The Origin and Evolution of Cultures*, edited by Robert Boyd and Peter J. Richerson, 251–82. Oxford: Oxford University.

Boyd, Robert, Peter J. Richerson, and Joseph Henrich. 2005b. "Why People Punish Defectors: Weak Conformist Transmission Can Stabilize Costly Enforcement Norms in Cooperative Dilemmas." In *The Origin and Evolution of Cultures*, edited by Robert Boyd and Peter J. Richerson, 189–203. Oxford: Oxford University.

Boyd, Robert, Peter J. Richerson, and Joseph Soltis. 2005. "Can Group-Functional Behaviors Evolve by Cultural Group Selection?" In *The Origin and Evolution of Cultures*, edited by Robert Boyd and Peter J. Richerson, 204–26. Oxford: Oxford University.

Bozek, Katarzyna, Yuning Wei, Zheng Yan, Xiling Liu, Jieyi Xiong, Masahiro Sugimoto, Masura Tomita, Svante Pääbo, Raik Pieszek, Chet C. Sherwood, et al. 2014. "Exceptional Evolutionary Divergence of Human Muscle and Brain Metabolomes Parallels Human Cognition and Physical Uniqueness." *PLoS Biology* 12:1–14.

Brakel, L. F. 1975. "State and Statecraft in 17th Century Aceh." In *Pre-Colonial State Systems in Southeast Asia: The Malay Peninsula, Sumatra, Bali-Lombok, South Celebes*, edited by A. Reid and L. Castles, 45–55. Monograph 6. Kuala Lampur: Malaysian Branch of the Royal Asiatic Society.

Braudel, Fernand. 1979. *Civilization and Capitalism, 15th–18th Century*. 3 vols. New York: Harper and Row.

Bräutigam, Deborah, Odd-Helge Fjeldstad, and Mick Moore, eds. 2008. *Taxation and State-Building in Developing Countries: Capacity and Consent*. Cambridge: Cambridge University Press.

Bray, Francesca. 1984. *Agriculture*. Part 2 of Biology and Biological Technology. Science and Civilization, vol. 6, edited by J. Needham. Cambridge: Cambridge University Press.

Bray, Francesca. 1997. *Technology and Gender: Fabrics of Power in Late Imperial China*. Berkeley: University of California Press.

Breckenridge, James D. 1968. *Likeness: A Conceptual History of Ancient Portraiture*. Evanston: Northwestern University Press.

Bridbury, A. R. 1986. "Markets and Freedom in the Middle Ages." In *The Market in History*, edited by B. L. Anderson and A J H Latham, 79–120. London: Croom Helm.

Britnell, Richard. 2004. *Britain and Ireland 1050–1530: Economy and Society*. Oxford: Oxford University Press.

Broda, Johanna. 1991. "The Sacred Landscape of the Aztec Calendar Festivals: Myth, Nature, and Society." In *Aztec Ceremonial Landscapes*, edited by Davíd Carrasco, 74–120. Boulder: University Press of Colorado.

Brook, Timothy. 1998. *The Confusions of Pleasure: Commerce and Culture in Ming China*. Berkeley: University of California Press.

Brook, Timothy. 2005. *The Chinese State in Ming Society*. London: Routledge.

Brooke, Christopher Nugent Lawrence. 1961. *From Alfred to Henry III, 871–1272*, vol. 2: *A History of England*. Edinburgh: Thomas Nelson and Sons.

Brothers, Leslie. 1997. *Friday's Footprint: How Human Society Shapes the Human Mind*. New York: Oxford University.

Brown, Donald E. 1988. *Hierarchy, History, and Human Nature: The Social Origins of Human Nature*. Tucson: University of Arizona Press.

Brown, Donald E. 2008. "Portraiture and Social Stratification." In *World Art Studies: Exploring Concepts and Approaches*, edited by Kitty Zijlmans and Wilfred van Damme, 325–42. Amsterdam: Valiz.

Brown, Norman O. 1947. *Hermes the Thief: The Evolution of a Myth*. Madison: University of Wisconsin Press.

Brown, Patricia Fortini. 1988. *Venetian Painting in the Age of Carpaccio*. New Haven: Yale University Press.

Brown, Patricia Fortini. 1997. *Art and Life in Renaissance Venice*. New York: Harry N. Abrams.

Bryson, Norman. 1983. *Vision and Painting: The Logic of the Gaze*. New Haven: Yale University Press.

Buller, David J., and Valerie Gray Hardcastle. 2006. "Modularity." In *Adapting Minds: Evolutionary Psychology and the Persistent Quest for Human Nature*, ed. David J. Buller and Valerie Gray Hardcastle, 127–200. Cambridge: MIT Press.

Burger, Richard L. 2013. "In the Realm of the Incas: An Archaeological Reconsideration of Household Exchange, Long-Distance Trade, and Marketplaces in the Pre-Hispanic Central Andes." In *Merchants, Markets, and Exchange in the Pre-Columbian World*, edited by Kenneth G. Hirth and Joanne Pillsbury, 319–34. Washington, DC: Dumbarton Oaks Research Library and Collection.

Burke, Peter. 1987. *Historical Anthropology of Early Modern Italy: Essays on Perception and Communication*. Cambridge: Cambridge University Press.

Butzer, Karl W. 1996. "Irrigation, Raised Fields, and State Management: Wittfogel Redux?" *Antiquity* 70:200–204.

Buxton, R.G.A. 1992. "Imaginary Greek Mountains." *Journal of Hellenic Studies* 112:1–15.

Byrne, Richard W. 1995. *The Thinking Ape: Evolutionary Origins of Intelligence*. Oxford: Oxford University Press.

Byrne, Richard W. 1997. "The Technical Intelligence Hypothesis: An Additional Evolutionary Stimulus to Intelligence?" In *Machiavellian Intelligence II: Extensions and Evaluations*, edited by Andrew Whiten and Richard W. Byrne, 289–311. Cambridge: Cambridge University.

Byrne, Richard W., and Andrew Whiten. 1997. "Machiavellian Intelligence." In *Machiavellian Intelligence II: Extensions and Evaluations*, edited by Andrew Whiten and Richard W. Byrne, 1–24. Cambridge: Cambridge University.

Call, Josep, and Laurie R. Santos. 2012. "Understanding Other Minds." In *The Evolution of Primate Societies*, edited by John C. Mitani, Josep Call, Peter M. Kappeler, Ryne A. Palombit, and Joan B. Silk, 664–81. Chicago: University of Chicago Press.

Calnek, Edward. 1976. "The Internal Structure of Tenochtitlan." In *The Valley of Mexico: Studies of Pre-Hispanic Ecology and Society*, edited by E. R. Wolf, 287–302. Albuquerque: University of New Mexico Press.

Calnek, Edward. 1978. "The Internal Structure of Cities in America: Pre-Columbian Cities: The Case of Tenochtitlan." In *Urbanization in the Americas from its Beginnings to the Present*, ed. Richard Schaedel, Jorge Hardoy, and Nora Scott-Kinzer, 315–26. The Hague: Mouton.

Calnek, Edward. 2003. "Tenochtitlan-Tlatelolco: The Natural History of a City." In *El Urbanismo en Mesoamérica: Urbanism in Mesoamerica*, edited by William T. Sanders, Alba Guadalupe Mastache, and Robert H. Cobean, 149–202. Mexico City: Instituto Nacional de Antropología e Historia.

Cameron, Catherine. 2008. *Invisible Citizens: Captives and Their Consequences*. Salt Lake City: University of Utah Press.

Cameron, Catherine M. 2011. "Captives and Culture Change: Implications for Archaeology." *Current Anthropology* 52:169–209.

Cameron, Catherine M. 2013. "How People Moved among Ancient Societies: Broadening the View." *American Anthropologist* 115:218–31.

Camp, John M. 1986. *The Athenian Agora: Excavations in the Heart of Classic Athens*. London: Thames and Hudson.

Camp, John M. 2001. *The Archaeology of Athens*. New Haven: Yale University Press.

Cannell, Fanella. 2010. "The Anthropology of Secularism." *Annual Review of Anthropology* 39:85–100.

Carballo, David M., ed. 2013a. *Cooperation and Collective Action: Archaeological Perspectives*. Boulder: University Press of Colorado.

Carballo, David M. 2013b. "Labor Collectives and Group Cooperation in Pre-Hispanic Central Mexico." In *Cooperation and Collective Action: Archaeological Perspectives*, edited by David Carballo, 243–74. Boulder: University Press of Colorado.

Carcopino, Jérôme. 1968. *Daily Life in Ancient Rome: The People and the City at the Height of the Empire*. New Haven: Yale University Press.

Carlton, Eric. 1977. *Ideology and the Social Order*. London: Routledge.

Carrasco, David, ed. 1991. *Aztec Ceremonial Landscapes*. Boulder: University Press of Colorado.

Carrasco, Pizana P. 1959. *Land and Polity in Tibet*. Seattle: American Ethnological Society and University of Washington Press.

Carrithers, Michael, Steven Collins, and Steven Lukes, eds. 1985. *The Category of the Person: Anthropology, Philosophy, History*. Cambridge: Cambridge University Press.

Carruthers, Peter. 2006. *The Architecture of the Mind: Massive Modularity and the Flexibility of Thought*. Oxford: Clarendon Press.

Carruthers, Peter, and Peter K. Smith. 1996a. "Introduction." In *Theories of Theories of Mind*, edited by Peter Carruthers and Peter K. Smith, 1–8. Cambridge: Cambridge University Press.

Carruthers, Peter, and Peter K. Smith, eds. 1996b. *Theories of Theories of Mind*. Cambridge: Cambridge University Press.

Cartledge, Paul. 1985. "The Greek Religious Festivals." In *Greek Religion and Society*, edited by P. E. Easterling and J. V. Muir, 98–127. Cambridge: Cambridge University Press.

Cartledge, Paul. 1997. "'Deep Plays': Theatre as a Process in Greek Civic Life." In *The Cambridge Companion to Greek Tragedy*, edited by P. E. Easterling, 3–35. Cambridge: Cambridge University Press.

Cartwright, John. 2008. *Evolution and Human Behavior: Darwinian Perspectives on Human Nature*. Cambridge: MIT Press.

Cassady, Ralph. 1968. "Negotiated Price-Making in Mexican Traditional Markets: A Conceptual Analysis." *America Indigena* 28:51–80.

Castagnoli, Ferdinando. 1971. *Orthogonal Town Planning in Antiquity*. Cambridge: MIT Press.

Castells, Manuel. 1978. *City, Class, and Power*. New York: St. Martin's Press.

Castriota, David. 1998. "Democracy and Art in Late Sixth- and Fifth-Century B. C. Athens." In *Democracy 2500? Questions and Challenges*, edited by Ian Morris and Kurt A. Raaflaub, 197–216. Archaeological Institute of America, Colloquia and Conference Papers, 2. Dubuque: Kendall/Hunt Publishing Company.

Chagnon, Napoleon. 1983. *Yanomamo: The Fierce People*. 3rd ed. New York: Holt, Rinehart, and Winston.

Chagnon, Napoleon. 1988. "Life Histories, Blood Revenge, and Warfare in a Tribal Population." *Science* 239:985–92.

Chambers, David S., and Brian Pullan. 2001. *Venice: A Documentary History, 1450–1630*. Toronto: University of Toronto Press.

Chan, Albert. 1962. "Peking at the Time of the Wan-Li Emperor (1572–1619)." *International Association of Historians of Asia, Second Biennial Conference*, Taipei.

Chandra, Satish. 1982. "Standard of Living: Mughal India." In *The Cambridge Economic History of India, Volume I: c. 1200 – c. 1750*, edited by T. Raychaudhuri and Irfan Habib, 458–71. Cambridge: Cambridge University Press.

Chatterjee, Anjan. 2010. "Neuroaesthetics: A Coming of Age Story." *Journal of Cognitive Neuroscience* 23:53–62.

Chaudhuri, K. N. 1978. "Some Reflections on the Town and Country in Mughal India." *Modern Asian Studies* 12:77–96.

Chaudhuri, K. N. 1982. "European Trade with India." In *The Cambridge Economic History of India*, vol. 1.: *c. 1200-c. 1750*, edited by T. Raychaudhuri and I. Habib, 382–407. Cambridge: Cambridge University Press.

Chaudhuri, K. N. 1985. *Trade and Civilization in the Indian Ocean: An Economic History from the Rise of Islam to 1750*. Cambridge: Cambridge University Press.

Cheibub, José Antonio, and James R. Vreeland. 2012. "Economic Development, Democratization, and Democracy." Paper presented at the 3rd International Conference on Democracy as Idea and Practice. University of Oslo, January 12–13. http://www.uio.no /english/research/interfaculty-research-areas/democracy/news-and-events/events/con ferences/2012/papers-2012/Cheibub-Vreeland-Wshop7.pdf.

Chen, Li-Fu. 1972. *The Confucian Way: A New and Systematic Study of the "Four Books."* Republic of China. Commercial Press.

Chi, Ch'ao-ting. 1936. *Key Economic Areas of Chinese History as Revealed in the Development of Public Works for Water Control.* London: George Allen and Unwin.

Choi, Jung-Kyoo, and Samuel Bowles. 2007. "The Coevolution of Parochial Altruism and War." *Science* 318:636–40.

Chong, Dennis. 1991. *Collective Action and the Civil Rights Movement.* Chicago: University of Chicago Press.

Chong, Dennis. 2000. *Rational Lives: Norms and Values in Politics and Society.* Chicago: University of Chicago Press.

Christie, Jan Wisseman. 1992. "Water from the Ancestors: Irrigation in Early Java and Bali." In *The Gift of Water: Water Management, Cosmology, and the State in South East Asia,* edited by J. Rigg, 7–25. London: School of Oriental and African Studies, University of London.

Chwe, Michael Suk-Young. 2001. *Rational Ritual: Culture, Coordination, and Common Knowledge.* Princeton: Princeton University Press.

Chwe, Michael Suk-Young. 2013. *Jane Austen, Game Theorist.* Princeton: Princeton University Press.

Clark, Gracia. 1994. *Onions Are My Husband: Survival and Accumulation by West African Market Women.* Chicago: The University of Chicago Press.

Clark, Gregory. 2007. *A Farewell to Alms: A Brief Economic History of the World.* Princeton: Princeton University Press.

Clunas, Craig. 1996. *Fruitful Sites: Garden Culture in Ming Dynasty China.* Durham: Duke University Press.

Clunas, Craig. 1997. *Pictures and Visuality in Early Modern China.* Princeton: Princeton University Press.

Clunas, Craig. 2007. *Empire of Great Brightness: Visual and Material Cultures of Ming China, 1368–1644.* Honolulu: University of Hawai'i Press.

Coaldrake, William H. 1981. "Edo Architecture and Tokugawa Law." *Monumenta Nipponica* 36:235–84.

Cohen, Abner. 1969. *Custom and Politics in Urban Africa: A Study of Hausa Migrants in Yoruba Towns.* Berkeley: University of California Press.

Cohen, Edward E. 1992. *Athenian Economy and Society: A Banking Perspective.* Princeton: Princeton University Press.

Collins, Randall. 2004. *Interaction Ritual Chains*. Princeton: Princeton University Press.

Colson, Elizabeth. 1969. "African Society at the Time of the Scramble." In *Colonialism in Africa, 1870–1960*, vol. 1: *The History and Politics of Colonialism, 1870–1914*, edited by L. H. Gann and P. Daignan, 27–65. Cambridge: Cambridge University Press.

Comrey, Andrew L. 1992. *A First Course in Factor Analysis*. 2nd ed. Hillsdale, NJ: Lawrence Erlbaum.

Connor, Robert W. 1996. "Civil Society, Dionysiac Festival, and the Athenian Democracy." In *Demokratia: A Conversation on Democracies, Ancient and Modern*, edited by Josiah Ober and Charles W. Hedrick. Princeton: Princeton University Press.

Contarini, Gasparo. (Original work published 1544) 1599. *The Commonwealth and Government of Venice*. Translated by Lewes Lewkenor. Early English Books Online. http://quod.lib.umich.edu/e/eebogroup/.

Conway, Lucien Gideon, III, and Mark Schaller. 2002. "On the Verifiability of Evolutionary Psychology Theories: An Analysis of the Psychology of Scientific Persuasion." *Personality and Social Psychology Review* 6:152–66.

Cook, Karen S., Russell Hardin, and Margaret Levi. 2005. *Cooperation without Trust?* New York: Russell Sage Foundation.

Cook, Scott, and Martin Diskin, eds. 1976. *Markets in Oaxaca*. Austin: University of Texas Press.

Coomaraswamy, Ananda K. 1975. *Rajput Painting: Being and Account of the Hindu Paintings of Rajasthan and the Panjab Himalayas from the Sixteenth to the Nineteenth Centuries*. New York: Hacker Art Books.

Coon, Matthew S. 2009. "Variation in Ohio Hopewell Political Economies." *American Antiquity* 74:149–76.

Coppedge, Michael. 1999. "Thickening Thin Concepts and Theories: Combining Large N and Small in Comparative Politics." *Comparative Politics* 31:465–76.

Cowgill, George L. 1997. "State and Society at Teotihuacan, Mexico." *Annual Review of Anthropology* 26:129–61.

Cowgill, George L. 2004. "Origins and Development of Urbanism: Archaeological Perspectives." *Annual Review of Anthropology* 33:525–49.

Crary, Jonathan. 1990. *Techniques of the Observer: On Vision and Modernity in the Nineteenth Century*. Cambridge: MIT Press.

Creel, Herrlee. 1964. "The Beginnings of Bureaucracy in China: The Origin of the *Hsien*." *Journal of Asian Studies* 23:155–83.

Creel, Herrlee. 1970. *The Origins of Statecraft in China*, vol. 1: *The Western Chou Empire*. Chicago: University of Chicago Press.

Cronk, Lee, and Beth L. Leech. 2013. *Meeting at Grand Central: Understanding the Social and Evolutionary Roots of Cooperation*. Princeton: Princeton University Press.

Cunningham, Frank. 2002. *Theories of Democracy: A Critical Introduction*. London: Routledge.

Curtin, Philip. 1971. "Pre-Colonial Trading Networks and Traders: The Diakhanké." In *The Development of Indigenous Trade and Markets in West Africa*, edited by Claude Meillassoux and Daryll Forde, 228–39. Oxford: Oxford University Press.

Curtin, Philip. 1984. *Cross-Cultural Trade in World History*. Cambridge: Cambridge University Press.

Dahl, Robert A. 1989. *Democracy and Its Critics*. New Haven: Yale University Press.

Dahl, Robert A., and Bruce Stinebrickner. 2003. *Modern Political Analysis*. 6th ed. New Jersey: Prentice-Hall, Upper Saddle River.

Dahlin, Bruce H., Christopher T. Jensen, Richard E. Terry, David R. Wright, and Timothy Beach. 2007. "In Search of an Ancient Maya Market." *Latin American Antiquity* 18:363–84.

D'Altroy, Terence N. 2002. *The Incas*. Malden, MA: Blackwell Publishers.

D'Altroy, Terence N., and Timothy K. Earle. 1992. "Staple Finance, Wealth Finance, and Storage in the Inka Political Economy." In *Inka Storage Systems*, edited by T. Y. LeVine, 31–61. Norman: University of Oklahoma Press.

D'Andrade, Roy. 1992. "Cognitive Anthropology." In *New Directions in Psychological Anthropology*, edited by Theodore Schwartz, Geoffrey M. White, and Catherine A. Lutz, 47–58. Cambridge: Cambridge University Press.

D'Andrade, Roy. 1995. "Moral Models in Anthropology." *Current Anthropology* 36:399–408.

D'Andrade, Roy. 2000. "The Sad Story of Anthropology 1950–1999." *Cross-Cultural Research* 34:219–32.

Danziger, Eve. 2006. "The Thought That Counts: Interactional Consequences of Variation in Cultural Theories of Meaning." In *Roots of Human Sociality: Culture, Cognition and Interaction*, edited by N. J. Enfield and Stephen C. Levinson, 259–78. Oxford: Berg.

Darwin, Charles. 1874. *The Descent of Man and Selection in Relation to Sex*. 2nd ed. New York: Burt.

Davidson, Richard J., and Sharon Begley. 2012. *The Emotional Life of Your Brain*. New York: A Plume Book.

Davis, James. 2012. *Medieval Market Morality: Life, Law, and Ethics in the English Marketplace, 1200–1500*. Cambridge: Cambridge University Press.

Davis, William G. 1973. *Social Relations in a Philippine Market: Self-Interest and Subjectivity*. Berkeley: University of California Press.

Deacon, Terrence W. 1997. *The Symbolic Species: The Co-Evolution of Language and the Brain*. New York: W. W. Norton & Company.

Degler, Carl. 1991. *In Search of Human Nature: The Decline and Revival of Darwinism in American Social Thought*. Oxford: Oxford University Press.

de Ligt, L. 1993. *Fairs and Markets in the Roman Empire: Economic and Social Aspects of Periodic Trade in a Pre-Industrial Society*. Amsterdam: J. C. Gieben.

de Maria, Blake. 2010. *Becoming Venetian: Immigrants and Arts in Early Modern Venice*. New Haven: Yale University Press.

Deng, Kent G. 2012. "The Continuation and Efficiency of the Chinese Fiscal State, 700 BC–AD 1911." In *The Rise of Fiscal States: A Global History 1500–1914*, edited by Bartolomé Yun-Casalilla and Patrick K. O'Brien, 335–52. Cambridge: Cambridge University Press.

Dewey, Alice G. 1962. *Peasant Marketing in Java*. New York: Free Press of Glencoe.

Dexter, Thomas F. G. 1930. *The Pagan Origin of Fairs*. Perranporth, Cornwall: New Knowledge Press.

Díaz del Castillo, Bernal. (Original work published 1560) 1963. *The Conquest of New Spain*. Baltimore: Penguin.

de Zorita, Alonso. 1994. *Life and Labor in Ancient Mexico: The Brief and Summary Relation of the Lords of New Spain*. Norman: University of Oklahoma Press.

Dilley, Roy, ed. 1992. *Contesting Markets: Analyses of Ideology, Discourse, and Practice*. Baltimore: Edinburgh University Press.

Dimen-Schein, Muriel. 1977. *The Anthropological Imagination*. New York: McGraw-Hill.

Dimmock, Spencer. 2007. "English Towns and the Transition, c. 1450–1550." In *Rodney Hilton's Middle Ages: An Exploration of Historical Themes*, edited by Christopher Dyer, Peter Coss, and Chris Wickham, 270–85. Oxford: Oxford University Press.

Dirks, Nicholas B. 1987. *The Hollow Crown: Ethnohistory of an Indian Kingdom*. Cambridge: Cambridge University Press.

Divale, William T., and Marvin Harris. 1976. "Population, Warfare, and the Male Supremacist Complex." *American Anthropologist* 78:521–38.

Dodds, E. R. 1951. *The Greeks and the Irrational*. Berkeley: University of California Press.

Donham, Donald L. 1981. "Beyond the Domestic Mode of Production." *Man, New Series* 16:515–40.

Douglas, Mary. 1966. *Purity and Danger: An Analysis of Concepts of Pollution and Taboo*. New York: Praeger.

Douglas, Mary. 1986. *How Institutions Think*. Syracuse: Syracuse University Press.

Douglas, Mary. 1992. *Risk and Blame: Essays in Cultural Theory*. London: Routledge.

Douglas, Mary, and Aaron Wildavsky. 1982. *Risk and Culture: An Essay on the Selection of Technical and Environmental Dangers*. Berkeley: University of California Press.

Dover, K. J. 1974. *Greek Popular Morality in the Time of Plato and Aristotle*. Berkeley: University of California Press.

Dray-Novey, Alison. 1993. "Spatial Order and Police in Imperial Beijing." *Journal of Asian Studies* 52:885–922.

Driver, Harold E. 1969. *Indians of North America*. 2nd ed. Chicago: University of Chicago Press.

Dueppen, Stephen A. 2012. *Approaches to Anthropological Archaeology: Egalitarian Revolution in the Savanna: The Origins of a West African Political System*. Sheffield: Equinox Publishing Ltd.

Dumont, Louis. 1977. *From Mandeville to Marx: The Genesis and Triumph of Economic Ideology*. Chicago: University of Chicago Press.

Dumont, Louis. 1985. "A Modified View of Our Origins: The Christian Beginnings of Modern Individualism." In *The Category of the Person: Anthropology, Philosophy, History*, edited by Michael Carrithers, Steven Collins, and Steven Lukes, 93–122. Cambridge: Cambridge University Press.

Dunbar, Robin, I. M. 2003. "The Social Brain: Mind, Language, and Society in Evolutionary Perspective." *Annual Review of Anthropology* 32:163–81.

Dunbar, Robin I. M. 2007. "The Social Brain Hypothesis and Its Relevance to Social Psychology." In *Evolution and the Social Mind: Evolutionary Psychology and Social Cognition*, edited by Joseph P. Forgas, Marie G. Haselton, and William von Hippel, 21–32. New York: Psychology Press.

Dunbar, Robin I. M., and S. Schultz. 2007. "Evolution in the Social Brain." *Science* 317:1344–47.

Dunn, John. 1988. "Trust and Political Agency." In *Trust: Making and Breaking Cooperative Relations*, edited by Diego Gambetta, 73–93. Oxford: Basil Blackwell.

Dunning, Thad. 2008. *Crude Democracy: Natural Resource Wealth and Political Regimes*. Cambridge: Cambridge University Press.

Durán, Diego. 1994. *The History of the Indies of New Spain*. Translated by Doris Heyden. Norman: University of Oklahoma Press.

Durkheim, Emile. (Original work published 1915) 1965. *The Elementary Forms of the Religious Life*. Translated by J. W. Swain. New York: Free Press.

Duyvendak, J. J. L. 1928. *The Book of Lord Shang: A Classic of the Chinese School of Law*. Chicago: University of Chicago Press.

Dyer, Christopher. 1989. *Standards of Living in the Later Middle Ages: Social Change in England c. 1200–1520*. Cambridge: Cambridge University Press.

Dyer, Christopher. 2000. *Everyday Life in Medieval England*. London: Hambledon and London.

Dyer, Christopher. 2002. *Making a Living in the Middle Ages: The People of Britain 850–1520*. New Haven: Yale University Press.

Dyer, Christopher. 2007. "The Ineffectiveness of Lordship in England, 1200–1400." In *Rodney Hilton's Middle Ages: An Exploration of Historical Themes*, edited by Christopher Dyer, Peter Coss, and Chris Wickham, 69–100. Oxford: Oxford University Press.

Dyer, John. (Original work published 1761) 1969. *Poems, Book III: Fleece*. Westmead, Farnborough, England: Gregg International Publishers.

Eakin, Emily. 2014. "Capital Man: Thomas Piketty Is Economics' Biggest Sensation. He Is Also the Field's Fiercest Critic." *Chronicle of Higher Education Review*, May 16, 2014, B6–B10.

Earle, Timothy. 2002. *Bronze Age Economics: The Beginnings of Political Economies*. Boulder, CO: Westview Press.

Eder, Herbert M. 1976. "Markets as Mirrors: Reflectors of the Economic Activity and the Regional Culture of Coastal Oaxaca." In *Markets in Oaxaca*, edited by Scott Cook and Martin Diskin, 67–80. Austin: University of Texas Press.

Edgerton, William F. 1947. "The Government and the Governed in the Egyptian Empire." *Journal of Near Eastern Studies* 6:152–60.

Ehrenberg, Victor. 1951. *The People of Aristophanes: A Sociology of Old Attic Comedy*. Cambridge, MA: Harvard University Press.

Ehrenreich, Robert M., Carol L. Crumley, and Janet E. Levy, eds. 1995. *Heterarchy and the Analysis of Complex Societies. Archaeological Papers of the American Anthropological Association 6*. Washington, DC: American Anthropological Association.

Eisenstadt, S. N., ed. 1986. *The Origins and Diversity of the Axial Age Civilizations*. Albany: State University of New York Press.

Eisenstadt, S. N., ed. 1996. *Japanese Civilization: A Comparative View*. Chicago: University of Chicago Press.

Elman, Benjamin A. 1991. "Political, Social, and Cultural Reproduction via Civil Service Examinations in Late Imperial China." *Journal of Asian Studies* 50:7–28.

Elster, Jon. 1989. *The Cement of Society: A Study of Social Order*. Cambridge: Cambridge University Press.

Elster, Jon. 2000. "Review: Rational Choice History: A Case of Excessive Ambition." *American Political Science Review* 94:685–95.

Elvin, Mark. 1972. "The High-Level Equilibrium Trap: The Causes of the Decline of Invention in the Traditional Chinese Textile Industries." In *Economic Organization in Chinese Society*, edited by W. E. Willmott, 136–72. Stanford: Stanford University Press.

Elvin, Mark. 1973. *The Pattern of the Chinese Past*. Stanford: Stanford University Press.

Elvin, Mark. 1985. "Between the Earth and Heaven: Conceptions of the Self in China." In *The Category of the Person: Anthropology, Philosophy, History*, edited by Michael Carrithers, Steven Collins, and Steven Lukes, 157–89. Cambridge: Cambridge University Press.

Ember, Carol R., and Melvin Ember. 2001. *Cross-Cultural Research Methods*. Lanham, MD: AltaMira Press.

Ember, Carol R., Marc Howard Ross, Michael L. Burton, and Candice Bradley. 1991. "Problems of Measurement in Cross-Cultural Research Using Secondary Data." *Behavior Science Research* 25:187–216.

Ember, Melvin. 1963. "The Relationship between Economic and Political Development in Non-Industrialized Societies." *Ethnology* 2:228–48.

Ember, Melvin, and Carol R. Ember. 1979. "Male-Female Bonding: A Cross-Species Study of Mammals and Birds." *Behavior Science Research* 14:37–56.

Ember, Melvin, Carol Ember, and Bruce Russett. 1992. "Peace between Participatory Polities: A Cross-Cultural Test of the 'Democracies Rarely Fight Each Other' Hypothesis." *World Politics* 44:573–99.

Emerson, Richard M. 1962. "Power-Dependence Relations." *American Sociological Review* 27:31–41.

Emery, Nathan. 2000. "The Eyes Have It: The Neuroethology, Function, and Evolution of Social Gaze." *Neuroscience and Biobehavioral Reviews* 24:581–604.

Emery, Nathan J., and Nicola S. Clayton. 2004. "The Mentality of Crows: Convergent Evolution of Intelligence in Corvids and Apes." *Science* 306:1903–7.

Emirbayer, Mustafa. 1997. "Manifesto for a Relational Sociology." *American Journal of Sociology* 103:281–317.

Enfield, N. J., and C. Stephen Levinson, eds. 2006. *Roots of Human Sociality: Culture, Cognition, and Interaction*. Oxford: Berg.

Engels, Frederick. 1972. *The Origin of the Family, Private Property, and the State*. New York: International Publishers.

Englehardt, Joshua D., and Donna M. Nagle. 2011. "Variations on a Theme: Dual-Processual Theory and the Foreign Impact on Mycenaean and Classic Maya Architecture." *American Journal of Archaeology* 115:355–82.

Ensminger, Jean. 1992. *Making a Market: The Institutional Transformation of an African Society*. Cambridge: Cambridge University Press.

Ensminger, Jean. 1997. "Transaction Costs and Islam: Explaining Conversion in Africa." *Journal of Institutional and Theoretical Economics* 153:4–29.

Erasmus, J. Charles. 1977. *In Search of the Common Good: Utopian Experiments Past and Present*. New York: Free Press.

Eriksson, Lina. 2011. *Rational Choice Theory: Potential and Limits*. New York: Palgrave Macmillan.

Ermer, Elsa, Scott A. Guerin, Leda Cosmides, John Tooby, and Michael B. Miller. 2007. "Theory of Mind Broad and Narrow: Reasoning about Social Exchange Engages ToM Areas, Precautionary Reasoning Does Not." In *Theory of Mind: A Special Issue of Social Neuroscience*, edited by Rebecca Saxe and Simon Baron-Cohen, 196–219. New York: Psychology Press.

Ertman, Thomas. 1997. *Birth of the Leviathan: Building States and Regimes in Medieval and Early Modern Europe*. Cambridge: Cambridge University Press.

Evensky, Jerry. 2005. *Adam Smith's Moral Philosophy: A Historical and Contemporary Perspective on Markets, Law, Ethics, and Culture*. New York: Cambridge University Press.

Everitt, Alan. 1967. "The Marketing of Agricultural Produce." In *The Agrarian History of England and Wales*, vol. 4: *1500–1640*, edited by Joan Thirsk, 466–592. Cambridge: Cambridge University Press.

Fafchamps, Marcel. 2004. *Market Institutions in Sub-Saharan Africa: Theory and Evidence*. Cambridge: MIT Press.

Fargher, Lane F. 2009. "A Comparison of the Spatial Distribution of Agriculture and Craft Specialization in Five State-Level Societies." *Journal of Anthropological Research* 65:353–87.

Fargher, Lane F., and Richard E. Blanton. 2007. "Revenue, Voice, and Public Goods in Three Pre-Modern States." *Comparative Studies in Society and History* 49:848–82.

Fargher, Lane F., and Richard E. Blanton. 2012. "Segmentacíon y accíon colectiva: Un acercamiento cultural-comparativo sobre la voz y el poder compartido en los estados premodernos." In *El poder compartido: Ensayos sobre la arqueología de organizaciones políticas segmentarias y oligárquicas*, edited by Annick Daneels and Gerardo Gutiérrez Mendoza, 205–36. Tlalpan, Mexico: Centro de Investigaciones y Estudios Superiores en Antropología Social and El Colegio de Michoacán.

Fargher, Lane F., Richard E. Blanton, and Verenice Y. Heredia Espinoza. 2010. "Egalitarian Ideology and Political Power in Prehispanic Central Mexico: The Case of Tlaxcallan." *Latin American Antiquity* 21:227–51.

Fargher, Lane, Richard E. Blanton, Verenice Y. Heredia Espinoza, John Millhauser, Nezahualcoyotl Xiuhtecutli, and Lisa Overholtzer. 2011. "Tlaxcallan: The Archaeology of an Ancient Republic in the New World." *Antiquity* 85:172–86.

Fargher, Lane, and Verenice Y. Heredia Espinoza. 2012. "Ripping Up the Stilts: Problematizing Romantic, Ethnocentric Legacies in Mesoamerican Archaeology." Paper presented at the 77th Annual Meeting of the Society for American Archaeology.

Fargher, Lane F., and Verenice Y. Heredia Espinoza, eds. 2016. *Alternative Pathways to Complexity: Households, Markets, World Systems, and Political Economy*. Boulder: University Press of Colorado.

Farmer, Edward L. 1976. *Early Ming Government: The Evolution of Dual Capitals*. Cambridge, MA: Harvard University Press.

Farmer, Mary K. 1992. "On the Need to Make a Better Job of Justifying Rational Choice Theory." *Rationality and Society* 4:411–20.

Farooque, Abul K. M. 1977. *Roads and Communications in Mughal India*. Delhi: Idarah-i-Adabiyat-I Delli.

Faroqhi, Suraiya. 1994. "Social Life in Cities." In *An Economic and Social History of the Ottoman Empire, 1300- 1914*, edited by H. Inalçik and D. Quataert, 576–608. New York: Cambridge University Press.

Faroqhi, Suraiya. 2000. *Subjects of the Sultan: Culture and Daily Life in the Ottoman Empire*. New York: I.B. Tauris.

Favro, Diane. 1992. "'Pater Urbis': Augustus as City Father of Rome." *Journal of the Society of Architectural Historians* 51:61–84.

Favro, Diane. 1993. "Reading the Augustan City." In *Narrative and Event in Ancient Art*, edited by Peter J. Holliday, 230–57. Cambridge: Cambridge University Press.

Fei, Si-yen. 2009. *Negotiating Urban Space: Urbanization and Late Ming Nanjing*. Cambridge, MA: Harvard University Press.

Feil, D. K. 1987. *The Evolution of Highland Papua New Guinea Societies*. Cambridge: Cambridge University.

Feinberg, Matthew, Robb Willer, Olga Antobenko, and Oliver D. John. 2012. "Liberating Reason from Passions: Overriding Intuitionist Moral Judgements through Emotional Reappraisal." *Psychological Science* 23:788–95.

Feinberg, Richard. 2009. "Bridging Science and Humanism." *Anthropology News* 50:4, 8.

Feinman, Gary M. 1995. "The Emergence of Inequality: A Focus on Strategies and Process." In *Foundations of Social Inequality*, edited by T. Douglas Price and Gary M. Feinman, 255–80. New York: Plenum Press.

Feinman, Gary M. 1998. "Scale and Social Organization: Perspectives on the Archaic State." In *Archaic States*, edited by Gary M. Feinman and Joyce Marcus, 95–134. Santa Fe: School of American Research Press.

Feinman, Gary M. 2000. "Dual-Processual Theory and Social Formations in the Southwest." In *Alternative Leadership Strategies in the Prehispanic Southwest*, edited by Barbara J. Mills, 207–29. Tucson: University of Arizona Press.

Feinman, Gary M. 2001. "Mesoamerican Political Complexity: The Corporate-Network Dimension." In *From Leaders to Rulers*, edited by Jonathan Haas, 151–75. New York: Kluwer Academic/Plenum.

Feinman, Gary M. 2011. "Size, Complexity, and Organizational Variation: A Comparative Approach." *Cross-Cultural Research* 45:37–58.

Feinman, Gary M., and Christopher P. Garraty. 2010. "Preindustrial Markets and Marketing: Archaeological Perspectives." *Annual Review of Anthropology* 39:167–91.

Feinman, Gary M., and Linda M. Nicholas. 2012. "The Late Prehispanic Economy of the Valley of Oaxaca, Mexico: Weaving Threads from Data, Theory, and Subsequent History." *Research in Economic Anthropology* 32:225–58.

Finley, M. I. 1962. *The World of Odysseus. Hammondsworth*. Penguin Books.

Finley, M. I. 1973. *The Ancient Economy*. Berkeley: University of California Press.

Finley, M. I. 1974. "Aristotle and Economic Analysis." In *Studies in Ancient Society*, edited by M. I. Finley, 26–51. London: Routledge and Kegan Paul.

Fix, Alan. 2002. "Foragers, Farmers, and Traders in the Malayan Peninsula: Origins of Cultural and Biological Diversity." In *Forager-Traders in South and Southeast Asia: Long-Term Histories*, edited by Kathleen D. Morrison and Laura L. Junker, 185–202. Cambridge: Cambridge University Press.

Fleming, Daniel E. 2004. *Democracy's Ancient Ancestors: Mari and Early Collective Governance*. Cambridge: Cambridge University Press.

Fletcher, Roland. 1995. *The Limits of Settlement Growth*. Cambridge: Cambridge University Press.

Fogg, Walter. 1932. "The Suq: A Study of the Human Geography of Morocco." *Geography (Sheffield, England)* 17:257–67.

Fogg, Walter. 1936. "The Economic Revolution in the Countryside of French Morocco." *Journal of the Royal African Society* 35:123–29.

Fogg, Walter. 1942. "The Organization of a Moroccan Tribal Market." *American Anthropologist* 44:47–61.

Forman, Shepard, and Joyce Riegelhaupt. 1970. "Market Place and Marketing System: Toward a Theory of Peasant Economic Integration." *Comparative Studies in Society and History* 12:188–212.

Fox, Richard. 1977. *Urban Anthropology: Cities in Their Cultural Settings*. Englewood Cliffs, NJ: Prentice-Hall.

Frank, Andre Gunder. 1998. *ReOrient: Global Economy in the Asian Age*. Berkeley: University of California Press.

Frank, Robert H. 1988. *Passions within Reason: The Strategic Role of the Emotions*. New York: W. W. Norton.

Fraser, Douglas, and Herbert M. Cole, eds. 1972. *African Art and Leadership*. Madison: University of Wisconsin Press.

Freedberg, David. 1989. *The Power of Images: Studies in the History and Theory of Response*. Chicago: University of Chicago Press.

Freedberg, David, and Vittorio Gallese. 2007. "Motion, Emotion, and Empathy in Esthetic Experience." *Trends in Cognitive Sciences* 11:197–203.

Freedman, Paul. 1999. *Images of the Medieval Peasant*. Stanford: Stanford University Press.

Fried, Morton H. 1967. *The Evolution of Political Society*. New York: Random House.

Friedland, Roger, and A. F. Robertson. 1990. "Beyond the Marketplace." In *Beyond the Marketplace: Rethinking Economy and Society*, edited by Roger Friedland and A. F. Robertson, 3–52. New York: Aldine de Gruyter.

Frier, B. W. 1999. "Roman Demography." In *Life, Death, and Entertainment in the Roman Empire*, edited by D. S. Potter and D. J. Mattingly, 85–112. Ann Arbor: University of Michigan Press.

Fukuyama, Francis. 1995. *Trust: The Social Virtues and the Creation of Prosperity*. New York: Simon and Schuster.

Fukuyama, Francis. 2011. *The Origins of Political Order: From Prehuman Times to the French Revolution*. New York: Farrar, Straus, and Giroux.

Fuma, Susamu. 1993. "Late Ming Urban Reform and the Popular Uprising in Hangzhou." In *Cities of Jiangnan in Late Imperial China*, edited by Linda Cooke Johnson, translated by Michael Lewis, 47–79. Albany: State University of New York Press.

Galinier, Jacques, Aurore Monod Mecquelin, Guy Bordin, Laurent Fontane, Francine Fourmaux, Juliet Roullet Ponce, Piero Salzurolo, Philippe Simonnot, Michèle Therrien, and Iole Zilli. 2010. "Anthropology of the Night: Cross-Disciplinary Investigations." *Current Anthropology* 51:819–47.

Gallese, Vittorio, and Alvin Goldman. 1998. "Mirror Neurons and the Simulation Theory of Mind-Reading." *Trends in Cognitive Sciences* 2:493–551.

Gallese, Vittorio, and Corrado Sinigaglia. 2011. "What Is So Special about Embodied Simulation?" *Trends in Cognitive Sciences* 15:512–19.

Galsterer, Harmut. 2000. "Local and Provincial Institutions and Government." In *The Cambridge Ancient History, Second Edition*, vol. 11: *The High Empire, A.D. 70–192*, edited by A. K. Bowman, P. Garnsey, and D. Rathbone, 344–60. Cambridge: Cambridge University Press.

Garraty, Christopher, and Barbara Stark, eds. 2010. *Archaeological Approaches to Market Exchange in Ancient Societies*. Boulder: University Press of Colorado.

Gates, Charles. 2003. *Ancient Cities: The Archaeology of Urban Life in the Ancient Near East and Egypt, Greece and Rome*. New York: Routledge.

Gay, Peter. 1954. "The Enlightenment in the History of Political Theory." *Political Science Quarterly* 69:374–89.

Geertz, Clifford. 1973. *The Interpretation of Cultures*. New York: Basic Books.

Geertz, Clifford. 1978. "The Bazaar Economy: Information and Search in Peasant Marketing." *Supplement to the American Economic Review* 68:28–32.

Geertz, Clifford. 1979. "Suq: The Bazaar Economy in Sefrou." In *Meaning and Order in Moroccan Society: Three Essays in Cultural Analysis*, by Clifford Geertz, Hildred Geertz, and Lawrence Rosen, 123–313. Cambridge: Cambridge University Press.

Geertz, Clifford. 1980. *Negara: The Theatre State in Nineteenth-Century Bali*. Princeton: Princeton University Press.

Geertz, Clifford. 1983a. "Centers, Kings, and Charisma: Reflections on the Symbolics of Power." In *Local Knowledge: Further Essays in Interpretive Anthropology*, edited by Clifford Geertz, 121–46. New York: Basic Books.

Geertz, Clifford. 1983b. "'From the Native's Point of View': On the Nature of Anthropological Understanding." In *Local Knowledge: Further Essays in Interpretive Anthropology*, edited by Clifford Geertz, 55–70. New York: Basic Books.

Gell, Alfred. 1998. *Art and Agency: An Anthropological Theory*. Clarendon: Oxford University Press.

Gellner, Ernest. 1972. "Political and Religious Organization of the Berbers of the Central High Atlas." In *Arabs and Berbers: From Tribe to Nation in North Africa*, edited by Ernest Gellner and Charles Micaud, 59–66. Lexington, MA: Lexington Books.

Gerring, John. 2012. *Social Science Methodology: A Unified Framework*. 2nd ed. Cambridge: Cambridge University Press.

Gibson, Kathleen. 2005. "Epigenesis, Brain Plasticity, and Behavioral Versatility: Alternatives to Standard Evolutionary Psychology Models." In *Complexities: Beyond Nature and Nurture*, edited by Susan McKinnon and Sydel Silverman, 23–42. Chicago: University of Chicago.

Gillespie, Susan D. 1989. *The Aztec Kings: The Construction of Rulership in Mexica History*. Tucson: University of Arizona Press.

Gintis, Herbert. 2012. "Role of Cognitive Processes in Unifying the Behavioral Sciences." In *Grounding Social Sciences in Cognitive Sciences*, edited by Ron Sun, 415–43. Cambridge, MA: MIT Press.

Gintis, Herbert, Samuel Bowles, Robert Boyd, and Ernst Fehr, eds. 2005. *Moral Sentiments and Material Interests: The Foundations of Cooperation in Economic Life*. Cambridge, MA: MIT Press.

Gluckman, Max. 1941. *Economy of the Central Barotse Plain. The Rhodes-Livingston Papers 7*. Livingston: Northern Rhodesia.

Gluckman, Max. 1943. *Essays on Lozi Land and Royal Property. The Rhodes-Livingston Papers 10*. Livingston: Northern Rhodesia.

Gluckman, Max. 1961. "The Lozi of Barotseland in North-Western Rhodesia." In *Seven Tribes of British Central Africa*, edited by E. Colson and M. Gluckman, 1–93. Manchester: Manchester University Press.

Godelier, Maurice. 1978. "The Concept of the 'Asiatic Mode of Production' and Marxist Models of Social Evolution." In *Relations of Production: Marxist Approaches to Economic Anthropology*, edited by D. Seddon, 209–58. London: Frank Cass.

Goldhill, Simon. 1990. "The Great Dionysia and Civic Ideology." In *Nothing to Do with Dionysos? Athenian Drama and Its Social Context*, edited by John J. Winkler and Froma I. Zeitlin, 97–129. Princeton: Princeton University Press.

Goldschmidt, Walter. 2011. "Notes toward a Human Nature for the Third Millennium." In *Origins of Altruism and Cooperation*, edited by Robert W. Sussman and C. Robert Cloninger, 271–81. New York: Springer.

Goldstone, Jack A. 2002. "Efflorescences and Economic Growth in World History: Rethinking the 'Rise of the West' and the Industrial Revolution." *Journal of World History* 13:323–89.

Goleman, Daniel. 2013. *Focus: The Hidden Driver of Excellence*. New York: HarperCollins Publishers.

Goodall, Jane. 1971. *In the Shadow of Man*. Boston: Houghton Mifflin.

Goody, Jack. 1996. *The East in the West*. Cambridge: Cambridge University Press.

Gordon, Robert M. 1996. "Radical Simulationism." In *Theories of Theories of Mind*, edited by Peter Carruthers and Peter K. Smith, 11–21. Cambridge: Cambridge University Press.

Goren-Inbar, Naama, Nira Alperson, Moredechai Kislev, Orit Simchoni, Yoel Melamed, Ardi Ben-Nun, and Ella Werker. 2004. "Evidence of Hominid Control of Fire at Gesher Benot Ya'aqov, Israel." *Science* 304:725–27.

Gorski, Philip S. 2003. *The Disciplinary Revolution: Calvinism and the Rise of the State in Early Modern Europe*. Chicago: University of Chicago Press.

Gould, Stephen Jay. 1980. "Sociobiology and the Theory of Natural Selection." In *Sociobiology: Beyond Nature/Nurture?* edited by George W. Barlow and James Silverberg, 257–69. Washington, DC: American Association for the Advancement of Science.

Granovetter, Mark. 1985. "Economic Action and Social Structure: The Problem of Embeddedness." *American Journal of Sociology* 91:481–510.

Granovetter, Mark. 1990. "The Old and the New Economic Sociology: A History and an Agenda." In *Beyond the Marketplace: Rethinking Economy and Society*, edited by Roger Friedland and A. F. Robertson, 89–112. New York: Aldine de Gruyter.

Granovetter, Mark. 1992. "The Nature of Economic Relations." In *Understanding Economic Process*, edited by Sutti Ortiz and Susan Lees, 21–37. Society for Economic Anthropology, Monographs in Economic Anthropology 10. Lanham, MD: University Press of America.

Grant, Jill. 2001. "The Dark Side of the Grid: Power and Urban Design." *Planning Perspectives* 16:219–41.

Great Britain India Office. 1878. *A Catalogue of Manuscript and Printed Reports, Field Books, Memoirs, Maps, etc., of the Indian Surveys Deposited in the Map Room of the India Office.*

Greenberg, James B. 1981. *Santiago's Sword: Chatino Peasant Religion and Economics*. Berkeley: University of California Press.

Greenberg, James B. 1989. *Blood Ties: Life and Violence in Rural Mexico*. Tucson: University of Arizona Press.

Gregory, C. A. 1982. *Gifts and Commodities*. London: Academic Press.

Greif, Avner. 2006. *Institutions and the Path to Modernity: Lessons from the Medieval Trade*. Cambridge: Cambridge University Press.

Grinin, Leonid E., and Andrey V. Korotayev. 2011. "Chiefdoms and Their Analogues: Alternatives of Social Evolution at the Societal Level of Medium Cultural Complexity." *Social Evolution and History* 10:276–335.

Grover, B. R. 1994. "An Integrated Pattern of Commercial Life in the Rural Society of North India during the Seventeenth and Eighteenth Centuries." In *Money and Market in India, 1100–1700*, edited by Sanjay Subrahmanyam, 219–55. Delhi: Oxford University Press.

Gulick, C. B. 1973. *The Life of the Ancient Greeks, with Special Reference to Athens*. New York: Cooper Square Publishers.

Gullick, J. M. 1958. *Indigenous Political Systems of Western Malaya*. London: University of London and Athlone Press.

Guy, John, and Jorrit Britschgi. 2011. *Wonder of the Age: Master Painters of India, 1100–1900*. New York: The Metropolitan Museum of Art.

Habib, Irfan. 1963. *The Agrarian System of Mughal India (1556–1707)*. Bombay: Asia Publishing House.

Habib, Irfan. 2002. "The Economy." In *The Magnificent Mughals*, edited by Zeenut Ziad, 269–80. Oxford: Oxford University Press.

Haidt, Jonathan. 2001. "The Emotional Dog and Its Rational Tail: A Social Intuitionist Approach to Moral Judgment." *Psychological Review* 108:814–34.

Hall, John W. 1991a. "Introduction." In *The Cambridge History of Japan*, vol. 4: *Early Modern Japan,* edited by J. W. Hall, 1–39. Cambridge: Cambridge University Press.

Hall, John W. 1991b. "The *Bakuhan* System." In *The Cambridge History of Japan*, vol. 4: *Early Modern Japan*, edited by John W. Hall, 128–82. Cambridge: Cambridge University Press.

Hall, Peter Geoffrey. 1988. *Cities in Civilization*. New York: Pantheon Books.

Hanley, Susan B. 1987. "Urban Sanitation in Preindustrial Japan." *Journal of Interdisciplinary History* 18:1–26.

Hannestad, Niels. 1988. *Roman Art and Imperial Policy*. Aarhus: Aarhus University Press.

Hansen, Mogens Herman. 1996. "The Ancient Athenian and the Modern Liberal View of Liberty as a Democratic Ideal." In *Demokratia: A Conversation on Democracies, Ancient and Modern*, edited by Josiah Ober and Charles W. Hedrick, 91–104. Princeton: Princeton University Press.

Hansen, Mogens Herman. 1999. *The Athenian Democracy in the Age of Demosthenes: Structure, Principles, and Ideology*. 2nd rev. ed. Norman: University of Oklahoma Press.

Hanson, F. Allan. 2004. "The New Superorganic." *Current Anthropology* 45:467–82.

Hanson, Victor Davis. 1999. *The Other Greeks: The Family Farm and the Agrarian Roots of Western Civilization*. 2nd ed. Berkeley: University of California Press.

Hardin, Russell. 1982. *Collective Action*. Baltimore: Johns Hopkins University Press.

Hardin, Russell. 1991. "Acting Together, Contributing Together." *Rationality and Society* 3:365–80.

Harding, Thomas G. 1967. *Voyagers of the Vitiaz Strait. The American Ethnological Society Monographs 44*. Seattle: University of Washington Press.

Harman, Oren. 2015. "The Altruism Game." *The Chronicle Review, The Chronicle of Higher Education*: Section B, February 13.

Harris, Marvin. 1968. *The Rise of Anthropological Theory*. New York: T. Y. Crowell.

Hart, Gillian. 1992. "Imagined Unities: Constructions of 'The Household' in Economic Theory." In *Understanding Economic Process*, edited by Sutti Ortiz and Susan Lees,

111–30. Society for Economic Anthropology, Monographs in Economic Anthropology 10. Lanham, MD: University Press of America.

Hart, Keith. 1988. "Kinship, Contract, and Trust: The Economic Organization of Migrants in an African City Slum." In *Trust: Making and Breaking Cooperative Relationships*, edited by Diego Gambetta, 176–93. Oxford: Basil Blackwell.

Haruko, Wakita. 1997. "Fêtes et communautés urbaines dans le Japon Médiéval: La Fête de Gion à Kyôto." *Annales. Histoire, Sciences Sociales, 52e Année* 5:1039–56.

Harvey, H. R. 1991. "The Oztotipac Land Map: A Reexamination." In *Land and Politics in the Valley of Mexico: A Two-Thousand Year Perspective*, edited by H. R. Harvey, 163–85. Albuquerque: University of New Mexico Press.

Hasan, Ibn. 1936. *The Central Structure of the Mughal Empire and Its Practical Working up to the Year 1657*. London: Oxford University Press.

Hassall, Mark. 2000. "The Army." In *The Cambridge Ancient History, Second Edition*, vol. 2: *The High Empire, A. D. 70–192*, edited by A. K. Bowman, P. Garnsey, and D. Rathbone, 320–43. Cambridge: Cambridge University Press.

Hassig, Ross. 1985. *Trade, Tribute, and Transportation: The Sixteenth-Century Political Economy of the Valley of Mexico*. Norman: University of Oklahoma Press.

Hawkes, David. 2001. *Idols of the Marketplace: Idolatry and Commodity Fetishism in English Literature, 1580–1680*. New York: Palgrave.

Hawkes, Kristen. 1993. "Why Hunter-Gatherers Work." *Current Anthropology* 34:341–61.

Hearn, M. K. 2008. *How to Read Chinese Painting*. New York: Metropolitan Museum of Art, New York.

Hechter, Michael. 1983. "A Theory of Group Solidarity." In *The Microfoundations of Macrosociology*, edited by Michael Hechter, 16–57. Philadelphia: Temple University Press.

Hechter, Michael. 1987. *Principles of Group Solidarity*. Berkeley: University of California Press.

Hechter, Michael. 1990a. "On the Inadequacy of Game Theory for the Solution of Real-World Collective Action Problems." In *The Limits of Rationality*, edited by Karen Schweers Cook and Margaret Levi, 240–49. Chicago: University of Chicago Press.

Hechter, Michael. 1990b. "The Emergence of Cooperative Social Institutions." In *Social Institutions: Their Emergence, Maintenance, and Effects*, edited by Michael Hechter, Karl-Dieter Opp, and Reinhard Wippler, 13–33. New York: Aldine de Gruyter.

Hechter, Michael, and William Brustein. 1980. "Regional Modes of Production and Patterns of State Formation in Western Europe." *American Journal of Sociology* 85:1061–94.

Heesterman, J. C. 1998. "The Conundrum of the King's Authority." In *Kingship and Authority in South Asia*, edited by John F. Richards, 13–40. Delhi: Oxford University Press.

Heijdra, Martin. 1998. "The Socio-Economic Development of Rural China during the Ming." In *The Cambridge History of China*, vol. 8: *The Ming Dynasty, 1368–1644, Part 2*, edited by Dennis Twitchett and F. W. Mote, 417–578. Cambridge: Cambridge University Press.

Hejeebu, Santhi, and Deirdre McCloskey. 1999. "The Reproving of Karl Polanyi." *Critical Review* 13:285–314.

Henrich, Joseph. 2004. "Cultural Group Selection, Coevolutionary Processes, and Large-Scale Cooperation." *Journal of Economic Behavior & Organization* 53:3–35.

Henrich, Joseph, Robert Boyd, Samuel Bowles, Colin Camerer, Ernst Fehr, and Herbert Gintis, eds. 2004. *Foundations of Human Sociality: Economic Experiments and Ethnographic Evidence from Fifteen Small-Scale Societies*. Oxford: Oxford University.

Henrich, Joseph, Jean Ensminger, Richard McElreath, Abigail Barr, Clark Barrett, Alexander Bolyanatz, Juman Camilo Cardenas, Michael Gurven, Edwins Gwako, Natalie Henrich, et al. 2010. "Markets, Religion, Community Size, and the Evolution of Fairness and Punishment." *Science* 327:1480–84.

Henrich, Joseph, Steven J. Heine, and Ara Norenzayan. 2010. "The Weirdest People in the World?" *Behavioral and Brain Sciences* 33:61–83.

Henrich, Joseph, and Natalie Henrich. 2007. *Why Humans Cooperate: A Cultural and Evolutionary Explanation*. New York: Oxford University Press.

Hernes, Gudmund. 1976. "Structural Change in Social Processes." *American Journal of Sociology* 82:513–47.

Herrmann, Benedikt, Christian Thöni, and Simon Gächter. 2008. "Antisocial Punishment across Societies." *Science* 319:1362–67.

Herskovits, Melville J. 1938. *Dahomey: An Ancient West African Kingdom*. New York: J. J. Augustine.

Heyden, Doris. 1991. "Dryness before the Rains: Toxcatl and Tezcatlipoca." In *Aztec Ceremonial Landscapes*, edited by Davíd Carrasco, 188–204. Boulder: University Press of Colorado.

Heyes, Cecilia M., and Chris D. Frith. 2014. "The Cultural Evolution of Mind Reading." *Science* 344:1243091. http://dx.doi.org/10.1126/science.1243091.

Hickerson, Nancy P. 1996. "Kiowa: An Emergent People." In *Portraits of Culture*, edited by Melvin Ember, Carol Ember, and David Levinson, 63–92. Englewood Cliffs, NJ: Prentice Hall.

Hill, Kim R., Robert S. Walker, Miran Bozicevic, James Eder, Thomas Headland, Barry Hewlett, A. Magdalena Hurtado, Frank Marlowe, Polly Weissner, and Brian Wood. 2011. "Co-Residence Patterns in Hunter-Gatherer Societies Show Unique Human Social Structure." *Science* 331:1286–89.

Hill, Polly. 1966. "Notes on Traditional Market Authority and Market Periodicity in West Africa." *Journal of African History* 7:295–311.

Hill, Polly. 1970. *Studies in Rural Capitalism in West Africa*. Cambridge: Cambridge University Press.

Hill, Polly. 1971. "Two Types of West African House Trade." In *The Development of Indigenous Trade and Markets in West Africa*, edited by Claude Meillassoux and Daryll Forde, 303–18. Oxford: Oxford University Press.

Hillier, Bill. 1989. "The Architecture of the Urban Object." *Ekistics* 56:5–21.

Hillier, Bill. 1996. *Space Is the Machine: A Configurational Theory of Architecture*. Cambridge: Cambridge University Press.

Hilton, Alison. 1978. "The Revolutionary Theme in Russian Realism." In *Art and Architecture in the Service of Politics*, edited by Henry A. Millon and Linda Nochlin, 108–27. Cambridge, MA: MIT Press.

Hilton, Rodney. 1985. *Class Conflict and the Crisis of Feudalism: Essays in Medieval Social History*. London: Hambledon Press.

Hilton, Rodney. 1992. *English and French Towns in Feudal Society: A Comparative Study*. Cambridge: Cambridge University Press.

Himmelfarb, Gertrude. 2001. "Two Enlightenments: A Contrast in Social Ethics." *Proceedings of the British Academy* 117:297–324.

Hirata, Satoshi. 2006. "Tactical Deception and Understanding of Others in Chimpanzees." In *Cognitive Development in Chimpanzees*, edited by T. Matsuzawa, M. Tomonaga, and M. Tanaka, 265–78. Tokyo: Springer-Verlag.

Hirschman, Albert O. 1970. *Exit, Voice, and Loyalty: Responses to Decline in Firms, Organizations, and States*. Cambridge, MA: Harvard University Press.

Hirschman, Albert O. 1977. *The Passions and the Interests: Political Arguments for Capitalism before Its Triumph*. Princeton: Princeton University Press.

Hirschman, Albert O. 1982. "Rival Interpretations of Market Society: Civilizing, Destructive, or Feeble?" *Journal of Economic Literature* 20:1463–84.

Hirschman, Albert O. 1992. *Rival Views of Market Society and Other Recent Essays*. Cambridge, MA: Harvard University Press.

Hirth, Kenneth G., and Joanne Pillsbury, eds. 2013. *Merchants, Markets, and Exchange in the Pre-Columbian World*. Washington, DC: Dumbarton Oaks Research Library and Collection.

Hitchner, R. Bruce. 2005. "The Advantages of Wealth and Luxury." In *The Ancient Economy: Evidence and Models*, edited by J. G. Manning and Ian Morris, 207–22. Stanford: Stanford University Press.

Ho Ping-ti. 1962. *The Ladder of Success in Imperial China: Aspects of Social Mobility, 1368–1911*. New York: Columbia University Press.

Ho Ping-ti. 1966. "Lo-yang, A.D. 495–534: A Study of Physical and Socio-Economic Planning of a Metropolitan Area." *Harvard Journal of Asiatic Studies* 26:52–101.

Hobbes, Thomas. (Original work published 1651) 1996. *Leviathan*. Edited by J.C.A. Gaskin. Oxford: Oxford University Press.

Hobsbaum, Eric. 1964. "Introduction." In *Karl Marx: Pre-Capitalist Economic Formations*, by Karl Marx, 1–67. New York: International Publishers.

Hodder, B. W. 1962. "The Yoruba Rural Market." In *Markets in Africa*, edited by Paul Bohannon and George Dalton, 103–17. Evanston: Northwestern University Press.

Hollan, Douglas. 1992. "Cross-Cultural Differences in the Self." *Journal of Anthropological Research* 48:283–300.

Holmberg, A. R. 1969. *Nomads of the Long Bow*. New York: Natural History Press.

Holmes, George. 1962. *A History of England*. Vol. 3. The Later Middle Ages, 1272–1485. Edinburgh: Thomas Nelson and Sons.

Holmes, Stephen. 1990. "The Secret History of Self Interest." In *Beyond Self-Interest*, edited by Jane Mansbridge, 267–86. Chicago: University of Chicago Press.

Hölscher, Tonio. 1991. "The City of Athens: Space, Symbol, and Structure." In *City States in Classical Antiquity and Medieval Italy*, edited by A. Molho, K. Raaflaub, and J. Emlen, 355–80. Ann Arbor: University of Michigan Press.

Honour, Hugh, and John Fleming. 1982. *The Visual Arts: A History*. Englewood Cliffs, NJ: Prentice-Hall.

Hope, Valerie. 2000. "The City of Rome: Capital and Symbol." In *Experiencing Rome: Culture, Identity, and Power in the Roman Empire*, edited by J. Huskinson, 63–94. New York: Routledge.

Hopkins, Keith. 1980. "Taxes and Trade in the Roman Empire." *Journal of Roman Studies* 70:101–25.

Hopkins, Keith. 1995–1996. "Rome, Taxes, Rents, and Trade." *Kodai: Journal of Ancient History* 6/7:41–75.

Horden, Peregrine, and Nicholas Purcell. 2000. *The Corrupting Sea: A Study of Mediterranean History*. Oxford: Blackwell.

House-Midamba, Bessie, and Feliz K. Ekechi. 1995. *African Market Women and Economic Power: The Role of Women in African Economic Development*. Westport, CT: Greenwood Press.

Howes, David. 1991. "Introduction: To Summon All the Senses." In *The Varieties of Sensory Experience: A Sourcebook in the Anthropology of the Senses*, edited by David Howes, 3–21. Toronto: University of Toronto Press.

Howes, David, and Constance Classen. 2014. *Ways of Sensing: Understanding the Senses in Society*. London: Routledge.

Hrdy, Sarah Blaffer. 2009. *Mothers and Others: The Evolutionary Origins of Mutual Understanding*. Cambridge, MA: Harvard University Press.

Huang, Ray. 1998. "The Ming Fiscal Administration." In *The Cambridge History of China*, vol. 8: *the Ming Dynasty, 1368–1644, Part 2*, edited by D. Twitchett and F. W. Mote, 9–105. Cambridge: Cambridge University Press.

Hucker, Charles O. 1978. *The Ming Dynasty: Its Origins and Evolving Institutions*. Ann Arbor: University of Michigan, Center for Chinese Studies.

Hucker, Charles O. 1998. "Ming Government." In *The Cambridge History of China*, vol. 8: *The Ming Dynasty, 1368–1644, Part 2*, edited by D. Twitchett and F. W. Mote, 9–105. Cambridge: Cambridge University Press.

Hui, Victoria Tin-Bor. 2005. *War and State Formation in Ancient China and Early Modern Europe*. Cambridge: Cambridge University Press.

Hume, David. (Original work published 1739) 1978. *A Treatise on Human Nature*, ed. L. A. Selby-Bigge. Oxford: Clarendon Press.

Humphrey, Caroline, and Stephen Hugh-Jones, eds. 1992. *Barter, Exchange, and Value: An Anthropological Approach*. Cambridge: Cambridge University Press.

Humphreys, S. C. 1978. *Anthropology and the Greeks*. London: Routledge and Kegan Paul.

Hunt, Robert C. 1988. "Size and Structure of Authority in Canal Irrigation Systems." *Journal of Anthropological Research* 44:325–55.

Hutson, Scott R. 2000. "Carnival and Contestation in the Aztec Marketplace." *Dialectical Anthropology* 25:123–49.

Iannaccone, Laurence. 1992. "Sacrifice and Stigma: Reducing Free-Riding in Cults, Communes, and Other Collectivities." *Journal of Political Economy* 100:271–91.

Inalçik, Halil. 1973. "Istanbul." In *Encyclopedia of Islam*, edited by E. van Donzel, B. Lewis, and C. Pellat, 2nd ed., vol. 4. Leiden: E. J. Brill.

Inalçik, Halil. 1994. "The Ottoman State: Economy and Society, 1300–1600." In *An Economic and Social History of the Ottoman Empire, 1300–1914*, edited by Halil Inalçik and D. Quataert, 9–410. Cambridge: Cambridge University Press.

Ingold, Tim. 1999. "On the Social Relations of the Hunter-Gatherer Band." In *The Cambridge Encyclopedia of Hunters and Gatherers*, edited by Richard B. Lee and Richard Daly, 399–410. Cambridge: Cambridge University Press.

Isaac, Barry L. 1993. "AMP, HH & OD: Some Comments." In *Economic Aspects of Water Management in the Prehispanic New World*, edited by Vernon Scarborough, 429–71. Greenwich, CT: JAI Press.

Isaac, Barry L. 2005. "Karl Polanyi." In *A Handbook of Economic Anthropology*, edited by James G. Carrier, 14–25. Cheltenham, UK: Edward Elgar.

Ivanhoe, Philip J. 2000. *Confucian Moral Self-Cultivation*. 2nd ed. Indianapolis: Hackett Publishing Company.

Jackson, Jean E. 1983. *The Fish People: Linguistic Exogamy and Tukanoan Identity in Northwest Amazonia*. Cambridge: Cambridge University Press.

Jacobsen, Thorkild. 1943. "Primitive Democracy in Ancient Mesopotamia." *Journal of Near Eastern Studies* 2:159–72.

James, T.G.H. 1984. *Pharaoh's People: Scenes from Life in Imperial Egypt*. London: Bodley Head.

Jensen, Nathan, and Leonard Wantchekon. 2004. "Resource Wealth and Political Regimes in Africa." *Comparative Political Studies* 37:816–41.

Johnson, Gregory A. 1978. "Information Sources and the Development of Decision-Making Organizations." In *Social Archaeology: Beyond Subsistence and Dating*, edited by C. L. Redman, J. Berman, E. V. Curtin, W. T. Langehorn Jr., N. M. Versaggi, and J. C. Wanser, 87–112. New York: Academic Press.

Johnson, Gregory A. 1983. "Decision-Making Organization and Pastoral Nomad Camp Size." *Human Ecology* 11:175–99.

Jones, Doug. 2000. "'Group Nepotism' and Human Kinship." *Current Anthropology* 41:779–809.

Jones, James Holland. 2009. "Anthropology as Biosocial Science: The Future of Cross-Cutting Research." *American Anthropological Association, Anthropology News* 50:5.

Jorgensen, Joseph G. 1980. *Western Indians: Comparative Environments, Languages, and Cultures of 172 Western American Indian Tribes*. San Francisco: W. H. Freeman and Company.

Jost, John T. 2012. "Left and Right, Right and Wrong." *Science* 337:525–26.

Julien, Catherine J. 1982. "Inca Decimal Administration in the Lake Titicaca Region." In *The Inca and Aztec States, 1400–1800: Anthropology and History*, edited by G. A. Collier, R. I. Rosaldo, and J. D. Wirth, 119–51. New York: Academic Press.

Kafescioglu, Çigdem. 1999. "'In the Image of Rum': Ottoman Architectural Patronage in Sixteenth-century Aleppo and Damascus." *Muqarnas* 16:70–96.

Kaiser, Alan. 2011. *Roman Urban Street Networks*. New York: Routledge.

Kandel, Eric R. 2012. *The Age of Insight: The Quest to Understand the Unconscious in Art, Mind, and Brain from Vienna 1900 to the Present*. New York: Random House.

Kaphan, Deborah A. 1996. *Gender in the Market: Moroccan Women and the Revoicing of Tradition*. Philadelphia: University of Pennsylvania Press.

Kaplan, Hillard, and Kim Hill. 1985. "Food Sharing among Foragers: Tests of Explanatory Hypotheses." *Current Anthropology* 26:223–46.

Kaplan, Leonard V. 1995. "Intention and Responsibility: The Attenuation of Evil, the Unfairness of Justice." In *Other Intentions: Cultural Contexts and the Attribution of Inner States*, edited by Lawrence Rosen, 119–40. Santa Fe: School of American Research Press.

Karmiloff-Smith, Annette. 2000. "Why Babies' Brains Are Not Swiss Army Knives." In *Alas, Poor Darwin: Arguments against Evolutionary Psychology*, edited by Hilary Rose and Steven Rose, 173–87. New York: Harmony Books.

Kaufman, Daniel, Aart Kraay, and Pablo Zoido-Lobatón. 2002. "Governance Matters II: Updated Indicators for 2000/01." World Bank and Stanford University. http://sitere sources.worldbank.org/DEC/Resources/WPS2772_2002.pdf

Kerridge, Eric. 1986. "Early Modern English Markets." In *The Market in History*, edited by B. L. Anderson and A.J.H. Latham, 121–54. London: Croom Helm.

Khuri, Fuad I. 1968. "The Etiquette of Bargaining in the Middle East." *American Anthropologist* 70:698–706.

Kiang, Heng Chye. 1999. *Cities of Aristocrats and Bureaucrats: The Development of Chinese Cityscapes*. Honolulu: University of Hawai'i Press.

King, Adam. 2003. *Etowah: The Political History of a Chiefdom Capital*. Tuscaloosa: University of Alabama Press.

Kiser, Edgar. 1999. "Comparing Varieties of Agency Theory in Economics, Political Science, and Sociology: An Illustration from State Policy Implementation." *Sociological Theory* 17:146–70.

Kiser, Edgar, and Shawn Bauldry. 2005. "The Contribution of Rational Choice Theory to Political Sociology." In *Handbook of Political Sociology*, edited by Thomas Janoski, Robert Alford, Alexander Hicks, and Mildred Schwartz, 172–86. Cambridge: Cambridge University Press.

Kiser, Larry L., and Elinor Ostrom. 2000. "The Three Worlds of Action: A Metatheoretical Synthesis of Institutional Approaches." In *Polycentric Games and Institutions: Readings from a Workshop in Political Theory and Policy Analysis*, edited by Michael D. McGinnis, 56–88. Ann Arbor: University of Michigan Press.

Kishigami, Nobuhiro. 2004. "A New Typology of Food-Sharing Practices among Hunter-Gatherers, with a Special Focus on Inuit Examples." *Journal of Anthropological Research* 60:341–58.

Kitcher, Philip. 1985. *Vaulting Ambition: Sociobiology and the Quest for Human Nature*. Cambridge, MA: MIT Press.

Knapp, Ronald. 1986. *China's Traditional Rural Architecture: A Cultural Geography of the Common House*. Honolulu: University of Hawaii Press.

Kobayashi, Hiromi, and Shiro Kohshima. 2001. "Unique Morphology of the Human Eye and Its Adaptive Meaning: Comparative Studies on External Morphology of the Primate Eye." *Journal of Human Evolution* 40:419–35.

Koenig, William J. 1990. *The Burmese Polity, 1752–1819: Politics, Administration, and Social Organization in the Early Kon-baung Period. Michigan Papers on South and Southeast Asia 34*. Ann Arbor: Center for South and Southeast Asian Studies.

Kopytoff, Igor. 1987. "The Internal African Frontier: The Making of African Political Culture." In *The African Frontier: The Reproduction of Traditional African Societies*, edited by Igor Kopytoff, 3–84. Bloomington: Indiana University Press.

Kopytoff, Igor, and Suzanne Miers. 1977. "African 'Slavery' as an Institution of Marginality." In *Slavery in Africa: Historical and Anthropological Perspectives*, edited by Suzanne Miers and Igor Kopytoff, 3–81. Madison: University of Wisconsin Press.

Kornai, János. 1992. *The Socialist System: The Political Economy of Communism*. Princeton: Princeton University Press.

Korotayev, Andrey V. 1995. "Mountains and Democracy: An Introduction." In *Alternative Pathways to Early State*, edited by N. N. Kradin and V. A. Lynsha, 60–74. Vladivostik: Dal'nauka.

Kostof, Spiro. 1991. *The City Shaped: Urban Patterns and Meanings through History*. Boston: Little, Brown, and Company.

Kostof, Spiro. 1992. *The City Assembled: The Elements of Urban Form through History*. Boston: Bullfinch Press.

Kottack, Conrad. 1972. "Ecological Variables in the Origin and Evolution of African States: The Buganda Example." *Comparative Studies in Society and History* 14:351–80.

Kowalewski, Stephen. 2006. "Coalescent Societies." In *Light on the Path: The Anthropology and History of the Southeastern Indians*, edited by Thomas J. Pluckhahn and Robbie Ethridge, 94–122. Tuscaloosa: University of Alabama Press.

Kowalewski, Stephen. 2012. "A Theory of the Ancient Mesoamerican Economy." *Research in Economic Anthropology* 32:187–224.

Kradin, Nikolay N. 2011. "Heterarchy and Hierarchy among the Ancient Mongolian Nomads." *Social Evolution and History* 10:187–214.

Kristan-Graham, Cynthia. 1993. "The Business Narrative at Tula: An Analysis of the Vestibule Frieze, Trade, and Ritual." *Latin American Antiquity* 4:3–21.

Krugman, Paul. 2009. "How Did Economists Get It So Wrong?" *New York Times Magazine*, September 6: 36–43.

Kubat, Ayse S. 1999. "The Morphological History of Istanbul." *Urban Morphology* 3:28–41.

Kuper, Adam. 2002. "Culture." *Proceedings of the British Academy* 112:87–102.

Kuran, Aptullah. 1996. "A Spatial Study of Three Ottoman Capitals: Bursa, Edirne, and Istanbul." *Muqarnas* 13:114–31.

Kusserow, Adrie Suzanne. 1999. "Crossing the Great Divide: Anthropological Theories of the Western Self." *Journal of Anthropological Research* 55:541–62.

Labovitz, Sanford. 1967. "Some Observations on Measurement and Statistics." *Social Forces* 46:151–60.

Labovitz, Sanford. 1970. "The Assignment of Numbers to Rank Order Categories." *American Sociological Review* 35:515–24.

Lacovara, Peter. 1997. *The New Kingdom Royal City*. London: Kegan Paul International.

Landa, Janet T. 1981. "A Theory of the Ethnically Homogeneous Middleman Group: An Institutional Alternative to Contract Law." *Journal of Legal Studies* 10:349–62.

Lane, Frederic C. 1973. *Venice: A Maritime Republic*. Baltimore: Johns Hopkins University Press.

Langlois, John D., Jr. 1998. "Ming Law." In *The Cambridge History of China*, vol. 8: *The Ming Dynasty, 1368–1644, Part 2*, edited by D. Twitchett and F. W. Mote, 172–220. Cambridge: Cambridge University Press.

Lansing, J. Stephen. 1987. "Balinese 'Water Temples' and the Management of Irrigation." *American Anthropologist* 89:326–41.

Larmore, Charles. 2004. "History & Truth." *Daedalus* 133:46–94.

Law, Robin. 1977. *The Oyo Empire c.1600—c.1836: A West African Imperialism in the Era of the Atlantic Slave Trade*. Oxford: Clarendon Press.

Lee, Hui-Shu. 2010. *Empresses, Art, and Agency in Song Dynasty China*. Seattle: University of Washington Press.

Le Goff, Jacques. 1980. *Time, Work, and Culture in the Middle Ages*. Translated by Arthur Goldhammer. Chicago: University of Chicago Press.

Levi, Margaret. 1988. *Of Rule and Revenue*. Berkeley: University of California Press.

Levi, Margaret. 1997. *Consent, Dissent, and Patriotism*. Cambridge: Cambridge University Press.

Levi, Margaret. 2002. "The State of the Study of the State." In *Political Science: The State of the Discipline*, edited by Ira Katznelson and Helen V. Milner, 33–55. New York: W. W. Norton.

Levine, Frances. 1991. "Economic Perspectives on the Comanche Trade." In *Farmers, Hunters, and Colonists: Interaction between the Southwest and the Southern Plains*, edited by Katherine A. Spielmann, 155–69. Tucson: University of Arizona Press.

Levinson, Stephen C. 2006. "On the Human 'Interaction Engine.'" In *Roots of Human Sociality: Culture, Cognition, and Interaction*, edited by N. J. Enfield and Stephen C. Levinson, 39–69. Oxford: Berg.

Lévi-Strauss, Claude. 1963. *Structural Anthropology*. Translated by Claire Jacobson and Brooke Grundfest Schoepf. New York: Basic Books.

Lévi-Strauss, Claude. 1974. *Tristes tropiques*, New York: Atheneum.

Lewis, Martin W. 1989. "Commercialization and Community Life: The Geography of Market Exchange in a Small-Scale Philippine Society." *Annals of the Association of American Geographers* 79:390–410.

Lichbach, Mark I. 1994. "What Makes Rational Peasants Revolutionary? Dilemma, Paradox, and Irony in Peasant Collective Action." *World Politics* 46:383–418.

Lichbach, Mark I. 1995. *The Rebel's Dilemma*. Ann Arbor: University of Michigan Press.

Lichbach, Mark I. 1996. *The Cooperator's Dilemma*. Ann Arbor: University of Michigan Press.

Little, Anthony C., Benedict C. Jones, and Lisa M. DeBruine, eds. 2011. "Theme Issue. Face Perception: Social, Neuropsychological, and Comparative Perspectives." *Philosophical Transactions of the Royal Society* B 366.

Little, Daniel. 1991. "Rational Choice Models and Asian Studies." *Journal of Asian Studies* 50:35–52.

Liu, Li. 2004. *The Chinese Neolithic: Trajectories to Early States*. Cambridge: Cambridge University Press.

Livingstone, Margaret. 2002. *Vision and Art: The Biology of Seeing.* New York: Abrams.

Locke, John. 1689. "Letter Concerning Toleration." Unpublished letter.

Locke, John. 1975. "(orig. 1689)." In *An Essay Concerning Human Understanding,* ed. Peter H. Nidditch. Oxford: Oxford University Press.

Lockhart, James. 1992. *The Nahuas after the Conquest: A Social and Cultural History of the Indians of Central Mexico, Sixteenth through Eighteenth Centuries.* Stanford: Stanford University Press.

Lopez, Robert S. 1976. *The Commercial Revolution of the Middle Ages, 950–1350.* Cambridge: Cambridge University Press.

López Austin, Alfredo. 1988. *The Human Body and Ideology: Concepts of the Ancient Nahuas.* Translated by Thelma Ortiz de Montellano and Bernardo Ortiz de Montellano, 2 vols. Salt Lake City: University of Utah Press.

Lorenz, Konrad. 1963. *On Aggression.* New York: Bantam Books.

Lott, J. Bert. 2004. *The Neighborhoods of Augustan Rome.* Cambridge: Cambridge University Press.

Lukasik, Christopher J. 2004. "The Face of the Public." *Early American Literature* 39:413–65.

Lukasik, Christopher J. 2011. *Discerning Characters: The Culture of Appearance in Early America.* Philadelphia: University of Pennsylvania Press.

Lukes, Steven. 1973. *Individualism.* New York: Harper and Row.

Lybyer, Albert H. 1966. *The Government of the Ottoman Empire in the Time of Suleiman the Magnificent.* New York: Russell and Russell.

Lyle, Henry F., III, and Eric A. Smith. 2012. "How Conservative Are Evolutionary Anthropologists? A Survey of Political Attitudes." *Human Nature (Hawthorne, N.Y.)* 23:306–22.

Lynch, Kevin. 1960. *The Image of the City.* Cambridge, MA: MIT Press.

Lyttkens, Carl Hampus. 2013. *Economic Analysis of Institutional Change and Ancient Greece: Politics, Taxation, and Rational Behavior.* London: Routledge.

Machiavelli, Niccolo. (Original work published 1513) 2005. *The Prince.* Translated by P. Bondanella. Oxford: Oxford University Press.

MacKinnon, Katherine C., and Augustín Fuentes. 2012. "Primate Social Cognition, Human Evolution, and Niche Construction: A Core Case for Neuroanthropology." In *The Encultured Brain: An Introduction to Neuroanthropology,* edited by Daniel H. Lende and Greg Downey, 67–102. Cambridge, MA: MIT Press.

Maine, Henry. 1872. *Village Communities in the East and West.* London: John Murray.

Malafouris, Lambros. 2013. *How Things Shape the Mind: A Theory of Material Engagement.* Cambridge, MA: MIT Press.

Malinowski, Bronislaw. 1932. *Argonauts of the Western Pacific.* London: Routledge.

Malinowski, Bronislaw. 1944. *A Scientific Theory of Culture and Other Essays.* Chapel Hill: University of North Carolina Press.

Mandeville, Bernard. (Original work published 1732) 1924. *The Fable of the Bees: Or, Private Vices, Publick Benefits*. Oxford: Clarendon Press.

Margolis, Howard. 1993. *Paradigms and Barriers: How Habits of Mind Govern Scientific Beliefs*. Chicago: University of Chicago Press.

Marlowe, Frank W. 2004. "What Explains Hadza Food Sharing?" *Research in Economic Anthropology* 23:69–88.

Marmé, Michael. 1993. "Heaven on Earth: The Rise of Suzhou, 1127–1550." In *Cities of Jiangnan in Late Imperial China*, edited by Linda Cooke Johnson, 16–45. Albany: State University of New York Press.

Marmé, Michael. 2005. *Suzhou: Where the Goods of All the Provinces Converge*. Stanford: Stanford University Press.

Marshall, Robert C., ed. 2010. *Cooperation in Economy and Society. Monograph of the Society for Economic Anthropology 28*. Lanham, MD: AltaMira Press.

Martin, Isaac William, Ajay K. Mehrotra, and Monica Prasad, eds. 2009. *The New Fiscal Sociology: Taxation in Comparative and Historical Perspective*. Cambridge: Cambridge University Press.

Martin, Ronald. 1981. *Tacitus*. Berkeley: University of California Press.

Marwell, Gerald, and Pamela Oliver. 1993. *The Critical Mass in Collective Action: A Micro-Social Theory*. Cambridge: Cambridge University Press.

Marx, Karl. 1973. *Grundrisse: Introduction to the Critique of Political Economy*. New York: Vintage Books.

Mason, Penelope. 2005. *History of Japanese Art*. 2nd ed., revised by Donald Dinwiddie. Upper Saddle River, NJ: Pearson/Prentice Hall.

Matsuzawa, T., M. Tomonaga, and M. Tanaka, eds. 2006. *Cognitive Development in Chimpanzees*. Tokyo: Springer-Verlag.

Mattingly, D. J. 1988. "Oil for Export? A Comparison of Libyan, Spanish, and Tunisian Olive Oil Production in the Roman Empire." *Journal of Roman Archaeology* 1:33–56.

Mauss, Marcel. (Original work published 1925) 1967. *The Gift: Forms and Functions of Exchange in Archaic Societies*. Translated by E. E. Evans-Pritchard. New York: Norton.

Mauss, Marcel. 1985. "A Category of the Human Mind: The Notion of Person; the Notion of Self." In *The Category of the Person: Anthropology, Philosophy, History*, edited by Michael Carrithers, Steven Collins, and Steven Lukes, translated by W. D. Halls., 1–25. Cambridge: Cambridge University Press.

Mayer, Enrique. 2013. "In the Realm of the Incas." In *Merchants, Markets, and Exchange in the Pre-Columbian World*, edited by Kenneth G. Hirth and Joanne Pillsbury, 309–17. Washington, DC: Dumbarton Oaks Research Library and Collection.

Mayr, Ernst. 1982. *The Growth of Biological Thought: Diversity, Evolution, and Inheritance*. Cambridge, MA: Harvard University Press.

McCafferty, Sharisse, and Geoffrey G. McCafferty. 1988. "Powerful Women and the Myth of Male Dominance in Aztec Society." *Archaeological Review from Cambridge* 7:46–59.

McCaskie, T. C. 1995. *State and Society in Pre-Colonial Asante*. Cambridge: Cambridge University Press.

McCloskey, Donald N. 1976. "English Open Fields as Behavior towards Risk." In *Research in Economic History: An Annual Compilation of Research*, edited by Paul Uselding, 124–70. Greenwich, CT: JAI Press.

McDermott, Joseph P. 1999. "Emperor, Élites, and Commoners: The Community Pact Ritual of the Late Ming." In *State and Court Ritual in China*, edited by Joseph P. McDermott, 299–351. Cambridge: Cambridge University Press.

McDowell, Nancy. 1991. *The Mundugumor: From the Field Notes of Margaret Mead and Reo Fortune*. Washington, DC: Smithsonian Institution Press.

McGuire, Martin C., and Mancur Olson, Jr. 1996. "The Economics of Autocracy and Majority Rule: The Invisible Hand and the Use of Force." *Journal of Economic Literature* 34:72–96.

McIntosh, Susan Keech. 1999. "Pathways to Complexity: An African Perspective." In *Beyond Chiefdoms: Pathways to Complexity in Africa*, edited by Susan McIntosh, 1–30. Cambridge: Cambridge University Press.

McKenzie, Evan. 1994. *Privatopia: Homeowner Associations and the Rise of Residential Private Government*. New Haven: Yale University Press.

McKinnon, Susan. 2005. *Neo-Liberal Genetics: The Myths and Moral Tales of Evolutionary Psychology*. Chicago: Prickly Paradigm Press.

Mead, Margaret. 1935. *Sex and Temperament in Three Primitive Societies*. New York: William Morrow.

Meek, Ronald L. 1962. *The Economics of Physiocracy: Essays and Translations*. London: George Allen & Unwin Ltd.

Meier, Christian. 1990. *The Greek Discovery of Politics*. Trans. D. McClintock. Cambridge, MA: Harvard University Press.

Meier, Richard. 1962. *A Communications Theory of Urban Growth*. Cambridge, MA: MIT Press.

Melcher, David, and Patrick Cavanagh. 2013. "Pictorial Cues in Art and Visual Perception." In *Art and the Senses*, edited by Francesca Bacci, 359–94. Oxford: Oxford University Press.

Melling, A. I., C. Lacrette, and J. D. Barbié. 1819. *Voyage Pittoresque de Constantinople et de Bosphore*. Paris: Chez les Édiiteurs.

Mesoudi, Alex. 2011. *Cultural Evolution: How Darwinian Theory Can Explain Human Culture and Synthesize the Social Sciences*. Chicago: University of Chicago Press.

Midgley, Mary. 2000. "Why Memes?" In *Alas, Poor Darwin: Arguments against Evolutionary Psychology*, edited by Hilary Rose and Steven Rose, 79–100. New York: Harmony Books.

Mikulincer, Mario, and Philip R. Sharer, eds. 2010. *Prosocial Motives, Emotions, and Behavior: The Better Angels of Our Nature*. Washington, DC: American Psychological Association.

Milgrom, Paul R., Douglass C. North, and Barry R. Weingast. 1990. "The Role of Institutions in the Revival of Trade: The Law Merchants, Private Judges, and the Champagne Fairs." *Economics and Politics* 2:1–20.

Miller, Edward, and John Hatcher. 1978. *Medieval England—Rural Society and Economic Change 1086–1348*. London: Longman.

Miller, Greg. 2008. "The Roots of Morality." *Science* 320:734–37.

Miller, Joan G. 1994. "Cultural Diversity in the Morality of Caring: Individually-Oriented Versus Duty-Based Interpersonal Moral Codes." *Cross-Cultural Research* 28:3–39.

Miller, Naomi. 2000. *Mapping Cities*. Seattle: University of Washington Press.

Mills, Barbara J., ed. 2000. *Alternative Leadership Strategies in the Prehispanic Southwest*. Tucson: University of Arizona Press.

Mills, C. Wright. 1959. *The Sociological Imagination*. London: Oxford University Press.

Mintz, Sidney W. 1971. "Men, Women, and Trade." *Comparative Studies in Society and History* 13:247–69.

Miracle, Marvin P. 1962. "African Markets and Trade in the Copper Belt." In *Markets in Africa*, edited by Paul Bohannon and George Dalton, 698–738. Evanston: Northwestern University Press.

Mitchell, Robert W. 1999. "Deception and Concealment as Strategic Script Violation in Great Apes and Humans." In *The Mentalities of Gorillas and Orangutans: Comparative Perspectives*, edited by Sue Taylor Parker, Robert W. Mitchell, and H. Lyn Miles, 295–315. Cambridge: Cambridge University Press.

Mithen, Steven. 2010. "Excavating the Prehistoric Mind: The Brain as a Cultural Artefact and Material Culture as Biological Extension." In *Social Brain, Distributed Mind*, edited by Robin Dunbar, Clive Gamble, and John Gowlett, 481–503. Proceedings of the British Academy 158. Oxford: Oxford University Press.

Moertono, Soemarsaid. 1981. *State and Statecraft in Old Java: A Study of the Later Mataram Period, 16th to 19th Centuries. Monograph Series 43*. Ithaca: Cornell University, Modern Indonesia Project.

Moholy-Nagy, Sibyl. 1968. *Matrix of Man: An Illustrated History of Urban Environment*. New York: Praeger.

Momigliano, A. 1985. "Marcel Mauss and the Quest for the Person in Greek Biography and Autobiography." In *The Category of the Person: Anthropology, Philosophy, History*, edited by Michael Carrithers, Steven Collins, and Steven Lukes, 83–92. Cambridge: Cambridge University Press.

Monson, Andrew, and Walter Scheidel. 2015. "Studying Fiscal Regimes." In *Fiscal Regimes and the Political Economy of Premodern States*, ed. Andrew Monson and Walter Scheidel, 3–28. Cambridge: Cambridge University Press.

Montesquieu, Charles de Secondat. (Original work published 1748) 1989. *The Spirit of the Laws*. Translated and edited by Anne M. Cohler, Basia Carolyn Miller, and Harold Samuel Stone. Cambridge: Cambridge University Press.

Moore, Henrietta, and Todd Sanders, eds. 2006. *Anthropology in Theory: Issues in Epistemology*. Oxford: Blackwell Publishing.

Moore, Mick. 2008. "Between Coercion and Contract: Competing Narratives on Taxation and Governance." In *Taxation and State-Building in Developing Countries: Capacity and Consent*, ed. Deborah Bräutigam, Odd-Helge Fjeldstad, and Mick Moore, 34–63. Cambridge: Cambridge University Press.

Morris, Craig. 1982. "The Infrastructure of Inka Control in the Peruvian Central Highlands." In *The Inca and Aztec States, 1400–1800: Anthropology and History*, edited by George A. Collier, Renato I. Rosaldo, and John D. Wirth, 153–71. New York: Academic Press.

Morris, Desmond. 1967. *The Naked Ape*. New York: Dell Publishing.

Morris, Ian. 1997. "An Archaeology of Equalities? The Greek City-States." In *The Archaeology of City-States: Cross-Cultural Approaches*, edited by Deborah Nichols and Thomas Charlton, 91–105. Washington, DC: Smithsonian Institution Press.

Morris, Ian. 1999. "Negotiated Peripherality in Iron Age Greece: Accepting and Resisting the East." In *World Systems Theory in Practice*, ed. P. N. Kardulias, 63–83. Lanham, MD: Rowman and Littlefield.

Morris, Ian. 2004. "Economic Growth in Ancient Greece." *Journal of Institutional and Theoretical Economics* 160:709–42.

Morris, Ian. 2005. "Archaeology, Standards of Living, and Greek Economic History." In *The Ancient Economy: Evidence and Models*, edited by Joseph G. Manning and Ian Morris, 91–126. Stanford: Stanford University.

Morris, Ian. 2006. "The Growth of Greek Cities in the First Millennium BC." In *Urbanism in the Preindustrial World: Cross-Cultural Approaches*, edited by Glenn R. Storey, 26–51. Tuscaloosa: University of Alabama Press.

Morris, Ian. 2010. *Why the West Rules—For Now: The Patterns of History, and What They Reveal about the Future*. New York: Farrar, Straus, and Giroux.

Morris, William A. 1940. "Introduction." In *The English Government at Work, 1327–1336*, vol. 1: *Central and Prerogative Administration*, edited by William A. Morris, 3–81. Cambridge: Mediaeval Academy of America.

Morrison, Kathleen D. 2001. "Coercion, Resistance, and Hierarchy: Local Processes and Imperial Strategies in the Vijayanagara Empire." In *Empires: Perspectives from Archaeology and History*, edited by Susan E. Alcock, Terence N. D'Altroy, Kathleen D. Morrison, and Carla M. Sinopoli, 252–78. Cambridge: Cambridge University Press.

Morrison, Kathleen D., and Laura L. Junker, eds. 2002. *Forager-Traders in South and Southeast Asia: Long-Term Histories*. Cambridge: Cambridge University Press.

Mote, Frederick W. 1968. "Chinese Political Thought." In *International Encyclopedia of the Social Sciences*, vol. 2. edited by D. L. Sills, 394–408. New York: MacMillan.

Mouffe, Chantal. 2000. *The Democratic Paradox*. London: Verso.

Muir, Edward. 1981. *Civic Ritual in Renaissance Venice*. Princeton: Princeton University Press.

Mukhia, H. 2004. *The Mughals of India*. Oxford: Blackwell.

Mumford, Lewis. 1961. *The City in History: Its Origins, Its Transformations, and Its Prospects*. New York: Harcourt, Brace, and World.

Munro, Donald J. 1969. *The Concept of Man in Early China*. Stanford: Stanford University Press.

Murra, John Victor. 1980. *The Economic Organization of the Inka State. Research in Economic Anthropology, Supplement 1*. Greenwich, CT: JAI Press.

Musgrave, Richard A. 1959. *The Theory of Public Finance*. New York: McGraw-Hill.

Nadel, S. F. 1942. *A Black Byzantium: The Kingdom of Nupe in Nigeria*. London: Oxford University Press.

Nafissi, Mohammad. 2005. *Ancient Athens and Modern Ideology: Value, Theory, and Evidence in Historical Sciences: Max Weber, Karl Polanyi, and Moses Finley. Bulletin of the University of London, Supplement 80*. London: Institute of Classical Studies.

Nakayama, Ken. 2011. "Introduction: Vision Going Social." In *The Science of Social Vision*, edited by Reginald B. Adams Jr., Nalini Ambody, Ken Nakayama, and Shinsuke Shimojo, xv–xxix. Oxford: Oxford University Press.

Naohiro, Asao. 1991. "The Sixteenth Century Unification." In *The Cambridge History of Japan*, vol. 4: *Early Modern Japan*, edited by J. W. Hall, 40–95. Cambridge: Cambridge University Press

Naquin, Susan. 2000. *Peking: Temples and City Life, 1400–1900*. Berkeley: University of California Press.

Neal, Peter. 2003. *Urban Villages and the Making of Communities*. London: Spon Press.

Nelson, Brian R. 2006. *The Making of the Modern State: A Theoretical Evolution*. New York: Palgrave Macmillan.

Nesse, Randolph M. 2001. "Natural Selection and the Capacity for Commitment." In *Evolution and the Capacity for Commitment*, edited by Randolph M. Nesse, 1–44. New York: Russell Sage Foundation.

Netting, Robert Mc. 1990. "Reconsidering the Alpine Village as Ecosystem." In *The Ecosystem Approach in Anthropology: From Concept to Practice*, edited by Emilio Moran, 229–46. Ann Arbor: University of Michigan Press.

Neugebauer, O. 1952. *The Exact Sciences in Antiquity*. Princeton: Princeton University Press.

Newett, M. Margaret. 1907. "The Sumptuary Laws of Venice in the Fourteenth and Fifteenth Centuries." In *Historical Essays: Commemoration of the Jubilee of the Owens*

College, Manchester, edited by T. F. Tout and James Tait, 245–78. Manchester: Manchester University Press.

Nicholson, Harold B. 2001. *Topiltzin Quetzalcoatl: The Once and Future Lord of the Toltecs.* Boulder: University Press of Colorado.

Nobuhiko, Nakai, and James L. McClain. 1991. "Commercial Change and Urban Growth in Early Modern Japan." In *The Cambridge History of Japan*, vol. 4: *Early Modern Japan*, edited by J. W. Hall, 519–95. Cambridge: Cambridge University Press.

Nochlin, Linda. 1989. *The Politics of Vision: Essays on Nineteenth-Century Art and Society.* New York: Harper and Row.

North, Douglass C. 1981. *Structure and Change in Economic History.* New York: W. W. Norton.

North, Douglass C. 1990. *Institutions, Institutional Change, and Economic Performance.* Cambridge: Cambridge University Press.

North, Douglass C., John Joseph Wallis, and Barry R. Weingast. 2009. *Violence and Social Orders: A Conceptual Framework for Interpreting Recorded Human History.* Cambridge: Cambridge University Press.

Norwich, John J. 1982. *A History of Venice.* New York: Alfred A. Knopf.

Nowak, Martin A. 2006. "Five Rules for the Evolution of Cooperation." *Science* 314:1560–63.

Nowak, Martin A., with Roger Highfield. 2011. *Supercooperators: Altruism, Evolution, and Why We Need Each Other to Succeed.* New York: Free Press.

Nowell, April, and Iain Davidson, eds. 2010. *Stone Tools and the Evolution of Human Cognition.* Boulder: University Press of Colorado.

Ober, Josiah. 1994. "Civic Ideology and Counterhegemonic Discourse: Thucydides on the Sicilian Debate." In *Athenian Ideology and Civic Ideology*, edited by Alan L. Boegehold and Adele C. Scafuro, 102–26. Baltimore: Johns Hopkins University Press.

Ober, Josiah. 1995. "Greek Horoi: Artifactual Texts and the Contingency of Meaning." In *Methods in the Mediterranean: Historical and Archaeological Views on Texts and Archaeology*, edited by David B. Small, 91–123. Leiden: E. J. Brill.

Ober, Josiah. 1998. *Political Dissent in Democratic Athens: Intellectual Critics of Popular Rule.* Princeton: Princeton University Press.

Ober, Josiah. 2006. "From Epistemic Diversity to Common Knowledge: Rational Rituals and Publicity in Democratic Athens." *Episteme* 3:214–33.

Ober, Josiah. 2008. *Democracy and Knowledge: Innovation and Learning in Classic Athens.* Princeton: Princeton University Press.

Ober, Josiah. 2010. "Wealthy Helas." *Transactions of the American Philological Association* 140:241–86.

Ober, Josiah, and Barry Strauss. 1990. "Drama, Political Rhetoric, and the Discourse of Athenian Democracy." In *Nothing to Do with Dionysos? Athenian Drama and Its Social*

Context, edited by John J. Winkler and Froma I. Zeitlin, 237–70. Princeton: Princeton University Press.

O'Connor, David B. 1983. "New Kingdom and Third Intermediate Period, 1552–664 B. C." In *Ancient Egypt: A Social History,* edited by Bruce G. Trigger, Barry Kemp, David B. O'Connor, and A. B. Lloyd, 183–278. Cambridge: Cambridge University Press.

O'Connor, David B. 1990. *Ancient Egyptian Society.* Pittsburgh: Carnegie Museum of Natural History.

O'Connor, Richard A. 1995. "Agricultural Change and Ethnic Succession in Southeast Asian States: A Case for Regional Anthropology." *Journal of Asian Studies* 54:968–96.

Offner, Jerome A. 1981. "On the Inapplicability of 'Oriental Despotism' and the 'Asiatic Mode of Production' to the Aztecs of Texcoco." *American Antiquity* 46:43–61.

Offner, Jerome A. 1983. *Law and Politics in Aztec Mexico.* Cambridge: Cambridge University Press.

Oka, Rahul, and Augustín Fuentes. 2010. "From Reciprocity to Trade: How Cooperative Infrastructures Form the Basis of Human Socioeconomic Evolution." In *Cooperation in Economy and Society,* edited by Robert C. Marshall, 3–28. Society for Economic Anthropology, Monographs in Economic Anthropology 28. Lanham, MD: AltaMira Press.

Olson, Mancur. 1965. *The Logic of Collective Action: Public Goods and the Theory of Groups.* Cambridge, MA: Harvard University Press.

Olson, Mancur. 1993. "Democracy, Dictatorship, and Development." *American Political Science Review* 87:567–75.

Ortner, Sherry. 1984. "Theory in Anthropology since the 1960s." *Comparative Studies in Society and History* 26:126–66.

Ortner, Sherry. 1995. "Resistance and the Problem of Ethnographic Refusal." *Comparative Studies in Society and History* 37:173–93.

Orum, Anthony M. 1998. "The Urban Imagination of Sociologists: The Centrality of Place." *Sociological Quarterly* 39:1–10.

Osborne, Robin. 1985. *Demos: The Discovery of Classical Attika.* Cambridge: Cambridge University Press.

Osborne, Robin. 2008. "Idealism, The Body, and the Beard in Classical Greek Art." In *Past Bodies: Body-Centered Research in Archaeology,* edited by D. Boric and John Robb, 29–36. Oxford: Oxbow Books.

Ostojic, Ljerka, Rachel C. Shaw, Lucy G. Cheke, and Nicola S. Clayton. 2013. "Evidence Suggesting That Desire-State Attribution May Govern Food Sharing in Eurasian Jays." *Proceedings of the National Academy of Sciences of the United States of America* 110:4123–28.

Ostrom, Elinor. 1986. "An Agenda for the Study of Institutions." *Public Choice* 48:3–25.

Ostrom, Elinor. 1990. *Governing the Commons: The Evolution of Institutions for Collective Action.* Cambridge: Cambridge University Press.

Ostrom, Elinor. 1998. "A Behavioral Approach to the Rational Choice Theory of Collective Action." *American Political Science Review* 92:1–22.

Ostrom, Elinor. 2000. "An Agenda for the Study of Institutions." In *Polycentric Games and Institutions: Readings from a Workshop in Political Theory and Policy Analysis*, edited by Michael D. McGinnis, 89–113. Ann Arbor: University of Michigan Press.

Ostrom, Elinor. 2005. "Policies That Crowd Out Reciprocity and Collective Action." In *Moral Sentiments and Material Interests: The Foundations of Cooperation in Economic Life*, edited by H. Gintis, S. Bowles, R. Boyd, and E. Fehr, 253–76. Cambridge, MA: MIT Press.

Ostrom, Elinor. 2007. "Collective Action Theory." In *The Oxford Handbook of Comparative Politics*, edited by Carles Boix and Susan C. Stokes, 186–208. Oxford: Oxford University.

Ostrom, Eleanor. 2010. "Beyond Markets and States: Polycentric Governance of Complex Economic Systems." *American Economic Review* 100:641–72.

Ostrom, Elinor, and James Walker. 2000. "Neither Markets nor States: Linking Transformation Process in Collective Action Arenas." In *Polycentric Games and Institutions: Readings from a Workshop in Political Theory and Policy Analysis*, edited by Michael D. McGinnis, 427–71. Ann Arbor: University of Michigan Press.

Ostrom, Elinor, James Walker, and Roy Gardner. 1992. "Covenants with and without a Sword: Self-Governance Is Possible." *American Political Science Review* 86:404–17.

Packer, James E. A. 1967. "Housing and Population in Imperial Ostia and Rome." *Journal of Roman Studies* 57:80–95.

Palmer, Robert E. A. 1990. "Studies of the Northern Campus Martius in Ancient Rome." *Transactions of the American Philosophical Society* 80:1–64.

Panksepp, J. 2007. "Affective Neuroscience and the Ancestral Sources of Human Feelings." In *Consciousness and Cognition: Fragments of Mind and Brain*, edited by Henri Cohen and Brigitte Stemmer, 173–88. Amsterdam: Elsevier.

Parker, Sue Taylor, Robert W. Mitchell, and H. Lyn Miles, eds. 1999. *The Mentalities of Gorillas and Orangutans: Comparative Perspectives*. Cambridge: Cambridge University Press.

Parkinson, William A., and Michael L. Galaty. 2007. "Primary and Secondary States in Perspective: An Integrated Approach to State Formation in the Prehistoric Aegean." *American Anthropologist* 109:113–29.

Parry, Jonathan. 1986. "The Gift, the Indian Gift, and the 'Indian' Gift." (New Series) *Man* 21:453–73.

Parry, Jonathan. 1989. "On the Moral Perils of Exchange." In *Money and the Morality of Exchange*, edited by Jonathan Parry and Maurice Bloch, 64–93. Cambridge: Cambridge University Press.

Parry, Jonathan, and Maurice Bloch, eds. 1989. *Money and the Morality of Exchange*. Cambridge: Cambridge University Press.

Pauketat, Timothy R. 2007. *Chiefdoms and Other Archaeological Delusions. Issues in Eastern Woodland Archaeology*. Lanham, MD: AltaMira Press.

Paul, Robert A. 1995. "Act and Intention in Sherpa Culture and Society." In *Other Intentions: Cultural Contexts and the Attribution of Inner States*, edited by Lawrence Rosen, 15–45. Santa Fe: School of American Research Press.

Peltonen, Markku. 2002. "Citizenship and Republicanism in Elizabethan England." In *Republicanism: A Shared European Heritage*, ed. Martin van Gelderen and Quentin Skinner, 85–106. Cambridge: Cambridge University Press.

Peregrine, Peter N. 2013. "Science and Narrative in the Postmodern World." *American Anthropologist* 155:645.

Perez, Louis G. 2002. *Daily Life in Early Modern Japan*. Westport, CT: Greenwood Press.

Perinbaum, B. Marie. 1980. "The Julas in Western Sudanese History: Long-Distance Traders and Developers of Resources." In *West African Cultural Dynamics: Archaeological and Historical Perspectives*, edited by B. K. Swartz and Raymond E. Dumette, 455–75. The Hague: Mouton.

Peterson, Nicolas. 1993. "Demand Sharing: Reciprocity and Pressure for Generosity among Foragers." *American Anthropologist* 95:860–74.

Pfaff, Donald W. 2015. *The Altruistic Brain: How We Are Naturally Good*. Oxford: Oxford University Press.

Pietilä, Tuulikki. 2007. *Gossip, Markets, and Gender: How Dialogue Constructs Moral Value in Post-Socialist Kilimanjaro*. Madison: The University of Wisconsin Press.

Pinker, Steven. 2011. *The Better Angels of Our Nature: Why Violence Has Declined*. New York: Viking.

Pinker, Steven. 2012. "The False Allure of Group Selection." http://edge.org/conversation /the-false-allure-of-group-selection.

Platt, Colin. 1982. *The Castle in Medieval England and Wales*. New York: Charles Scribner's Sons.

Plucknett, Theodore F. T. 1940. "Parliament." In *The English Government at Work, 1327–1336,*vol. 1: *Central and Prerogative Administration*, edited by W. A. Morris, 82–128. Cambridge: Mediaeval Academy of America.

Pohl, John M. D., John Monaghan, and Laura Stiver. 1997. "Religion, Economy, and Factionalism in the Mixtec Boundary Zones." In *Códices y documentos sobre México: Segundo Simposio*, vol. 1, edited by Salvadore Rueda Smithers, Constanza Vega Sosa, and Rodrigo Martínez Baracs, 205–32. Mexico City: Instituto Nacional de Antropología e Historia y Dirección General de Publicaciones del Consejo Nacional Para la Cultura y las Artes.

Polanyi, Karl. 1944. *The Great Transformation: The Political and Economic Origins of Our Time*. New York: Rinehart & Company.

Polanyi-Levitt, Kari, ed. 1990. *The Life and Work of Karl Polanyi*. Montreal: Black Rose Books.

Pomeranz, Kenneth. 2000. *The Great Divergence: Europe, China, and the Making of the Modern World Economy*. Princeton: Princeton University Press.

Pope, Stephen J. 2004. "Primate Sociality and Natural Law Theory: A Case Study for the Relevance of Science for Ethics." In *The Origins and Nature of Sociality*, edited by Robert W. Sussman and Audrey R. Chapman, 313–31. New York: Aldine de Gruyter.

Popkin, Samuel L. 1979. *The Rational Peasant: The Political Economy of Rural Society in Vietnam*. Berkeley: University of California Press.

Popkin, Samuel L. 1988. "Political Entrepreneurs and Peasant Movements in Vietnam." In *Rationality and Revolution*, edited by Michael Taylor, 9–62. Cambridge: Cambridge University Press.

Popper, Karl R. (Original work published 1945) 1962. *The Open Society and Its Enemies*. London: Routledge and Kegan Paul.

Porter, Martin. 2005. *Windows on the Soul: Physiognomy in European Culture 1470–1780*. Oxford: Clarendon Press.

Possehl, Gregory L. 1998. "Sociocultural Complexity without the State: The Indus Civilization." In *Archaic States*, edited by Gary M. Feinman and Joyce Marcus, 261–92. Santa Fe: School of American Research Press.

Pounds, Norman J. G. 1969. "The Urbanization of the Classic World." *Annals of the Association of American Geographers* 59:135–57.

Povinelli, Daniel. 1996. "Chimpanzee Theory of Mind? The Long Road to Strong Inference." In *Theories of Theories of Mind*, edited by Peter Carruthers and Peter K. Smith, 293–329. Cambridge: Cambridge University Press.

Premack, David. 2004. "Is Language the Key to Human Intelligence?" *Science* 303:318–20.

Price, Michael E. 2012. "Group Selection Theories Are Now More Sophisticated But Are They More Predictive?" *Evolutionary Psychology* 10:45–49.

Price, T. Douglas, and Gary M. Feinman, eds. 2010. *Pathways to Power: New Perspectives on the Emergence of Social Inequality*. New York: Springer.

Prins, A.H.J. 1967. *The Swahili-Speaking Peoples of Zanzibar and the East African Coast (Arabs, Shirazi, and Swahili.) Ethnographic Survey of Africa, East Central Africa 12*. London: International African Institute.

Prins, A.H.J. 1971. *Didemic Lamu: Social Stratification and Spatial Structure in a Muslim Maritime Town*. Groningen, Netherlands: Institut voor Culturele Anthropologie der Rijksvuniversiteit.

Prins, Gwyn. 1980. *The Hidden Hippopotamus: Reappraisal in African History: The Early Colonial Experience in Western Zambia*. Cambridge: Cambridge University Press.

Pritchard, David M. 2010. "The Symbiosis between Democracy and War: The Case of Ancient Athens." In *War, Democracy, and Culture in Ancient Athens*, edited by David Pritchard, 1–62. Cambridge: Cambridge University Press.

Pullan, Brian. 1971. *Rich and Poor in Renaissance Venice: The Social Institutions of a Catholic State, to 1620*. Cambridge, MA: Harvard University Press.

Pyysiäinen, Ilka. 2001. "Cognition, Emotion, and Religious Experience." In *Religion in Mind: Cognitive Perspectives on Religious Belief, Ritual, and Experience*, edited by Jensine Andresen, 70–93. Cambridge: Cambridge University Press.

Rabibhadana, Akin. 1969. *The Organization of Thai Society in the Early Bangkok Period, 1782–1873. Cornell University Southeast Asia Program, Data Paper 74*. Ithaca: Cornell University.

Rahman, Zia Haider. 2014. *In the Light of What We Know*. New York: Farrar, Straus and Giroux.

Rapoport, Amos. 1980–81. "Neighborhood Homogeneity or Heterogeneity: The Field of Man-Environment Studies." *Architecture and Behavior* 1:65–77.

Rappaport, Roy A. 1978. "Maladaptation in Social Systems." In *The Evolution of Social Systems*, edited by J. Friedman and M. J. Rowlands, 49–72. Pittsburgh: University of Pittsburgh.

Rappaport, Roy A. 1979. "The Obvious Aspects of Ritual." In *Ecology, Meaning, and Religion*, edited by Roy A. Rappaport, 173–222. Richmond, CA: North Atlantic Books.

Rattray, R. S. 1923. *Ashanti*. Oxford: Clarendon Press.

Rattray, R. S. 1929. *Ashanti Law and Constitution*. Oxford: Clarendon Press.

Rawski, Evelyn S. 1972. *Agricultural Change and the Peasant Economy of South China*. Cambridge, MA: Harvard University Press.

Rawski, Evelyn S. 1985. "Economic and Social Foundations of Late Imperial China." In *Popular Culture in Late Imperial China*, edited by David G. Johnson, Andrew J. Nathan, and Evelyn S. Rawski, 3–33. Berkeley: University of California Press.

Rawson, Elizabeth. 1994. "Caesar: Civil War and Dictatorship." In *The Cambridge Ancient History: Second Edition*, vol. 9: *The Last Age of the Roman Republic, 146–43 B. C.*, edited by J. A. Crook, A. Lintott, and E. Rawson, 421–67. Cambridge: Cambridge University Press.

Raybeck, Douglas, and Paul Y. L. Ngo. 2011. "Behavior and the Brain: Mediation of Acquired Skills." *Cross-Cultural Research* 45:178–207.

Raymond, André. 1984. "Cairo's Area and Population in the Early Fifteenth Century." *Muqarnas* 2:21–31.

Raymond, André. 1995. "The Role of the Communities (Tawa'if) in the Administration of Cairo in the Ottoman Period." In *The State and Its Servants: Administration in Egypt from Ottoman Times to the Present*, edited by Nelly Hanna, 32–43. Cairo: American University in Cairo Press.

Read, Dwight. 2010. "From Experiential-Based to Relational-Based Forms of Social Organization: A Major Transition in the Evolution of Homo Sapiens." In *Social Brain, Distributed Mind*, edited by Robin Dunbar, Clive Gamble, and John Gowlett, 199–229. Proceedings of the British Academy 158. Oxford: Oxford University Press.

Redfield, James M. 1986. "The Development of the Market in Archaic Greece." In *The Market in History*, edited by B. L. Anderson and A. J. H. Latham, 29–58. London: Croom Helm.

Reid, Anthony. 1975. "Trade and the Problem of Royal Power in Aceh: Three Stages: c. 1550–1700." In *Pre-Colonial State Systems in Southeast Asia*, edited by Anthony Reid and L. Castles, 45–55. Monographs of the Malaysian Branch of the Royal Asiatic Society 6. Kuala Lampur: Royal Asiatic Society.

Reid, Anthony. 1980. "The Structure of Cities in Southeast Asia, Fifteenth to Seventeenth Centuries." *Journal of Southeast Asian Studies* 11:235–50.

Reid, Anthony. 1988. *Expansion and Crisis*. Vol. 2. Southeast Asia in the Age of Commerce, 1450–1680. New Haven: Yale University Press.

Reid, Anthony. 1993. "Introduction, A Time and Place." In *Southeast Asia in the Early Modern Era: Trade, Power, and Belief*, edited by A. Reid, 1–19. Ithaca: Cornell University Press.

Reill, Peter Hanns. 1975. *The German Enlightenment and the Rise of Historicism*. Berkeley: University of California Press.

Renfrew, Colin. 1975. "Trade as Action at a Distance: Questions of Integration and Communication." In *Ancient Civilization and Trade*, edited by Jeremy A. Sabloff and C. C. Lamberg-Karlovsky, 3–60. Albuquerque: University of New Mexico Press.

Rhodes, P. J. 2003. "Nothing to Do with Democracy: Athenian Drama and the Polis." *Journal of Hellenic Studies* 123:104–19.

Reyna, S. P. 1990. *Wars without End*. Hanover, NH: University Press of New England.

Richards, John F. 1998. "The Formulation of Imperial Authority under Akbar and Jahangir." In *Kingship and Authority in South Asia*, edited by J. F. Richards, 285–326. Delhi: Oxford University Press.

Richards, John F. 2012. "Fiscal States in Mughal and British India." In *The Rise of Fiscal States: A Global History 1500–1914*, edited by Bartolomé Yun-Casalilla and Patrick K. O'Brien, 410–41. Cambridge: Cambridge University Press.

Richerson, Peter J., and Robert T. Boyd. 1999. "Complex Societies: The Evolutionary Origins of a Crude Superorganism." *Human Nature (Hawthorne, N.Y.)* 10:253–89.

Roberts, Andrew. 1970. "Nyamwezi Trade." In *Pre-Colonial African Trade: Essays on Trade in Central and Eastern Africa Before 1900*, edited by Richard Gray and David Birmingham, 39–74. New York: Oxford University Press.

Roberts, Sam G. B. 2010. "Constraints on Social Networks." In *Social Brain, Distributed Mind*, edited by Robin Dunbar, Clive Gamble, and John Gowlett, 115–34. Proceedings of the British Academy 158. Oxford: Oxford University Press.

Robertshaw, Peter. 1999. "Women, Labor, and State Formation in Western Uganda." In *Complex Polities in the Ancient Tropical World*, edited by E. A. Bacus and L. J. Lucero, 51–65. Washington, DC: American Anthropological Association.

Robertshaw, Peter. 2003. "The Origins of the State in East Africa." In *East African Archaeology: Foragers Potters, Smiths, and Traders*, ed. Chopururkha M. Kusimba and Sibel B. Kusimba, 149–66. Philadelphia: The University of Pennsylvania Museum of Archaeology and Anthropology.

Robinson, Roger. 1976. *Ways to Move: A Geography of Networks and Accessibility*. Cambridge: Cambridge University Press.

Romano, Dennis. 1987. *Patricians and Popolani: The Social Foundations of the Venetian Renaissance State*. Baltimore: Johns Hopkins University Press.

Roscoe, John. 1923. *The Bakitara or Banyoro*. Cambridge: Cambridge University Press.

Roscoe, John. 1965. *The Baganda: An Account of Their Native Customs and Beliefs*. 2nd ed. London: Frank Cass.

Rose, Hilary, and Steven Rose, eds. 2000. *Alas Poor Darwin: Arguments against Evolutionary Psychology*. New York: Harmony Books.

Rose, Steven. 2000. "Escaping Evolutionary Psychology." In *Alas Poor Darwin: Arguments against Evolutionary Psychology*, edited by Hilary Rose and Steven Rose, 299–320. New York: Harmony Books.

Rosen, Lawrence. 1995. "The Cultural Analysis of Others' Inner States." In *Other Intentions: Cultural Contexts and the Attribution of Inner States*, edited by Lawrence Rosen, 3–11. Santa Fe: School of American Research Press.

Rosenberg, Jakob, Seymour Slive, and Engelbert H. ter Kuile. 1966. *Dutch Art and Architecture, 1600 to 1800*. Baltimore: Penguin.

Ross, Marc Howard. 1992. "Social Structure, Psychological Dispositions, and Violent Conflict: Extensions from a Cross-Cultural Study." In *Aggression and Peacefulness in Humans and Other Primates*, edited by James Silverberg and J. Patrick Gray, 271–93. New York: Oxford University Press.

Ross, Michael L. 1999. "The Political Economy of the Resource Curse." *World Politics* 51:297–322.

Rossi, Paolo. 1970. *Philosophy, Technology, and the Arts in the Early Modern Era*. Translated by Salvator Attanasio. New York: Harper & Row.

Rothstein, Bo. 2005. *Social Traps and the Problem of Trust*. Cambridge: Cambridge University Press.

Ruggiero, Guido. 1980. *Violence in Early Renaissance Venice*. New Brunswick: Rutgers University Press.

Runciman, W. G. 1982. "Origins of States: The Case of Archaic Greece." *Comparative Studies in Society and History* 24(3):351–77.

Russell, Josiah C. 1948. *British Medieval Population*. Albuquerque: University of New Mexico Press.

Ryan, Jason, and Theresa Cook. 2007. "U.S. Spy Chief: 9/11 'Could Have Been Prevented.'" http://abcnews.go.com/TheLaw/story?id=3621517.

Rykwert, Joseph. 1998. *The Idea of a Town: The Anthropology of Urban Form in Rome, Italy, and the Ancient World*. Cambridge, MA: MIT Press.

Sahagún, Fray Bernardino de. 1950–82. *Florentine Codex: General History of the Things of New Spain*. Translated by Charles E. Dibble and Arthur J. O. Anderson. Austin: University of Texas Press.

Sahlins, Marshall. 1965. "On the Sociology of Primitive Exchange." In *The Relevance of Models for Social Anthropology*, edited by Michael Banton, 139–236. A.S.A. Monograph 1. London: Tavistock.

Sahlins, Marshall. 1972. *Stone Age Economics*. Chicago: Aldine-Atherton.

Sahlins, Marshall. 1976. *The Use and Abuse of Biology: An Anthropological Critique of Sociobiology*. Ann Arbor: University of Michigan Press.

Said, Edward. 1978. *Orientalism*. Harmondsworth: Penguin.

Saletore, B. A. 1934. *Social and Political Life in the Vijayanagara Empire (AD 1346–AD 1646)*. 2 vols. Madras: B. G. Paul and Company.

Salisbury, Robert. 1969. "An Exchange Theory of Interest Groups." *Midwest Journal of Political Science* 13:1–32.

Sanders, William T. 2003. "The Population of Tenochtitlan-Tlatelolco." In *El Urbanismo en Mesoamérica: Urbanism in Mesoamerica*, edited by William T. Sanders, Alba Guadalupe Mastache, and Robert H. Cobean, 203–16. Mexico City: Instituto Nacional de Antropología e Historia.

Sanders, William T., and Barbara Price. 1968. *Mesoamerica: The Evolution of a Civilization*. New York: Random House.

Sanderson, Alexis. 1985. "Purity and Power among the Brahmans of Kashmir." In *The Category of the Person: Anthropology, Philosophy, History*, edited by Michael Carrithers, Steven Collins, and Steven Lukes, 190–216. Cambridge: Cambridge University Press.

Sarkar, Jadunath. 1963. *Mughal Administration*. 5th ed. Calcutta: M. C. Sarkar and Sons.

Sawyer, Peter. 1986. "Early Fairs and Markets in England and Scandinavia." In *The Market in History*, edited by B. L. Anderson and A. J. H. Latham, 59–78. London: Croom Helm.

Saxe, Rebecca, and Simon Baron-Cohen, eds. 2007. *Theory of Mind, A Special Issue of Social Neuroscience*. Hove, East Sussex: Psychology Press.

Scagnetti, F., and G. Grande. 1978. *Pianta Topografica a Colori di Roma Antica*. Rome: ME di Maggiore Cristina.

Schegloff, Emanuel A. 2006. "Interaction: The Infrastructure for Social Institutions, the Natural Ecological Niche for Language and the Arena in Which Culture Is Enacted." In *Roots of Human Sociality: Culture, Cognition, and Interaction*, edited by N. J. Enfield and Steven Levinson, 70–96. Oxford: Berg.

Scheidel, Walter. 2010. "Real Wages in Early Economies: Evidence for Living Standards from 1800 BCE to 1300 CE." *Journal of Economic and Social History of the Orient* 53:425–62.

Schmidt, Karen L., and Jeffrey F. Cohn. 2001. "Human Facial Expressions as Adaptations: Evolutionary Questions in Facial Expression Research." *Yearbook of Physical Anthropology* 44:3–24.

Schneewind, Sarah. 2006. *Community Schools and the State in Ming China.* Stanford: Stanford University Press.

Schofield, N. 1985. "Anarchy, Altruism, and Cooperation." *Social Choice and Welfare* 2:207–19.

Schrieke, B. 1957. *Indonesian Sociological Studies, Part Two: Ruler and Realm in Early Java.* The Hague: W. van Hoere.

Schulte-Nordholt, Henk. 1996. *The Spell of Power: A History of Balinese Politics, 1650–1940.* Leiden: KITLV Press.

Schumpeter, Joseph A. 1991. "The Crisis of the Tax State." In *Joseph A. Schumpeter: The Economics and Sociology of Capitalism,* edited by Richard Swedberg, 99–140. Princeton: Princeton University Press.

Schwartz, Theodore. 1963. "Systems of Areal Integration: Some Considerations Based on the Admiralty Islands of Northern Melanesia." *Anthropological Forum* 11:56–97.

Scott, James C. 1976. *The Moral Economy of the Peasant: Rebellion and Subsistence in Southeast Asia.* New Haven: Yale University Press.

Scott, James C. 1990. *Domination and the Arts of Resistance: Hidden Transcripts.* New Haven: Yale University Press.

Scott, James C. 1998. *Seeing Like a State: How Certain Schemes to Improve the Human Condition Have Failed.* New Haven: Yale University Press.

Scott, James C. 2009. *The Art of Not Being Governed: An Anarchist History of Upland Southeast Asia.* New Haven: Yale University Press.

Sefton, Martin, Robert Shupp, and James M. Walker. 2007. "The Effect of Rewards and Sanctions on the Provision of Public Goods." *Economic Inquiry* 45:671–90.

Segalen, Martine. 1986. *Historical Anthropology of the Family.* Cambridge: Cambridge University Press.

Sen, Amartya. 1977. "Rational Fools: A Critique of the Behavioral Foundations of Economic Theory." *Philosophy & Public Affairs* 6:317–44.

Sen, Amartya. 1987. *On Ethics and Economics.* Oxford: Basil Blackwell.

Sen, Amartya. 2002. *Rationality and Freedom.* Cambridge, MA: Harvard University Press.

Sen, Amartya. 2005. *The Argumentative Indian: Writings on Indian History, Culture, and Identity.* New York: Farrar, Straus and Giroux.

Sen, Geeti. 1984. *Paintings from the Akbar Nama: A Visual Chronicle of Mughal India.* Calcutta: Lustre Press Pvt. Ltd.

Sewell, William H., Jr. 1985. "Ideologies and Social Revolutions: Reflections on the French Case." *Journal of Modern History* 57:57–85.

Sewell, William H., Jr. 1992. "A Theory of Structure: Duality, Agency, and Transformation." *American Journal of Sociology* 98:1–29.

Seyfarth, Robert M., and Dorothy L. Cheney. 2012. "Knowledge of Social Relations." In *The Evolution of Primate Societies*, edited by John C. Mitani, Josep Call, Peter M. Kappeler, Ryne A. Palombit, and Joan B. Silk, 628–42. Chicago: University of Chicago Press.

Shatzman-Steinhardt, Nancy. 1986. "Why Were Chang'an and Beijing so Different?" *Journal of the Society of Architectural Historians* 45:339–57.

Shaw, Brent D. 1981. "Rural Markets in North Africa and the Political Economy of the Roman Empire." *Antiquités Africaines* 17:37–83.

Shelach, Gideon, and Yuri Pines. 2008. "Secondary State Formation and the Development of Local Identity: Change and Continuity in the State of Qin (770–221 B.C.)." In *Archaeology of Asia*, edited by Miriam T. Stark, 202–30. Hoboken, NJ: Blackwell Publishing.

Shen, Chen. 2003. "Compromises and Conflicts: Production and Commerce in the Royal Cities of Eastern Zhou, China." In *The Social Construction of Ancient Cities*, edited by Monica L. Smith, 290–310. Washington, DC: Smithsonian Books.

Shennan, Stephen. 1988. *Quantifying Archaeology*. San Diego: Academic Press.

Shepherd, William R. 1911. *Historical Atlas*. New York: Henry Holt.

Shils, Edward A. 1961. "Centre and Periphery." In *The Logic of Personal Knowledge: Essays Presented to Michael Polanyi on His Seventieth Birthday*, edited by Edward A. Shils, 117–30. Glencoe, IL: Free Press.

Sickman, Laurence C. S., and Alexander C. Soper. 1960. *The Art and Architecture of China*. Baltimore: Penguin.

Siegel, Bernard J., and Alan R. Beals. 1962. "Pervasive Factionalism." *American Anthropologist* 62:394–417.

Silver, Morris. 1983. "Karl Polanyi and Markets in the Ancient Near East: The Challenge of the Evidence." *Journal of Economic History* 43:795–825.

Silverman, Marilyn, and Richard F. Salisbury, eds. 1977. *A House Divided? Anthropological Studies of Factionalism. Institute of Social and Economic Research, Social and Economic Papers 9. Newfoundland, Canada*. St. John's: Memorial University of Newfoundland.

Simon, Herbert A. 1969. *The Sciences of the Artificial*. Cambridge, MA: MIT Press.

Simpson, Jeffrey A., and Lane Beckes. 2010. "Evolutionary Perspectives on Prosocial Behavior." In *Prosocial Motives, Emotions, and Behavior: The Better Angels of Our Nature*, edited by Mario Mikulincer and Philip R. Sharer, 35–53. Washington, DC: American Psychological Association.

Sinha, D. P. 1963. "The Role of the Phariya in Tribal Acculturation in a Central Indian Market." *Ethnology* 2:170–79.

Sinopoli, Carla M. 1994. "Political Choices and Economic Strategies in the Vijayanagara Empire." In *The Economic Anthropology of the State*, edited by Elizabeth Brumfiel,

223–42. Society for Economic Anthropology, Monographs 11. Lanham, MD: University Press of America.

Sjoberg, Gideon. 1960. *The Preindustrial City, Past and Present*. Glencoe: Free Press.

Skinner, Elliott P. 1962. "Trade and Markets among the Mossi People." In *Markets in Africa*, edited by Paul Bohannon and George Dalton, 190–210. Evanston, IL: Northwestern University Press.

Skinner, G. William. 1964. "Marketing and Social Structure in Rural China, Part I." *Journal of Asian Studies* 24:3–43.

Skinner, G. William. 1965a. "Marketing and Social Structure in Rural China, Part II." *Journal of Asian Studies* 24:195–228.

Skinner, G. William. 1965b. "Marketing and Social Structure in Rural China, Part III." *Journal of Asian Studies* 24:363–99.

Skinner, G. William. 1971. "Chinese Peasants and the Closed Community: An Open and Shut Case." *Comparative Studies in Society and History* 13:270–81.

Skinner, G. William. 1985. "Rural Marketing in China: Revival and Reappraisal." In *Markets and Marketing*, edited by Stuart Plattner, 7–48. Society for Economic Anthropology. Monographs in Economic Anthropology 4. Lanham, MD: University Press of America.

Skinner, G. William, ed. 1977. *The City in Late Imperial China*. Stanford: Stanford University Press.

Slicher van Bath, B. H. 1963. *The Agrarian History of Western Europe*. Translated by Olive Ordish. London: Edward Arnold.

Small, David B. 2009. "The Dual-Processual Model in Ancient Greece: Applying a Post-Neoevolutionary Model to a Data-Rich Environment." *Journal of Anthropological Archaeology* 28:205–21.

Smelser, Neil J., and Richard Swedberg. 2005. "Introducing Economic Sociology." In *The Handbook of Economic Sociology*, 2nd ed., edited by Neil J. Smelser and Richard Swedberg, 3–25. Princeton: Princeton University Press.

Smith, Adam. (Original work published 1759) 1969. *The Theory of Moral Sentiments*. New Rochelle, NY: Arlington House.

Smith, Adam. (Original work published 1776) 1993. *An Inquiry into the Nature and Causes of the Wealth of Nations: A Selected Edition*. Edited by Kathryn Sutherland. Oxford: Oxford University Press.

Smith, Carol A. 1974. "Economics of Marketing Systems: Models from Economic Geography." *Annual Review of Anthropology* 3:167–201.

Smith, Carol A. 1976. "Regional Economic Systems: Linking Geographical Models and Socioeconomic Problems." In *Regional Analysis*, vol. 1: *Economic Systems*, edited by Carol A. Smith, 3–68. New York: Academic Press.

Smith, Carol A. 1985. "How to Count Onions: Methods for a Regional Analysis of Marketing." In *Markets and Marketing*, edited by Stuart Plattner, 49–78. Society for

Economic Anthropology, Monographs in Economic Anthropology 4. Lanham, MD: University Press of America.

Smith, Henry D. 1978. "Tokyo as an Idea: An Exploration of Japanese Urban Thought until 1945." *Journal of Japanese Studies* 4:45–80.

Smith, M. Brewster. 1985. "The Metaphorical Basis of Selfhood." In *Culture and Self: Asian and Western Perspectives*, edited by Anthony J. Marsella, George DeVos, and Francis L. K. Hsu, 56–88. New York: Tavistock Publications.

Smith, Michael E. 1987. "Household Possessions and Wealth in Agrarian States: Implications for Archaeology." *Journal of Anthropological Archaeology* 6:297–335.

Smith, Michael E. 2003. *The Aztecs*. 2nd ed. Malden, MA: Blackwell.

Smith, Michael E. 2007. "Form and Meaning in the Earliest Cities: A New Approach to Ancient Urban Planning." *Journal of Planning History* 6:3–47.

Smith, Michael E. 2010. "The Archaeological Study of Neighborhoods and Districts in Ancient Cities." *Journal of Anthropological Archaeology* 29:137–54.

Smith, Michael E. 2011. "Empirical Urban Theory for Archaeologists." *Journal of Archaeological Method and Theory* 18:167–92.

Smith, Michael E., and Frances F. Berdan, eds. 2003. *The Postclassic Mesoamerican World*. Salt Lake City: University of Utah Press.

Smith, Peter K. 1996. "Language and the Evolution of Mind-Reading." In *Theories of Theories of Mind*, edited by Peter Carruthers and Peter K. Smith, 344–54. Cambridge: Cambridge University Press.

Smith, Stuart T. 1995. *Askut in Nubia: The Economics and Ideology of Egyptian Imperialism in the Second Millennium B. C.* London: Kegan Paul International.

Smith-Doerr, Laurel, and Walter W. Powell. 2005. "Networks and Economic Life." In *The Handbook of Economic Sociology*, 2nd ed., edited by Neil J. Smelser and Richard Swedberg, 379–402. Princeton: Princeton University Press.

Snodgrass, Anthony. 1981. *Archaic Greece: The Age of Experiment*. Berkeley: University of California Press.

Snow, Dean R. 2009. "The Multidisciplinary Study of Human Migration." In *Ancient Human Migrations: A Multidisciplinary Approach*, ed. Peter N. Peregrine, Ilia Peiros, and Marcus Feldman, 6–20. Salt Lake City: The University of Utah Press.

Solso, Robert. 2003. *The Psychology of Art and the Evolution of the Conscious Brain*. Cambridge, MA: MIT Press.

Sosis, Richard, and Candace Alcorta. 2003. "Signaling, Solidarity, and the Sacred: The Evolution of Religious Behavior." *Evolutionary Anthropology* 12:264–74.

Sosis, Richard, and Eric R. Bressler. 2003. "Cooperation and Commune Longevity: A Test of the Costly Signaling Theory of Religion." *Cross-Cultural Research* 37:211–39.

Spawforth, Antony J. S. 1996. "Markets and Fairs." In *The Oxford Classical Dictionary*, edited by Simon Hornblower and Antony Spawforth, 926. New York: Oxford University Press.

Spielmann, Katherine Ann. 1986. "Interdependence among Egalitarian Societies." *Journal of Anthropological Archaeology* 5:279–312.

Spiro, Melford E. 1993. "Is the Western Concept of the Self 'Peculiar' within the Context of World Cultures?" *Ethos (Berkeley, Calif.)* 21:107–53.

Spufford, Margaret. 1984. *The Great Reclothing of Rural England: Petty Chapmen and Their Wares in the Seventeenth Century*. London: Hambledon Press.

Stallybrass, Peter, and Allon White. 1986. *The Politics and Poetics of Transgression*. Ithaca: Cornell University Press.

Stark, Barbara L. 2014. "Ancient Open Space, Gardens, and Parks: A Comparative Study of Mesoamerican Urbanism." In *Making Ancient Cities: Space and Place in Early Urban Societies*, edited by Andrew T. Creekmore, III, and Kevin D. Fisher, 370–406. Cambridge: Cambridge University Press.

Steiner, Christopher B. 1990. "Body Personal and Body Politic: Adornment and Leadership in Cross-Cultural Perspective." *Anthropos* 85:431–45.

Steinhardt, Nancy S. 1990. *Chinese Imperial City Planning*. Honolulu: University of Hawaii Press.

Sterling, Richard W., and William C. Scott. 1985. *Plato: The Republic*. New York: W. W. Norton.

Stiglitz, Joseph E. 2002. *Globalization and its Discontents*. New York: W. W. Norton.

Stocking, George W., Jr. 2001. *Delimiting Anthropology*. Madison: University of Wisconsin Press.

Stone, Elizabeth C. 2008. "A Tale of Two Cities: Lowland Mesopotamia and Highland Anatolia." In *The Ancient City: New Perspectives on Urbanism in the Old and New World*, edited by Joyce Marcus and Jeremy A. Sabloff, 141–64. Santa Fe: School for Advanced Research.

Stone, Valerie E. 2006. "Theory of Mind and the Evolution of Social Intelligence." In *Social Neuroscience: People Thinking about Thinking People*, edited by John T. Cacioppo, Penny S. Visser, and Cynthia L. Pickett, 103–29. Cambridge, MA: MIT Press.

Storey, Glenn R. 1997. "The Population of Ancient Rome." *Antiquity* 71:966–78.

Storey, Glenn R. 2002. "Regionaries-Type Insulae 2: Architectural/Residential Units at Rome." *American Journal of Archaeology* 106:411–34.

Storey, Glenn R. 2006a. "Introduction: Urban Demography of the Past." In *Urbanism in the Pre-Industrial World*, edited by Glenn R. Storey, 1–26. Tuscaloosa: University of Alabama Press.

Storey, Glenn R., ed. 2006b. *Urbanism in the Pre-Industrial World*. Tuscaloosa: University of Alabama Press.

Storey, Rebecca. 1992. *Life and Death in the Ancient City of Teotihuacan*. Tuscaloosa: University of Alabama Press.

Strassmann, Beverly I. 2011. "Cooperation and Competition in a Cliff-Dwelling People." *Proceedings of the National Academy of Sciences of the United States of America* 108 (Supplement 2): 10894–901.

Strathern, Andrew. 1982. "Two Waves of African Models in the New Guinea Highlands." In *Inequality in New Guinea Highlands Societies*, edited by Andrew Strathern, 35–49. Cambridge: Cambridge University Press.

Strayer, Joseph R. 1947. "Introduction." In *The English Government at Work, 1327–1336*, vol. 2: *Fiscal Administration*, edited by W. A. Morris and J. R. Strayer, 3–40. Cambridge: Mediaeval Academy of America.

Stuart-Fox, David J. 1991. "Pura Besakih: Temple-State Relations from Precolonial to Modern Times." In *State and Society in Bali: Historical, Textual, and Anthropological Approaches*, edited by Hildred Geertz, 11–41. Leiden: KITLV Press.

Subrahmanyam, Sanjay, ed. 1998. *Money and Market in India 1100–1700*. Delhi: Oxford University Press.

Sung-hsing, Wang. 1985. "On the Household and Family in Chinese Society." In *The Chinese Family and Its Ritual Behavior*, edited by H. Jih-Chang and C. Ying-Chang, 50–58. Taipei: Academica Sinica, Institute of Ethnology.

Sussman, Robert W., and Audrey R. Chapman. 2004. "The Nature and Evolution of Sociality." In *The Origins and Nature of Sociality*, edited by Robert W. Sussman and Audrey R. Chapman, 3–19. New York: Aldine de Gruyter.

Sussman, Robert W., and Paul A. Garber. 2004. "Rethinking Sociality: Cooperation and Aggression among Primates." In *The Origins and Nature of Sociality*, edited by Robert W. Sussman and Audrey R. Chapman, 161–90. New York: Aldine de Gruyter.

Sweet, Dennis. 1999. "The Birth of Tragedy." *Journal of the History of Ideas* 60 (2): 345–59.

Tambiah, Stanley Jeyaraja. 1976. *World Conqueror and World Renouncer: A Study of Buddhism and Polity in Thailand against a Historical Background*. Cambridge: Cambridge University Press.

Tambiah, Stanley Jeyaraja. 1985. "A Performative Approach to Ritual." In *Culture, Thought, and Social Action: An Anthropological Perspective*, edited by Stanley Tambiah, 123–66. Cambridge, MA: Harvard University Press.

Tatsuya, Tsuji. 1991. "Politics in the Eighteenth Century." In *The Cambridge History of Japan*, vol. 4: *Early Modern Japan*, edited by J. W. Hall, 425–77. Cambridge: Cambridge University Press.

Taylor, Michael. 1982. *Community, Anarchy, and Liberty*. Cambridge: Cambridge University Press.

Taylor, Romeyn. 1998. "Official Religion in the Ming." In *The Cambridge History of China, Volume 8, The Ming Dynasty, 1368–1644, Part 2*, edited by Dennis Twitchett and F. W. Mote, 840–92. Cambridge: Cambridge University Press.

Temin, Peter. 2013. *The Roman Market Economy*. Princeton: Princeton University Press.

Thackston, Wheeler M. 2002. "Literature." In *The Magnificent Mughals*, edited by Z. Zeenut, 83–112. Oxford: Oxford University Press.

Thapar, Romila. 1992. *Interpreting Early India*. Delhi: Oxford University Press.

Thirsk, Joan. 1967. "The Farming Regions of England." In *The Agrarian History of England and Wales*, vol. 4: *1500–1640*, edited by Joan Thirsk, 1–112. Cambridge: Cambridge University Press.

Thompson, E. P. 1971. "The Moral Economy of the English Crowd in the Eighteenth Century." *Past & Present* 50:76–136.

Thompson, Homer A., and R. E. Wycherley. 1972. "The Agora of Athens: The History, Shape and Uses of an Ancient City Center." *Athenian Agora* 14:iii–257.

Thompson, Michael, Richard Ellis, and Aaron Wildavsky. 1990. *Cultural Theory*. Boulder: Westview Press.

Thurnwald, Richard. 1932. *Economics in Primitive Communities*. Oxford: Oxford University Press.

Thurston, Tina L. 2001. *Landscapes of Power, Landscapes of Conflict: State Formation in the South Scandinavian Iron Age*. New York: Kluwer Academic/Plenum Publishers.

Thurston, Tina L. 2010. "Bitter Arrows and Generous Gifts: What Was a 'King' in the European Iron Age?" In *Pathways to Power: New Perspectives on the Emergence of Social Inequality*, edited by T. Douglas Price and Gary Feinman, 193–254. New York: Springer.

Thurston, Tina L., and Christopher T. Fisher, eds. 2007. *Seeking a Richer Harvest: The Archaeology of Subsistence Intensification, Innovation, and Change*. New York: Springer Science+Business Media.

T'ien, Ju-K'ang. 1953. *The Chinese of Sarawak: A Study of Social Structure*. London: London School of Economics and Political Science, Department of Anthropology.

Tilly, Charles. 1975a. "Reflections on the History of European State-Making." In *The Formation of National States in Western Europe*, edited by Charles Tilly, 3–83. Princeton: Princeton University Press.

Tilly, Charles. 1975b. "Western State-Making and Theories of Political Transformation." In *The Formation of National States in Western Europe*, edited by Charles Tilly, 601–38. Princeton: Princeton University Press.

Tilly, Charles. 1985. "War Making and State Making as Organized Crime." In *Bringing the State Back*, edited by Peter B. Evans, Dietrich Rueschemeyer, and Theda Skocpol, 169–91. Cambridge: Cambridge University Press.

Tilly, Charles. 1990. *Coercion, Capital, and European States, AD 990–1990*. Oxford: Basil Blackwell.

Tomlinson, Richard A. 1992. *From Mycenae to Constantinople: The Evolution of the Ancient City*. London: Routledge.

Tooby, John, and Leda Cosmides. 1992. "The Psychological Foundations of Culture." In *The Adapted Mind: Evolutionary Psychology and the Generation of Culture*, edited by Jerome H. Barkow, Leda Cosmides, and John Tooby, 19–136. New York: Oxford University.

Topsfield, Andrew. 2008. *Paintings from Mughal India*. Oxford: Bodleian Library, University of Oxford.

Tosh, John. 1970. "The Northern Interlacustrine Region." In *Pre-Colonial African Trade: Essays on Trade in Central and Eastern Africa Before 1900*, edited by Richard Gray and David Birmingham, 103–18. New York: Oxford University Press.

Toshio, Furushima. 1991. "The Village and Agriculture during the Edo Period." In *The Cambridge History of Japan*, vol. 4: *Early Modern Japan*, edited by J. W. Hall, 478–515. Cambridge: Cambridge University Press.

Trigger, Bruce G. 2003. *Understanding Early Civilizations: A Comparative Study*. Cambridge: Cambridge University Press.

Trivers, Robert L. 1971. "The Evolution of Reciprocal Altruism." *Quarterly Review of Biology* 46 (4): 35–57.

Trivers, Robert L. 1974. "Parent-Offspring Conflict." *American Zoologist* 14:249–64.

Trubitt, Mary Beth D. 2000. "Mound Building and Prestige Goods Exchange: Changing Strategies in the Cahokia Chiefdom." *American Antiquity* 675:669–90.

Turchin, Peter. 2006. *War and Peace and War: The Life Cycles of Imperial Nations*. New York: Pi Press.

Turner, Bryan S. 1983. *Religion and Social Theory: A Materialist Perspective*. London: Heinemann Educational Books.

Turner, Jonathan H., and Alexandra Maryanski. 1979. *Functionalism*. Menlo Park, CA: Benjamin/Cummings Publishing Company.

Turner, Victor. 1969. *The Ritual Process: Structure and Anti-Structure*. Ithaca: Cornell University Press.

Turner, Victor, and Edith L. B. Turner. 1978. *Image and Pilgrimage in Christian Culture*. New York: Columbia University Press.

Tyler, Stephen A. 2006. "The Antinomies." In *Anthropology in Theory: Issues in Epistemology*, edited by Henrietta Moore and Todd Sanders, 305–10. Oxford: Blackwell.

Umberger, Emily. 2014. "Tezcatlipoca and Huitzilopochtli: Political Dimensions of Aztec Deities." In *Tezcatlipoca: Trickster and Supreme Deity*, edited by Elizabeth Baquedano, 83–112. Boulder: University Press of Colorado.

Uslaner, Eric M. 2000. "Producing and Consuming Trust." *Political Science Quarterly* 115:569–90.

van Aert, Laura. 2006. "Trade and Gender Emancipation: Retailing Women in Sixteenth-Century Antwerp." In *Buyers and Sellers: Retail Circuits and Practices in Medieval and Early Modern Europe*, edited by Bruno Blondé, 297–313. Turhout, Belgium: Brepols Publishers.

van Gennep, Arnold. 1909. *The Rites of Passage.* Translated by Monika B. Vizedom and Gabrielle L. Caffee. London: Routledge and Kegan Paul.

Vansina, Jan. 1973. *The Tio Kingdom of the Middle Congo, 1880–1892.* London: International African Institute and Oxford University Press.

van Tilburg, Cornelius. 2007. *Traffic and Congestion in the Roman Empire.* London: Routledge.

Van Zanden, Jan Luiten. 2009. *The Long Road to the Industrial Revolution: The European Economy in Global Perspective, 1000–1800.* Leiden: Brill.

van Zantwijk, Rudolf A. M. 1985. *The Aztec Arrangement: The Social History of Pre-Spanish Mexico.* Norman: University of Oklahoma Press.

Vaporis, Constantine N. 1997. "To Edo and Back: Alternate Attendance and Japanese Culture in the Early Modern Period." *Journal of Japanese Studies* 23:25–67.

Vasina, Jan. 1978. *The Children of Woot: A History of the Kuba Peoples.* Madison: University of Wisconsin Press.

Vella, Walter F. 1957. *Siam under Rama III, 1824–1851.* New York: Augustin, Locust Valley.

Verdery, Katherine. 1991. "Theorizing Socialism: A Prologue to the 'Transition.'" *American Ethnologist* 18:419–39.

Verma, S. D. 1994. *Mughal Painters and Their Work: A Biographical Survey and Comprehensive Catalogue.* Delhi: Oxford University Press.

Veyne, Paul. 1990. *Bread and Circuses: Historical Sociology and Political Pluralism.* Trans. B. Pearce. London: Penguin Books.

Vidal-Naquet, Pierre. 1981. *The Black Hunter: Forms of Thought and Forms of Society in the Greek World.* Translated by Andrew Szegedy-Maszak. Baltimore: Johns Hopkins University Press.

Vinograd, Richard. 1992. *Boundaries of the Self: Chinese Portraits, 1600–1900.* Cambridge: Cambridge University Press.

Vitkin, Mikhail A. 1981. "Marx and Weber on the Primary State." In *The Study of the State,* edited by H.J.M. Claessen and P. Skalník, 443–54. The Hague: Mouton.

von Glahn, Richard. 1991. "Municipal Reform and Urban Social Conflict in Late Ming Jiangnan." *Journal of Asian Studies* 50:280–307.

von Grunebaum, G. E. 1961. *Islam: Essays in the Nature and Growth of a Cultural Tradition.* New York: Barnes and Noble.

von Herder, Johann Gottfried. (Original work published 1774) 1978. "Yet Another Philosophy of History." In *Main Currents of Western Thought: Readings in Western European Intellectual History from the Middle Ages to the Present,* edited by Franklin Le Van Baumer, 495–97. New Haven: Yale University Press.

Wagley, Charles. 1969. "Cultural Influences on Population: A Comparison of Two Tupí Tribes." In *Environment and Cultural Behavior: Ecological Studies in Cultural Anthropology,* edited by Andrew P. Vayda, 268–80. New York: Natural History Press.

Walker, Kathy Le Mons. 1999. *Chinese Modernity and the Peasant Path: Semicolonialism in the Northern Yangzi Delta*. Stanford: Stanford University Press.

Wallace, Robert. 1998. "Solonian Democracy." In *Democracy 2500? Questions and Challenges*, edited by Ian Morris and Kurt Raaflaub, 11–29. Archaeological Institute of America, Colloquia and Conference Papers 2. Dubuque, IA: Kendall/Hunt Publishing Company.

Ward-Perkins, Bryan. 2005. *The Fall of Rome and the End of Civilization*. New York: Oxford University Press.

Watanabe, John M., and Barbara B. Smuts. 1999. "Explaining Religion without Explaining It Away: Trust, Truth, and the Evolution of Cooperation in Roy Rappaport's 'The Obvious Aspects of Ritual.'" *American Anthropologist* 101:98–112.

Watanabe, John M., and Barbara B. Smuts. 2004. "Cooperation, Commitment, and Communication in the Evolution of Human Sociality." In *The Origins and Nature of Sociality*, edited by Robert W. Sussman and Audrey R. Chapman, 288–309. New York: Aldine de Gruyter.

Watson, William. 2000. *The Arts of China 900–1620*. New Haven: Yale University Press.

Watts, David P. 2002. "Reciprocity and Interchange in the Social Relationships of Wild Male Chimpanzees." *Behaviour* 139:343–70.

Waugh, Scott L. 1991. *England in the Reign of Edward III*. Cambridge: Cambridge University Press.

Weber, Max. 1946. *From Max Weber: Essays in Sociology*. Edited and translated by H. H. Gerth and C. Wright Mills. New York: Oxford University Press.

Weber, Max. 1947. *The Theory of Social and Economic Organization*. Translated by A. M. Henderson and Talcott Parsons. New York: Free Press.

Weber, Max. (Original work published 1922) 1978. *Economy and Society*. Edited by Guenther Roth and Claus Wittich. Berkeley: University of California Press.

Wegner, Daniel. 2009. "How to Say, Think, or Do the Precisely Worst Thing for Any Occasion." *Science* 325:48–50.

Wei-ming, Tu. 1985. "Selfhood and Otherness in Confucian Thought." In *Culture and the Self: Asian and Western Perspectives*, edited by Anthony J. Marsella, George DeVos, and Francis L. K. Hsu, 231–51. New York: Tavistock Publications.

West, Stuart A., Claire El Mouden, and Andy Gardner. 2011. "Sixteen Common Misconceptions about the Evolution of Cooperation in Humans." *Evolution and Human Behavior* 32:231–62.

Weston, Dagmar Motycka. 2012. "Greek Theatre as an Embodiment of Cultural Meaning." In *The Cultural Role of Architecture: Contemporary and Historical Perspectives*, edited by Paul Emmons, John Hendrix, and Jane Lomholt, 5–17. New York: Routledge.

Wheatley, Paul. 1971. *The Pivot of the Four Quarters: A Preliminary Inquiry into the Origins and Character of the Ancient Chinese City*. Chicago: Aldine Publishing Company.

Whitby, Michael. 1998. "The Grain Trade of Athens in the Fourth Century BC." In *Trade, Traders, and the Ancient City*, edited by Helen Parkins and Christopher J. Smith, 99–124. New York: Routledge.

White, Leslie. 1949. *The Science of Culture*. New York: Grove Press.

Whitehead, Jane. 1993. "The 'Cena Trimalchionis' and Biographical Narration in Roman Middle-Class Art." In *Narrative and Event in Ancient Art*, edited by Peter J. Holliday, 299–325. Cambridge: Cambridge University Press.

Whiten, Andrew. 1996. "When Does Smart Behavior-Reading Become Mind Reading?" In *Theories of Theories of Mind*, edited by Peter Carruthers and Peter K. Smith, 277–92. Cambridge: Cambridge University Press.

Whiten, Andrew, and Richard W. Byrne, eds. 1997. *Machiavellian Intelligence II: Extensions and Evaluations*. Cambridge: Cambridge University.

Whitley, James. 2001. *The Archaeology of Ancient Greece*. Cambridge: Cambridge University Press.

Wiens, Mi Chu. 1988. "Social Change and Fiscal Reform in the Fifteenth Century." *Ming Studies* 26:18–36.

Wiessner, Polly. 1982. "Risk, Reciprocity and Social Influences on! Kung San Economics." In *Politics and History in Band Societies*, edited by Eleanor Leacock and Richard Lee, 61–84. Cambridge: Cambridge University Press.

Wilcox, David. 1991. "Changing Contexts of Pueblo Adaptations: A. D. 1250–1600." In *Farmers, Hunters, and Colonists: Interaction between the Southwest and the Southern Plains*, edited by Katherine A. Spielmann, 128–54. Tucson: University of Arizona Press.

Wilkinson, Bertie. 1940. "The Chancery." In *The English Government at Work, 1327–1336*, vol. 1: *Central and Prerogative Administration*, edited by W. A. Morris, 162–205. Cambridge: Mediaeval Academy of America.

Wilks, Ivor. 1975. *Asante in the Nineteenth Century: The Structure and Evolution of a Political Order*. Cambridge: Cambridge University Press.

Wilks, Ivor. 1993. *Forests of Gold: Essays on the Akan and the Kingdom of Asante*. Athens: Ohio University Press.

Willett, Frank. 1972. "Ife, The Art of an Ancient Nigerian Aristocracy." In *African Art and Leadership*, edited by Douglas Fraser and Herbert M. Cole, 209–26. Madison: University of Wisconsin Press.

Williams, Barbara J., and Herbert R. Harvey. 1988. "Content, Provenience, and Significance of the Codex Vergara and the Codice de Santa Maria Asunción." *American Antiquity* 53:337–51.

Williams, Barbara J., and María del Carmen Jorge y Jorge. 2008. "Aztec Arithmetic Revisited: Land-Area Algorithms and Acolhua Congruence Arithmetic." *Science* 320:72–77.

Williamson, Oliver E. 1975. *Markets and Hierarchies: Analysis of Antitrust Implications: A Study in the Economics of Internal Organization*. New York: Free Press.

Wilmsen, Edwin N., and James R. Denbow. 1990. "Paradigmatic History of San-Speaking Peoples and Current Attempts at Revision." *Current Anthropology* 31:489–523.

Wilson, David Sloan. 2002. *Darwin's Cathedral: Evolution of Religion, and the Nature of Society*. Chicago: University of Chicago.

Wilson, Edward O. 1975. *Sociobiology: The New Synthesis*. Cambridge: Harvard University Press.

Wilson, Edward O. 2013. Commentary, U. S. Edition of the *Wall Street Journal*, April 6, C2.

Wittfogel, Karl A. 1957. *Oriental Despotism: A Study of Total Power*. New Haven: Yale University Press.

Wolf, Eric R. 1951. "The Social Organization of Mecca and the Origins of Islam." *Southwestern Journal of Anthropology* 7:329–56.

Wolf, Eric R. 1957. "Closed Corporate Peasant Communities in Mesoamerica and Central Java." *Southwestern Journal of Anthropology* 13:1–18.

Wolf, Eric R. 1974. "Foreword." In *In Search of the Primitive*, edited by Stanley Diamond, xi–xiii. Brunswick, NJ: Transaction Books.

Wolf, Eric R. 1982. *Europe and the People without History*. Berkeley: University of California Press.

Wong, R. Bin. 1991. "Chinese Traditions of Grain Storage." In *Nourish the People: The State Civilian Granary System in China, 1650–1850*, edited by Pierre-Etienne Will and R. Bin Wong, 1–18. Ann Arbor: University of Michigan Center for Chinese Studies.

Wong, R. Bin. 1997. *China Transformed: Historical Change and the Limits of European Experience*. Ithaca: Cornell University Press.

Wong, R. Bin. 2012. "Taxation and Good Governance in China 1500–1914." In *The Rise of Fiscal States: A Global History 1500–1914*, edited by Bartolomé Yun-Casalilla and Patrick K. O'Brien, 353–77. Cambridge: Cambridge University Press.

Wrigley, Christopher. 1996. *Kingship and State: The Buganda Dynasty*. Cambridge: Cambridge University Press.

Wrong, Dennis. 1961. "The Oversocialized Conception of Man in Modern Sociology." *American Sociological Review* 26:183–96.

Wycherley, R. E. 1978. *The Stones of Athens*. Princeton: Princeton University Press.

Wynn, Thomas. 1995. "Handaxe Enigmas." *World Archaeology* 27:10–24.

Wynne-Edwards, Vero C. 1962. *Animal Dispersion in Relation to Social Behavior*. New York: Hafner Publishing Company.

Xu, Yinong. 2000. *The Chinese City in Space and Time: The Development of Urban Form in Suzhou*. Honolulu: University of Hawaii Press.

Yang, Anand A. 1998. *Bazaar India: Markets, Society, and the Colonial State in Gangetic Bihar*. Berkeley: University of California Press.

Yengoyan, Aram. 1968. "Demographic and Ecological Influences on Aboriginal Australian Marriage Sections." In *Man the Hunter*, edited by Richard Lee and Irvine DeVore, 186–99. Chicago: Aldine.

Ylvisaker, Marguerite. 1979. *Lamu in the Nineteenth Century: Land, Trade, and Politics. African Research Studies Number 13*. Boston: African Studies Center, Boston University.

York, Abigail M., Michael E. Smith, Benjamin W. Stanley, Barbara L. Stark, Juliana Novic, Sharon L. Harlan, George L. Cowgill, and Christopher G. Boone. 2010. "Ethnic and Class Clustering through the Ages: A Transdisciplinary Approach to Urban Neighborhood Social Patterns." *Urban Studies (Edinburgh, Scotland)* 48:2399–415.

Young, Rodney S. 1951. "An Industrial District of Ancient Athens." *Hesperia* 20:135–288.

Yun-Casalilla, B., and Patrick K. O'Brien, eds. 2012. *The Rise of Fiscal States: A Global History 1500–1914*. Cambridge: Cambridge University Press.

Zafirovski, Milan. 1999. "What Is Really Rational Choice? Beyond the Utilitarian Concept of Rationality." *Current Sociology* 47:47–113.

Zahari, Amotz. 1975. "Mate Selection—A Selection for Handicap." *Journal of Theoretical Biology* 53:205–14.

Zanker, Paul. 1988. *The Power of Images in the Age of Augustus*. Ann Arbor: University of Michigan Press.

Zurndorfer, Harriet T. 2011. "Cotton Textile Manufacture and Marketing in Late Imperial China and the 'Great Divergence.'" *Journal of Economic and Social History of the Orient* 54:701–38.

Index

www.ingramcontent.com/pod-product-compliance
Lightning Source LLC
Chambersburg PA
CBHW060019030426
42334CB00019B/2101